Problems and Materials
on Secured Transactions

ASPEN CASEBOOK SERIES

PROBLEMS AND MATERIALS ON SECURED TRANSACTIONS

TENTH EDITION

DOUGLAS J. WHALEY
PROFESSOR EMERITUS
MORITZ COLLEGE OF LAW
THE OHIO STATE UNIVERSITY

STEPHEN M. MCJOHN
PROFESSOR OF LAW
SUFFOLK UNIVERSITY LAW SCHOOL

Wolters Kluwer

Published by Wolters Kluwer in New York.

Wolters Kluwer Legal & Regulatory US serves customers worldwide with CCH, Aspen Publishers, and Kluwer Law International products. (www.WKLegaledu.com)

To contact Customer Service, e-mail customer.service@wolterskluwer.com, call 1-800-234-1660, fax 1-800-901-9075, or mail correspondence to:

Wolters Kluwer
Attn: Order Department
PO Box 990
Frederick, MD 21705

Printed in the United States of America.

1 2 3 4 5 6 7 8 9 0

ISBN: 978-1-4548-8606-8

Library of Congress Cataloging-in-Publication Data

Names: Whaley, Douglas J., author. | McJohn, Stephen M., author.
Title: Problems and materials on secured transactions / Douglas J. Whaley, Professor Emeritus, Moritz College of Law, The Ohio State University; Stephen M. McJohn, Professor of Law, Suffolk University Law School.
Description: Tenth edition. | New York : Wolters Kluwer, [2016] | Includes bibliographical references and index.
Identifiers: LCCN 2016040705 | ISBN 9781454886068
Subjects: LCSH: Security (Law)—United States. | LCGFT: Casebooks
Classification: LCC KF1050 .W465 2016 | DDC 346.7307/4—dc23
LC record available at https://lccn.loc.gov/2016040705

About Wolters Kluwer Legal & Regulatory US

Wolters Kluwer Legal & Regulatory US delivers expert content and solutions in the areas of law, corporate compliance, health compliance, reimbursement, and legal education. Its practical solutions help customers successfully navigate the demands of a changing environment to drive their daily activities, enhance decision quality and inspire confident outcomes.

Serving customers worldwide, its legal and regulatory portfolio includes products under the Aspen Publishers, CCH Incorporated, Kluwer Law International, ftwilliam.com and MediRegs names. They are regarded as exceptional and trusted resources for general legal and practice-specific knowledge, compliance and risk management, dynamic workflow solutions, and expert commentary.

Dedicated to Clayton and Maria Whaley

— Douglas Whaley

For Lorie, Ian, and the Fiddlehead Bridge
Corps of Engineers

— Stephen McJohn

Summary of Contents

Contents

This book explores the law of secured transactions primarily through a series of Problems designed to encourage the student to concentrate on the exact statutory language in the Uniform Commercial Code and related federal statutes. Unfortunately, students reared on the case method sometimes have trouble concentrating on Problem after Problem. Such an attitude here can be academically fatal. As a guide to the degree of concentration required, we have used a hierarchy of signals. When the Problem states "Read §9-203," we mean "Put down this book, pick up the Uniform Commercial Code, and study §9-203 carefully." When the instruction is "See §9-203," the reader need look at the cited section only if unsure of the answer. "Cf. §9-203" or simply "§9-203" are lesser references, included as a guide for the curious.

We have edited the footnotes out of most cases; the ones that remain have been stripped of their original numbering and have been consecutively numbered with our own footnotes. Unless clearly indicated otherwise, all footnotes in the cases are the court's own.

Everyone writing in this area owes an enormous debt to the late Professor Grant Gilmore for his peerless two-volume treatise, *Security Interests in Personal Property* (1965). We are among that group (and in fact the work so impressed Whaley that he once wrote Professor Gilmore an unabashed fan letter). If not nonexistent, this book would be a great deal shorter and considerably less interesting but for the Gilmore treatise.

We also thank the good people at Aspen Publishers for all their work. This is the tenth edition of this casebook with Aspen, and we are much impressed by the constant dedication of the company to putting out quality books.

Finally, we must express our gratitude to our students, who through the years have taught us as much about secured transactions as we have taught them.

Douglas J. Whaley
Columbus, Ohio

Stephen M. McJohn
Boston, Massachusetts

September 2016

PROBLEMS AND MATERIALS ON SECURED TRANSACTIONS

CHAPTER 1

INTRODUCTION TO THE UNIFORM COMMERCIAL CODE

I. A BIT OF HISTORY

During medieval times, commercial law varied widely from place to place throughout the trading world, and the statutes of the various countries either didn't address the relevant issues that traders cared about or reached results that were at odds with what those traders thought either realistic or fair. During much of English history, for example, the common law courts were lumbered by such arcane rules of procedure that justice was either unavailable or so slow as to come far too late.

To solve this dilemma the traders developed their own legal system, the so-called "law merchant" (or "lex mercatoria" in Latin). By agreement they created their own courts, chose their own judges, and developed those mercantile understandings that made trade efficient and fair (in their own eyes). At some point the real courts became aware that they were being bypassed and began to incorporate the law merchant into their own rules. During the time of the American Revolution, the English court system had as its Chief Justice the great jurist Lord Mansfield. He believed in pragmatism in his courtroom, and during his tenure the law merchant was given much influence in English decisions. Lord Mansfield would call merchants into court to testify as to what mercantile understandings were about the matter

LORD MANSFIELD.

before the court, and was not above putting merchants on the jury and then asking them questions as cases proceeded.

II. *THE CREATION OF THE UNIFORM COMMERCIAL CODE*

Starting in the 1940s, two private bodies, the American Law Institute (ALI) and the National Conference of Commissioners on Uniform State Law (NCCUSL), decided it was time to modernize the state laws on commercial matters. Over the coming years, they gathered together the greatest commercial experts in the country to draft a new giant statute that would supersede existing ones for the areas that were covered. Chief draftsman was Professor Karl N. Llewellyn, the leading voice for the "legal realism" school of jurisprudence (very much in Lord Mansfield's tradition), and he led a

Karl Llewellyn
Photograph courtesy of
Yale Law School

drafting team that by 1952 produced the first version of what was called the "Uniform Commercial Code."

The Uniform Commercial Code went through various versions from that day to this. The UCC (or, in this course, simply the Code) is divided into "Articles" covering different aspects of commercial law. It is important to appreciate that the UCC is not federal law. Instead, the two drafting bodies submitted it for adoption to the states, and it had to be individually enacted into law state by state. The idea was that if commercial law were uniform throughout the country, commerce would be more certain and efficient (the same goals animating the law merchant centuries before). Most states did adopt the Code with few changes (though some have sneaked in through the years, and you, budding lawyer, should always check your own state's enactment to make sure some evil alteration hasn't muddled what you've learned in this course). By the end of the last quarter of the twentieth century, all states and most U.S. territories had adopted the UCC completely, though Louisiana, with its French law, Napoleonic Code, tradition did not enact Article 2 on the Sale of Goods, but has its own civil law version thereof.

III. FEDERAL LAW

The federal government, of course, has a great interest in commercial matters, and thus has enacted a wide number of statutes that exist alongside the states' UCC mandates. Federal law supersedes inconsistent state laws, and in this book we will explore these collisions as they occur.

IV. ARTICLE 1 OF THE CODE

The first Article of the UCC covers "General Provisions," and it applies to all UCC matters unless a more specific section elsewhere in the Code says otherwise. Article 1's most recent rewrite occurred in 2001, and that version, now adopted by most of the states, is the one referred to in this book.

Look at §1-103 and let's highlight some of what it says. Subsection 1-103(a)(1) tells us that the UCC shall be "liberally construed." This is not a political statement, but instead is meant to combat the old presumption that the common law (meaning the law as created by precedent with no statutory guidance) was thought so wise that a rule of statutory construction arose stating that "statutes in derogation of the common law are to be *strictly* construed" so as to change the common law result as little as possible. Karl Llewellyn was having none of that: the UCC is to be read broadly, the common law be damned.

Subsection 1-103(a)(3) commands the courts of the various states to work to make the law "uniform" throughout the country. This gives the attorney finding a favorable ruling in one state a strong argument that it's a good precedent in another—a valuable thing to remember.

Finally §1-103(b) preserves all of the common law rules (including the rules of equity and even the law merchant) to the extent that they do not contradict the statutory rules contained in the UCC. If the UCC doesn't speak to an issue, then attorneys must look to other laws to find the desired result.

One of the most important sections in the Code is §1-201, which is a huge definition section containing definitions for 43 different words. You will consult it often when exploring the matters we'll discuss in later chapters. Section 1-202 has complicated definitions of "notice" and "knowledge" that answer important questions such as what the two terms mean and at what moment a notice is effective (when sent? when received?). Section 1-204 defines "value" and §1-205 explores the issues of "reasonable time" and "seasonable."

There's a choice of law provision in §1-301 that generally applies the law of the enacting state if "appropriate," but allows the parties by agreement to choose the law of any state having a "reasonable relation" to the transaction.

Another important section, often referred to in this book and the case law, is §1-303, which explains what are sometimes called "construction" terms: the items that make up the understanding of the parties as to what the contract means. Section 1-303(c) explains that a "usage of trade" is a *custom* within the industry (sort of a throwback to the law merchant) and this custom binds all of those who should know about it, sometimes including even consumers. Ask yourself this: is it the "usage of trade" that car dealers can lie about the attributes of the vehicle being sold and therefore get away with that? [Of course not—a usage of trade can't violate the law, and such lies would be fraud.] "Course of dealing" in §1-303(b) refers to what the parties did in their *past* contacts with one another. If the parties have dealt with each other in prior dealings, that history creates an expectation of what will happen in this contract, and the Code thusly recognizes it. Finally "course of performance" in §1-303(a) means what the parties do in performing this one particular contract, especially important where the contract goes on over a period of time and creates its own history and expectations. The common law called "course of performance" by the term "practical construction" and found it gave great guidance to the true boundaries of the contract. Then, in §1-303(e), there is a hierarchy of importance of these construction terms, with the more relevant ones beating out the less relevant. Under this idea, express terms control course of performance, but course of performance is more important than both course of dealing or usage of trade, and course of dealing beats out an inconsistent usage of trade. One caveat to this little list: §1-303(f) explains that an express term in a contract ("deliveries must be made on time or the contract is breached") can be *waived* by course of performance (accepting late deliveries without protest means one cannot suddenly call a breach for this reason—a result codified by §2-209 for the sale of goods).

Section 1-304 provides that "Every contract or duty within the Uniform Commercial Code imposes an obligation of good faith in its performance and enforcement." The definition of "good faith" is "honesty in fact and the observance of reasonable commercial standards of fair dealing." §1-201(b)(20). So good faith has a subjective component (honesty in fact) and an objective component (observance of reasonable commercial standards of fair dealing). This standard has changed over time. Some states have kept to the old definition of good faith, which required only "honesty in fact." Failure to act in good faith, by itself, "does not support an independent cause of action." Official Comment to §1-304; See, e.g., Brooklyn Bagel Boys, Inc. v. Earthgrains Refrigerated Dough Products, Inc, 212 F.3d 373 (7th Cir. 2000). Courts have held that failure to act in good faith, by itself, does not make a party liable, but a party that has performed in bad faith may be unable to assert rights under the Code. In one case, for example, a creditor who behaved in a blatantly evil manner had the usual Article 9 priorities reversed and ended up losing its collateral; see Ninth Dist. Prod. Credit Assn. v. Ed Duggan, Inc., 821 P.2d 788 (Colo. 1991), a case that we'll return to later in this book.

V.   THE OFFICIAL COMMENTS

All of the sections of the Code are followed by the Official Comments (such as the one quoted in the previous paragraph) which explain how the drafters wanted the sections to be interpreted. These Comments, the courts have said clearly, are not the law, but they are important in understanding the meaning of the relevant section and are to be studied in that light. If in a future case you have an Official Comment in your favor, you will, of course, call it to the court's attention and remind the court that this Comment was written by the very experts who wrote the statute and therefore it should be given great weight. If the relevant Comments hurts your case and has, annoyingly, been raised by the other side, remind the court that the Comments are not the law, and that sometimes these Comments have the look of "Oops, we meant to say this, but knew we couldn't get it through the legislature so we're trying to amend the law through a more devious channel."

CHAPTER 2

INTRODUCTION TO SECURED TRANSACTIONS

"Secured Transactions" is an imposing term, but it merely refers to a business transaction in which a credit extension is protected (secured) by collateral given by the debtor to better backup the loan. Much can go wrong here: the parties may not specify the collateral exactly, or the creditor may fail to make the loan, other parties (buyers, other creditors, the debtor's trustee in bankruptcy) may make claims to the property, etc. Article 9 of the Uniform Commercial Code resolves these and other issues. It is not the most interesting subject to study, but it is logical and fits together well. And what knowledge you gain here is very important. You, future attorney, will often extend credit to your clients and it might be to your advantage to demand collateral to protect that debt. And no matter how dull secured transactions might seem in law school it will (a) likely be tested on the bar exam, (b) help you find a job, and (c) become the most fascinating subject you've ever looked at when the senior partner of your firm tells you that because you know Article 9 (from this course) you're in charge of making sure nothing goes wrong on the $5 million deal the firm is handling for its largest client.

It is understandable that someone extending credit in a sale or loan transaction wants to be sure of repayment. Some debtors are so solvent and/or trustworthy that the creditor demands nothing more than the debtor's promise to pay (sometimes called a *signature loan*); creditors doing this are said to be *unsecured*. In many transactions the creditor is less sanguine about the debtor's ability or desire to repay and may demand that the debtor either obtain a surety (called by various names: a *co-signor,* a *guarantor,* or, in Article 3 of the Uniform Commercial Code, an *accommodation party*) or *secure* the debt by nominating some of the debtor's current or future property as collateral. If the debtor defaults, the collateral may be seized and sold and the proceeds of the sale used to pay the debt.

A basic problem with mastering the law of secured transactions has always been in understanding the terminology: *lien, pledge, perfection, purchase money security interest,* etc. The terminology is complex because historically what we now call *secured transactions* have their source in many separate business devices, each with an individual set of descriptive terms. In addition, Article 9 of the Uniform Commercial Code adds a new and different nomenclature. To understand the pre-Code cases and the Code commentators' references to these pre-Code devices, it is necessary to have some minimal appreciation of how creditors protected their interests prior to the adoption of the UCC.

The core problem is that when a debtor cannot pay the bills, creditors must look to the debtor's property for whatever satisfaction they will get. These creditors must compete with other claimants for the property: donees, buyers, and (if financial death has occurred) the debtor's bankruptcy trustee. Worse yet, the creditors must compete with each other, and the law must somehow provide rules to determine who among all these individuals is to receive the property. As fast as the lawmakers create one set of statutes, those in business and their advisors think up new contractual arrangements that the statutes do not cover, and the law is chaotic until a new group of statutes can be added to those already regulating similar practices.

The original version of Article 9 of the Uniform Commercial Code, dealing with these "secured" transactions, was promulgated in 1962 and has twice been substantially rewritten: in 1972 and most recently in 1999, the version considered in this book. In most states the 1999 revision went into effect on July 1, 2001. The transition rules from the old version to the next can be found in the 9-700s. Official Comment 4 to §9-101 has a concise summary of the changes that the 1999 revision makes to the earlier version of the statute. This book also covers the minor revisions promulgated in 2010, which all 50 states had adopted by the end of 2015.

We start with some basic definitions.

A *lien* is an interest in the debtor's property given by the law to protect a creditor. If the debtor voluntarily grants such an interest, a *consensual* lien is created. If a consensual lien is taken in the debtor's real property, the lien is called a *mortgage.* A consensual lien in personal property or fixtures is called a *security interest* and is governed by Article 9 of the Uniform Commercial Code. Involuntary liens can also be imposed against the debtor's property.

If the lien arises from judicial proceedings (the creditor sues, recovers judgment, and sends the sheriff out to seize the defendant's property), a *judicial lien* is created. A *statutory lien* is one imposed by either a statute or the common law in favor of certain creditors the law deems worthy of protection. Examples are the liens given to landlords, to artisans repairing personal property (the garage mechanic, for example), and to a host of others, such as ostlers, innkeepers, and even attorneys. A mechanic's lien is a statutory lien in favor of those who perform construction work. And if you do not pay your taxes, the federal government will file the awesome federal tax lien, a statutory lien that reaches *all* of the taxpayer's property, a matter we treat at length in a later chapter.

Although it is impossible to make a categorical statement, generally the prior statutes regulating these matters established a hierarchy of heady contenders in the derby to divide up the debtor's assets. Assuming a claimant qualifies, a "bona fide purchaser [BFP] in the ordinary course of business" was (and still is under Article 9) a favorite in the race. Another current favorite is the bankruptcy trustee, who represents all of the bankrupt's unsecured creditors and to whom the federal bankruptcy statute gives an awesome arsenal of weapons with which to attack the supposed interests that secured creditors assert in the estate's property. Under what is called the *strong arm clause* (§544(a) of the Bankruptcy Code), as of the date of the filing of the bankruptcy petition, the trustee (and all the claims the trustee represents) is conclusively presumed to occupy the legal position of a judicial lien creditor who has levied on all of the bankrupt's property. As we shall see, secured creditors whose security interests are *unperfected* at this moment lose the right to claim the collateral. But if a creditor's claim to the property will survive the attack of the bankruptcy trustee, the creditor's security interest (lien) is said to be *perfected*. Perfection of the security interest then becomes the ultimate goal of any creditor taking an interest in the debtor's collateral. And—again this is a generality—creditors with perfected security interests not only beat out the bankruptcy trustee but also win over non-BFPs—creditors without perfected security interests, creditors whose security interests were perfected later in time, and creditors with no security interests at all (called, in bankruptcy parlance, *general creditors*: typically, for example, the corner grocer, the family doctor).

How is a creditor's security interest perfected? The answer depends on the nature of the collateral, the technical steps required by the statutes (or the courts if the legislature has not yet acted), and the particular moment in history in which the question is asked. Before embarking on a description of the major pre-Code security devices, there follows a brief outline of the bankruptcy rules against which the validity of these devices (and Article 9) must be viewed.

I. *BANKRUPTCY*

The United States Constitution states that Congress shall pass laws pertaining to bankruptcy; the result is the Bankruptcy Reform Act of 1978, 11 U.S.C. §101 et seq. (hereinafter the Bankruptcy Code). There are four primary types of bankruptcy: Chapter 7, straight bankruptcy (a pure liquidation proceeding); Chapter 11, a reorganization proceeding for businesses; Chapter 12, a reorganization proceeding for farmers; and Chapter 13, a debt repayment plan for individuals. The vast majority of bankruptcies are straight bankruptcies, and over 90 percent of those are filed by individuals, as opposed to businesses. Consequently, the rest of this discussion is a sketch of the proceedings in straight bankruptcy.

To commence bankruptcy, the debtor (a *voluntary* bankruptcy) or the debtor's creditors (an *involuntary* bankruptcy) file a petition with the bankruptcy court. This is a federal court under the direction of the local federal district court. The date on which the petition is filed is important because it is the measuring moment for many of the Bankruptcy Code's sections. Along with the petition the debtor will file lists (called *schedules*), showing assets and creditors. The creditors are then summoned to a meeting (called, not inaptly, the *first meeting of creditors* or, because of its Bankruptcy Code number, a *§341 meeting*) at which they elect someone (the *trustee*) to gather up the debtor's property, sell it, and represent the creditors' interests in the distribution of the proceeds. If the debtor's property must be tended to *before* the first meeting of creditors (say, for instance, a circus goes bankrupt—someone must see to it that the menagerie doesn't run loose), a temporary custodian (an *interim trustee*), who acts until the trustee can take over, is appointed.[1]

The trustee collects the debtor's property. This can be a more complicated task than it may seem. If other people claim the property (creditors, a relative who was the recipient of a very generous birthday gift, or even the bankrupt, should there be an argument over *exempt* assets), the trustee may have to litigate the issue either before the bankruptcy judge or in the state or federal court. Property exempt from bankruptcy under federal or—in some jurisdictions—state law and worthless property (the bankrupt's cat, for example) are returned to the bankrupt. The bankrupt then petitions the bankruptcy judge for a *discharge* (read *forgiveness*) of all the scheduled debts so that the bankrupt's life can be resumed financially unburdened.

---

1. The interim trustee automatically becomes the trustee unless someone else is elected trustee at the first meeting of creditors. Bankruptcy Code §702(d).

With certain exceptions, bankrupts usually receive a discharge from most (but not all) debts.[22]

When the trustee gathers the estate's property, either the trustee surrenders the encumbered collateral to the secured creditors or, if the trustee elects to sell the collateral, creditors with perfected security interests get their debts paid *first* from the proceeds of the sale. The unencumbered assets of the estate are also sold, and those proceeds are used to pay the expenses of the bankruptcy proceeding, wages of the bankrupt's employees, some tax claims, certain other priority claimants, and, finally, the general creditors (who get nothing until all the above are paid in full).

The trustee need not accept the creditor's statement that the creditor has a perfected security interest; the validity (*perfection*) of the security interest is a matter of state law and will be measured by state standards. If the security interest is finally determined to be *unperfected,* the interest is destroyed, and the creditor becomes just another general (*unsecured*) creditor. Not only is the trustee armed (as has been mentioned) with the position of a perfected *lien creditor* coming into existence on the date of the petition filing (Bankruptcy Code §544(a)), but also the trustee occupies the same legal position as any actual existing creditor (Bankruptcy Code §544(b)). Further, the Bankruptcy Code codifies the old common law maxim that a debtor must "be just before he is generous." Section 547 of the Bankruptcy Code condemns as a *preference* the following type of conduct:

> On January 1, Alice owed to Tom, Dick, and Harry $1,000 each for past due loans. On May 1, she paid Tom $1,000, and the next day she filed a voluntary petition in bankruptcy.

Section 547 provides that many payments made by an insolvent debtor to an existing creditor within 90 days of the date of the filing of the petition are void as *preferences*. The trustee can recover the payment from the preferred creditor. (The fairness of §547 to Dick and Harry should be obvious.)

A final practical note worth remembering: in most bankruptcies the unsecured creditors receive *nothing*. For this reason most creditors want security (collateral) for their debts, and they want their lawyers to advise them how they can perfect that security against other creditors and the bankruptcy trustee.

2. See Bankruptcy Code §§523, 727.

II. PRE-CODE SECURITY DEVICES

Students who know nothing other than Article 9 (and, as to real property creditor conflicts, know only what they learned in their basic property course) may not appreciate the wide variety of devices the UCC replaced. Such a student may ask why all these devices, particularly those that were very similar, were needed. The answer is historical. Our legal ancestors (lawyers, judges, and legislators) had some rigid ideas about what was transferable property (a diamond ring) and what was not (a right to sue your customer if the bill wasn't paid) and about the propriety of certain business practices that now seem commonplace. We begin our study with a famous case.

Benedict v. Ratner

United States Supreme Court, 1925
268 U.S. 353

BRANDEIS, J.

The Hub Carpet Company was adjudicated bankrupt by the federal court for southern New York in involuntary proceedings commenced September 26, 1921. Benedict, who was appointed receiver and later trustee, collected the book accounts of the company. Ratner filed in that court a petition in equity praying that the amounts so collected be paid over to him. He claimed them under a writing given May 23, 1921—four months and three days before the commencement of the bankruptcy proceedings. By it the company purported to assign to him, as collateral for certain loans, all accounts present and future. Those collected by the receiver were, so far as appears, all accounts which had arisen after the date of the assignment, and were enumerated in the monthly list of accounts outstanding which was delivered to Ratner September 23. Benedict resisted the petition on the ground that the original assignment was void under the law of New York as a fraudulent conveyance; that, for this reason, the delivery of the September list of accounts was inoperative to perfect a lien in Ratner; and that it was a preference under the Bankruptcy Act. He also filed a cross-petition in which he asked that Ratner be ordered to pay to the estate the proceeds of certain collections which had been made by the company after September 17 and turned over to Ratner pursuant to his request made on that day. The company was then insolvent and Ratner had reason to believe it to be so. These accounts also had apparently been acquired by the company after the date of the original assignment.

The District Judge decided both petitions in Ratner's favor. He ruled that the assignment executed in May was not fraudulent in law; that it created an equity in the future acquired accounts; that because of this equity, Ratner was entitled to retain, as against the bankrupt's estate, the proceeds of the accounts which had been collected by the company in September and turned over to him; that by delivery of the list of the accounts outstanding on September 23, this equity in them had ripened into a perfect title to the remaining accounts; and that the title so perfected was good as against the supervening bankruptcy. Accordingly, the District Court ordered that, to the extent of the balance remaining unpaid on his loans, there be paid to Ratner all collections made from accounts enumerated in any of the lists delivered to Ratner; and that the cross-petition of Benedict be denied. There was no finding of fraud in fact. On appeal, the Circuit Court of Appeals affirmed the order. 282 Fed. 12. A writ of certiorari was granted by this Court. 259 U.S. 579.

The rights of the parties depend primarily upon the law of New York. Hiscock v. Varick Bank of N.Y., 206 U.S. 28. It may be assumed that, unless the arrangement of May 23 was void because fraudulent in law, the original assignment of the future acquired accounts became operative under the state law, both as to those paid over to Ratner before the bankruptcy proceedings and as to those collected by the receiver; and that the assignment will be deemed to have taken effect as of May 23. Sexton v. Kessler, 225 U.S. 90, 99. That being so, it is clear that, if the original assignment was a valid one under the law of New York, the Bankruptcy Act did not invalidate the subsequent dealings of the parties. Thompson v. Fairbanks, 196 U.S. 516; Humphrey v. Tatman, 198 U.S. 91. The sole question for decision is, therefore, whether on the following undisputed facts the assignment of May 23 was in law fraudulent.

The Hub Carpet Company was, on May 23, a mercantile concern doing business in New York City and proposing to continue to do so. The assignment was made there to secure an existing loan of $15,000, and further advances not exceeding $15,000 which were in fact made July 1, 1921. It included all accounts receivable then outstanding and all which should thereafter accrue in the ordinary course of business. A list of the existing accounts was delivered at the time. Similar lists were to be delivered to Ratner on or about the 23rd day of each succeeding month containing the accounts outstanding at such future dates. Those enumerated in each of the lists delivered prior to September, aggregated between $100,000 and $120,000. The receivables were to be collected by the company. Ratner was given the right, at any time, to demand a full disclosure of the business and financial conditions; to require that all amounts collected be applied in payment of his loans; and to enforce the assignment although no loan had matured. But until he did so, the company was not required to apply any of the collections to the repayment of Ratner's loan. It was not required to replace accounts collected by other collateral of equal value. It was not required to account in any way to Ratner. It was at liberty to use the proceeds of all accounts collected as it might see fit. The existence of the assignment was to be kept secret. The business was to be conducted as theretofore. Indebtedness was to be incurred, as usual, for the purchase of merchandise and otherwise in the ordinary course of business. The amount of such indebtedness unpaid at the time of the commencement of the bankruptcy proceedings was large. Prior to September 17, the company collected from accounts so assigned about $150,000, all of which it applied to purposes other than the payment of Ratner's loan. The outstanding accounts enumerated in the list delivered September 23 aggregated $90,000.

Under the law of New York a transfer of property as security which reserves to the transferor the right to dispose of the same, or to apply the proceeds thereof, for his own uses is, as to creditors, fraudulent in law and void. This is true whether the right of disposition for the transferor's use be reserved in the instrument or by agreement in pais, oral or written; whether the right of disposition reserved be unlimited in time or be expressly terminable by the happening of an event; whether the transfer cover all the property of the debtor or only a part; whether the right of disposition extends to all the property transferred or only to a part thereof; and whether the instrument of transfer be recorded or not.

If this rule applies to the assignment of book accounts, the arrangement of May 23 was clearly void; and the equity in the future acquired accounts, which it would otherwise have created, did not arise. Whether the rule applies to accounts does not appear to have been passed upon by the Court of Appeals of New York. But it would seem clear that whether the collateral consists of chattels or of accounts, reservation of dominion inconsistent with the effective disposition of title must render the transaction void. Ratner asserts that the rule stated above rests upon ostensible ownership, and argues that the doctrine of ostensible ownership is not applicable to book accounts. That doctrine raises a presumption of fraud where chattels are mortgaged (or sold) and possession of the property is not delivered to the mortgagee (or vendee). The presumption may be avoided by recording the mortgage (or sale). It may be assumed, as Ratner contends, that the doctrine does not apply to the assignment of accounts. In their transfer there is nothing which corresponds to the delivery of possession of chattels. The statutes which embody the doctrine and provide for recording as a substitute for delivery do not include accounts. A title to an account good against creditors may be transferred without notice to the debtor or record of any kind. But it is not true that the rule stated above and invoked by the receiver is either based upon or delimited by the doctrine of ostensible ownership. It rests not upon seeming ownership because of possession retained, but upon a lack of ownership because of dominion reserved. It does not raise a presumption of fraud. It imputes fraud conclusively because of the reservation of dominion inconsistent with the effective disposition of title and creation of a lien.

The nature of the rule is made clear by its limitations. Where the mortgagor of chattels agrees to apply the proceeds of their sale to the payment of the mortgage debt or to the purchase of other chattels which shall become subject to the lien, the mortgage is good as against creditors, if recorded. The mortgage is sustained in such cases "upon the ground that such sale and application of proceeds is the normal and proper purpose of a chattel mortgage, and within the precise boundaries of its lawful operation and effect. It does no more than to substitute the mortgagor as the agent of the mortgagee to do exactly what the latter had the right to do, and what it was his privilege and his duty to accomplish. It devotes, as it should, the mortgaged property to the payment of the mortgage debt." The permission to use the proceeds to furnish substitute collateral "provides only for a shifting of the lien from one piece of property to another taken in exchange." Brackett v. Harvey, 91 N.Y. 214, 221, 223. On the other hand, if the agreement is that the mortgagor may sell and use the proceeds for his own benefit, the mortgage is of no effect although recorded. Seeming ownership exists in both classes of cases because the mortgagor is permitted to remain in possession of the stock in trade and to sell it freely. But it is only where the unrestricted dominion over the proceeds is reserved to the mortgagor that the mortgage is void. This dominion is the differentiating and deciding element. The distinction was recognized in Sexton v. Kessler, 225 U.S. 90, 98, 32 S. Ct. 657, where a transfer of securities was sustained. It was pointed out that a reservation of full control by the mortgagor might well prevent the effective creation of a lien in the mortgagee and that the New York cases holding such a mortgage void rest upon that doctrine.

The results which flow from reserving dominion inconsistent with the effective disposition of title must be the same whatever the nature of the property transferred. The doctrine which imputes fraud where full dominion is reserved must apply to assignments of accounts although the doctrine of ostensible ownership does not. There must also be the same distinction as to degrees of dominion. Thus, although an agreement that the assignor of accounts shall collect them and pay the proceeds to the assignee will not invalidate the assignment which it accompanies, the assignment must be deemed fraudulent in law if it is agreed that the assignor may use the proceeds as he sees fit.

In the case at bar, the arrangement for the unfettered use by the company of the proceeds of the accounts precluded the effective creation of a lien and rendered the original assignment fraudulent in law. Consequently the payments to Ratner and the delivery of the September list of accounts were inoperative to perfect a lien in him, and were unlawful preferences.

On this ground, and also because the payment was fraudulent under the law of the State, the trustee was entitled to recover the amount. . . .

Reversed.

The evil under attack in Benedict v. Ratner is the *secret lien* that other creditors do not know about. If it is enforced by the courts, the other creditors who were deceived by the debtor's apparently unencumbered prosperity are hurt. But, although the Court in this case ruled against the creditor's security interest, most creditors took comfort from the decision because the Court had indicated methods by which the lien *would* have survived the trustee's attack. By requiring the creditor to *police* the debtor's conduct (record the mortgage, pay over collections to the creditor, etc.), the Court paved the way for increased commercial financing. Once the creditors knew what the rules were, they were more willing to extend credit.

Did the rule of Benedict v. Ratner survive the enactment of Article 9? Read §9-205 and its Official Comment 2. Article 9 solves the secret lien problem by making sure that the creditor's interest in the debtor's property is obvious so that no later creditors are deceived (typically by the filing of a notice, called a *financing statement,* in the public records, though there are other methods, such as taking possession of the collateral, that serve the same function). Note that in a sale of goods transaction it still is a bad idea for the seller to retain possession of the sold objects for a long period of time after the sale is over; read §2-402(2).

One way around the problems encountered in this famous case was to permit the creditor to have physical possession of the property (a *pledge*; see below), though this is a solution only where the collateral has tangible form, which accounts receivable, of course, do not. Other ways were suggested by the opinion itself. A very brief summary of the major devices follows.

A.   *Pledge*

In a *pledge*[3] the debtor (called a *pledgor*) gives physical possession of the collateral to the creditor (called the *pledgee*) until the debt is paid. Possession then *perfects* the creditor's interest in the collateral (even against the bankruptcy trustee). Obviously when the creditor has possession of, say, a diamond ring, the whole world is on notice that the creditor has some legal interest therein. Pledging is a superior way to perfect the creditor's security interest, but it has two drawbacks: (1) only tangible objects can be pledged,

---

3. A pledge is sometimes called a *hypothecation.*

and a business debtor may want to borrow money against intangible collateral (such as accounts receivable due from existing customers); and (2) for some types of collateral the debtor needs to keep possession (the machines used in manufacturing, for example). It was therefore necessary to create *non*possessory security interests.

B.   Chattel Mortgage

The debtor could always mortgage land, so why not have something similar for personal property (*chattels*)? And, as with real property, the mortgage given by the debtor (the *mortgagor*) to the creditor (the *mortgagee*) was recorded in a designated place and indexed under the name of the debtor so that other potential creditors could check and see whether the collateral was encumbered. Thus, the debtor could have possession, but the secret lien problem so dreaded in Benedict v. Ratner was avoided because the mortgage was (through the recording system) witness to the creditor's very public interest in the property.

C.   Conditional Sale

Here's a surprise. Without first reading the text that follows, form an opinion as to the answer to this Problem.

PROBLEM 1

Honest John sold Nancy Debts a used car for $900, to be paid off in three payments of $300 each. The contract was oral. Nancy missed the second payment, and one of Honest John's employees repossessed the car and returned it to the seller. Nancy sued Honest John for conversion. Who should win? After forming your initial opinion, read §2-702 and see if that has any bearing on your answer.

Most people assume that the unpaid seller always has a right to repossess. *This is untrue.* The unpaid seller may repossess in only three circumstances: (1) when §2-702 (which you have just read and about which more later) applies; (2) when the buyer has specifically granted the seller a *security interest* in the object sold; and (3) when the seller sues, recovers judgment, and has the sheriff seize the property as part of the execution of the seller's judgment. (When an unsecured creditor sues and acquires a judgment and then sends the sheriff out to levy on the defendant's property, the creditor is called, variously, a *judgment creditor,* a *judicial creditor,* or simply a *lien creditor.*)

Of course, prior to the UCC, the seller could take a chattel mortgage in the property sold and file to record this interest, but that was a lot of trouble. Another way was to have a *conditional sale* whereby the buyer got possession of the property but the seller reserved full and complete title to it until the buyer paid in full (the *condition* in *conditional sale* was this payment before the buyer got any title). A conditional sale has the Benedict v. Ratner problem of the debtor-in-possession and a secret lien in the seller's favor, and the fictitious title retention theory had as short a life here as it did in the real property mortgage situation. The upshot was that in many states the seller's "title" was treated as nothing more than an unperfected security interest, so that the seller lost to later judicial creditors, to creditors who perfected their security interests, and to the buyer's trustee in bankruptcy. That is certainly the result in Article 9; see §9-202. In most states the seller's interest in a conditional sale had to be filed to be perfected.

Some sellers still use *conditional sale* terminology in their contracts. What effect does the seller's retention of title have under the UCC? Read §§2-401(1), second sentence, and 1-201(b)(35), second-to-last sentence in the first paragraph.

D. *Trust Receipt*

A strained use of trust law principles helped the retail automobile dealer finance (*floor plan*) purchases of vehicles from the manufacturer. In trust receipt financing, the car dealer would ask a bank to buy the cars from the manufacturer. The bank would then turn them over to the dealer after two things happened: (1) the bank filed a notice in the appropriate place announcing its intention to engage in trust receipt financing with this particular dealer; and (2) the dealer signed a *trust receipt* (thereby becoming a *trustee*; the bank was called an *entruster*), acknowledging receipt of the vehicles and granting the bank a security interest therein. As the cars[4] were sold, the bank's interest was paid off, and, when paid in full, the trust receipt was canceled. Various complications could arise, the most common of these being a sale "out of trust," meaning that the dealer did not remit the proceeds of the car sales as required by the agreement, which often happened if the bank failed to police the debtor's activities. Trust receipt financing rules were codified in the Uniform Trust Receipts Act, a very difficult statute that was adopted in two-thirds of the states.

---

4. Trust receipt financing was, of course, used in financing the acquisition of inventory other than automobiles but was available only where the inventory consisted of easily identifiable separate items—for instance, those having serial numbers.

E. Factor's Lien

The word *factor* originally meant any selling agent (wholesaler or retailer) who helped finance the principal's business. As time went on, the factor's selling function died out, and the factor became a financing entity who loaned money against inventory the manufacturer put up as collateral. In return, the factor was granted a lien (a security interest) in the inventory, but this security interest had to be filed to be perfected under most states' factor lien statutes. Most of these statutes contained this drawback: The lien did not extend to new additions to the inventory (*after-acquired property*); that is, it was not a *floating lien* that attached to the changing objects in the inventory. If the after-acquired property in the inventory was to become collateral for the factor, a new security agreement and, typically, a filing of the same were prerequisites to perfection.

F. Field Warehousing

In Benedict v. Ratner the primary evil was that the debtor was in possession of property that secretly belonged to the creditor. With a pledge, possession of the collateral is in the creditor, and no deception problem arises. If the collateral is too big to be conveniently left in the creditor's possession (say, for instance, the collateral is an inventory of Christmas tree ornaments waiting for the Christmas season), one way of pulling off a pledge was for the debtor to store the goods in a warehouse and have the warehouse company issue a negotiable warehouse receipt made out to *bearer*. Such a warehouse receipt (a *document of title*, now regulated by Article 7 of the UCC) has to be surrendered before the warehouse company will turn over the goods to anyone (§7-403); in effect, this rule makes the warehouse receipt take the place of the goods, and thus the receipt was pledged to the creditor in return for the loan of money. Possession of a negotiable document of title (a warehouse receipt or a bill of lading) perfected the creditor's security interest. A *field warehouse* is the same thing as a normal warehouse with one difference: The warehouse comes to the goods instead of vice versa. If the goods are too bulky to move easily, the field warehouseman goes to the goods, stakes them out in some way, issues a warehouse receipt therefor, and guards them (even the debtor, on whose premises they remain, is not supposed to be able to get to the goods). The receipt is then pledged to a financing agency; when the debt is repaid, the warehouse receipt is returned to the debtor, who presents it to the field warehouse agent, who surrenders the goods and then packs up and leaves the debtor's property. (The field warehouse agent is frequently only temporarily hired by the field warehouse company and is actually a regular employee of the debtor. The resulting loyalty conflicts often gave rise to warehouseman misbehavior and, inevitably, lawsuits.)

G. *Conclusion*

Article 9 of the Code replaced all these devices (though some of the practices, such as a pledge or field warehousing, live on) with new rules as to creation of the security interest, the collateral to which it can attach, and the steps necessary for perfection. It is meant to be all-inclusive to cover all possible security interests in personal property and fixtures (see §9-109(c) and (d) for a list of transactions excluded from Article 9's dominion).

When Article 9 was being created the drafters were worried that it would prove politically difficult to adopt because it did away with so many other statutes (Chattel Mortgage, Factors Act, Uniform Trust Receipts Act, and others), and replaced them with a completely new system that lawyers would have to learn. To their surprise Article 9 turned out to be a chief selling point during the state by state adoption of the Uniform Commercial Code because it was one logical system and did not require understanding a hodgepodge of other laws, and lawyers were relieved to have to master only one set of well-structured rules.

THE SCOPE OF ARTICLE 9

It is particularly important for an attorney to appreciate which transactions Article 9 will apply to and those it will not. The scope provisions of the Article are considered next, starting with definitions, transactions at the borders of the Article, and exclusions from its coverage.

Article 9 focuses on secured transactions in personal property. Its rules state what a debtor and creditor must do to make the transaction effective (*attachment* or *creation*); what the creditor must do to give notice making the transaction effective against other parties, such as other creditors, buyers, or a bankruptcy trustee (*perfection*); who wins if creditors, buyers, or other parties contest rights in the collateral (*priority*); and what the creditor may and may not do to repossess the collateral and sell it to get paid (*default*).

I. SECURITY INTEREST DEFINED

Read §1-201(b)(35) (defining *security interest*) and §9-109(a) (General Scope of Article).

PROBLEM 2

Assume that a state statute gives someone doing repairs a possessory artisan's lien on the property repaired. Mr. Baker took his car into Mack's Garage for repair but, being strapped for funds, couldn't pay the full bill, and Mack wouldn't let him have the car back. Is Mack's artisan's lien an Article 9 *security interest*? See §9-109(d)(2). If, prior to the repair work, Mr. Baker signed a statement giving Mack's Garage a right to repossess the car if the bill wasn't paid, does this agreement create a *security interest* under the Code? See §9-109(a)(1).

PROBLEM 3

To raise money, Farmer Brown's Fresh Vegetables Roadside Stand sold all of its accounts receivable to Nightflyer Finance Company, which notified the customers that henceforth all payments should be made directly to Nightflyer. (Note that this is not a loan from the finance company to the farmer with the accounts put up as collateral; it is an outright *sale*. If it were a loan, and if the collectible accounts exceeded the amount of the loan, the excess would be returned to Farmer Brown; in an actual sale, Nightflyer can keep the surplus. See §9-608(b).) Is this sale nonetheless an Article 9 "security interest"? See §9-109(a)(3). If so, even though Farmer Brown has no further obligations to Nightflyer, he would of necessity be termed an Article 9 "debtor." See §9-102(a)(28)(B). Then Nightflyer would have to file an Article 9 financing statement to perfect its interest against later parties. Why would the Code drafters have brought an outright sale of accounts (and *chattel paper, payment intangibles,* and *promissory notes,* all defined below) under the coverage of Article 9? Remember Benedict v. Ratner? See Official Comment 4 to §9-109; Major's Furniture Mart, Inc. v. Castle Credit Corp., 602 F.2d 538 (3d Cir. 1979).

For the practicing attorney, the possibility that a business transaction with no apparent *loan* or *collateral* may still fall within Article 9 is a matter of great concern. If the transaction creates an Article 9 *security interest,* the attorney's client had better have taken whatever steps Article 9 requires for perfection, or the client may lose the property to later creditors. If the attorney has not advised the client of this possibility, the client's thoughts may turn to malpractice actions.

PROBLEM 4

The loan agreement between Dickens Publishing, Inc., and Octopus National Bank contained a negative pledge clause. Dickens agreed not to use any of its property as collateral for debt to other creditors. Is the transaction governed by Article 9? Cf. Chase Manhattan Bank, N.A. v. Gems-By-Gordon, Inc., 649 F.2d 710 (9th Cir. 1981). Suppose Dickens had agreed as follows: "Dickens agrees to repay Lender the entire principal of $18,000 on or before April 1, 2015. If Dickens cannot refinance its current debt to cover this amount or if another source of funds is unavailable, Dickens agrees to sell its inventory and equipment in order to repay Lender." Is the transaction governed by Article 9? See In re Ryalls, 2007 WL 1228789 (Bankr. N.D. Cal. 2007).

A few of the obviously troublesome areas where Article 9 may or may not apply are discussed next.

II. CONSIGNMENTS

A true consignment is neither a *sale* nor a *security device;* it is a marketing procedure by which the owner of goods (the *consignor*) sends (*consigns*) them to a retailer (the *consignee*) for sale to the public. The retailer does not *buy* the goods (so no sale takes place when the consignor delivers the goods to the consignee). If the retailer cannot sell them, they are returned to the consignor. In effect, the consignee is the selling agent for the consignor, or, looked at another way, the consignee is a bailee with the ability to sell the bailor's goods. The advantages to the consignor of a true consignment over an outright sale (with reservation of a security interest so the goods can be reclaimed if the retailer does not pay for them) is that the consignor retains control over the terms of the retail sale (and thus can dictate the retail price), and, at least at common law, there is no requirement that the consignor file a notice anywhere announcing that a consignment is going on. (Why, the consignors argue, should they have to notify anyone that they have claimed an interest in their own property?) At common law, this argument tended to prevail, with the consignors able to reclaim the consigned goods from the inventory of the consignee over the objections of the consignee's other creditors; see Ludwigh v. American Woolen Co., 231 U.S. 522 (1913); In re Haley & Steele, Inc., 20 Mass. L. Rptr. 204, 2005 WL 3489869 (Mass. Super. 2005).

Nonetheless, consignments have the Benedict v. Ratner problem: the retailer appears to be the unfettered owner of goods in inventory that actually belong to someone else (the consignor). The retailer's other creditors may wish to extend credit with the inventory as collateral, but there is no place they can go to check whether some or all of the inventory is actually held on consignment.

Further, some consignments are not *true consignments* at all but are sales on credit (i.e., secured transactions) disguised as consignments in order to escape the filing requirements. If the retailer must pay for the goods whether or not able to resell them, this is not a true consignment, even if called that; it is the creation of a security interest in goods. If a *security interest* is intended, then it is not a true consignment at all; see §9-102(a)(20)(D).[1] Article 9 *must be* complied with (perfection by filing, etc.).

In the end, the drafters of the revised version of Article 9 decided to take some kinds of true consignments and treat them as Article 9 matters, thus requiring the usual steps for perfecting a security interest in someone else's inventory (see "Purchase Money Security Interests" in Chapter 7) but leaving some true consignments outside the Code (and thus protected by the common law rule that favored the consignor). Read §9-102(a)(20).

PROBLEM 5

Antiques R Us was the largest antiques store in the city, well known as a place where antique dealers could hire out space and exhibit their wares, with the store handling the sales and taking a commission on each one and returning to the dealers items that remained unsold. When the store takes out a loan from Octopus National Bank and uses as collateral "all its property," will the bank's security interest reach the items in the store that belong to the dealers if the dealers have never taken the steps required of consignors under Article 9? See §9-102(a)(20)(A)(iii).

The "not generally known by its creditors to be substantially engaged in selling the goods of others" test from §9-102(a)(20)(A)(iii) is taken from an identical provision in the former language of §2-326, which also exempted such retail transactions from the necessity of compliance with the perfection rules of Article 9. If the consignor failed to take these steps, the consignor would frequently appeal to this factual test as a last resort but, as the case below indicates, it was a slim reed on which to lean.

---

1. This so-called "consignment" would typically create a purchase money security interest, requiring the steps yet to be discussed for its perfection. Because Article 9 consignments are also given this treatment, this distinction, carefully preserved in the statute, is much ado about nothing.

In re Fabers, Inc.

United States District Court, District of Connecticut,
Bankruptcy Division, 1972
1972 WL 20789

SEIDMAN, Ref. Bankr.

The bankrupt is a retail carpet and rug merchant. On May 31, 1971, the petitioner, Mehdi Dilmaghani & Company, Inc. (dealer), shipped oriental rugs to the bankrupt on consignment. Subsequent deliveries of rugs on a similar basis were made on May 5, 1971, October 4, 1971, October 5, 1971, October 7, 1971, December 6, 1971, and December 23, 1971. All of the rugs so shipped had an identifying label attached. On each label was printed "MD. & CO., INC., Reg. No. R.N. 22956, 100% wool pile, No. _____, Quality _____, Size _____, Sq. Feet _____, Made in Iran." The consignment agreement provided that title to the rugs remained in the dealer until fully paid for; that the consignee had the right to sell the rugs in the ordinary course of business and only at a price in excess of the invoice price; that the proceeds of any sale were the property of the dealer and held in trust for the dealer; that the proceeds of any sale were to be remitted to the dealer immediately with a report of the sale; [and] that all rugs were held at the risk of the consignee.

No effort was made to comply with the provisions of the Uniform Commercial Code relating to security interests. The dealer does not assert a security interest in the rugs, claiming only that the rugs are and always were the property of the dealer under a "true consignment" and, therefore, not subject to the provisions of the Code relating to security interests. . . .

The dealer's claim is that the consignment was not intended for security and is, therefore, not subject to the requirements of Article 9. The logic of this argument escapes the court. If the dealer did not want the agreement to provide it with security for either the payment of the rugs or their return, what other purpose could there have been? The agreement describes the rugs as belonging to the dealer, but the risk of loss or damage is on the consignee. This is inconsistent with the liability of a bailee. The proceeds of the sales were to be the property of the dealer, but the consignee is described as holding the proceeds in trust. A trustee has *title* to the trust estate. The agreement impliedly permitted the consignee to mingle the proceeds with his own funds before remitting. At any rate, there was no requirement of a separate account. This is inconsistent with a true trust. . . .

The principal claim of the dealer is that the transaction was a true consignment, that at all times the consignee was acting as the agent of the dealer and, therefore, the transaction came under the exception allowed in §2-326. . . . To protect itself from the claims of creditors, the dealer could have complied with the filing provisions of Article 9, §2-326(3)(c), but it admittedly did not. The only other exceptions are compliance with an applicable Connecticut law providing for a consignor's interest by a sign (there apparently is no such law) or establishing that the consignee-bankrupt was generally known by his creditors to be substantially engaged in selling the goods of others.

In support of the latter theory, evidence was submitted that the dealer never dealt in oriental rugs prior to May 1971 and that an advertisement in the local newspapers on October 12, 1971, included a picture of Mr. Mehdi Dilmaghani together with the narrative: "By Special Arrangement, we proudly introduce: A distinctive collection of Mehdi Dilmaghani . . . renown importer of genuine handmade Oriental, India, and Petit-Point Rugs. . . ." This hardly complies with the requirement that the bankrupt "is generally known *by his creditors* to be substantially engaged in selling the goods of others." (Emphasis added.) There was no evidence of any notification to any of the bankrupt's creditors to that effect. In fact, it is found that the contrary was true. The bankrupt was not substantially engaged in selling the goods of others.

The dealer argues that the oriental rugs were not the kind of goods in which the bankrupt dealt. They may not have been of the same quality or price range as the other rugs and carpets sold by the bankrupt, but they were all of the same kind of goods—to wit: floor coverings. The trade name of the bankrupt was "Faber's World of Carpets." Other than the reference to the collection by Dilmaghani in the newspaper advertisement there was nothing to suggest any possible connection with the dealer. In fact, this advertisement is no different from that of a department store advertising a full line of "Frigidaire" appliances, or a collection of Pierre Cardin's new spring line. This is a far cry from the situation in In re Griffin, 1 U.C.C. Rep. Serv. 492, where the bankrupt had a sign in his window advertising used furniture and the court found that under the particular circumstances, this was notice that goods of others were being sold. In the instant case, there was no such notice.

There was evidence that the members of the Oriental Rug Dealers Association usually sold their rugs on consignment. This was well known to the members of the association. There was no evidence that this was the universal invariable practice in the trade, or that the creditors of the bankrupt who apparently did not deal in oriental rugs knew anything about the custom of the members of the Oriental Rug Dealers Association. As between the parties, the transaction was a consignment agreement. As to the creditors, it was a sale or return and bound by the provisions of Section 2-326. Since the petitioner does not come under the exceptions in this section, it was required to comply with the filing provisions of Article 9 to preserve its secured position. Admittedly, this was not done.

It is found that the agreement was intended for security and subject to the requirements of §2-326. There was no perfection of the security interest and the agreement did not come under the exceptions set forth in §2-326(3). Accordingly, it is held that the goods are subject to the claims of creditors, §2-326(2). The reclamation petition is denied, and it is so ordered.

PROBLEM 6

When Luke Skywalker, an artisan who handcrafted his wares, finished creating a large jeweled sword, he took it down to Weapons of the World (WOW), a large gun and weapon dealer which mostly sold items that it either manufactured itself or bought from other dealers around the globe. The sword was appraised as being worth over $25,000. Luke asked WOW to sell the sword for him. Is this an Article 9 consignment so that Luke needs to take Article 9 steps to protect himself from WOW's other creditors who have an interest in the store's inventory?

III.   LEASES

A problem similar to the applicability of Article 9 to consignments occurs when the parties disguise a secured sale as a lease.

PROBLEM 7

BIG Machines, Inc., leased a duplicating machine to Connie's Print Shop. The lease was for five years, and the rental payments over this period exactly equaled the current market price of the machine. The lease contract further provided that at the end of the five years Connie's Print Shop could purchase the machine outright by paying BIG Machines $5. BIG Machines did not file an Article 9 financing statement. Thereafter Connie's Print Shop borrowed money from the Octopus National Bank and signed a security agreement with the bank granting it an interest in all of the print shop's "equipment." Octopus National duly perfected its security interest by filing a financing statement in the appropriate place. When Connie's Print Shop failed to repay the loan, Octopus National seized all the shop's equipment, including the duplicating machine. In the lawsuit Octopus National Bank v. BIG Machines, Inc., who gets the machine? Read §1-201(b)(35).

Parties may wish to cast a transaction as a lease rather than a sale for many reasons. At various times in the tortured history of tax law (a history that is changing so fast that your authors express no opinion as to the current status of the issue under the Internal Revenue Code), rental payments on a *true lease* could be deducted from gross income, but in a *sale,* the "lessee" could take only depreciation on the object purchased. Tax lawyers developed much experience wrestling with the distinctions between a true lease and a disguised sale, witness:

> At the time of this writing, the use of many millions (and probably billions) of dollars' worth of equipment is being obtained through a medium of tax-oriented leases where the ability of the lessor to take accelerated depreciation and obtain the Investment Tax Credit [is] so crucial that the lease will not be entered into without a ruling by the Commissioner on this point, or at the very least, an unqualified opinion by tax counsel, who necessarily must err only on the side of caution. Tax counsel and administrators have developed a lore of their own for distinguishing a true lease from a disguised sale. One point of interest is their emphasis upon the necessity for the lessor's retention of a residual of significant and measurable value. Although this element is seldom stressed as such in chattel security literature, it is suggested that if UCC draftsmen ever deem it feasible to devise something better than either old U.S.C.A. section 1(2) or abandoned section 7-403, study should be directed toward the possibility of devising a formula based on the value of the residual to be returned at the end of the lease term. A rule of thumb in tax rulings and in super-cautious opinions of lessors' tax counsel is (1) that the lease must come to an end at a time when at least two years or twenty percent of the useful life of the leased item remains, and (2) that this residual must be valued at not less than 15 percent of the purchase price. The lessor's tax counsel is likely to insist that there be no options, or only an option to purchase at the market value as determined when the option is exercised. This position is based on the premise that risk of an increase or decrease in value of the residual is an incident of the lessor's ownership and that he should, therefore, bear this risk.

P. Coogan, Leases of Equipment and Some Other Unconventional Security Devices: An Analysis of UCC Section 1-207(37) and Article 9, 1973 Duke L.J. 909, 966-967. For other IRS tests, see Rev. Rul. 55-540, 1955-2 Cum. Bull. 39; Rev. Proc. 75-21, 26 C.F.R. §601.201 (1975). The same issue comes up when books must be maintained:

> From an accounting point of view, the true lease has had the advantage to the lessee of providing him with "off balance sheet financing." That is to say, the lease obligates him to pay rent and not to buy goods. Accordingly, the leased property is not shown as an asset on the lessee's balance sheet, and, consistently, the obligation to pay rent is not listed as a liability. This

treatment tends to improve the balance sheet ratios commonly used in determining the lessee's financial strength. Additionally, the obligations of a lessee under a true lease usually are not subject to restrictions on the amount of money he may borrow contained in existing loan agreements, corporate charters and so forth.

W. Hawkland, The Proposed Amendments to Article 9 of the UCC—Part 5: Consignments and Equipment Leases, 77 Com. L.J. 108, 113 (1972). The tax/accounting tests tend to focus on the "intention of the parties" and on two other factors: (1) the "equity" the lessee builds in the leased property; and (2) the value of the property surrendered to the lessor at the end of the term.

Finally, for various statutory reasons, lessors fare better in bankruptcy than do sellers. See discussion in In re Grubbs Constr. Co., 319 B.R. 698 (Bankr. M.D. Fla. 2005).

The drafters of the Uniform Commercial Code deal with the issue in the complicated definition of "security interest" in §1-203. The drafters' task was to give some concrete guidance to the difference between a sale on credit disguised as a lease (security interest) and a true lease. Take a deep breath and wade through that definition now, with the hope that the following materials will make it seem less formidable than appears at first glance.

What are we to make of this definition? The happiest thing about it (despite its size) is that it does draw some bright lines to help attorneys distinguish leases from secured transactions:

1.   If at the end of the lease period the lessee becomes the owner of the property for little or no consideration, a secured transaction and not a lease has been created.
2.   If the contract contains a clause that permits the lessee to terminate the lease at any time and return the leased goods, a true lease has resulted. Such a right of termination is not an attribute of a sale of goods.
3.   If the lease is for the entire economic life of the leased goods, with or without renewal, a disguised sale has occurred. This is sometimes called the *junk pile* test because goods that are worthless at the end of the lease are simply tossed out.

Other than that, each lease must be evaluated on its own. It does not necessarily answer the central question if the lessee pays consideration equal to or even greater than the fair market value of the leased goods as long as the lease does not cover the total economic life of the goods. Nor does the lessee's assumption of major duties (taxes, risk of loss, etc.) necessarily indicate either a lease or a sale of goods.

Use the definition and the above tests to answer the following Problem.

PROBLEM 8

Business Corporation leased a massive copier from Copies, Inc., for a five-year period. At the outset of the lease the copier had a fair market value of $300,000 and a predicted ten-year useful life. Over the course of the five-year lease the rental payments would total to $330,000. The lease provides that Business Corporation has the option to become the owner of the copier at the end of the five-year period by paying Copies, Inc., the amount of $10,000. Is this a true lease or a secured sale? Would we reach a different result if the copier's useful life were only five years?

Gibraltar Financial Corp. v. Prestige Equipment Corp.

Supreme Court of Indiana, 2011
949 N.E.2d 314

SULLIVAN, Justice.

The parties to this lawsuit claim rights to a punch press used in the manufacturing business of now-defunct Vitco Industries, Inc. Gibraltar Financial Corp. holds a perfected security interest in Vitco's tangible and intangible property, including its equipment. The other parties claim that the security interest does not cover the press because the press was not Vitco's equipment; rather, it had been leased to Vitco by Key Equipment Finance, Inc. We find that genuine issues of material fact exist regarding whether the press was leased.

BACKGROUND

Vitco Industries, Inc., was a manufacturer of porcelain enameled goods in Napanee, Indiana. In April, 2004, Vitco paid $243,000 for a punch press to use in its business. Roughly eight months later, in December, 2004, Vitco entered into a transaction with Key Equipment Finance, Inc. ("Finance"), in which Finance paid Vitco the same amount, $243,000, and Finance and Vitco executed a contract under which Vitco was entitled to use the punch press in exchange for monthly payments. Finance and Vitco called this contract a "Master Lease Agreement," which we will refer to in this opinion as the "Lease." Consistent with the lease nomenclature, Finance did not file a financing statement in connection with the transaction.

The Lease had the following terms:

- Term: Six years.
- Rent: $3,591.91 per month ($43,102.92 per annum).
- Net Lease Terms: Vitco was required to maintain insurance, pay all personal property taxes, bear all risk of loss, and perform all repairs and maintenance with regard to the press.

- Early Buyout Option ("EBO"): Vitco was entitled to buy the press after five years for $78,464.70 (32.29% of the total cost of the equipment), a price that the Lease recited represented "the parties['] present best estimate of the fair market value of the Equipment on the EBO Date determined by using commercially reasonable methods which are standard in the industry." Appellant's App. 121.
- End-of-Term Options: In the event Vitco did not exercise the EBO, Vitco was required to continue paying monthly rent during the sixth year (total of $43,102.92). At the end of the Lease's six-year term, Vitco could do one of four things:
  (1) buy the press for fair market value; or
  (2) renew the Lease for the fair market renewal rental value; or
  (3) continue the Lease month-to-month at the current monthly rental rate; or
  (4) return the press to Finance (in which case Vitco would pay for the press's removal and return to Finance, or Finance could attempt to sell the press directly from Vitco's facility).

For purposes of the End-of-Term Options, the Lease defined "fair market value" as "the Equipment's value as determined between Lessor and Lessee, based upon a price which would be obtained in an arm's-length transaction between an informed and willing lessor or seller . . . and an informed and willing lessee or buyer." Id. at 114.

Vitco never made it to the point where it could exercise the EBO or otherwise complete the terms of the Lease. By 2007, Vitco was no longer in business and had defaulted under the Lease.

Independent of its dealings with Finance, Vitco had entered into several loan agreements with Gibraltar Financial Corp. pursuant to which it had granted Gibraltar a security interest in virtually all of its tangible and intangible property, including its equipment. It is undisputed that Gibraltar perfected its security interest. In a separate lawsuit filed against Vitco in July, 2007, Gibraltar was awarded possession of the collateral in which it had a perfected security interest, including Vitco's equipment. Gibraltar sold that equipment and credited Vitco with the sale proceeds, but Vitco still owed Gibraltar almost $580,000.

In the meantime, Finance repossessed the press and sold it in July, 2007, for $160,000 to National Machinery Exchange, Inc. ("NME"), in a joint venture with Prestige Equipment Corp.

In May, 2008, Gibraltar filed this action against Prestige to recover the value of the press, alleging that Prestige had acquired the press subject to Gibraltar's security interest. A series of third-party complaints and amendments followed, as detailed in the margin. The parties agreed after a pretrial conference that the dispute turned on whether the Lease was a true lease (as argued by the Defendants) or a sale subject to a security interest (as argued by Gibraltar). The trial court granted summary judgment in favor of the Defendants after concluding that the Lease was a true lease.

The Court of Appeals affirmed the trial court's grant of summary judgment. Gibraltar Fin. Corp. v. Prestige Equip. Corp., 925 N.E.2d 751 (Ind. Ct. App. 2010). Gibraltar sought transfer to this Court, arguing, in part, that the decision of the Court of Appeals in this case conflicted with the prior decision of the Court of Appeals in Gangloff Industries, Inc. v. Generic Financing & Leasing Corp., 907 N.E.2d 1059 (Ind. Ct. App. 2009). We have granted transfer to reconcile any conflict between these two cases and to clarify Indiana law in distinguishing true leases from sales subject to security interests. . . .

DISCUSSION

I

Court decisions, treatises, and articles on commercial law are replete with declarations of the difficulty in distinguishing between "true" leases and sales subject to security agreements. For example, the court in the epic WorldCom bankruptcy case was forced to observe that though the concepts of lease and security agreement "are rather easily defined, the means to distinguish between them in a rigorous manner has often eluded the courts." WorldCom, Inc. v. Gen. Elec. Global Asset Mgmt. Servs. (In re WorldCom, Inc.), 339 B.R. 56, 64 (Bankr. S.D.N.Y. 2006). For their part, White and Summers say that whether a transaction in the form of a lease is characterized as a lease or a sale subject to a security interest is "one of the most frequently litigated issues under the Uniform Commercial Code." 4 James J. White & Robert S. Summers, Uniform Commercial Code 17 (6th ed. 2010).

Our review of the history of these disputes suggests that much of the difficulty arose under the pre-1987 version of the Uniform Commercial Code ("U.C.C."), a uniform law adopted in some version by all 50 states. See In re Edison Bros. Stores, Inc., 207 B.R. 801, 809 n.7 (Bankr. D. Del. 1997) (noting that the U.C.C. has been adopted by all 50 states). The pre-1987 U.C.C. emphasized the subjective intent of the parties entering into a lease agreement at the time the agreement was made. The Official Comment to post-1987 U.C.C. §1-203 discusses this problem:

> Reference to the intent of the parties to create a lease or security interest led to unfortunate results. In discovering intent, courts relied upon factors that were thought to be more consistent with sales or loans than leases. Most of these criteria, however, were as applicable to true leases as to security interests. . . . Accordingly, [the 1987 revision of the U.C.C.] contains no reference to the parties' intent.

U.C.C. §1-203 cmt. 2 (2001) (formerly U.C.C. §1-201(37)), 1 U.L.A. 28 (2004).

The parties agree that this dispute is governed by Colorado law. Two sections of the U.C.C. as adopted by Colorado are applicable here. First, the Colorado U.C.C. defines the term "lease" as follows:

> "Lease" means a transfer of the right to possession and use of goods for a term in return for consideration, but a sale, including a sale on approval or a sale or return, or retention or creation of a security interest is not a lease. . . .

Colo. Rev. Stat. §4-2.5-103(j) (2010). The key thing to note about this definition is that it specifies that a transaction creating a lease and a transaction retaining or creating a security interest are mutually exclusive. E. Carolyn Hochstadter Dicker & John P. Campo, FF & E and the True Lease Question: Article 2A and Accompanying Amendments to UCC Section 1-201(37), 7 Am. Bankr. Inst. L. Rev. 517, 521 (1999).

Colorado has adopted the following provision of the U.C.C. that sets forth rules for distinguishing a transaction creating a lease and a transaction retaining or creating a security interest: [The court quoted §1-203.] . . .

II

Although Colorado §1-203(a) provides that "[w]hether a transaction in the form of a lease creates a lease or security interest is determined by the facts of each case," §1-203(b) dictates that if its specifications are met, the transaction will be deemed to have created a security interest. Thus, Colorado §1-203(b) provides that if its bright-line test is met, the issue is decided—the transaction has created a security interest and no further inquiry is required.

The bright-line test of §1-203(b) has two prongs which, if both satisfied, dictate that a transaction creates a security interest. The first prong is satisfied "if the consideration that the lessee is to pay the lessor for the right to possession and use of the goods is an obligation for the term of the lease and is not subject to termination by the lessee." Colo. Rev. Stat. §1-203(b). As one commentator has observed, this prong is satisfied if the lease "requires the lessee to make rental payments to the lessor 'come hell or high water.' " Dicker & Campo, supra, at 534 (footnote omitted).

The Defendants maintain that the Lease was subject to early termination by Vitco by virtue of Vitco being able to terminate the lease by exercising the EBO. But the Court of Appeals rejected this argument, pointing out that a termination clause differs from a buyout clause. *Gibraltar*, 925 N.E.2d at 755-56. We agree with the Court of Appeals and its analysis on this point—the consideration Vitco was obligated to pay was an obligation for the term of the lease and was not subject to termination by Vitco. Thus, the first prong of the bright-line test is satisfied.

The second prong of the bright-line test of §1-203(b) is satisfied if any one of the four "Residual Value Factors" listed in §1-203(b)(1) through (4) are found to exist. In re QDS Components, Inc., 292 B.R. 313, 332 & n.9 (Bankr. S.D. Ohio 2002). Gibraltar acknowledges that the first three factors do not apply to the Lease. Appellant's Br. 18. But it contends that the fourth factor does, arguing that the Lease provided Vitco with "an option to become the owner of the goods for no additional consideration or for nominal additional consideration upon compliance with the [Lease]." Colo. Rev. Stat. §4-1-203(b)(4). If so, both prongs of the bright-line test would be satisfied and the transaction would have created a security interest.

As discussed under Background, supra, the Lease gave Vitco two opportunities to become the owner of the punch press—at the end of the Lease and upon exercise of the EBO.

At the end of the Lease, Vitco had the right to purchase the press for its "fair market value"; no specific amount was provided. Did this provision give Vitco the right to buy the press "for no additional consideration or for nominal additional consideration"?

The statute provides that "[a]dditional consideration is not nominal if: . . . the price is stated to be the fair market value of the goods determined at the time the option is to be performed." 322 Colo. Rev. Stat. §4-1-203(d)(2).

The price "stated" for Vitco to purchase the press at the end of the lease was its "fair market value," in so many words, and so the consideration in this circumstance was not nominal. As such, the provisions of the end-of-term option did not cause the transaction to create a security interest.

The provisions of the EBO, however, were quite different. Under the EBO, Vitco had the right to buy the press after five years for the specific amount of $78,464.70. And as described in Background, supra, the Lease did declare that the parties agreed that this amount represented their best estimate of what the fair market value of the equipment would be on the EBO date. The Defendants argue that this language had the effect of "stat[ing]" that Vitco could purchase for fair market value within the meaning §1-203(d)(2). For the same reason the provisions of the end-of-term option did not cause the transaction to create a security interest, the Defendants contend, so too for the EBO.

The Court of Appeals rejected this contention, holding that "the EBO applie[d] a fixed price [(the $78,000 amount)] to the value of the Punch Press rather than permitting the price to be determined at the time the option [was] to be performed." *Gibraltar*, 925 N.E.2d at 757. The Court of Appeals was correct in concluding that for §1-203(d)(2) to operate, the fair market value of the goods must be determined at the time the option is to be performed. But, at the same time, §1-203(e) directs that "'reasonably predictable' . . . fair market value . . . shall be determined with reference to the facts and circumstances at the time the transaction is entered into." Even if we were to conclude, reading these two provisions together, that fair market value could be specified in advance under the Fair Market Value Test, we think that for the Defendants to be entitled to summary judgment on this point, they were required to set forth material facts demonstrating that the $78,000 price constituted the expectations of Vitco and Finance at the time the transaction was entered into as to what the fair market value of the punch press would be on the EBO date.

Except for the recitation in the contract itself, there was no evidence presented to the trial court of the expectations of Vitco and Finance at the time the transaction was entered into as to what the fair market value of the punch press would be on the EBO date. There was evidence presented by Gibraltar's expert that the value of the press near the time of the EBO date was at least $100,000. Appellant's App. 229. And there was evidence that after Vitco's default, Finance sold the press for $160,000 approximately two-and-a-half years after the Lease was executed. Id. at 110. While these facts are not relevant to establishing the expectations of Vitco and Finance at the time the transaction was entered into, they are enough to keep us from crediting the contract recitation alone as reflecting the parties' actual expectations. We agree with the Court of Appeals that Finance failed to establish that the $78,000 EBO price is not nominal under the Fair Market Value Test.

While the Court of Appeals did not find §1-203(d)(2) applicable here, it came to the ultimate conclusion that Vitco did not have an option to become the owner of the punch press for only nominal additional consideration upon compliance with the EBO. It reached this result by applying the test embodied in the first sentence of §1-203(d)—referred to in the cases as the "Option Price/Performance Cost Test"—and concluding that the $78,000 price was greater than Vitco's reasonably predictable cost of performing if the EBO was not exercised. *Gibraltar*, 925 N.E.2d at 756-57 (citing In re QDS Components, 292 B.R. at 335). We agree. Had Vitco declined to exercise the EBO, it would have been required to pay an additional approximately $43,000 in rent. The only evidence in the record indicates that the cost to return the punch press would have equaled approximately $19,500, although that figure was not estimated at the time the parties entered into the agreement. Appellant's App. 228. In any event, the $78,000 price is not less than even the sum of these two amounts and, therefore, not nominal within the meaning of §1-203(d). *Gibraltar*, 925 N.E.2d at 757; see also In re QDS Components, 292 B.R. at 335-340 (detailing the proper method of applying the "Option Price/Performance Cost Test" of §1-203(d)).

To review, we have applied the objective, bright-line test of §1-203(b) and concluded that the Lease did not create a security interest per se. Even though it was not subject to termination by Vitco, compliance with the

Lease required Vitco to pay more than nominal consideration to become the owner of the press. This is because the $78,000 EBO price was not less than Vitco's reasonably predictable cost of performance under the Lease had the EBO not been exercised within the meaning of the Option Price/Performance Cost Test of §1-203(d).

III

A

Under the objective, bright-line test of §1-203(b), the Lease did not create a security interest per se. But because §1-203(a) provides "[w]hether a transaction . . . creates a lease or security interest is determined by the facts of each case," the facts of this case may nevertheless dictate that the Lease did create a security interest. In re WorldCom, 339 B.R. at 70; Sankey v. ABCO Leasing, Inc. (In re Sankey), 307 B.R. 674, 680 (Bankr. D. Alaska 2004) (citing In re QDS Components, 292 B.R. at 333).

If a court finds that a transaction did not create a security interest per se, it must then "consider the economic reality of the transaction in order to determine . . . whether the transaction is more fairly characterized as a lease or a secured financing arrangement." Duke Energy Royal, LLC v. Pillowtex Corp. (In re Pillowtex), 349 F.3d 711, 719 (3d Cir. 2003). Unfortunately, the U.C.C. does not provide any explicit test or methodology for assessing the economic reality of the transaction. As a result, the cases contain a plethora of formulations and approaches which we will briefly survey.

The majority of courts and commentators recite that the principal inquiry in this regard is " 'whether the lessor has retained a meaningful reversionary interest in the goods.' " In re WorldCom, 339 B.R. at 71 (emphasis in original) (citation omitted). However, again, the U.C.C. does not provide for assessing whether a lessor has retained a "meaningful reversionary interest." In re QDS Components, 292 B.R. at 341. Nevertheless, the *WorldCom* court explained the rationale for the "meaningful reversionary interest" test as follows:

> If the lessor does not possess a meaningful reversionary interest, the lessor has no interest in the economic value or remaining useful life of the goods, and therefore the lessor transferred title to the goods, in substance if not in form. In other words, the parties did not create a lease where the putative lessor does not have the interest, the entrepreneurial stake, in the goods that a true lessor would have.

339 B.R. at 72. But as the *WorldCom* court itself acknowledged, this reasoning by itself is "circular." Id. In point of fact, the absence of any accepted method of determining whether a meaningful reversionary interest exists

renders such a determination more a statement of conclusion—that the transaction is a lease—than a method of analysis.

For its part, the Court of Appeals recognized that the cases provide no "'consistent set of factors for identifying a lessor's residual interest.'" *Gibraltar,* 925 N.E.2d at 758 (quoting In re Gateway Ethanol, L.L.C., 415 B.R. 486, 504 (Bankr. D. Kan. 2009)). Following the *Gateway* court, it "decline[d] to apply a laundry list of factors identified by other courts [and instead focused] on the economic factors of the Lease."[2]

In sorting through these various formulations, we first conclude that the U.C.C. has rejected the laundry list approach in an apparent effort to "overrule a series of bad decisions under the pre-1987 version of section 1-201(37)." 4 White & Summers, supra, at 30. This was done because many of the factors considered under the old approach were just as applicable to true leases as they were to security interests. *Kimco Leasing,* 656 N.E.2d at 1218 n.15; In re QDS Components, 292 B.R. at 326.

Nonetheless, the U.C.C. does not explicitly prohibit consideration of these factors. Rather, it provides that "[a] transaction in the form of a lease does not create a security interest merely because" of the presence of any one or more of the six factors. Colo. Rev. Stat. §1-203(c)(1)-(6) (emphasis added). Indeed, the Court of Appeals in Gangloff Industries, Inc. v. Generic Financing & Leasing, Corp. relied on this language in concluding that certain factors were not prohibited from consideration. 907 N.E.2d at 1066 n.8; see also In re WorldCom, 339 B.R. at 71 (noting that the factors are "characterized as not sufficient alone to establish that a security interest has been created." . . . Leading scholars, on the other hand, have opined that with the exception of the first,[3] the conditions are not only "not enough," but are simply not relevant in distinguishing between true leases and security interests. 4 White & Summers, supra, at 33.

---

2. Similar to the Court of Appeals in this case, the Indiana Tax Court has rejected the "laundry list" approach and instead identified two considerations in determining whether the lessor retained a meaningful residual interest: "1) whether the lease contains an option to purchase for no or nominal consideration, and 2) whether the lessee develops equity in the leased property such that the only sensible decision economically for the lessee is to exercise the purchase option." Kimco Leasing, Inc. v. State Bd. of Tax Comm'rs, 656 N.E.2d 1208, 1218 & n.15 (Ind. Tax Ct. 1995); see also In re QDS Components, 292 B.R. at 342-43 (noting that California law considers similar factors). We note that the first consideration duplicates the second prong of the bright-line test contained in §1-203(b)(4). See In re QDS Components, 292 B.R. at 343 n.20 (noting the redundancy in considering the nominality of the option price a second time in the meaningful-residual-interest analysis).

3. The first condition considers the amount of rent the lessee is required to pay as compared to the fair market value of the goods at the time the lease is entered into. Colo. Rev. Stat. §1-203(c)(1). We agree with these scholars that the exclusion of the first condition is "puzzling" because "[n]ormally one would assume that when [the first condition] is met the parties have a secured sale, not a lease." 4 White & Summers, supra, at 30-31.

B

To be entitled to summary judgment, the Defendants bear the burden of demonstrating the absence of any genuine issue of material fact as to whether the economic realities of the transaction dictate that it is a lease as a matter of law. Ind. Trial Rule 56(C). The Court of Appeals concluded that the Defendants were entitled to summary judgment because Finance had retained a meaningful reversionary interest in the punch press. This was so, according to the Court of Appeals, primarily because the equipment would still have had significant value had Vitco decided to return it at the end of the six-year Lease. It reached this conclusion because the useful life of the punch press was apparently fifteen to twenty years. *Gibraltar*, 925 N.E.2d at 758.

The putative lessor in the *Pillowtex* case made a similar argument. In that case, the Third Circuit found

> that under certain circumstances, the fact that transferred goods have a useful life extending beyond the term of the transferring agreement could reveal the transferor's expectation of retaining residual value in those goods. Such an inference would only be proper, however, where the evidence showed a plausible intent by the transferor to repossess the goods.

In re Pillowtex, 349 F.3d at 720. In *Pillowtex,* the court found no likelihood that the transferor would repossess the fixtures in question because their removal would have been prohibitively expensive. Id. at 720-21. That is certainly not the situation with the punch press. But *Pillowtex*'s analysis does lead us to conclude that the punch press's useful life extending beyond the term of the Lease does not by itself establish that the transaction was a true lease.

C

In the end, we "focus on economics." U.C.C. §1-203 cmt. 2 (2001), 1 U.L.A. 29 (2004). This includes "all the economic factors which drove the transaction and which were the prime impetus to the ultimate decision to enter into the transaction and the reasons for structuring the transaction as it was done." Am. President Lines, Ltd. v. Lykes Bros. Steamship Co., Inc. (In re Lykes Bros. Steamship Co., Inc.), 196 B.R. 574, 580 (Bankr. M.D. Fla. 1996); see, e.g., United Airlines, Inc. v. HSBC Bank USA, N.A., 416 F.3d 609, 617 (7th Cir. 2005) (finding as determinative the measure for rent, the presence of a balloon payment, the effect of prepayment, and the lessee already having the asset and using it for an extension of credit); Kentuckiana Med. Ctr. LLC v. The Leasing Group Pool II, LLC (In re Kentuckiana Med. Ctr. LLC), No. 10-93039-BHL-11, 2011 Bankr. LEXIS 1702, 2011 WL 1750769, at *7 (Bankr. S.D. Ind. May 6, 2011) (noting that the leases were structured in such a way as to make lessee's cost of returning the collateral exceed the cost of purchasing it); In re Grubbs Constr. Co., 319 B.R. 698, 720 (Bankr. M.D.

Fla. 2005) (noting the key factor for entering into the transaction was the effective interest rate charged for financing); *Gangloff Indus.*, 907 N.E.2d at 1065 (citing evidence that consideration was based on the price plus interest divided by months). Other factors may include, but are not limited to, the total amount of rent required of the lessee, whether the lessee acquired equity or any pecuniary interest in the goods, the useful life of the goods, the practical limitations on the lessee's ability to remove and return the leased goods, and the ability of the lessor to market the equipment. In re Uni Imaging Holdings, LLC, 423 B.R. 406, 418-20 (Bankr. N.D. N.Y. 2010) (citing In re Gateway Ethanol, 415 B.R. at 505); In re WorldCom, 339 B.R. at 74; In re Grubbs Constr. Co., 319 B.R. at 718-721.

At least some of these factors are present in this case. Pointing toward the transaction creating a security interest is the fact that Vitco already owned the punch press when it entered into the Lease with Finance (and it may have used it as security for an extension of credit). Pointing toward the transaction creating a lease are the useful life of the punch press, the absence of limitations on its removal, and the ability of Finance to market it.

What we are not able to determine, however, is whether the payment provisions of the Lease are more indicative of a lease or of a secured financing arrangement. We know that the purchase price of the press at the time of the transaction was $243,000. We know that Vitco had the option of purchasing it after five years for a total outlay of roughly $294,000 (60 monthly payments of $3,591.91 plus the EBO price of $78,464.70). And we know that if Vitco had not exercised the EBO, it would have been required to make twelve additional monthly payments totaling $43,102.92 (a total outlay of roughly $259,000), and thereafter it could have purchased the punch press for its then-appraised value.

The economics of the transaction can certainly be cast to demonstrate a lease: The parties agreed that Vitco would lease the punch press for 72 months at $3,592 per month with an option to buy at fair market value at the end. Under this approach, the EBO is an aside — an agreement as to the option price if Vitco wanted to exercise the option after 60 months.

On the other hand, the economics could also be cast to demonstrate a sale subject to a security interest: Vitco agreed to buy the punch press for $294,000 with 60 monthly payments of $3,592 plus a balloon payment of $78,000. Under this approach, the language regarding the sixth year was mere surplusage — paying the $78,000 was the only economically sensible course for Vitco to take.

A bankruptcy case discussed by both sides in their briefs illustrates this point. In that case, a construction company had entered into several equipment leases. In re Grubbs Constr. Co., 319 B.R. 698. Under the leases' early buyout options, the "price was determined in advance and in no way depended on a future valuation." Id. at 720-21. In holding that the equipment leases had created security interests, the court found that "the only economically sensible course for [the company], absent default, was to exercise the Early Buyout Option" and acquire the equipment. Id. at 721.

As the movants for summary judgment, the Defendants had the burden of establishing the absence of any genuine issue of material fact as to the economic realities of the transaction dictating that it was a lease as a matter of law. To do so required evidence of the expectations of Vitco and Finance at the time the transaction was entered into as to such factors as the value of the punch press on the EBO and lease expiration dates, the discount rate, and whether the "only economically sensible course" for Vitco would have been to exercise the EBO. We regret having to remand this case for further proceedings, but the authorities are clear that "[f]oresight not hindsight controls." 4 White & Summers, supra, at 33; see also In re Uni Imaging Holdings, 423 B.R. at 417 ("In determining whether 'additional consideration' is nominal, the Court is to examine the economic realities of the transaction and the expectations of the parties concerning the projected value of the equipment at the time they entered into the agreement. . . ." (citing In re Gateway Ethanol, 415 B.R. at 500)). We see no way of resolving this case without this evidence. Because such evidence was not presented, summary judgment was not appropriate.

CONCLUSION

For the foregoing reasons, the judgment of the trial court is reversed and the case is remanded for proceedings consistent with this opinion.

———————————

In close cases the advising attorney may wish to tell the lessor (or the alleged consignor in quasi-consignment problems) to play it safe and file a financing statement even if it is believed that a true lease/non-consignment has been created. This may create a danger, however, that the Article 9 filing is an admission (for tax/accounting purposes) that only a secured transaction is involved. To avoid this admission problem, the drafters gave us §9-505, which is a "fail-safe" provision, allowing the protective filing without it being in any way an admission that a secured transaction is intended.

IV. OTHER TRANSACTIONS

PROBLEM 9

When Mercy Hospital's administrators decided to build a new addition, they hired a general contractor named Crash Construction Co. and required it to get a surety to guaranty the performance of the construction job and the payment of all the workers and material suppliers (to avoid a mechanic's lien on the hospital). Standard Surety issued such a performance and payment bond covering Crash's obligation to Mercy Hospital. To finance the construction, Crash borrowed money from Octopus National Bank (ONB) and gave as collateral the right to collect the progress payments from Mercy Hospital as they came due. ONB duly filed an Article 9 financing statement. Halfway through the job, Crash went bankrupt, and Standard Surety had to finish and pay off the employees and suppliers. At this point, by virtue of the common law right to *subrogation* (the equitable right given to sureties to step into the legal shoes of persons they have paid), Standard Surety claimed a superior right to unpaid monies retained by Mercy Hospital, which were to be paid to Crash. ONB also claimed this fund, pointed to its filed security interest, and stated that Standard Surety's subrogation right was only an unfiled Article 9 security interest. Who should win? See New Mexico State Highway and Transp. Dept. v. Gulf Ins. Co., 996 P.2d 424(N.M. App. 1999); Comment, Equitable Subrogation—Too Hardy a Plant to Be Uprooted by Article 9 of the UCC? 1971 U. Pitt. L. Rev. 580.

V.   *EXCLUSIONS FROM ARTICLE 9*

Read §9-109(c) and (d).

A.   *Federal Statutes*

It is no surprise that the Uniform Commercial Code, a state statute, cannot displace federal law. From the way §9-109(c)(1) is worded, however, note that the UCC *does* apply to the extent that the federal statute does not answer the problem presented. See G. Gilmore, Security Interests in Personal Property, ch. 13 (1965) (hereinafter G. Gilmore); for a list of such statutes, see J. White & R. Summers, Uniform Commercial Code (6th ed. 2010) [hereinafter White & Summers, a leading treatise on the meaning of the UCC] §22-11. With the exception of the federal tax lien statute, Internal Revenue Code §§6321-6325, most federal statutes (for example, the Ship Mortgage Act of 1920 and the Civil Aeronautics Act's provisions on security interests in aircraft) do not cover the field and are constantly supplemented by Article 9 provisions in litigation.

In United States v. Kimbell Foods, 440 U.S. 715(1979), the Supreme Court decided that, as a matter of *federal* law, the relative priority of private consensual liens arising in favor of the U.S. government under various lending programs is to be decided under non-discriminatory state law (i.e., the UCC), unless a federal statute clearly provides otherwise.

For the practitioner, the important thing to remember is that certain matters must be researched on a federal as well as a state level. Ship mortgages, aircraft titles, railroad equipment, and some interstate commercial vehicles (such as trucks and buses registered with the Interstate Commerce Commission) are, in part, governed by federal statutes. Creditors (and their attorneys) who simply think an Article 9 filing will perfect their interest in, say, an airplane, end up as unsecured creditors whose only cause of action may be against their state-law–minded attorneys. See Feldman v. Chase Manhattan Bank, N.A., 368 F. Supp. 1327 (S.D.N.Y. 1974) (assignment of airplane lease with Article 9 filing not effective against bankruptcy trustee where creditor failed to file with FAA as required by Federal Aviation Act). Exciting efforts are under way to create an international registration system for rail, planes, and satellites, and some parts of the plan are already in place; see http://www.unidroit.org/work-in-progress-studies/studies/security-interests.

Further, certain federal statutes may void some security interests. Section 125 of the Truth in Lending Act, 15 U.S.C. §1635 (1980), for instance, destroys any security interest taken in a consumer's home as part of a credit transaction if the credit seller does not notify the consumer of a three-day right to rescind the contract (and supply the consumer with other truth-in-lending disclosures).

Some federal statutes may be more friendly to creditors than Article 9. In one case Magnacom Wireless bought FCC radio spectrum licenses on credit, but was unable to pay the price when due. The FCC revoked the licenses and resold them, for $249 million more than Magnacom owed. Had Article 9 applied, Magnacom would have been entitled to the surplus. But under the governing federal law, the FCC was entitled to keep the surplus. See In re Magnacom Wireless, LLC, 503 F.3d 984(9th Cir. 2007).

NOTE ON INTELLECTUAL PROPERTY AS COLLATERAL

Strangely enough, there is great confusion as to whether security interests in various types of intellectual property are to be perfected under federal or state law. The federal trademark, patent, and copyright statutes all provide that security interests may be recorded in the relevant federal office (the U.S. Patent and Trademark Office or the Copyright Office). But none of the three statutes is clear on whether federal filing is required to perfect the security interest. Courts have reached a variety of conclusions on the issues. See In re Together Dev. Corp., 227 B.R. 439 (Bankr. D. Mass. 1998) (trademarks should be filed under Article 9); In re Cybernetic Services, Inc., 252 F.3d 1039 (9th Cir. 2001) (patents should be filed under Article 9); Rhone-Poulenc Argo, S.A. v. DeKalb Genetics Corp., 284 F.3d 1323 (Fed.

Cir. 2002) (stating that federal filing would govern priority in patent rights); In re World Auxiliary Power Co., 303 F.3d 1120 (9th Cir. 2002) (security interest in *unregistered* copyrights should be filed under Article 9); In re Peregrine Entertainment, Ltd., 116 B.R. 194 (C.D. Cal. 1990) (security interest in *registered* copyrights should be filed in Copyright Office).The matter is of some real practical importance. If a UCC filing is all that is required, one filing in the name of the debtor will do it for all the intangible rights he/she owns; if a federal filing is necessary, it will have to be done for *each* patent, copyright, or trademark, a much more expensive undertaking. Cf. White & Summers §22-11.

PROBLEM 10

Pollution Solutions, Inc., took out a loan from Octopus National Bank (ONB), putting up as collateral its copyrights, patents, and trademarks. Where *should* ONB file to be sure it has a perfected security interest? No one knows where ONB *must* file to perfect its security interest, but the question here is slightly different.

Philko Aviation, Inc. v. Shacket

United States Supreme Court, 1983
462 U.S. 406

Justice WHITE delivered the opinion of the Court.

This case presents the question whether the Federal Aviation Act of 1958 (Act), 49 U.S.C. §§1301 et seq., prohibits all transfers of title to aircraft from having validity against innocent third parties unless the transfer has been evidenced by a written instrument, and the instrument has been recorded with the Federal Aviation Administration (FAA). We conclude that the Act does have such effect.

On April 19, 1978, at an airport in Illinois, a corporation operated by Roger Smith sold a new airplane to respondents. Respondents, the Shackets, paid the sale price in full and took possession of the aircraft, and they have been in possession ever since. Smith, however, did not give respondents the original bills of sale reflecting the chain of title to the plane. He instead gave them only photocopies and his assurance that he would "take care of the paperwork," which the Shackets understood to include the recordation of the original bills of sale with the FAA. Insofar as the present record reveals, the Shackets never attempted to record their title with the FAA.

Unfortunately for all, Smith did not keep his word but instead commenced a fraudulent scheme. Shortly after the sale to the Shackets, Smith purported to sell the same airplane to petitioner, Philko Aviation. According to Philko, Smith said that the plane was in Michigan having electronic equipment installed. Nevertheless, Philko and its financing bank were satisfied that all was in order, for they had examined the original bills of sale and had checked the aircraft's title against FAA records. At closing, Smith gave Philko the title documents, but, of course, he did not and could not have given Philko possession of the aircraft. Philko's bank subsequently recorded the title documents with the FAA.

After the fraud became apparent, the Shackets filed the present declaratory judgment action to determine title to the plane. Philko argued that it had title because the Shackets had never recorded their interest in the airplane with the FAA. Philko relied on §503(c) of the Act, 49 U.S.C. §1403(c), which provides that no conveyance or instrument affecting the title to any civil aircraft shall be valid against third parties not having actual notice of the sale, until such conveyance or other instrument is filed for recordation with the FAA. However, the District Court awarded summary judgment in favor of the Shackets, 497 F. Supp. 1262 (N.D. Ill. 1980), and the Court of Appeals affirmed, reasoning that §503(c) did not preempt substantive state law regarding title transfers, and that, under the Illinois Uniform Commercial Code, Ill. Rev. Stat., ch. 26, §§1-101 et seq., the Shackets had title but Philko did not. 681 F.2d 506 (CA7 1982). We granted certiorari, ____ U.S. ____ (1982), and we now reverse and remand for further proceedings.

Section 503(a)(1) of the Act, 49 U.S.C. §1403(a)(1), directs the Secretary of Transportation to establish and maintain a system for the recording of any "conveyance which affects the title to, or any interest in, any civil aircraft of the United States." Section 503(c), 49 U.S.C. §1403(c), states:

> No conveyance or instrument the recording of which is provided for by [§503(a)(1)] shall be valid in respect of such aircraft . . . against any person other than the person by whom the conveyance or other instrument is made or given, his heir or devisee, or any person having actual notice thereof, until such conveyance or other instrument is filed for recordation in the office of the Secretary of Transportation.

The statutory definition of "conveyance" defines the term as "a bill of sale, contract of conditional sale, mortgage, assignment of mortgage, or other instrument affecting title to, or interest in, property." 49 U.S.C. §1301(20) (Supp. V, 1981). If §503(c) were to be interpreted literally in accordance with the statutory definition, that section would not require every transfer to be documented and recorded, it would only invalidate unrecorded title *instruments,* rather than unrecorded title *transfers.* Under this interpretation, a claimant might be able to prevail against an innocent third party by establishing his title without relying on an instrument. In the present case, for example, the Shackets could not prove their title on the basis of an unrecorded bill of sale or other writing purporting to evidence a transfer of title to them, even if state law did not require recordation of such instruments, but they might still prevail, since Illinois law does not require written evidence of a sale "with respect to goods for which payment has been made and accepted or which have been received and accepted." Ill. Rev. Stat., ch. 26, §2-201(3)(c).

We are convinced, however, that Congress did not intend §503(c) to be interpreted in this manner. Rather, §503(c) means that *every* aircraft transfer must be evidenced by an instrument, and *every* such instrument must be recorded, before the rights of innocent third parties can be affected. Furthermore, because of these federal requirements, state laws permitting undocumented or unrecorded transfers are preempted, for there is a direct conflict between §503(c) and such state laws, and the federal law must prevail.

These conclusions are dictated by the legislative history. The Senate, House, and Conference committee reports, and the section-by-section analysis of one of the bill's drafters, all expressly declare that the federal statute "requires" the recordation of "every transfer of any interest in a civil aircraft." The Senate report explains: "This section requires the recordation with the Authority of every transfer made after the effective date of the section, of any interest in a civil aircraft of the United States. The conveyance evidencing *each such transfer* is to be recorded with an index in a recording system to be established by the Authority." Thus, since Congress intended to require the recordation of a conveyance evidencing *each transfer* of an interest in aircraft, Congress must have intended to preempt any state law under which a transfer without a recordable conveyance would be valid against innocent transferees or lienholders who have recorded.

Any other construction would defeat the primary congressional purpose for the enactment of §503(c), which was to create "a central clearing house for recordation of titles so that a person, wherever he may be, will know where he can find ready access to the claims against, or liens, or other legal interests in an aircraft." Hearings Before the House Comm. on Interstate and Foreign Commerce, 75 Cong., 3d Sess., 407 (April 1, 1938) (testimony of F. Fagg, Director of Air Commerce, Dept. of Commerce). Here, state law does not require any documentation whatsoever for a valid transfer of an aircraft to be effected. An oral sale is fully valid against third parties once the buyer takes possession of the plane. If the state law allowing this result were not preempted by §503(c), then any buyer in possession would have absolutely no need or incentive to record his title with the FAA, and he could refuse to do so with impunity, and thereby prevent the "central clearing house" from providing "ready access" to information about his claim. This is not what Congress intended.

In the absence of the statutory definition of conveyance, our reading of §503(c) would be by far the most natural one, because the term "conveyance" is first defined in the dictionary as "the action of conveying," i.e., "the act by which title to property . . . is transferred." Webster's Third New International Dictionary 499 (P. Gove ed. 1976). Had Congress defined "conveyance" in accordance with this definition, then §503(c) plainly would have required the recordation of every transfer. Congress' failure to adopt this definition is not dispositive, however, since the statutory definition is expressly not applicable if "the context otherwise requires." 49 U.S.C. §1301. Even in the absence of such a caveat, we need not read the statutory definition mechanically into §503(c), since to do so would render the recording system ineffective and thus would defeat the purpose of the legislation. A statutory definition should not be applied in such a manner. Lawson v. Suwannee S.S. Co., 336 U.S. 198, 201 (1949). Accordingly, we hold that state laws allowing undocumented or unrecorded transfers of interests in aircraft to affect innocent third parties are preempted by the federal Act.

In support of the judgment below, respondents rely on Matter of Gary Aircraft Corp., 681 F.2d 365 (CA5 1982), which rejected the contention that §503 preempted all state laws dealing with priority of interests in aircraft. The Court of Appeals held that the first person to record his interest with the FAA is not assured of priority, which is determined by reference to state law. We are inclined to agree with this rationale, but it does not help the Shackets. Although state law determines priorities, all interests must be federally recorded before they can obtain whatever priority to which they are entitled under state law. As one commentator has explained, "The only situation in which priority appears to be determined by operation of the [federal] statute is where the security holder has failed to record his interest. Such failure invalidates the conveyance as to innocent third persons. But recordation itself merely validates, it does not grant priority." Scott, Liens in Aircraft: Priorities, 25 J. Air L. & Com. 193, 203 (1958). Accord, Sigman, The Wild Blue Yonder: Interests in Aircraft Under Our Federal System, 46 So. Cal. L. Rev. 316, 324-325 (1973) (although recordation does not establish priority, "failure to record . . . serves to subordinate"); Note, 26 Wash. & Lee L. Rev. 205, 212-213 (1979).

In view of the foregoing, we find that the courts below erred by granting the Shackets summary judgment on the basis that if an unrecorded transfer of an aircraft is valid under state law, it has validity as against innocent third parties. Of course, it is undisputed that the sale to the Shackets was valid and binding as between the parties. Hence, if Philko had actual notice of the transfer to the Shackets or if, under state law, Philko failed to acquire or perfect the interest that it purports to assert for reasons wholly unrelated to the sale to the Shackets, Philko would not have an enforceable interest, and the Shackets would retain possession of the aircraft. Furthermore, we do not think that the federal law imposes a standard with which it is impossible to comply. There may be situations in which the transferee has used reasonable diligence to file and cannot be faulted for the failure of the crucial documents to be of record. But because of the manner in which this case was disposed of on summary judgment, matters such as these were not considered, and these issues remain open on remand. The judgment of the Court of Appeals is reversed, and the case is remanded for further proceedings consistent with this opinion.

So ordered.

NOTE

For the resolution of this case on retrial, see Shacket v. Philko Aviation, Inc., 841 F.2d 166 (7th Cir. 1988) (second purchaser, alas, still lost because of failure to investigate suspicious circumstances).

B.   Landlord's Lien and Other Statutory Liens

Subsections (d)(1) and (2) of §9-109 exclude statutory liens (like the one in Problem 2) from Article 9; but what about the following situation?

PROBLEM 11

When Christopher Morley opened his bookshop, the landlord wanted security for the rent. They signed a lease agreement providing that all of the inventory (the books) would be subject to a lien in the landlord's favor and could be seized and sold if Christopher defaulted on the rent payments. Is the landlord's lien required to be perfected under Article 9? See Persky, Shapiro, Salim, Esper, Arnoff & Nolfi Co., L.P.A. v. Guyuron, 2000 WL 1867407 (Ohio App. 2000).

C.   Wage Assignments

Claims to wages were once a fertile source of collateral, but special statutory regulation has all but killed off wage assignments. Thus, some states absolutely prohibit the assignment of future wages (see, e.g., Ala. Code tit. 39, §201; such assignments are *void*); some permit them in limited circumstances if the employer consents (see, e.g., Del. Code Ann. tit. 5, §2115; N.C. Gen. Stat. §95-31); and some states require the consent of both the employer and the spouse (see, e.g., Ind. Code §22-2-7). Employers always disliked having to bother with direct payments to an employee's creditors (and further disliked the idea that employees had little or no equity left in their own paychecks). The special statutes on the matter survive the enactment of Article 9; §9-109(d)(3).

PROBLEM 12

Carl Jugular was an independent insurance agent who sold policies for many companies, though his primary sales were the life and automobile policies of the Montana Insurance Association (MIA). In order to float a loan to buy a car, Carl gave the lending bank a security interest in "all present and future commissions earned or to be earned" from the MIA. Does Article 9 cover this assignment? See Massachusetts Mut. Life Ins. Co. v. Central Pa. Natl. Bank, 372 F. Supp. 1027 (E.D. Pa. 1974).

D.   Non-Financing Assignments

The §9-109(d)(4) through (7) exclusions of some transfers of accounts, chattel paper, payment intangibles, and promissory notes are each meant to be an exclusion of all such assignments of a non-financing nature. See G. Gilmore §10-5. Generally, as we have seen, such sales would be Article 9 matters, but in the listed situations no one would think to comply with Article 9, and the possibility of the deception of later parties is small.

PROBLEM 13

When David Vargo sold his lucrative art business to Manny Flowers, he sold not only all the tangible assets but his outstanding accounts receivables as well. Must the buyer take the steps required by Article 9 of a secured party? See §§9-102(a)(72)(D) and 9-109(d)(4). If Vargo received a commission to paint the portrait of the city's mayor but decided he was too busy to perform the task and (with the mayor's permission) transferred the job (and the right to the payment for it) to another artist, must the new artist take Article 9 steps? See §9-109(d)(6). When one of Vargo's clients refused to pay for a delivered painting, Vargo sold the account to Trash Collection Agency. Must Trash comply with Article 9? See §9-109(d)(5). Finally, pressed by his art supplies store for payment of his outstanding tab, Vargo transferred to the store the money due him from a client whose portrait he had painted the month before. Must the art supplies store take Article 9 steps? See §9-109(d)(7).

E. Real Estate

Except for fixtures, real estate security interests are not covered by Article 9, but what happens when the paperwork creating them (the mortgage and the promissory note the debtor signs) is used as security when the mortgagee seeks a loan?

PROBLEM 14

Local Loan Company (LLC) needed to borrow money, and Octopus National Bank agreed to loan it the requisite amount, taking into ONB's possession as collateral the real property mortgages and accompanying promissory notes given to LLC by its borrowers. Need ONB do anything either in the real property recording office or under the UCC's Article 9 to protect its interest in this collateral? Compare §9-109(d)(11) and (b); read Official Comment 7 to §9-109; see the helpful discussion in R. Bowmar, Real Estate Interests as Security Under the UCC: The Scope of Article Nine, 12 UCC L.J. 99 (1979); and see §§9-203(g) and 9-308(e). See Prime Fin. Servs. LLC v. Vinton, 279 Mich. App. 245, 260 (Mich. Ct. App. 2008).

F. Other Exclusions

PROBLEM 15

Octopus National Bank issued Connie Consumer a credit card. As collateral for the credit card debts, ONB took a security interest in all items she purchased using the card, as well as in her personal checking account with the bank. Does Article 9 apply to the bank's rights in this account? See §9-109(d)(13).

Would Article 9 apply if she used her consumer bank account as collateral for a business loan? See §9-102(a)(26).

PROBLEM 16

Debtors assigned to Octopus National Bank "all sums recovered by Debtors, directly or indirectly," from their lawsuit against Meep Corporation for breach of a sales contract. Meep Corporation settled the lawsuit, and agreed to pay Debtors the claimed amount. Is the assignment subject to Article 9? See §9-109(d)(9). See Goldberg & Connolly v. New York Cmty. Bancorp, Inc., 565 F.3d 66 (2d Cir. 2009).

Section 9-109(d) lists some other items that are excluded from Article 9 coverage in whole or in part (insurance, certain tort claims, etc.). We will consider these matters as they arise in other contexts.

CHAPTER 3   ASSESSMENT: MULTIPLE CHOICE QUESTIONS

1. UCC Article 9 provides a comprehensive scheme for regulating security interests in personal property. To which of the following transactions would Article 9 apply?
   a. Pemulis Auto borrowed money from Wolters Bank, with the parties agreeing that Pemulis Auto's inventory, equipment, and accounts receivable would be collateral for the loan.
   b. Von Richthofen provided aerial photography services for Konstantin Farms, to guide irrigation and planting decisions. A state statute gave Von Richthofen a lien on Konstantin Farm's crops, to secure payment for those services.
   c. Williams Bank purchases the accounts receivable of Fitzherbert Spa, which are the debts owed by customers for spa services.
   d. Turing, unable to sell his Enigma supercomputer on eBay, delivers it to a local electronics retailer. The parties agree that if the retailer sells the Enigma, they will split the proceeds, and if not Turing will take the Enigma back.
   e. All of the above.

2. To which of the following transactions does Article 9 apply?
   a. Baldwin put up his house on Strivers Row as collateral for a loan from Empire Bank.
   b. Stewart used her life insurance policy as a security for a debt to Fateful Finance.
   c. Darrow, a lawyer, assigned a long-unpaid account receivable, for collection to Persistent Servicing.
   d. Cannon leased a car for a day.
   e. None of the above.

3. Sasha had a samovar, which had been in the family several generations. He took it to Karl's Konsignments, who agreed to attempt to sell it on Sasha's behalf, for a percentage. Not long after, Karl's Konsignments went into bankruptcy. If Article 9 applied, as we will see in later chapters, that means Sasha would lose the samovar to the bankruptcy trustee. Did Article 9 apply?
   a. Yes. Article 9 applies to consignments.
   b. No. This transaction did not fit in the Article 9 definition of consignments, because it was a consignment of consumer goods.
   c. No. Sasha did not borrow money from Karl's Konsignments.

d. No. Karl's Konsignments did not borrow money from Sasha.

4. Pemulis Auto offers to sell Lloyd, an Uber driver, a Somme Sedan for a down payment of $1,000, along with 36 monthly payments of $400. Lev likes those terms, but would prefer a lease, on the theory that he could deduct the lease payments as a business expense. So Pemulis Auto offers a Lease Agreement, under which Lloyd ("Lessee") pays down $1,000 and is obliged to make 36 monthly lease payments of $400 to Pemulis Auto ("Lessor"), and then will have an option to purchase the car for $1. The Lease Agreement further provides that if Lev fails to make the payments, Pemulis Auto may repossess the car. Lev signs and hands over $1,000. Pemulis Auto signs the papers to have the car registered in Lloyd's name and reminds him to get insurance on the car. Is the transaction subject to Article 9?

   a. No. It is a lease, not a secured loan, consignment, sale of accounts, or agricultural lien.
   b. Yes. In substance, the transaction is a sale of the car on credit, with the car serving as collateral.
   c. No. Article 9 does not apply to cars, which are regulated by Lemon laws and the like.
   d. No. Article 9 does not apply to true leases, and the parties have drafted an agreement using only lease terminology.

5. Chang Equipment was negotiating a one-year loan of $50,000 at 10% interest from Nightflyer Finance, putting up equipment worth $120,000 as collateral. Nightflyer wished to avoid the complexities of debtor-creditor law. Creatively, the parties crafted the following transaction. Chang Equipment agreed to sell the equipment to Nightflyer for $50,000, although Chang Equipment retained use of the equipment. In one year, Chang has the option to buy the equipment back for $55,000. If it does not buy the equipment back, Nightflyer gets the equipment. Does Article 9 apply to the transaction?

   a. Yes. The transaction, in substance if not form, is a secured loan.
   b. No. The transaction is a sale of equipment with an option to buy back, with no debt or collateral.
   c. No. The transaction is a true lease.
   d. No. Article 9 applies only to consumer transactions.

ANSWERS

1. *E* is the best answer. Section 9-109 states the transactions to which Article 9 applies. Answer A is a classic secured transaction, a party agrees to use personal property as collateral for a debt, covered by §9-109(a). But §9-109 makes Article 9 apply more broadly, to transactions that also raise

issues common to secured transactions. B is an agricultural lien, therefore covered by §9-109(b). C is a sales of accounts, within §9-109(c). Even though that is not a secured transaction, it is brought within Article 9 in order to require Williams Bank to comply with the protections that Article 9 provides, such as notice to other creditors (thereby avoiding the secret lien of *Benedict v. Ratner*). D is a consignment. This transaction is also not a secured transaction. The retailer is not borrowing money and the Enigma is not collateral. But the hazard of the secret lien still exists: the retailer's creditors might not realize that the Enigma does not belong to the retailer. Bringing such consignments within Article 9 means that Turing will (as later chapters will discuss) need to file a UCC financing statement to maintain priority in the Enigma, should other creditors go after the Enigma or should the retailer file bankruptcy.

2. *E* is the best answer. This question gives some of the transactions excluded from Article 9 by §9-109. There was already well-established law dealing with mortgages, so Article 9 excludes transactions where the collateral is real estate. Insurance as collateral is specifically excluded. Although assignments of accounts generally are made subject to Article 9, some assignments are excluded because the protections of Article 9 are not necessary. The assignment of an account for collection is excluded. That is not an assignment of which Darrow's creditors need notice. True leases are not secured transactions, although a lease that has the effect of a secured transaction is within Article 9. A one-day car rental is a true lease, not a disguised secured transaction.

3. *B* is the best answer. Article 9 generally applies to consignments, but its definition of consignment excludes various consignments to which the policy of giving notice to creditors is weaker. See §9-102(20). The definition excludes consignments where the consignor and consignee have the same name (so creditors would likely not be affected), where the consignee is an auctioneer (whose creditors would not expect to go after the goods the auctioneer sells for others), or where the creditors know the consignee generally takes goods on consignments (and so the creditor do not need notice of that fact). It also excludes consignments of less than $1,000 in value and excludes consignments (as in this question) of consumer goods, because we do not expect consumers to know about Article 9 and comply with it.

4. *B* is the best answer. Article 9 applies to "a transaction, regardless of its form, that creates a security interest in personal property or fixtures by contract." §9-109(a). Regardless of the legal form used (lease, sale, trust, assignment, etc.), Article 9 will apply if the substance of the transaction is that personal property is used as collateral for an obligation. Here, the form of the transaction was a lease, but the substance was a secured sale. The business deal was that Lev was obliged to pay for the car and was

entitled to keep it, subject to Pemulis Auto's right of repossession in the event of default. In substance, that is a sale of a car on credit, with the car serving as collateral. It was not a true lease, contrary to D. C is misleading. Other laws apply to cars, but they do not displace Article 9.

5. *A* is the best answer. The transaction is just the secured loan under another name. The terms are the same: Nightflyer hands over $50,000 and in one year Chang Equipment pays $55,000 or loses its equipment. C and D are red herrings. Although the parties used only sales terms, the substance governs over form, contrary to B.

What difference does it make that Article 9 applies? The following chapters will tell, but here is a preview. Article 9 requires that Nightflyer Finance would have to file a UCC financing statement to give constructive notice to the world of its security interest in the equipment. If Nightflyer Finance does not do so, it will lose its right to the collateral if Chang Equipment goes into bankruptcy, or sells the equipment, or is faced with a judgment creditor after the equipment. In addition, Article 9 limits the rights of a creditor on default. Nightflyer Finance would not be entitled to simply keep the equipment (worth $120,000) if Chang Equipment did not make its payments (of $55,000). Article 9 imposes other rules that Nightflyer Finance might violate if it does not realize that Article 9 applies. This chapter, then, introduces an important skill for any lawyer that deals with transactions, whether negotiating, closing, or litigating them. A lawyer must recognize whether Article 9 applies, irrespective of the business terms the parties use, and protect her client accordingly.

THE CREATION OF A SECURITY INTEREST

The client tells the attorney "Protect my interest in the collateral," and that instruction triggers the rules of this chapter. The attorney immediately begins thinking about how the law classifies this collateral and what steps are required to make sure the client's interest will prevail over other claimants to the property. It is easy to make mistakes at this stage and create very unhappy clients.

I. CLASSIFYING THE COLLATERAL

Article 9 divides *collateral* (defined in §9-102(a)(12)) into many different categories:

Goods (read §9-102(a)(44); cf. §2-105):
    Consumer Goods (read §9-102(a)(23));
    Equipment (read §9-102(a)(33));
    Farm Products (read §9-102(a)(34)); and
    Inventory (read §9-102(a)(48)).

Quasi-Tangible Property (pieces of paper used as collateral):
    Instruments (read §§9-102(a)(47) and 3-104).[1]
    Investment Property (stocks and bonds and rights to accounts containing same) (read §9-102(a)(49));
    Documents (warehouse receipts and bills of lading) (read §§9-102(a)(30) and 1-201(b)(16));
    Chattel Paper (read §9-102(a)(11)); and
    Letter of Credit Rights (read §9-102(a)(51)).

Intangible Property (property having no significant physical form):
    Accounts (read §9-102(a)(2));
    Commercial Tort Claims (read §9-102(a)(13));
    Deposit Accounts (read §9-102(a)(29));
    General Intangibles (read §9-102(a)(42));
    Health-Care–Insurance Receivables (read §9-102(a)(46) — these are a subcategory of "accounts"); and
    Payment Intangibles (read §9-102(a)(61) — these are a subcategory of "general intangibles").

Note that *equipment* is defined not according to its usual meaning but rather as a catchall category for any goods that do not fit into the other three goods categories. Similarly, *general intangibles* include all intangible collateral not falling into another category.

Classification of the collateral is central because many provisions of Article 9 make legal distinctions based on the type of collateral. For example, the technical steps required to *perfect* a security interest in a negotiable instrument, a family car, or a hardware store's inventory are completely different, as we shall explore when we address the issue of perfection.

It is important to note that it is the *debtor's* announced use of the collateral that determines its classification.

PROBLEM 17

Fill in the blanks with the proper classifications of these items of collateral:
(a) A professional pianist's piano: _____ (see In re Symons, 1967 WL 8983 (Ref. Bankr., E.D. Mich. 1967)).
(b) Cattle fattened by a farmer for sale: _____ (see In re Cadwell, Martin Meat Co., 1970 WL 12561 (Ref. Bankr., E.D. Cal. 1970)); the farmer's tractor: _____ (see Central Natl. Bank v. Wonderland Realty Corp., 38 Mich. App. 76, 195 N.W.2d 768 (1972)); the farmer's chickens: _____

---

1. Promissory notes, defined in §9-102(a)(65), are a subcategory of instruments.

(see United States v. Pete Brown Enter., Inc., 328 F. Supp. 600 (N.D. Miss. 1971)); manure from the dairy herd: _____ (see Miller, Farm Collateral Under the UCC: "Those Are Some Mighty Tall Silos, Ain't They Fella?" 20 S.D. L. Rev. 514, 526 (1975)).

(c) A mobile home: _____ (compare §9-102(a)(53)).

(d) A right to sue someone for breach of contract: _____ (see Friedman, Lobe & Block v. C.L.W. Corp., 9 Wash. App. 319, 512 P.2d 769 (1973)); a right to sue someone for negligence arising out of an automobile accident: _____ (see §9-109(d)(12)); a right to sue a corporation for wooing away a trusted employee: _____ (see §9-102(a)(13)); a security interest in a lawsuit plaintiff has already won and that has been reduced to a settlement agreement: _____ (see §9-109, Official Comment 15).

(e) Pencils and other stationery supplies used by Sears or a similar large retailer in its credit offices: _____ (see §9-102, Official Comment 4(a), fourth paragraph).

(f) A liquor license: _____ (see In re Chris-Don, Inc., 308 B.R. 214 (Bankr. D.N.J. 2004)); a right to the return of a security deposit held by a landlord: _____ (see United States v. Samel Ref. Corp., 461 F.2d 941, (3d Cir. 1972)); a newspaper carrier's right to payments for papers already delivered: _____; a newspaper carrier's right to payments for papers to be delivered in the future: _____.

(g) Curtains bought by a lawyer for the law office: _____ (see In re Bonnema, 1967 WL 9011 (N.D. Ohio 1967)). What if after purchasing the curtains the lawyer decides to use them at home? Do they become consumer goods? See §9-507(b) and the next case; cf. In re McClain, 447 F.2d 241 (10th Cir. 1971).

(h) Aunt Augusta loaned her nephew $5,000 with an oral agreement he would repay the money the following year. If she wants to use this agreement as collateral, how would it be classified?

(i) Patents, trademarks, and copyrights: _____ (see, e.g., Matter of Roman Cleanser, 43 B.R. 940 (Bankr. Mich. 1984)).

(j) Lottery winnings: _____ (see Tex. Lottery Commn. v. First State Bank of DeQueen, 254 S.W.3d 677 (Tex. App. 2008)).

In re Troupe

United States District Court, Western District of Oklahoma,
Bankruptcy Division, 2006
340 B.R. 86, 2006 WL 689515

T.M. WEAVER, Chief Judge.
Presented by the parties' cross-motions for summary judgment is the issue of whether the debtors' tractor, in which the defendant has a purchase

money security interest, is consumer goods under Article 9 of the UCC. If it is, the defendant's security interest is perfected even though the defendant did not file a financing statement. If not, the defendant's security interest is unperfected and subject to avoidance. Because of representations in the security agreement regarding the debtors' intended personal use of the tractor, and for the other reasons herein stated, the court concludes that the tractor is consumer goods and that the defendant has a perfected security interest.

The Chapter 7 Trustee (the "trustee" or "plaintiff") brought this action against the defendant (the "creditor" or "Deere") seeking to avoid Deere's security interest in the tractor pursuant to Sections 544, 549 and 550 of the Bankruptcy Code. The trustee contends that Deere's admitted failure to file a financing statement renders Deere's purchase money security interest unperfected. The trustee asserts that the tractor was used and intended to be used for business, rather than personal, purposes and thus was not consumer goods under Article 9. The defendant maintains that the debtors' primary intended and actual use of the tractor was for personal, family and household purposes and hence was consumer goods. The parties acknowledge that a purchase money security interest in consumer goods is perfected upon attachment, without filing a financing statement. Conversely, they agree that with respect to non consumer goods, the filing of a financing statement is required for perfection of a non-possessory purchase money security interest. . . .

Undisputed Facts

The following material facts are undisputed:

1. On September 24, 2004 (the "petition date"), the debtors filed their voluntary Chapter 7 bankruptcy petition.

2. On the petition date, Robert O. Troupe and Dawn Lynn Troupe (the "debtors") owned a 2001 John Deere 4300 MFWD tractor, with loader and blade (collectively, the "tractor").

3. The debtors purchased the tractor from Deere's dealer on or about July 13, 2001.

4. At the time of the purchase, the debtors lived on a 10-acre tract of land in Colorado.

5. Prior to the purchase of the tractor, the debtors applied for credit with Deere and submitted a credit application dated July 2, 2001.

6. The credit application signed by the debtors stated that the debtor Robert O. Troupe ("Robert") was not self-employed but was employed in a management position with an automotive company earning a gross salary of $4,500 per month. The credit application also stated that the debtor Dawn Lynn Troupe ("Dawn") was employed as a professional auto body estimator earning a gross income of $36,000 per year.

7. The debtors each worked at least 60 hours per week at their respective places of employment. Dawn testified on deposition that she worked approximately 75 hours per week at her job as an estimator and two other part-time jobs that she held at the same time.

8. Before purchasing the tractor, the debtors told the Deere's dealer's salesman that the debtors wanted to purchase a tractor to be used to fill irrigation ditches on their land. They also stated they wanted the tractor to be small enough to go through the gate of a horse stall. Dawn testified on deposition that she also represented to the salesman that they wanted to use the tractor for moving dirt, hay and snow.

9. Deere financed the debtors' purchase of the tractor. In connection with the financing, the debtors and Deere executed a security agreement by which the debtors granted to Deere a purchase money security interest in the tractor.

10. At the top of the first page of the executed security agreement, there were boxes labeled "Personal" and "Commercial," respectively. An "x" was placed in the box labeled "Personal," while the "Commercial" box was left blank.

11. The security agreement contained the following provision on the first page:

Unless I otherwise certify below, this is a consumer credit transaction and the Goods will be used primarily for personal, family or household purposes. (bold type on security agreement)

12. The security agreement also contained on the first page a conspicuous rectangular box running the entire width of the printed page within which appeared the following:

COMMERCIAL PURPOSE AFFIDAVIT. I/We being first duly sworn, affirm and represent to Seller and its assignees that this is a commercial credit transaction, as the Goods listed above will be used by the undersigned in his/her/its business primarily for commercial purposes and will not be used primarily for personal, family or household use.

Buyer's (Debtor's) Signature   Buyer's (Debtor's) Signature

The above signature lines were left blank.

13. The purchase price of the tractor was $16,539.00.

14. At the time of their purchase of the tractor, and for the several years thereafter, the debtors boarded horses and raised cattle and pigs on their acreage. This activity was done while they were working at their full-time jobs.

15. The debtors testified that they intended their farming and ranching activity on their acreage to be profitable financially.

16. On the debtors' tax returns for the years 2001, 2002 and 2003, the debtors took a deduction for depreciation on the tractor. The tax returns reflected that the tractor was used 100 percent for business.

17. The debtors' tax returns for each of the above years showed a substantial loss from ranching.

18. Marketing information on the website of the defendant shows the subject tractor to be in the category of residential equipment.

19. In their affidavits submitted in support of the trustee's motion for summary judgment, the debtors represented that their actual use and intended use of the tractor was for the business purpose of farming and ranching.

20. The debtors' deposition testimony is that the tractor was used 90 percent of the time for personal purposes and 10 percent for business. They considered personal use as being work performed on the homestead as opposed to work done to make a living.

CONCLUSIONS OF LAW AND DISCUSSION

This court has jurisdiction over this adversary proceeding pursuant to 28 U.S.C. §157, 1334 and 11 U.S.C. §544 and 550. This is a core proceeding under 28 U.S.C. §157(b)(2)(F).

The trustee brings this action asserting his rights under the "strong arm clause" of §544(a)(1). Under this provision, the trustee has the rights and powers of a hypothetical lien creditor who held a judicial lien on the property in question at the time of the commencement of the bankruptcy case, whether or not there actually is such a creditor. By exercising these rights, a trustee may avoid liens on property that a lien creditor without notice could avoid. Id.

In bankruptcy proceedings, state law governs issues of validity and priority of security interests [citing cases]. The parties do not dispute that Colorado law applies here. Under C.R.S. §4-9-317(a)(2), the holder of an unperfected security interest is subordinate to the rights of one who became a lien creditor before the security interest was perfected. A lien creditor includes a trustee in bankruptcy. C.R.S. §4-9-102(52). Thus, Deere must have held a perfected security interest to prevail over the trustee in bankruptcy. It is not disputed that if the tractor is classified as consumer goods under the UCC, Deere held a perfected purchase money security interest despite the fact that a financing statement was not filed. C.R.S. §4-9-309(1). If the tractor is not consumer goods, however, Deere is not perfected. C.R.S. §4-9-310.

Consumer goods are "goods that are used or bought for use primarily for personal, family or household purposes." C.R.S. §4-9-102(23). The other possible classification for the tractor, and the one supported by the trustee is that of equipment. Equipment is defined as "goods other than inventory, farm products or consumer goods." C.R.S. §4-9-102(33).

The classification of collateral is to be determined as of the time of the creation of the security interest. The classification does not change because of a later change in the manner in which the collateral is used [citing cases]. If the law were otherwise, a secured party would be required to continually monitor the use that was being made of the collateral.

From reviewing the affidavits of the debtors submitted in support of the trustee's motion for summary judgment, and their deposition testimony, it is not completely clear what oral representations the debtors may have made to Deere's dealer regarding their intended use of the collateral. Robert says he told the salesman that he needed a tractor that was large enough to move dirt to fill irrigation ditches on his land, but small enough to get through a horse stall door. Dawn says she told the salesman they wanted the tractor to do a number of other things on their land in addition to filling the irrigation ditches. Yet nowhere in the debtors' sworn testimony is there any evidence that they told Deere's representative that the tractor was to be used in any type of commercial activity.

The debtors state that they were in the farming and ranching business on their 10-acre tract. They testified that they boarded horses and raised some livestock. Their intention was to make a profit, they said. Their income tax returns reflected that they were involved in ranching, although it was not a profitable endeavor. While the tax returns indicated that the tractor was used 100 percent for business purposes, the debtors' deposition testimony is that 90 percent of the use was personal. Assuming that all of this testimony is true, it nevertheless relates to events subsequent to the attachment of the security agreement. The focus, however, must be on the intended use of the collateral when the security interest was granted.

At the outset, the debtors gave no indication to Deere that they were engaged in a business activity. Their credit application represented that they were both employed, together earning $90,000 per year. Robert represented in the credit application that he was not self-employed. They worked long hours at their jobs—Robert 60 hours per week and Dawn about 75 hours per week.

The security agreement that the debtors signed reflected that it was a "Personal" rather than a "Commercial" transaction. The body of the document stated unequivocally that it was a consumer credit transaction and that the tractor was intended to be used for personal, family or household purposes.

The case law is clear that where a debtor makes an affirmative representation in loan documents that he or she intends to use goods primarily for personal, family or household purposes, the creditor is protected even if the representation turns out to be erroneous. 1 Barkley Clark, The Law of Secured Transactions Under the Uniform Commercial Code ¶12-02 [3] (rev. ed. 2005). ("... just about every case that has dealt with this issue holds that the dealer ... can rely on the debtor's written 'consumer representation'"). In Sears, Roebuck & Co. v. Pettit (In re Pettit), 18 B.R. 8 (Bankr. E.D. Ark. 1981), the debtor bought goods for use in his rental business. Yet the debtor did not inform the seller of his intended use. The security agreement "affirmatively and unambiguously represented that the debtor was purchasing the collateral for personal, family or household purposes." Id. at 9. The bankruptcy court rejected the admission of extrinsic evidence to contradict the unambiguous representation in the security agreement of the debtor's intended use of the collateral. The *Pettit* court held that the seller's purchase money security interest was properly perfected without filing a financing statement, observing that the secured party was not required by the UCC to monitor the debtor's use of the collateral in order to determine its proper classification. In accord is McGehee v. Exchange Bank & Trust Co., 561 S.W.2d 926, 930 (Tex. App. 1978) ("the intent of the debtor-purchaser at the time of the sale when ... [the] security instrument attached to the collateral is controlling, and no creditor is required to monitor the use of the collateral in order to ascertain its proper classification.")

The rationale of *Pettit* is compelling. A debtor who makes representations in a security agreement regarding the intended use of the collateral should be bound by those representations. That is especially true where the debtors fail to inform the creditor that they intend to use the collateral for other than personal, family or household purposes. The classification of the collateral, for purposes of perfection of the security interest, is determined when the security interest attaches. The later use of the collateral for another purpose than as stated in the security agreement is irrelevant in determining whether the security interest is perfected.

According to the security agreement here, the debtors intended to use the tractor as consumer goods. Deere was entitled to rely on the debtors' representation. The debtors did not inform Deere of a different intended use. Therefore, Deere's purchase money security interest was perfected when it attached, and the filing of a financing statement was not required. The security interest remains perfected despite any subsequent use for purposes other than consumer, if indeed there was such other use.

The trustee argues that he should not be bound by the debtors' representations in the security agreement because the debtors did not know of the representations. However, one who signs an agreement is bound by its terms, although ignorant of them, absent fraud or false representation. Elsken v. Network Multi-Family Security Corporation, 49 F.3d 1470 (10th Cir. 1995). As there is no allegation of fraud or false representation regarding the security agreement, this argument is without merit.

For these reasons, the court holds that Deere has a perfected purchase money security interest in the tractor. Accordingly, the defendant's motion for summary judgment is granted, and the plaintiff's motion for summary judgment is denied.

QUESTIONS

What will be the result where a car buyer tells the seller he wants the car for personal family use, but is lying and really plans to resell it on his own lot? See Balon v. Cadillac Auto. Co., 113 N.H. 108, 303 A.2d 194397 (1973). Some creditors contemplating a loan to the debtor require that the debtor fill out an application that explains the intended use of the collateral. Is this legally wise from the creditor's point of view?

PROBLEM 18

Mercy Hospital needs financing and calls you, its attorney, with this question. Many of its patients are members of various health plans, and when they come in for treatment, they sign paperwork authorizing the hospital to seek payment from their health insurance coverage provider. The hospital always has a large number of such receivables in the process of collection. When the hospital borrows money, can it use the monies due it from the various health plans as collateral? See §§9-109(d)(8) and 9-102(a)(46).

PROBLEM 19

Passport Credit Card Company issued millions of credit cards internationally, sending them to cardholders, who then used them in millions of transactions with merchants. The merchants would then send the resulting paperwork to Passport for reimbursement (minus Passport's fee). You are the attorney for Passport. When Passport needs to borrow money, can it use these credit card transactions as collateral? See §9-102(a)(2). Remember that the outright sale of such property by Passport is also an Article 9 transaction; §9-109(a)(3).

PROBLEM 20

Fill in the blanks with the proper collateral classifications:
(a) Milk in the hands of the farmer: _____; in the hands of the grocery store: _____; in the hands of the grocery store's customer who is buying for consumption: _____. Would your answer to the

second question change if "restaurant" were used in place of "grocery store"? See §9-102, Official Comment 4(a), second paragraph.

(b) A certificate of deposit issued by a bank: _____ (compare §3-104(j), §9-102(a)(47), and Southview Corp. v. Kleberg First Natl. Bank, 512 S.W.2d 817 (Tex. Civ. App. 1974)). Would it make a difference if the certificate of deposit was transferable? See In re Perez, 440 B.R. 634 (Bankr. D.N.J. 2010), and Official Comment 12 to §9-102. An *airbill* issued by an airline as a receipt for frozen shrimp shipped by air: _____ (see §1-201(b)(6)); the receipt given to a farmer by a silo operator when the farmer stored grain there: _____.

(c) Rare coins bought by a hobbyist for addition to his collection: _____ (see In re Midas Coin Co., 264 F. Supp. 193 (E.D. Mo. 1967), *aff'd,* 387 F.2d 118 (8th Cir. 1968)).

(d) A tax refund: _____ (see In re American Home Furnishings Corp., 48 Bankr. 905 (Bankr. W.D. Wash. 1985)).

(e) A debenture bond issued by a corporation: _____ (see §§8-102(a)(15) and 9-102(a)(49)); a right to 100 shares of stock recorded on the books of the debtor's stockbroker: _____ (see §8-102(a)(17)).

(f) The checking account you have at your bank: _____ (see §9-102(a)(29)).

(g) A computer program: _____ (see §9-102(a)(44)).

(h) The monthly rental obligations owed to a landlord, who wants to use these obligations as collateral for a loan: _____ (compare §§9-102(a)(2), 9-109(d)(11)); the promissory notes signed for the tenants to pay their rent: _____ (§§9-102(a)(47), 9-109(b)).

Morgan County Feeders, Inc. v. McCormick

Colorado Court of Appeals, 1992
836 P.2d 1051

[Neil Allen made an agreement with James McCormick to sell him 56 head of cattle Allen owned. The cattle were subject to a perfected security interest in favor of Morgan County Feeders, Inc., which seized the cattle prior to their delivery to McCormick. Items sold in the "ordinary course of business" (i.e., *inventory*), as we shall see, pass to the buyer free of even perfected security interests; pieces of *equipment* generally do not. After stating the facts and noting that the trial court had ruled in favor of Morgan County Feeds, Judge Rothenberg continued as follows.]

McCormick first contends that the trial court erred in determining that the cattle purchased by Allen were equipment, rather than inventory. We disagree.

Under the Uniform Commercial Code, "goods" are defined as "all things which are movable at the time the security interest attaches. . . ." Section 4-9-105(1)(f), C.R.S. (1991 Cum. Supp.) [now §9-102(a)(44)—Eds.]. Goods are classified under four major types which are mutually exclusive. These include: consumer goods; equipment; farm products; and inventory. . . .

Here, the parties agree that the cattle constitute "goods" under the Uniform Commercial Code. They further agree that the cattle are not "farm products." Thus, the remaining issue surrounding the cattle is whether they should be designated as inventory or equipment. The distinction is important because buyers of inventory in the ordinary course of business take free of perfected security interests. [See §9-320—Eds.]

Section 4-9-109(2), C.R.S. [now §9-102(a)(33)—Eds.], provides that goods are equipment:

> if they are used or bought for use primarily in business (including farming or a profession) . . . or if the goods are not included in the definitions of inventory, farm products, or consumer goods.

In contrast, §4-9-109(4), C.R.S. [now §9-102(a)(48)—Eds.], provides that goods are inventory:

> if they are held by a person who holds them for sale or lease or to be furnished under contracts of service or if he has so furnished them, or if they are . . . materials used or consumed in a business. Inventory of a person is not to be classified as his equipment.

In ascertaining whether goods are inventory or equipment, the principal use of the property is determinative. Section 4-9-109, C.R.S. (Official Comment 2). The factors to be considered in determining principal use include whether the goods are for immediate or ultimate sale and whether they have a relatively long or short period of use in the business. Section 4-9-109, C.R.S. (Official Comment 3); First Colorado Bank & Trust v. Plantation Inn, Ltd., 767 P.2d 812 (Colo. App. 1988).

Goods used in a business are equipment when they are fixed assets or have, as identifiable units, a relatively long period of use. They are inventory, even though not held for sale, if they are used up or consumed in a short period of time in the production of some end product. First Colorado Bank & Trust v. Plantation Inn, Ltd., supra. . . .

At trial, the court determined that the longhorn cattle were "equipment" and not "inventory" because: "Allen did not acquire or hold them for the principal purpose of immediate or ultimate sale or lease. . . . Instead, the cattle were to be used principally for recreational cattle drives. . . . While Allen might have occasionally leased the cattle to other entrepreneurs, it was his intention to utilize the cattle principally in his own recreational business." Thus, the court concluded that McCormick bought the cattle subject to Morgan County Feeders' security interest.

Although we recognize that the classification of cattle as "equipment," rather than "inventory," is highly unusual, we also recognize that the evidence presented to the trial court disclosed unusual circumstances, and we conclude that the record supports the court's classification.

Allen testified that his purpose for purchasing the longhorn cows was to use them on cattle drives and that these cows have a relatively long period of use in comparison to rodeo calves and feeder cattle. Several other witnesses also testified that Allen had stated his intent to use the longhorn cows for recreational cattle drives. Thus, the trial court was justified in rejecting McCormick's contention that the cattle were purchased only for rodeos. And, it did not err in finding that, under these unique circumstances, the cattle should be classified as "equipment."

In light of this conclusion, we need not address McCormick's additional contention that the trial court erred in finding that McCormick was not a buyer in the ordinary course of business. . . .

The judgment is affirmed.

PROBLEM 21

Sam Ambulance was a lawyer who loved speculative investments. When Elvis Presley died, Ambulance managed to acquire one of the musician's guitars. He decided to keep it for years and let it appreciate in value (he did not himself play the guitar). If Ambulance uses the guitar as collateral for a loan needed to run his law practice, how is the guitar classified?

A Few Words About Chattel Paper. Chattel paper is an artificial construct of Article 9. Suppose, for example, that you run an automobile dealership and your business successfully sells a lot of cars each month on credit. The purchasers sign promissory notes in your favor and also sign a security agreement giving your dealership a security interest in the sold vehicle so that you (or your assignee) can repossess it in the event of default. This set of papers, taken collectively, is called *chattel paper* (note that it includes an instrument therein). Read §9-102(a)(11).[2] There is a huge market for such paper, so when your dealership needs money it can either sell the chattel paper outright or use it as collateral for a loan from a lending institution. Either way it

---

2. This is just one example of chattel paper, which is defined broadly enough to encompass the sale of most security interests from one secured party to another. Because the buying secured party takes possession of the paper, that is usually sufficient to satisfy the Article 9 rules on attachment and perfection.

is an Article 9 transaction and will require the purchaser/lending institution to take the steps required by Article 9 to protect its security interest in the paper; §9-109(a).

PROBLEM 22

How would you categorize the car lease contracts that Dime-A-Minute Rental Cars uses as collateral when it borrows money from a bank? If Dime-A-Minute moves into the computer age and stops using paper entirely, can the electronic version of this paperwork be used as collateral? See §9-102(a)(31) and its Official Comment 5(b). Article 9 provides that a secured party will be protected as to such electronic chattel paper if it has "control" over the paper, but, given that there is no actual writing, how could this possibly be done? Read §9-105.

PROBLEM 23

The State of Montana has enacted a statute giving unpaid crop dusters a lien on the crops of the farmer; Montana Statutes §71-3-901. This, of course, is a statutory lien (since it arises by statute and is not created by the consent of the debtor—the farmer). Is this nonetheless an Article 9 transaction requiring compliance with the usual Article 9 rules? See §§9-102(a)(5), 9-109(a)(2) and (d)(2).

II. TECHNICAL VALIDITY OF THE FORMS

The creation of an Article 9 security interest typically involves two documents: the *security agreement* and the *financing statement*. The security agreement is the *contract* between the debtor and the creditor by which the debtor grants to the creditor (the *secured party*) a security interest in the collateral. See §9-102(a)(74).[3] The financing statement is the *notice* that is filed in the place specified in §9-501 (and indexed under the debtor's name) in order to give later creditors an awareness that the collateral is encumbered. Thus, the purpose of the security agreement is to create property rights between

---

3. The 2010 revisions to Article 9 inserted a new definition of "public organic record" at §9-102(a)(68), so the numbers of the following subsections are all increased by 1.

the debtor and the creditor, and the purpose of a financing statement is to create property rights in the creditor against most of the rest of the world.

This section of the book explores the technical requirements for valid security agreements and financing statements. While not inherently interesting in and of themselves, these sections deserve your close attention. Much of the litigation involving Article 9 of the Code could have been avoided if the attorneys had done their jobs carefully when the documents were created. Imagine that you are a new associate at a major law firm that has just landed a multimillion-dollar account requiring Article 9 compliance. The senior partner confirms that you studied secured transactions in law school (this course) and puts you in charge of making sure that the client's interests are perfected in this big-ticket transaction. The partner tells you, unnecessarily, that the whole firm is trusting you not to make any mistakes. Now read §§9-203(a) and (b), 9-502(a), 9-509(a) and (b), and 9-521. *Record* (a new term in the 1999 revision) is defined broadly in §9-102(a)(70) with the hope that it will encompass all the possible future ways of memorializing legal arrangements.

A. The Security Agreement

Where the collateral is in the possession of the secured party (a *pledge*), no written security agreement is required by law (though one is probably still desirable for evidentiary reasons). Where, however, the property is to leave the creditor's control, §9-203 becomes relevant and creates technical problems.

If the collateral is not in the secured party's possession or control, the §9-203 security agreement must (1) be authenticated by the debtor (*authenticate* is defined in §9-102(a)(7)) and (2) describe the collateral (plus the land if timber is involved). The security agreement need not be in any particular form or contain any particular words. Cf. §1-201(b)(3), defining *agreement*. It needn't call itself a security agreement. See Official Comment 3 to §9-203 on the admissibility of parol evidence to establish the security nature of apparently absolute transactions.

PROBLEM 24

When Frederick Bean bought a new computer on credit from Centerboro Office Supply, before he could take it home the store made him sign a "Conditional Sale Contract," by which he agreed that title to the computer would remain with the store until he had fully paid for his purchase. The contract described the computer, but nowhere did it mention a security interest. Does the contract qualify as a security agreement under §9-203? See §1-201(b)(35), and §2-401(1), second sentence; Sommers v. International Bus. Machs., 640 F.2d 686 (5th Cir. 1981).

A good security agreement will, of course, spell out much more than §9-203 requires. It should identify the parties, describe the collateral, contain a grant by the debtor to the creditor of a security interest in the collateral, and specify the contractual understandings of the parties—in particular, naming what events will constitute *default* to permit the creditor to realize on the security interest by repossessing the collateral. Many more desirable clauses will be suggested by the materials that follow.

B. The Financing Statement

The financing statement—commonly called by its form number, "UCC-1"—is the document filed in the appropriate public office by the creditor (secured party) to *perfect* the creditor's rights in the collateral against later parties. Under the 1999 revision, the requirements for a financing statement have been significantly simplified. Per §9-502(a) it need be signed by no one (though the debtor must have *authorized* it, which follows automatically from the signing of the security agreement; §9-509), but it must identify the parties and indicate what collateral is covered. If realty interests are involved (timber, fixtures, minerals to be extracted from the ground), §9-502(b) adds other requirements—particularly that it describe the realty and the record owner of the realty (if he or she is not the obligor) and indicate that it be filed in the real property records (so that the filing officer sees that it gets to the right place).

In addition, §9-516 lists other things that need to be in the financing statement before the filing office will accept it. Read that section. Note, however, that if the filing office does take the financing statement not containing these things, the financing statement is effective nonetheless.

The financing statement has as its function the giving of notice to later creditors as to what property of the debtor is encumbered by prior liens. Consequently, the financing statement does not typically contain many details of the underlying transaction. Such things as the amount of the loan, the time periods of repayment, etc., are not required to be described in the financing statement. If later curious parties are to discover these details, they must find them out from the original parties, not the public record. This is facilitated by the fact that the financing statement will have on it the addresses of the debtor and secured party, so that those searching the files know how to contact the original participants and discover the current state of the described encumbrance.

Security agreements and financing statements serve different purposes, but they have several problems in common: who the *debtor* is, what a sufficient *description of the collateral* is, etc. Some of these issues are resolved identically for both documents, and some are not. The most common specific problems are explored next.

C.   The Debtor's Identity

When the financing statement is filed (typically in the Secretary of State's office), it will be indexed under the debtor's name. Because later possible creditors will search the records under that name, it is particularly important that it be correct.

PROBLEM 25

Harry Fellini ran a movie theater called "Fellini's Art Theater," but, because he was the sole proprietor, that was a trade name. He gave a security interest in the business's equipment to Sharkteeth Finance Company. The financing statement calls for a listing of the "debtor's name."

(a) Should the parties use the business name or individual name? Read §9-503.

(b) If the theater were run as a partnership, would the partnership's name be used as the debtor's name? See §9-503(a)(4) and (b)[4] and its Official Comment 2.

Determining the name of an individual has proven to be a nightmare for lenders, their attorneys, and the courts. The 2010 amendments to Article 9 gave the states two options to resolving the issue: in §9-503(a)(4)'s Alternative A [sometimes called the "Only If Rule"] or Alternative B [the "Safe Harbor Rule"]. To these alternative possibilities §9-506(a) adds that a financing statement that is in error but not "seriously misleading" is nonetheless effective, but that issue is complicated by the "search engine" test of §9-506(c), defining "seriously misleading" in a cyber fashion. Use these citations to resolve the following Problem.

---

4. Before the 2010 revisions to Article 9 this issue was governed by §9-503(a)(4)(A) and (b).

PROBLEM 26

Bob Wolton had always used "Bob" as his first name even though his birth certificate lists him as "Robert Edward Wolton." All of Bob's public records used "Bob Wolton," and that is the name on his driver's license. When Bob applied for a loan from a credit union, using his valuable comic book collection as collateral, will the credit union be perfected in an Alternative A state if its financing statement identifies him as "Bob Wolton"? In an Alternative B state? What if his driver's license lapses and he fails to get another one? Is the credit union now perfected in either state?

In re John's Bean Farm of Homestead, Inc.

United States Bankruptcy Court for the Southern District of Florida,
Miami Division, 2007
378 B.R. 385

LAUREL M. ISICOFF, Bankruptcy Judge.

[Creditor filed its financing statement under the name of "John Bean Farms, Inc.," instead of the Debtor's actual name of incorporation, "John's Bean Farm of Homestead, Inc."]

The matter under consideration is one of first impression in this district and concerns the degree of error necessary to render a financing statement "seriously misleading" under revised Uniform Commercial Code section 9-506, as adopted in Florida. . . .

PERFECT FINANCING STATEMENTS UNDER REVISED ARTICLE 9

A primary purpose of revised section 9-506 of the UCC, adopted in Florida as Fla. Stat. §679.5061, was to replace the former reasonableness standard with a clearer standard based on the computerized search logic of the filing office. This represents a significant shift from the prior law. Enacted to clarify the sufficiency of debtors' names in financing statements, the revision was "designed to discourage the fanatical and impossibly refined reading of statutory requirements in which courts occasionally have indulged themselves." Fla. Stat. §679.5061 cmt. 2. See In re Kinderknecht, 308 B.R. 71, 75 (B.A.P. 10th Cir. 2004) ("The intent to clarify when a debtor's name is sufficient shows a desire to foreclose fact-intensive tests, such as those that existed under former Article 9 of the UCC").

Courts in other states that have adopted revised Article 9 have recognized and emphasized the purpose and importance of this change in the search standard. The Supreme Court of Kansas analyzed its own state's adoption of revised UCC sections 9-503 and 9-506 (which adoption is virtually identical to the Florida language) and noted the importance of the accuracy of the name and the reasons behind the shift in focus of the revised Article 9:

> [T]he express provisions of the revised amendments read *in pari materia,* and the Official UCC Comments are all in accord that the primary purpose of the revision of the name requirement is to lessen the amount of fact-intensive, case-by-case determinations that plagued earlier versions of the UCC, and to simplify the filing system as a whole. The object of the revisions was to shift the responsibility to the filer by requiring the not too heavy burden of using the legal name of the debtor, thereby relieving the searcher from conducting numerous searches using every conceivable name variation of the debtor.

Pankratz Implement Co. v. Citizens Nat'l Bank, 281 Kan. 209, 227, 130 P.3d 57, 68 (Kan. 2006). Accord In re F. V. Steel and Wire Co., 310 B.R. 390, 393-94 (Bankr. E.D. Wis. 2004) ("A rule that would burden a searcher with guessing at misspellings and various configurations of a legal name would not provide creditors with the certainty that is essential in commercial transactions").

Under revised Article 9 what debtor misnomer is "seriously misleading" is statutorily defined as that which would not be discovered using the state's standard search logic. Thus, under the Safe Harbor provision, the discoverability of a financing statement expressly delimits permissible error. A financing statement is effective if a computer search run under the debtor's correct name produces the financing statement with the incorrect name. If it does not, then the financing statement is ineffective as a matter of law. This new standard is intended to

> reflect[] a balance between the need for some flexibility to allow for human error on the part of filers . . . and the avoidance of a rule that would cast an altogether inappropriate burden on searchers to have to try to divine potential errors and make searches under not only the correct name but also "foreseeable" or "likely" errors that a filer might have made[.]

Harry C. Sigman, Twenty Questions About Filing Under Revised Article 9: The Rules of the Game Under New Part 5, 74 Chi. Kent L. Rev. 861, 862-63 (1999). See also Steven O. Weise, An Overview of Revised Article 9, in the New Article 9 Uniform Commercial Code 7 (Corinne Cooper, ed., 2d ed. 2000).

> Revised Article 9 contains a statutory rule to determine when a mistake [sic] the debtor's name is so incorrect as to make the financing statement ineffective. The financing statement is effective if a computer search run under the debtor's correct name turns up the financing statement with the incorrect name. If it does not, then the financing statement is ineffective as a matter

of law. The court has no discretion to determine that the incorrect name is "close enough."

Id. (as quoted in In re F.V. Steel and Wire Co., 310 B.R. at 393-94).

Post-revision case law is fairly well settled that the burden is squarely on the creditor to correctly identify the name of the debtor.

> Revised Article 9 requires more accuracy in filings, and places less burden on the searcher to seek out erroneous filings. The revisions to Article 9 remove some of the burden placed on searchers under the former law, and do not require multiple searches using variations on the debtor's name. Revised Article 9 rejects the duty of a searcher to search using any names other than the name of the debtor indicated on the public record of the debtor's jurisdiction of organization.

In re Summit Staffing Polk County, Inc., 305 B.R. 347, 354-55 (Bankr. M.D. Fla. 2003). See Receivables Purchasing Co. v. R&R Directional Drilling, LLC, 263 Ga. App. 649, 652, 588 S.E.2d 831, 833 (Ga. 2003) ("[A] party filing a financing statement now acts at his peril if he files the statement under an incorrect name").

The majority of cases decided under revised Article 9 are unforgiving of even minimal errors. In In re Tyringham Holdings, Inc., 354 B.R. 363 (Bankr. E.D. Va. 2006), the creditor filed a financing statement covering 65 pieces of jewelry totaling $310,925 worth of consigned inventory. However, the creditor listed the name of the debtor as "Tyringham Holdings" rather than the debtor's legal corporate name, "Tyringham Holdings, Inc." Although the name error merely omitted the corporate suffix "Inc.," an official search under the debtor's actual name did not reveal the creditor's financing statement and the court held that, therefore, the financing statement was ineffective to perfect the security interest. The *Tyringham* court reasoned:

> [w]hile application of the filing office's standard search logic may lead to situations where it appears a relatively minor error in a financing statement leads to a security interest becoming unperfected, it is not that difficult to ensure that a financing statement is filed with the correct name of the debtor. Little more is asked of a creditor than to accurately record the debtor's name, and according to the statute, failure to perform this action clearly dooms the perfected status of a security interest.

354 B.R. at 368. Similarly, in Pankratz Implement Co. v. Citizens Nat'l Bank, 281 Kan. 209, 130 P.3d 57, the debtor purchased a tractor from the creditor, signed a security agreement, and the creditor misspelled the debtor's name on the financing statement by omitting a "d"—listing the debtor as "Roger House" instead of his legal name "Rodger House." The Supreme Court of

Kansas upheld summary judgment invalidating the prior interest represented by the faulty financing statement. In Host Am. Corp. v. Coastline Fin., Inc., 2006 U.S. Dist. LEXIS 35727, 2006 WL 159614 (D. Utah 2006), the court held that a financing statement was seriously misleading where the debtor, whose name was "K.W.M. Electronics Corporation" was identified in the financing statement as "K W M Electronics Corporation."

This canvas of history, commentary and application sets the background against which the adequacy of Klein's financing statement must be judged.

THE KLEIN FINANCING STATEMENT IS SERIOUSLY MISLEADING

Both the Trustee and Klein rely on In re Summit Staffing Polk County, Inc., 305 B.R. 347. In that case Chief Judge Glenn determined that a financing statement that identified the debtor as "Summit Staffing, Inc." rather than by the debtor's correct name of "Summit Staffing of Polk County, Inc." was not seriously misleading because, although using the standard search logic for Florida did not produce a page on which the financing statement appeared, the searcher only had to push the "previous" button one time and the financing statement was listed. Chief Judge Glenn held that the "reasonably diligent searcher" standard survives in some part. "Although Revised Article 9 does not require that a searcher exercise reasonable diligence in the selection of the names to be searched or the number of searches to conduct, the revisions to Article 9 do not entirely remove the duty imposed on a searcher to be reasonably diligent." Id. at 355. In Chief Judge Glenn's view, some burden is placed on the searcher to employ "reasonable diligence in examining the results of the search." Id.

In the *Summit Staffing* case, a creditor, Associated Receivables, filed a financing statement listing the debtor as Randy A. Vincent and "Summit Staffing," a sole proprietorship, as an additional debtor. Summit Staffing was subsequently incorporated as "Summit Staffing of Polk County, Inc." The corporation later filed for relief under Chapter 7 of the Bankruptcy Code. The Chapter 7 Trustee conducted a UCC search through the Florida Secured Transaction Registry website using the actual corporate name of the debtor, Summit Staffing of Polk County, Inc., and found no financing statement relating to the debtor's assets. The name "Summit Staffing" appeared at the top of the page displayed when a search under the debtor's correct name was made. By selecting the "previous" command to display the results page with alphabetical listings immediately prior to the page displayed, the Associated Receivables financing statement appeared. In determining the financing statement was not seriously misleading, and that Florida's standard search logic revealed the faulty financing statement, Chief Judge Glenn wrote:

> When a search is conducted in the Florida Secured Transaction Registry, a listing of debtors' names is produced. The listing is an alphabetical listing,

and 20 names are displayed. If the debtor's actual name is produced, it is at the top of the list. If the debtor's name is not found, the next succeeding name on the alphabetical list is at the top of the list. To see the next preceding name on the alphabetical list, the searcher must use the "Previous" command on the screen. In fact, at the top of the list is the statement: "Use the Previous and Next buttons *to display additional search results.*" (Emphasis supplied.) This statement directs the searcher to use the "Previous" command to see the immediately preceding names on the alphabetical list.

Certainly the searcher should do this. Since the name immediately following Summit Staffing of Polk County, Inc. is produced at the top of the alphabetical list, and since the filing office's directions state that the searcher should use the "Previous" command to display additional search results, clearly a searcher should check the preceding names on the alphabetical list.

305 B.R. at 353-354. However, Chief Judge Glenn noted that the obligation to push the "previous" button is not limitless.

Although it is clear that a searcher should check the immediately preceding names as well as the immediately succeeding names on an alphabetical list if there is not an exact match of the debtor's correct name, the issue of "reasonableness" develops at some point because the listing is an alphabetical listing. Although only three names begin with "Summit Staffing," there are several screens of debtors' names, with 20 names per screen, that begin with "Summit." Moreover, since the listing is an alphabetical listing, it is conceivable that one could use the "Previous" command to go to back to the beginning of the alphabetical list.

Id. at 354.

Here, the Trustee conducted a search of the Registry's online database. Using the Debtor's correct name, the Trustee's search yielded no matches. (Tr.'s Mot. Summ. J. Ex. CP 3.) It is undisputed that when the Debtor's correct name was inputted as the search term, the listing of 20 names on the initial search result screen did not disclose the Klein financing statement. (Tr.'s Mot. Summ. J. P 21; Klein Resp. n. 25.) Klein's financing statement was only found by striking the "previous" command 60 times. (Tr. Mot. Summ. J. P 22; Dubon Aff. PP 4-5; Klein Resp. n. 25.)

The Trustee relies on *Summit Staffing* arguing the case demonstrates that only the initial search result screen generated when the Debtor's correct name is input counts as the search result and, since Klein's financing statement did not appear on the initial page displayed, the financing statement is seriously misleading. Moreover, the Trustee argues, even if the search result goes beyond the initial result screen, then, as Chief Judge Glenn stated in *Summit Staffing,* the obligation to expand the search beyond the initial page displayed must be reasonable.

Klein also relies on *Summit Staffing*. Klein correctly points out that in *Summit Staffing*, the disputed financing statement did not appear on the initial page displayed, but rather the page displayed when the searcher pushed the "previous" command once. Thus, Klein argues, the results of "standard search logic" in Florida means something other than the initial result screen. However, Klein goes on to argue that Chief Judge Glenn improperly imposed a "reasonableness" requirement on the searcher's duty, that the statute is unambiguous, and has no "reasonableness" limitation. Since, by pushing the "previous" command (60 times) the Klein financing statement did eventually appear, Klein argues the financing statement is not seriously misleading.

The Trustee argues "[t]o require a secured creditor to search through numerous pages of names would defeat the salutary purpose of revised Article 9 and set dangerous precedent." (Tr. Mot. Summ. J. P 23.) Klein counters that since the plain language of the statute has no reasonableness requirement the court cannot impose a requirement that the statute doesn't provide. "Adding a reasonableness requirement would inevitably result in a situation where courts would have to delve into a host of case by case factual issues that were never contemplated by the legislative, and indeed, would require the courts to effectively rewrite the Safe Harbor Provision [Fla. Stat. §679.5061] in a manner that conflicts with the plain language." (Klein Resp. 11.) Thus, according to Klein's interpretation of the statute, any financing statement filed, no matter how far it may appear from the proper listing, would be sufficient so long as the statement could be found at some point in the pages preceding or following the initial displayed page. Under this interpretation, absent any reasonableness as to the distance between a proper and improper listing, a searcher would have to look through every page of the online database to determine whether or not a financing statement exists.

The crux of the dispute between the Trustee and Klein is what constitutes the search result using Florida's standard search logic. If my answer to this question is something other than the initial displayed page, then I must determine whether there is a limit on how much a searcher must search past the original display page. The debate between the Trustee and Klein centers on the meaning of "a search of the records of the filing office under the Debtor's correct name, using the filing office's standard search logic. . . ." As noted, the Trustee argues this refers to the initial page result; Klein argues there is a difference between a "search result" and a "display."

The only "search logic" in Florida is statutorily defined as a search by the debtor's name or document number. In order to determine what is the result of inputting that search logic, it is necessary and appropriate to understand what the Registry explains is a "result." The Registry, at its website, www.floridaucc.com, has a list of frequently asked questions. One of the questions listed is "How do I do my own search on the Internet." The answer to that question is:

> You can access the UCC filed records for the Florida Secured Transaction Registry on the Internet at: www.floridaucc.com. Click on the "Search" option. Choose one item in the "Select Search Type" box, then enter the appropriate data in the "Name/Document Number" box, and click on "search." *The exact name or number or the nearest alphabetical or numeric entry will be displayed.* Click on the number of the entry(ies) you are interested in.

Florida Secured Transaction Registry, UCC Frequently Asked Questions, http://www.floridaucc.com/faq.html (emphasis added). The same website has a Help menu that explains "UCC Filing Inquiry by Debtor Name." That section states in pertinent part:

> These transactions provide a list of UCC filings on the Florida Secured Transaction Registry beginning with the name that is closest to the key entered. This list also includes the document number and the type of each record. There are several inquiry functions available using the Debtor's Name, all of these inquiry functions will provide the user with an alphabetic listing beginning with the name closest to the key entered.

Id. at http://www.floridaucc.com/help.html#name.

I agree with Klein that the statute is unambiguous. Moreover, I agree with Klein that the statute does not include a reasonableness requirement. Indeed, as explained in great detail above, the very purpose of this statute was to eliminate the need for, indeed, the ability of, a judge to inject himself or herself in the determination of what is seriously misleading. However, I disagree with Klein's assertion that the initial page displayed is not the result of applying Florida's standard search logic. Florida's standard search logic is set by statute. The search logic clearly leads to one result—a single page on which names appear. For those, including Klein, that argue the search result is something more, the Registry website makes clear they are wrong. The Registry's own website unambiguously describes the page displayed when the search data is input as the result of the search. Nothing in the Registry's information page mentions the use of the "previous" or "next" page key in connection with conducting a search using the search criteria. Since it is undisputed that Klein's financing statement did not appear in the search result when the Debtor's correct name was input, the financing statement is seriously misleading and summary judgment in the Trustee's favor is appropriate.

Although I have found that Fla. Stat. §679.5061 is unambiguous, and that there is no implicit or explicit obligation of a searcher to go beyond the search result, I feel compelled to address what I view as Klein's incredible argument that the Florida statute unambiguously requires a searcher to scroll through the pages of the UCC search until the nonconforming financing statement is located. If Klein is correct, that the "search result" means something other than the page displayed when the required data is input, it does not follow that the statute requires a limitless search through the UCC database.

Klein argues that the case law is clear—when a statute is unambiguous on its face, it must be applied as written. However, Klein cavalierly casts aside as inapplicable the equally long and well established case law on statutory construction that reminds us —

> When applying the plain and ordinary meaning of statutory language "produces a result that is not just unwise but is clearly absurd, another principle comes into the picture. That principle is the venerable one that statutory language should not be applied literally if doing so would produce an absurd result."

Miedema v. Maytag Corp., 450 F.3d 1322, 1326 (11th Cir. 2006) (quoting Merritt v. Dillard Paper Co., 120 F.3d 1181, 1188 (11th Cir. 1997)).

Klein's argument that Florida's Safe Harbor provision clearly recognizes his financing statement was not seriously misleading, notwithstanding that it was listed 60 pages prior to the displayed search result (that is 1,200 entries), asks this Court to apply a meaning to the Safe Harbor provision that is "clearly absurd." Such an interpretation would eviscerate the purpose of the statute—that is, to create a framework for the perfection of security interests that is less arbitrary, that includes statutory guidance for simplifying the search, while allowing for "minor" errors.

Accordingly, if I am incorrect, and in fact, the Florida search result includes more than the initial page displayed, then, in order to interpret section 679.5061 so as to avoid an absurd result, I would be compelled alternatively to hold, as did Chief Judge Glenn, that there is a reasonable limit to the search, which I find is no more than one page "previous" or "next" from the initial result screen. Since Klein's financing statement appears 60 pages from the initial display, not one page, it is seriously misleading.

PROBLEM 27

EDM Corporation routinely did business as "EDM Equipment," and was commonly known by that name, so when the lender filed its financing statement it listed the debtor as "EDM CORPORATION D/B/A EDM EQUIPMENT." Does this correctly identify the debtor's name, and, to answer this question, is there something else you need to know? See Official Comment 2; In re EDM

Corp., 431 B.R. 459 (B.A.P. 8th Cir. 2010). In resolving this Problem it may be useful for you to see a common administrative rule used by most states as to search logic. Here is the one from Ohio:

Ohio Administrative Code §111-11-62 Search Methodology

Search results are produced by the application of search logic to the name presented to the filing officer. Human judgment does not play a role in determining the results of the search.

The following rules apply to searches:

(A) There is no limit to the number of matches that may be returned in response to the search criteria.

(B) No distinction is made between upper and lower case letters.

(C) Punctuation marks and accents are disregarded.

(D) Words and abbreviations at the end of a name that indicate the existence or nature of an organization as set forth in the "Ending Noise Words" list as promulgated and adopted by the international association of corporation administrators are disregarded.

(E) The word "the" at the beginning of the search criteria is disregarded.

(F) All spaces are disregarded.

(G) For first and middle names of individuals, initials are treated as the logical equivalent of all names that begin with such initials, and first name and no middle name or initial is equated with all middle names and initials. For example, a search request for "John A. Smith" would cause the search to retrieve all filings against all individual debtors with "John" or the initial "J" as the first name, "Smith" as the last name, and with the initial "A" or any name beginning with "A" in the middle name field. If the search request were for "John Smith" (first and last names with no designation in the middle name field), the search would retrieve all filings against individual debtors with "John" or the initial "J" as the first name, "Smith" as the last name and with any name or initial or no name or initial in the middle name field.

(H) After using the preceding rules to modify the name to be searched the search will reveal only names of debtors that are contained in unlapsed financing statements and exactly match the name requested, as modified.

[Here is the list of "Ending Noise Words":

IACA List of Ending Noise Words pursuant to Rule 503.4

The following words and abbreviations indicate the existence or nature of an entity. These business endings will be ignored in a UCC search.

• Agency • Association • Assn • Associates • Assc • Assoc • Attorneys at Law • Bank • National Bank • Business Trust • Charter • Chartered • Company • Co • Corporation • Corp • Credit Union • CU • Federal Savings

Bank • FSB • General Partnership • Gen part • GP • Incorporated • Inc •
Limited • Ltd • Ltee • Limited Liability Company • LC • LLC • Limited
Liability Partnership • LLP • Medical Doctors Professional Association
• MDPA • Medical Doctors Professional Corporation • MDPC • National
Association • NA • Partners • Partnership • Professional Association • Prof
Assn • PA • Professional Corporation • Prof Corp • PC • Professional Limited
Liability Company • Professional Limited Liability Co • PLLC • Railroad •
RR • Real Estate Investment Trust • REIT • Registered Limited Liability
Partnership • RLLP • Savings Association • SA • Service Corporation • SC •
Sole Proprietorship • SP • SPA • Trust • Trustee • As Trustee

Punctuation and accents are disregarded. "And" and "&" are
disregarded.]

PROBLEM 28

When World Wide Widgets was formed it filed a corporate name document with the State Corporate Registration Office, as required by law. That
document identified the company as "World Wide Wigets, Inc." (a typographical error), but the State's database correctly listed the company as "World
Wide Widgets, Inc." and that was the name in the State's Index of Registered
Corporations. What is the corporation's name for Article 9 filing purposes? See
§§9-503(a)(1), 9-102(a)(68)

In re PTM Technologies, Inc.

United States Bankruptcy Court, M.D.N.C., 2011
452 B.R. 165

WILLIAM L. STOCKS, Bankruptcy Judge.

* * *

On July 15, 2010, the Plaintiff [PTM Technologies, Inc.] filed an adversary proceeding against Maxus Capital, seeking to avoid its lien pursuant to
11 U.S.C. §544(a) on the basis that it was unperfected. That same day, the
Plaintiff also filed an adversary proceeding against GE Capital, seeking to
avoid its lien on the same basis. The Motion seeks summary judgment on
these section 544(a) claims.

PTM Technologies, Inc. is a duly organized corporation and that its
jurisdiction of organization is North Carolina, the state in which it was
organized. PTM Technologies, Inc. is the actual registered name of PTM
Technologies, Inc. in the office of the Secretary of State of North Carolina.

In 2008, PTM Technologies, Inc. sought certain financing from Maxus
Capital, and the parties closed on four separate loans subject to a master

security agreement. These documents granted Maxus Capital a security interest in the collateral described in the loan documents. Certain of these loans then were sold and assigned to GE Capital.

On August 23, 2010, GE Capital filed a proof of claim in the amount of $5,185,283.35. The documents attached to the proof of claim include a UCC financing statement that was filed in the North Carolina Secretary of State's office on May 7, 2008. The financing statement incorrectly listed the Debtor's name as "PTM Tecnologies, Inc."—omitting the "h" in "Technologies." The financing statement that was filed in the Secretary of State's office by Maxus Capital on the same date also incorrectly listed the Debtor's name by omitting the "h" in "Technologies."

The North Carolina Secretary of State maintains a website that may be accessed over the internet. One of the services available on that website is "UCC Research" that enables users to search the UCC financing statements that are on record with the Secretary of State. Navigating to the page of the website at which UCC searches may be conducted involves clicking on an entry on the opening page of the website entitled "UCC Records." That takes a user to a page on the website that lists the UCC "Business Services" available on the website. One of the business services listed is "UCC Research." By clicking on "UCC Research" a user accesses the website page on which research regarding UCC financing statements may be conducted. Two types of searches are available on the research page, namely, the "Standard RA9" search and the "Non-Standard RA9" search. When the research page is accessed, the Standard RA9 search is selected automatically. A standard search is then available by inserting the name of the organization in question and clicking on the word "Search." In order to conduct a non-standard search, it is necessary to click on "Non-Standard RA9."

The parties agree that a search of the Secretary of State's records under the Debtor's correct name, using the "Standard RA9" search, does not reveal the GE Capital or the Maxus Capital financing statement. The parties also agree that a search of the Secretary of State's records under the Debtor's correct name, using the "sounds like" feature of the "Non-Standard RA9" search does reveal the financing statements filed by GE Capital and Maxus Capital.[5]

ANALYSIS

In 2001, North Carolina adopted Revised Article 9 [RA9] of the Uniform Commercial Code, which included UCC sections 9-503 and 9-506(b) and (c). Under N.C. Gen.Stat. §25-9-503, if the debtor is a registered

---

5. When a user clicks on the Non–Standard search, the next step is to chose one of fives types of searches, namely, "Starting with," "Sounds Like," "All words," "Exact Match" and "Any Words".

organization, a financing statement sufficiently provides the debtor's name only if it lists the debtor's correct name as indicated on the public record. It is undisputed that the GE Capital and Maxus Capital financing statements do not sufficiently provide the debtor's name under this section because they misspell the Debtor's name and thus do not list the Debtor's name as it is shown in the public record in the Secretary of State's office.

N.C. Gen.Stat. §25-9-506(a) provides that "[a] financing statement substantially satisfying the requirements of this Part is effective, even if it has minor errors or omissions, unless the errors or omissions make the financing statement seriously misleading." Generally, "a financing statement that fails sufficiently to provide the name of the debtor in accordance with G.S. 25-9-503(a) is seriously misleading." N.C. Gen.Stat. §25-9-506(b). However, N.C. Gen. Stat. §25-9-506(c) provides a safe harbor for certain financing statements that fail to use the debtor's correct name.

> "If a search of the records of the filing office under the debtor's correct name, using the filing office's standard search logic, if any, would disclose a financing statement that fails sufficiently to provide the name of the debtor in accordance with G.S. 25-9-503(a), the name provided does not make the financing statement seriously misleading."

The issue in this proceeding is whether the GE Capital and Maxus Capital financing statements fall within the safe harbor provided under N.C. Gen. Stat. §25-9-506(c). Based upon the undisputed facts presented, the court concludes that the financing statements do not fall within the safe harbor provided by section 25-9-506(c) and that the Plaintiff's Motion should be granted and the Defendants' Cross-Motions denied.

The 2001 amendments were designed to eliminate the inconsistency that had developed in the court decisions regarding whether an error in the debtor's name made a financing statement seriously misleading. The amendments in Revised Article 9 eliminate such inconsistency by creating a clear delineation for determining when an incorrect name makes a financing statement seriously misleading. If the debtor's name is incorrect, then the financing statement is seriously misleading, unless a search using the filing office's standard search logic, if any, would nevertheless reveal the defective financing statement.

N.C. Gen. Stat. §25-9-526 gave the Secretary of State authority to "adopt and publish rules to implement the Secretary of State's responsibilities" under sections 25-9-503 and 25-9-506. Pursuant to this authority, the Secretary of State has adopted rules dealing with UCC searches that are found in Title 18 of the North Carolina Administrative Code and which may be accessed on the UCC search page of the Secretary of State's website by clicking on "Administrative Rules." These rules include 18 N.C.A.C.

5B.0503 which is entitled "Rules Applied to Search Requests," and which provides:

> Search results shall be produced by the application of standardized search logic to the name presented to the filing officer. Human judgment shall not play a role in determining the results of the search. The following rules shall apply to searches:
>
> (1) There shall be no limit to the number of matches that may be returned in response to the search criteria.
>
> (2) No distinction shall be made between upper and lower case letters.
>
> (3) Punctuation marks and accents shall be disregarded.
>
> (4) Words and abbreviations at the end of a name that indicate the existence or nature of an organization as set forth in the "Ending Noise Words" list as promulgated and adopted by IACA shall be disregarded. This list may be viewed or obtained by contacting the UCC Section.
>
> (5) The word "the" at the beginning of the search criteria shall be disregarded.
>
> (6) For first and middle names of individuals, initials shall be treated as the logical equivalent of all names that begin with such initials, and first name and no middle name or initial shall be equated with all middle names and initials. For example, a search request for "John A. Smith" shall cause the search to retrieve all filings against all individual debtors with "John" or the initial "J" as the first name, "Smith" as the last name, and with the initial "A" or any name beginning with "A" in the middle name field. If the search request were for "John Smith" (first and last names with no designation in the middle name field), the search shall retrieve all filings against individual debtors with "John" or the initial "J" as the first name, "Smith" as the last name and with any name or initial or no name or initial in the middle name field.
>
> (7) After using the preceding paragraphs of this Rule to modify the name to be searched, the search shall reveal only names of debtors that are contained in unlapsed financing statements and, exactly match the name requested, as modified.

Under this regulation, the seven rules stated therein constitute the "standardized search logic" that "shall" be applied to searches performed by the Secretary of State. As such, these rules describe the standard search logic employed in the North Carolina Secretary of State's office and hence constitute "the filing office's standard search logic" for purposes of N.C. Gen. Stat. §25-9-506(c). This means that if a search using these seven rules would reveal the defective GE Capital and Maxus Capital financing statements, then they would be saved by the safe harbor provision of section 25-9-506(c); conversely, if such a search would not reveal the financing statements, then the financing statements are seriously misleading as a matter of law under N.C. Gen. Stat. §25-9-506(b).

Rule 5B.0503 essentially creates a two-step process for applying the seven enumerated rules to the filing records. 18 N.C.A.C. 5B.0503. First, rules (1) through (6) are applied to ensure there is no limit on the number of matches returned and to expand the possible search results by treating the debtor's precise name more leniently. These rules expand the possible results by removing any distinction based on capitalization, disregarding punctuation marks, disregarding noise words such as "Company" at the end of the debtor's name, removing the word "the" from the beginning of a debtor's name, and modifying the debtor's name to account for initials if the debtor is an individual. Second, after applying the above rules to modify the debtor's name "the search shall reveal only names of debtors that are contained in unlapsed financing statements and, *exactly match the name requested,* as *modified.*" (Emphasis supplied). Under this search logic, the GE Capital and Maxus Capital financing statements clearly would not be disclosed in a search under the Debtor's correct name. A search using this search logic would modify the name to reveal a financing statement with incorrect capitalization, such as "ptm technologies, inc." It would disregard punctuation, and thus reveal a financing statement with no punctuation or different punctuation. It would remove ending noise words, and thus reveal a financing statement under the name "PTM Technologies." However, none of the rules defining the standard search logic would modify the debtor's name to correct for the missing "h" in the debtor's name. Thus, a search of the filing office's records under the debtor's correct name, using the foregoing standard search logic, would not reveal the defective financing statements filed by GE Capital and Maxus Capital, since after modifying the name accordingly, the name in the defective financing statements would not "exactly match the name requested." It follows, therefore, that the safe harbor of N.C. Gen. Stat. §25-9-506(c) is not available to GE Capital and Maxus Capital.

The same result flows from the results that occur when a "Standard RA9" search is conducted under the correct name of PTM Technologies, Inc. The designation of the "Standard RA9" search alternative as "Standard" sufficiently identifies that search alternative as the one employing the standard search logic described in Rule 5B.0503 and adopted as such by the Secretary of State. A "Standard RA9" search thus also dictates a decision in favor of the Plaintiff since the parties agree that a "Standard RA9" search at the Secretary of State's website does not reveal the defective financing statements. The parties also agree that a "Non-Standard RA9" search using the "sounds like" feature will reveal the financing statements. Given these results, in order for the Defendants to prevail on the merits, they would have to establish that the "Non-Standard RA9" search utilizes the "standard" search logic, while the "Standard RA9" search does not, a proposition that is illogical and contrary to the undisputed facts before the court.

CONCLUSION

Since the safe harbor of N.C. Gen. Stat. §25-9-506(c) does not apply, the GE Capital and Maxus Capital financing statements are seriously misleading as a matter of law, pursuant to N.C. Gen. Stat. §25-9-506(b), and therefore are insufficient to perfect the security interests claimed by GE Capital and Maxus Capital. The Plaintiff's Motion therefore should be granted and the Defendants' Cross-Motions denied. A separate order so providing is being entered pursuant to Rule 9021 of the Federal Rules of Bankruptcy Procedure.

PROBLEM 29

Barbara Song borrowed $50,000 from Octopus National Bank (ONB) in order to start a business called "Barb's Interiors," interior design being her specialty. ONB and Ms. Song signed a security agreement showing her as the debtor and giving ONB an interest in the inventory and equipment. ONB duly filed a financing statement. Subsequently, Ms. Song married Fred Dancer, and she changed her name to Barbara Dancer. She borrowed another $50,000 from the Nightflyer Finance Company, which loaned her the money after searching the records under "Dancer" and finding no prior encumbrances on the business's inventory and equipment. Did ONB lose its security interest because it failed to refile when her name changed? See §9-507(c) and its Official Comment 4.

PROBLEM 30

The Last National Bank filed a financing statement in the proper place to perfect its security interest in the accounts receivable of the American Electronics Store. When the latter ran into financial difficulty, its assets were sold to a new electronics concern, Voice of Japan, which moved into the same retail location. Must Last National refile to keep its security interest perfected in (1) the accounts actually transferred by American Electronics to Voice of Japan or (2) accounts thereafter acquired by Voice of Japan? See §9-507(a) and its Official Comment 3. Do we get the same result if American Electronics Store merges with Voice of Japan and the new entity is called "Voice of Electronics, Inc."? See §§9-102(a)(56), 9-203(d) and (e) and its Official Comment 7, and 9-508. What if the opposite happens, and the debtor remains the same, but Last National assigns its interest in the debtor's accounts to Octopus National Bank? Need the records be changed? Read §§9-310(c) and 9-511. Is Octopus National's interest superior to that of Last National's creditors? Consider that the transfer of the security interest from Last National to Octopus National is itself the transfer of an account or chattel paper; see Official Comment 4, Example 2 to §9-310.

PROBLEM 31

When Robin Oakapple found he could not get a loan unless he had collateral, he got permission from his foster brother, Richard Dauntless, to use Richard's yacht as collateral. Should the lender make both sign the security agreement (only Robin signed the promissory note)? Which of these parties is the "debtor" and which the "obligor"? Compare §§9-102(a)(28)(A) and 9-102(a)(59). Under whose name should the financing statement be filed?

D.   Description of the Collateral

One of the great fears of those opposed to Article 9's original adoption was that it would lead to creditor overreaching in demanding too much collateral.

PROBLEM 32

Peter Poor signed a security agreement and financing statement in favor of the Total Finance Company, giving the company a security interest in "all personal property debtor now owns or ever owns or even hopes to own between now and the end of the world or his death, whichever occurs first." Does this perfect an interest in his guitar? Compare §§9-108 and 9-504. Why would the drafters have drawn this distinction between the description in the security agreement and that in the financing statement?

In re Grabowski

Bankruptcy Division, Southern District of Illinois, 2002
277 B.R. 388

Kenneth J. Meyers, Bankruptcy Judge.

This case involves a priority dispute between defendants Bank of America and South Pointe Bank ("South Pointe") regarding their security interests in three items of farm equipment owned by the debtors.

Both lenders filed financing statements perfecting their interests. Bank of America, the first to file, described its collateral in general terms and listed the debtors' business address, rather than their home address where the collateral was located. South Pointe, by contrast, described the collateral more specifically and included the debtors' home address. South Pointe contends that Bank of America's description was ineffective to perfect the Bank's security interest in the equipment and that South Pointe has a superior interest by reason of its subsequently filed financing statement.

The facts are undisputed. In April 2001, debtors Ronald and Trenna Grabowski of Dubois, Illinois, filed this Chapter 11 proceeding to reorganize their farming operation in Washington and Perry counties, Illinois. The debtors have been engaged in farming at this location for the past 30 years. Beginning in 1993, the debtors also owned and operated a John Deere farm equipment business, Grabowski Tractor-Benton, Inc., at 12047 Highway 37, Benton, Illinois. During this time, debtor Trenna Grabowski, a certified public accountant, moved her accounting practice to the Benton dealership. Although the dealership was sold in 1999, Trenna Grabowski continues to conduct her accounting practice from the Benton location.

The debtors' schedules include a list of items of equipment used in their farming operation. The debtors filed the present proceeding to determine the validity, priority, and extent of liens held by various lenders in this equipment. Subsequently, the lenders reached an agreement concerning their respective interests in the farm equipment with the exception of three items. (See Stip., Doc. No. 20, filed February 1, 2002.) These items, as to which a dispute remains between Bank of America and South Pointe, consist of a John Deere 925 flex platform, a John Deere 4630 tractor, and a John Deere 630 disk. (See Stip. at 3-4.)

Bank of America claims a prior security interest in this equipment by virtue of a security agreement signed by the debtors in December 1998. The Bank's financing statement, filed on December 31, 1998, identifies the debtors as "Ronald and Trenna Grabowski" and lists their address as "12047 State Highway #37, Benton, Illinois 62812." The financing statement describes the Bank's collateral as:

All Inventory, Chattel Paper, Accounts, *Equipment* and General Intangibles[.]

(See Supplmntl. Stip., Doc. No. 15, Ex. B, filed Jan. 22, 2002) (emphasis added).

South Pointe subsequently obtained a lien on the debtors' equipment in January 2000. South Pointe's financing statement, filed January 18, 2000, identifies the debtors as "Ronald and Trenna Grabowski" at "P.O. Box 38, Dubois, Illinois 62831" and describes South Pointe's collateral as:

JD 1995 9600 combine . . . , *JD 925 FLEX PLATFORM* . . . , *JD 4630 TRACTOR* . . . , *JD 630 DISK 28' 1998* . . . referenced in South Pointe's financing statement.

(See Supplmntl. Stip., Doc. No. 15, Ex. C, filed Jan. 22, 2002) (emphasis added).

South Pointe asserts that Bank of America's financing statement, although prior in time, was insufficient to perfect the Bank's interest because it failed to place other lenders on notice of Bank of America's interest in the subject equipment. Specifically, South Pointe notes that the Bank's financing statement contained the address of the debtors' farm equipment business rather than that of the debtors' home where their farming operation is located and, further, that it failed to mention any specific items of equipment or even make reference to "farm equipment" or "farm machinery." South Pointe argues that, based on this description, a subsequent lender would reasonably conclude that Bank of America's intended security was the personal property of the debtors' business rather than equipment used in the debtors' farming operation. South Pointe maintains, therefore, that the Bank's financing statement did not reasonably identify the Bank's collateral as required to fulfill the notice function of a financing statement under Illinois' Uniform Commercial Code. . . .

The UCC sets forth the requirements for a creditor to obtain and perfect a security interest in personal property of the debtor.

Section 9-203 governs the attachment and enforcement of security interests through the parties' execution of a security agreement, while §9-502 relates to the requisites of a financing statement filed to perfect the creditor's interest against the interests of third parties. Both sections call for a description of the debtor's property. However, the degree of specificity required of such description depends on the nature of the document involved—whether it is a security agreement or financing statement—and the purpose to be fulfilled by such document. See 9A Hawkland, Uniform Commercial Code Series, [Rev.] §9-108:2, at 291-92; [Rev.] §9-108:2, at 294-96 (2001). While a security agreement defines and limits the collateral subject to the creditor's security interest, a financing statement puts third parties on notice that the creditor may have a lien on the property described and that further inquiry into the extent of the security interest is prudent. See Signal Capital Corp. v. Lake Shore Natl. Bank, 273 Ill. App. 3d 761, 210 Ill. Dec. 388, 652 N.E.2d 1364, 1371 (1995).

Section 9-108 sets forth the test for sufficiency of a description under the UCC, stating:

> (a) . . . a description of personal . . . property is sufficient, whether or not it is specific, *if it reasonably identifies what is described.*

810 Ill. Comp. Stat. 5/9-108(a) (emphasis added) (2001) (see former §9-110, 810 Ill. Comp. Stat. 5/9-110 (2000)). Examples of descriptions that meet this "reasonable identification" test include identification by "category" or by

"type of collateral defined in the UCC." See §9-108(b)(2), (3). In addition, identification "by any other method" is sufficient, "if the identity of the collateral is objectively determinable." See §9-108(b)(6). Only a super-generic such as "all the debtor's assets" or "all the debtor's personal property" is insufficient under the "reasonable identification" standard of §9-108. See 810 Ill. Comp. Stat. 5/9-108(c).

While §9-108 provides a flexible standard for determining the sufficiency of a description in a security agreement, §9-504 provides an even broader standard with regard to a financing statement. This section states:

> A financing statement sufficiently indicates the collateral that it covers if the financing statement provides:
> (1) a description of the collateral pursuant to Section 9-108; or
> (2) *an indication that the financing statement covers all assets or all personal property.*

810 Ill. Comp. Stat. 5/9-504 (2001) (emphasis added). Thus, in the case of a financing statement, a creditor may either describe its collateral by "type" or "category" as set forth in §9-108 or may simply indicate its lien on "all assets" of the debtor.

This exceedingly general standard for describing collateral in a financing statement, which is new to the UCC under revised Article 9, is consistent with the "inquiry notice" function of a financing statement under previous law. A financing statement need not specify the property encumbered by a secured party's lien, but need merely notify subsequent creditors that a lien may exist and that further inquiry is necessary "to disclose the complete state of affairs." Uniform Commercial Code Comment 2, 810 Ill. Comp. Stat. 5/9-502, Smith-Hurd Ann. at 385 (West Supp. 2002); see Matter of Little Brick Shirthouse, Inc., 347 F. Supp. 827, 829 (N.D. Ill. 1972); In re Swati, 54 B.R. 498, 501 (Bankr. N.D. Ill. 1985). In the present case, Bank of America filed a financing statement indicating it had a lien on the debtors' property consisting of "all inventory, chattel paper, accounts, equipment, and general intangibles." Despite the generality of the Bank's description, it was sufficient to notify subsequent creditors, including South Pointe, that a lien existed on the debtors' property and that further inquiry was necessary to determine the extent of the Bank's lien. For this reason, the Court finds no merit in South Pointe's argument that the description of the Bank's collateral was too general to fulfill the notice function of a financing statement under the UCC.

South Pointe asserts, however, that it was misled by the incorrect address contained in Bank of America's financing statement and "reasonably concluded" that the only equipment subject to the Bank's lien was that located at the debtors' farm equipment dealership. The Court disagrees that such conclusion was "reasonable." The debtors' business address was not part of the Bank's description of its collateral and, thus, did not serve to limit the collateral subject to the Bank's lien as South Pointe argues. In fact, Bank of America's financing statement indicated the Bank had a lien on the debtors' "equipment," with no indication that its interest was confined to equipment located in a particular place. Rather than serving to describe the Bank's collateral, therefore, the debtors' address merely provided a means by which subsequent lenders could contact the debtors to inquire concerning the Bank's lien. See 9 Hawkland, supra, §9-402:11, at 724-25.

While a subsequent creditor should not be imposed upon to be a "super-detective" in investigating prior secured transactions, the debtors' address in this case was an accurate and ready means of contacting the debtors. The Court notes, moreover, that even though the mailing address on the Bank's financing statement was that of the debtors' business, the debtors' names were listed as "Ronald and Trenna Grabowski," not "Grabowski Tractor-Benton, Inc.," the name of the debtors' business. Accordingly, the Court finds that a reasonably prudent lender would not be misled into believing that the collateral listed was property of the debtors' business, rather than that of the debtors individually.

For the reasons stated, the Court concludes that Bank of America's financing statement was sufficient to perfect its security interest in the subject farm equipment and that the Bank's interest, being prior in time, is superior to that of South Pointe. Accordingly, the Court finds in favor of Bank of America and against South Pointe on the debtors' complaint to determine validity, priority, and extent of liens in the debtors' farm equipment.

PROBLEM 33

Jeanne Angell sold 20 cows to Richard Baker, a dairy farmer, on credit. With each cow, Angell delivered a Certificate of Registration issued by Holstein Association USA, Inc. Each certificate stated the name of the cow, and included a sketch of the cow with its distinctive markings. Some of the certificates included handwritten ear tag identification numbers. Baker granted Angell a security interest in the cows for the unpaid price. Angell filed a financing statement, stating a name and ear tag identification number for each cow.

Some time later, it turned out that only four of the cows had ear tags with numbers that matched the financing statement. Ten cows had no tag and six cows had tags with numbers not matching those listed in the financing statement. Missing and inaccurate ear tags are common in the dairy industry. The cows, however, could be identified by name, using the certificates. Did the financing statement sufficiently describe the 20 cows? See In re Baker, 465 B.R. 359 (Bankr. N.D.N.Y. 2012).

PROBLEM 34

When you sign up for a credit card the agreement will often have this clause: "Cardholder hereby grants the Issuer a security interest in all goods purchased on your Account." Does this sufficiently describe the law books you subsequently buy with the card? Compare In re Murphy, 2013 WL 1856337 (Bankr. D. Kan. 2013), and In re Cunningham, 489 B.R. 602 (Bankr. D. Kan. 2013).

PROBLEM 35

The financing statement described the collateral as:

All assets of the Debtor including, but not limited to, any and all equipment, fixtures, inventory, accounts, chattel paper, documents, instruments, investment property, general intangibles, letter-of-credit rights and deposit accounts now owned and hereafter acquired by Debtor and located at or relating to the operation of the premises at 100 River Rock Drive, Suite 304, Buffalo, New York, together with any products and proceeds thereof including, but not limited to, a certain Komori 628 P+L Ten Color Press and Heidelberg B20 Folder and Prism Print Management System.

After the financing statement was filed and payment commenced the debtor moved everything in the business to a new location in Buffalo. No one thought to amend the financing statement. Will this description be sufficient to give the creditor a valid interest in the same assets at the new Buffalo location? See In re Sterling United, Inc., 2015 WL 7573240 (W.D.N.Y. 2015).

PROBLEM 36

Polly Travis owned a clothing store that was doing quite well, so she decided to open branches all over the state. She borrowed money to do so from Longhorn State Bank, which took a security interest (according to the filed financing statement) in "all inventory, accounts receivable, equipment, instruments, general intangibles, and personal property." The bank also made her pledge her extensive collection of jewelry to the bank, making her bring it from her home and putting it in the vault. A year later she asked to have the jewelry back so that she could wear it to a social occasion, and the bank gave it to her. Before she could return it to the bank, another creditor seized it by judicial process. You are the lawyer for Longhorn State Bank. Is their interest in the jewelry perfected by the filed financing statement? What will be your argument? See In re Boogie Enters., Inc., 866 F.2d 1172(9th Cir. 1989); Merchants Natl. Bank v. Halberstadt, 425 N.W.2d 429 (Iowa App. 1988).

A much-discussed issue facing the drafters of the Uniform Commercial Code was the wisdom of permitting debtors to encumber not only their current property, but also property that they would acquire in the future. In the end, freedom of contract prevailed, and debtors are allowed (with one exception involving consumer goods, discussed later) to use future as well as current property as collateral for a credit extension. Where this is done, the so-called "floating lien" arises, because the creditor's lien will attach to new property without the signing of any further paperwork. Read §9-204(a).

PROBLEM 37

The security agreement and the financing statement both described the collateral as "inventory." Does this limit the security interest to existing inventory only, or does the security interest extend to replacement for the original collateral? See In re Filtercorp, Inc., 163 F.3d 570 (9th Cir. 1998). If the security agreement had said "inventory now owned or after acquired" but the financing statement had simply mentioned "inventory," does this perfect a security interest in after-acquired inventory? See Official Comment 3 to §9-108 and Official Comment 2 to §9-502; Kubota Tractor Corp. v. Citizens & S. Natl. Bank, 198 Ga. App. 830, 403 S.E.2d 218 (1991) (similar issue where collateral was "all farm equipment"). The same problem arises if the collateral consists of accounts receivable. See In re Shenandoah Warehouse Co., 202 B.R. 871 (Bankr. W.D. Va. 1996).

Section 9-108 (read it along with its Official Comment 2) speaks to the faulty description problem in both the security agreement and the financing statement. The test adopted by the courts is the one from the Official Comment: "whether the description does the job assigned to it, i.e., make possible the identification of the thing described." Marine Midland Bank-Eastern Natl. Assn. v. Conerty Pontiac-Buick, Inc., 77 Misc. 2d 311, 352 N.Y.S.2d 953 (Sup. Ct. 1974). Or, because later potential creditors will be doing the records searching, would a "reasonable person" be put on inquiry as to the identity of the collateral? Ray v. City Bank & Trust Co., 358 F. Supp. 630 (S.D. Ohio 1973). The UCC adopts a system of *notice filing*, so that the description in the financing statement must be sufficient to alert the searcher to the necessity for further inquiry. "The description need only inform, it need not educate," *Marine Midland Bank*, supra, at 960; see also Official Comment 2 to §9-502.

PROBLEM 38

The financing statement's description said "Various Equipment, see attached list." No list was attached. Is the statement sufficient to perfect a security interest in the debtor's equipment? See Chase Manhattan Bank v. J. & L. Gen. Contractors, Inc., 832 S.W.2d 204 (Tex. App. 1992).

PROBLEM 39

The security agreement stated that the collateral was "machinery, equipment, furniture and fixtures." To this list the financing statement added "inventory and accounts receivable." The parties are all willing to testify that the loan was intended to be secured by inventory and accounts receivable as well as by the items listed in the security agreement. Other creditors object. Does the secured party's interest reach inventory and accounts receivable? See §9-203(b) and In re Martin Grinding & Mach. Works, Inc., 793 F.2d 592 (7th Cir. 1986) ($233,000 lost as a result of this error!).

PROBLEM 40

The loan officer at Octopus National Bank has sent you, the bank's attorney, an e-mail with the following question. The bank is planning to make a loan to Luddite Technology, Inc., and wants to take a security interest in all of the equipment of the debtor. However, Luddite's most important piece of equipment is the very expensive Abacus-12, which designs computer hardware. Should the security agreement be drafted to say that the debtor grants a security interest in "the Abacus-12 plus all other equipment," "all equipment, particularly the Abacus-12," or simply "all equipment"? Or do you have a better phraseology?

PROBLEM 41

The security agreement stated that the tractor buyer granted a security interest to "_____," but the seller forgot to fill in his name. The seller later filed a financing statement showing he had a secured interest in the buyer's tractor. Is the purported document with the blank a §9-203 security agreement? What about the financing statement? What about both? See In re Bollinger Corp., 614 F.2d 924 (3d Cir. 1980).

NOTE

To meet all the above objectives, the wise creditor will:

1. Make sure all the forms are correctly filled out in all particulars;
2. check the debtor's technical legal name now and in the immediate past and make sure it is correctly listed on all documents, and given the 2010 amendments to Article 9, take a close look at the debtor's driver's license;
3. refile if the debtor's name changes in any way;
4. describe the collateral as accurately and completely as possible in all documents; and
5. inquire into the source of the debtor's title to ensure that the former owner's creditors have no valid claims.

III.   ATTACHMENT OF THE SECURITY INTEREST

Attachment is the process by which the security interest in favor of the creditor becomes effective against the debtor. *Perfection* is the process by which the creditor's security interest becomes effective against most of the rest of the world. The steps involved in attachment are described in §9-203. They are:

1.   a security agreement must be "authenticated" (defined in §9-102(a)(7) to mean "signed" or some the electronic equivalent), or the creditor must have possession or control of the collateral, pursuant to an oral agreement with the debtor;

2.   the creditor must give *value* (defined in §1-204—after all, you shouldn't get a security interest unless you've done something to deserve it); and

3.   the debtor must have some rights in the collateral (one cannot give a security interest in property one does not own or have some legal interest in).

Read both §§9-203 and 9-204.

Border State Bank of Greenbush v. Bagley Livestock Exchange, Inc.

Court of Appeals of Minnesota, 2004
690 N.W.2d 326

LANSING, Judge.

This action arises from a dispute over the enforceability of a security interest and the interpretation of the cattle-sharing agreement that underlies the security interest. The district court, apparently relying on an incorrect argument that an ownership interest was necessary for the security interest to attach, made no findings on the disputed provisions of the agreement. We therefore reverse the district court's order directing a verdict against the bank, which attempted to enforce the security interest in a conversion claim, and remand for the court to address the disputed provisions. We affirm, however, the jury verdict adjudicating the claims between the cattlemen on the breach of the underlying cattle-sharing agreement. The record contains competent evidence to sustain the verdict, the special-verdict form conveyed a correct understanding of the law, and the damages assessed by the jury do not require remittitur.

FACTS

Bert Johnson, doing business as Johnson Farms, and Hal Anderson entered into an oral cattle-sharing contract in December 1997. Approximately one month later, they memorialized the oral contract in written form. Under the written instrument, Anderson agreed to care for and breed cattle owned by Johnson and Johnson would receive a "guaranteed" percentage of the annual calf crop. The contract further provided that the cattle Johnson placed with Anderson were "considered to be owned by Johnson Farms and any offspring is to be sold under Johnson Farms' name." The contract required Johnson Farms and Anderson mutually to agree when the calves would be sold and within thirty days of receiving money for the sale, Johnson Farms to pay the "remainder" to Anderson "for his keeping of [the] cattle."

In the fall of 1998 and 1999, calves bred under the contract were sold under the provisions of the written contract. Anderson testified that in October 1999, Johnson asked him to care for additional cattle on the same terms. Anderson initially declined, explaining to Johnson that he was ending his cattle business because of adverse personal circumstances. Anderson said that his father had died, his mother was in a nursing home, his partner, Linda Peterson, was caring for an ill family member, he had no additional help at his farm, he had insufficient feed for the cattle, and he had not planted hay for the coming winter. Nevertheless, according to Anderson, they continued to discuss their cattle-sharing contract, and he eventually agreed to continue based on certain modifications: (1) the share percentage would be a straight 40/60 split, without Johnson's "guaranteed" percentage; (2) Johnson would provide feed, including beet tailings; (3) Johnson would provide additional pasture; and (4) the agreement would include approximately 500 cattle, instead of the original 151 cattle.

Johnson testified that he discussed the cattle-sharing agreement with Anderson in October 1999 and that he agreed to send Anderson beet tailings, which were free to him, so long as Anderson paid the cost of shipping. Johnson also testified that he and Anderson agreed that approximately 500 cattle would be cared for under the cattle-sharing agreement, rather than the original 151 cattle. But Johnson denied that he had agreed to provide feed, other than the beet tailings, and denied that he had agreed to change the provision that "guaranteed" that his percentage of the calf crop would be calculated on the initial number of cows regardless of whether each produced a calf that survived.

In March 2000, Anderson negotiated with Border State Bank for loans totaling $155,528. To secure these loans, Anderson granted Border State Bank a security interest in, among other things, all of Anderson's "rights, title and interest" in all "livestock" then owned or thereafter acquired.

After the modification of the cattle-sharing contract, Johnson made a number of shipments of beet tailings to Anderson. When Johnson stopped the shipments, he sent checks totaling $55,000 to Anderson for the purchase of feed. In November 2000, Anderson encountered difficulty caring for the cattle due to heavy rainfall and lack of feed. The cattle were reclaimed by Johnson, but the calves remained with Anderson for sale. At trial, Anderson testified that some of the cattle that Johnson reclaimed were actually Anderson's cattle or were cattle that belonged to Evonne Stephens, another person with whom Anderson had a cattle-sharing contract.

In December 2000, 289 calves that had remained with Anderson were sold at Bagley Livestock Exchange. The livestock exchange knew of Border State's security interest in Anderson's livestock but, after discussing the agreement with Johnson, determined the security interest did not attach to the calves. The livestock exchange issued a check to Johnson Farms in the amount of $119,403. Thereafter, Johnson gave Anderson a check for $19,404, representing Anderson's share of the sale proceeds, less $55,000 that Johnson claimed as repayment for money advanced to Anderson to purchase feed.

Border State Bank sued Bagley Livestock Exchange and Johnson, contending that they had converted Border State Bank's perfected security interest in the calves sold in December 2000. In a third-party complaint, Johnson sought indemnity from Anderson, in the event that Border State Bank was successful on its conversion claim. Anderson served a counter-claim against Johnson, asserting breach of contract.

These claims were tried to a jury in September 2003. Following Border State Bank's case-in-chief, Johnson and Bagley Livestock Exchange moved for a directed verdict. The district court granted the motion, finding that, under the cattle-sharing agreement, Johnson did not "grant" Anderson an "ownership interest" in the calves. Border State Bank appeals from the directed verdict on its conversion claim.

Following the directed verdict, Anderson presented evidence on his breach-of-contract counterclaim against Johnson, and the counterclaim was submitted to the jury. In response to special-verdict questions, the jury determined that the written contract between Anderson and Johnson had been modified, Johnson breached the contract, and Johnson's breach directly caused damages to Anderson in the amount of $92,360. Johnson moved for judgment notwithstanding the verdict (JNOV), or, in the alternative, a new trial or remittitur. The district court denied Johnson's posttrial motions. Johnson appeals from that denial.

Issues

I. Did the district court err by issuing a directed verdict against Border State Bank?

II. Does the record contain competent evidence to sustain the verdict?

III. Did the district court abuse its discretion by denying Johnson's motion for new trial?

IV. Did the district court abuse its discretion by submitting to the jury a special-verdict form that conveyed an incorrect understanding of the law?

V. Were the damages assessed by the jury so unjustified that the district court abused its discretion in denying the posttrial motion for remittitur?

Analysis

I . . .

Article 9 of the Uniform Commercial Code, incorporated into Minnesota law, provides that a security interest attaches to collateral, and is enforceable against the debtor or third parties, when (1) value has been given; (2) the debtor "has rights in the collateral or the power to transfer rights"; and (3) the debtor has signed a security agreement that contains a description of the collateral. Minn. Stat. §336.9-203(b) (2002). To perfect the security interest, both the security agreement and financing statement must contain an adequate description of the collateral. Prod. Credit Assn. of W. Cent. Minn. v. Bartos, 430 N.W.2d 238, 240 (Minn. App. 1988). We liberally construe descriptions in the security agreement and financing statement because their essential purpose is to provide notice, not to definitively describe each item of collateral. World Wide Tracers, Inc. v. Metro. Prot. Inc., 384 N.W.2d 442, 447 (Minn. 1986).

The parties do not dispute that Anderson signed a security agreement and that value was given. The security agreement stated that the collateral included, in part, "all livestock owned or hereafter acquired" and Anderson's "rights, title and interest" in such livestock. The financing statements covered "all livestock," whether "now owned or hereafter acquired, together with the proceeds from the sale thereof." The parties also do not dispute the validity of these descriptions or the assertion that "livestock" includes cattle and calves. What is disputed is whether the bank's security interest attached to the 289 calves sold in December 2000 under Anderson and Johnson's cattle-sharing agreement. See Wangen v. Swanson Meats, Inc., 541 N.W.2d 1, 3 (Minn. App. 1995) (stating that if security interest attaches to collateral transferred to third party, secured party may repossess collateral or maintain action for conversion), review denied (Minn. Jan. 25, 1996).

In directing a verdict against Border State Bank's conversion claim, the district court did not issue a written order. The district court, instead, briefly stated the decision on the record at the conclusion of Border State Bank's case-in-chief, following arguments by counsel. Johnson's attorney couched his argument in terms of "who actually owned these cattle." The attorney for the cattle exchange cast his argument in terms of a "mutual mistake of fact as to the ownership" and also referred to an "ownership interest." Anderson's attorney, in response, argued that "[m]erely titling something in somebody's name" does not determine "ownership interest." And the bank's attorney asserted that the provisions in the contract did not "indicate who owns [the] calves." The district court stated on the record that the cattle-sharing contract had not "granted" Anderson an "ownership interest" in the calves, specifically finding that "the modifications testified to by Mr.

Anderson in the light most favorable to Border State Bank do not modify the terms of the agreement such that an ownership interest is granted." Based on the arguments presented, the district court apparently determined that, for Border State Bank's security interest to attach, Johnson would have had to grant Anderson an interest equivalent to ownership.

The provisions of the Uniform Commercial Code's Article 9, incorporated into Minnesota law, refer to "rights in the collateral," not solely the "ownership" of the collateral. Minn. Stat. §336.9-203(b)(2) (stating security interest may attach to collateral if "the debtor has rights in the collateral or the power to transfer rights in the collateral"). Rights in the collateral, as the term is used in Article 9, include full ownership and limited rights that fall short of full ownership. Minn. Stat. Ann. §336.9-203 U.C.C. cmt., para. 6 (West 2002) ("A debtor's limited rights in collateral, short of full ownership, are sufficient for a security interest to attach."); see also Greenbush State Bank v. Stephens, 463 N.W.2d 303, 306 (Minn. App. 1990) (explaining that "ownership" under the UCC can be shared, with each party possessing its own bundle of interests"), review denied (Minn. Feb. 4, 1991). Simply stated, the UCC "does not require that collateral be owned by the debtor." State Bank of Young Am. v. Vidmar Iron Works, Inc., 292 N.W.2d 244, 249 (Minn. 1980).

Other jurisdictions have cautioned against an interpretation that ownership rights are necessary for the attachment of a security interest. For purposes of the UCC, "sufficient rights" arise with far less than full ownership. Kinetics Tech. Intl. Corp. v. Fourth Natl. Bank of Tulsa, 705 F.2d 396, 398-99 (10th Cir. 1983). Ownership or title is not the relevant concern under Article 9; "the issue is whether the debtor has acquired sufficient rights in the collateral so that the security interest would attach." Fricke v. Valley Prod. Credit, Assn., 721 S.W.2d 747, 753 (Mo. Ct. App. 1986). The "rights in the collateral" language is a "gateway through which one looks to other law to determine the extent of the debtor's rights." Am. Bank & Trust v. Shaull, 678 N.W.2d 779, 788 (S.D. 2004). Thus, "[a]ll or some of owner's rights can be transferred by way of sale, lease, or license [and a] person with transferable rights can grant an enforceable security interest in those rights." Id. at 788, n.4. A "security interest will attach to the collateral only to the extent of the debtor's rights in the collateral"; mere possession of the collateral is insufficient to support an attachment, but the debtor need not have full ownership. Pleasant View Farms, Inc. v. Ness, 455 N.W.2d 602, 604 (S.D. 1990). "The common conceptualization of property rights as consisting of a bundle of sticks is helpful in understanding when a debtor has sufficient rights in an asset to grant an enforceable Article 9 security interest." First Natl. Bank of Philip, S.D. v. Temple, 642 N.W.2d 197, 204 (S.D. 2002) (quotation omitted).

The district court did not analyze the modified cattle-sharing contract to determine the nature of Anderson's rights in the calves or whether Anderson's interests or rights were sufficient to permit attachment of a security interest. We conclude that the standard relied on by the district court is inconsistent with Minnesota law. The application of the incorrect standard prematurely terminated the analysis of the cattle-sharing agreement, which is necessary to determine whether Anderson's rights in the collateral were sufficient for the bank's security interest to attach. Findings of fact that are controlled or influenced by errors of law are not final and must be set aside. Webb Bus. Promotions, Inc. v. Am. Elecs. & Entm't Corp., 617 N.W.2d 67, 73 (Minn. 2000). Because the district court applied a standard of ownership that is inconsistent with Minnesota law, its finding that the security interest did not attach was influenced by an error of law.

In applying the correct legal standard, the district court must initially determine whether the cattle-sharing agreement is ambiguous. Turner v. Alpha Phi Sorority House, 276 N.W.2d 63, 66 (Minn. 1979). The agreement suggests ambiguity by stating that the cattle provided by Johnson continue to be "owned" by Johnson, but, with respect to the calves, requiring only that they are to be sold in Johnson's "name." When contract language is susceptible to more than one meaning, the interpretation of the contract becomes a question of fact. Trondson v. Janikula, 458 N.W.2d 679, 681 (Minn. 1990). The parties whose interests are affected by this determination should have a full opportunity to argue whether the cattle-sharing contract is ambiguous. For these reasons, we reverse the district court's order that directed the verdict on Border State Bank's conversion claim. On remand, the district court shall consider the cattle-sharing agreement to determine whether Anderson had "rights" in the calves, to which the bank's security interest attached. . . .

DECISION

Minn. Stat. §336.9-203(b) (2002) refers to "rights in the collateral." The district court applied the wrong legal standard by limiting its inquiry to whether Anderson owned the cattle and erred in failing to address whether the debtor held "rights" in the collateral under the cattle-sharing agreement. We reverse the directed verdict on the bank's conversion claim and remand for further proceedings. Because the record contains competent evidence to sustain the verdict, the special-verdict form conveyed a correct understanding of the law, and the damages assessed by the jury did not so greatly exceed adequate compensation as to require remittitur, we affirm the district court's denial of Johnson's posttrial motions.

Affirmed in part, reversed in part, and remanded.

PROBLEM 42

Roy Gabriel decided to go into the music business and borrowed $35,000 from Octopus National Bank (ONB) in order to open his shop, named Gabriel's Trumpets. On January 6 he signed a security agreement with the bank, giving ONB an interest in all "existing and after-acquired inventory in the store." That same day he received the money. On January 6 his inventory consisted of four guitars and a pitch pipe. Gabriel did have a contract with Triumphant Trumpet Manufacturing Company (TTMC) to sell him 40 trumpets, which he paid for in advance of the delivery date (March 30). On March 15 TTMC packaged the 40 trumpets and marked them "For Shipment to Gabriel's Trumpet Store." On March 30 TTMC shipped them to Gabriel, who received them that day and displayed them in the store.

(a) On what day or days did the bank's security interest *attach* (that is, become effective) to the guitars, pitch pipe, and trumpets? See §9-203(a) and read §2-501. (Why is it relevant?)

(b) Does your answer change if we add the fact that the bank filed a proper financing statement covering Gabriel's inventory on January 7? Can a financing statement be filed before the security agreement is signed? Attached? See §9-502(d). Why would a creditor wish to file a financing statement before the security interest had attached? See §9-322(a)(1).

(c) If the bank did not advance any money until March 31 (the date the bank actually saw the trumpets in the store), and if the bank did not make any commitment (see §9-102(a)(69)) to advance any money until that date, when did the security interest attach?

PROBLEM 43

Daniel Huron loaned Jennifer Ontario money to buy a car. They agreed over the phone that the car would be collateral for the debt. After Huron sent a form to the Registry of Motor Vehicles, he was listed as a creditor on the car's certificate of title. Does he have a security interest in the car? Compare In re Crandall, 346 B.R. 220 (Bankr. M.D. Fla. 2006), with In re Westermeyer, 2012 WL 2952176 (Bankr. C.D. Ill. 2012).

PROBLEM 44

ACRO, Inc., owed considerable funds to its bank. The bank subsequently obtained possession of valuable promissory notes belonging to ACRO, and, because the transactions were closed in the bank's offices, the notes were put in the bank's vault. Did the notes become collateral for ACRO's debt to the bank? See In re ACRO Bus. Fin. Corp., 357 B.R. 785619 (Bankr. D. Minn. 2006); In re Debaeke, 2011 WL 5563543 (Bankr. E.D. Mich. 2011).

In re Howell Enterprises, Inc.

United States Court of Appeals, Eighth Circuit, 1991
934 F.2d 969

ROSENBAUM, J.

It all started simply enough. Howell Enterprises, Inc. (Howell) and Tradax America, Inc. (Tradax) both sell rice. A customer, Bar Schwartz Limited (Bar Schwartz), wanted to buy some rice and pay for it with a commercial letter of credit. But Bar Schwartz could not buy rice from Howell because Howell would not accept the commercial letter of credit as payment. This means of payment was acceptable to Tradax, but Bar Schwartz refused to buy rice from Tradax for reasons of its own. So, Howell and Tradax came up with a plan—Tradax would sell its rice to Bar Schwartz under Howell's name. This seemingly simple solution created the complex legal problem now before the court, a problem the parties clearly did not contemplate when the transaction took place.

I. BACKGROUND

Howell is an Arkansas corporation engaged in the business of buying, selling, storing, and milling rice. On June 20, 1986, Howell borrowed $2,100,000 from the First National Bank of Stuttgart, Arkansas (First National), and granted the bank a security interest in all accounts receivable.

Tradax is a New York corporation engaged in the business of buying and selling rice in the United States and abroad. Tradax transacted business with Howell on a regular basis in 1987. One of those transactions engendered this lawsuit.

On February 25, 1987, a contract was signed in the name of Howell, under which rice would be sold by Tradax to Bar Schwartz. Payment was to be accomplished by a one-year commercial letter of credit. Names were used interchangeably throughout the transaction: Tradax was listed as the owner on some shipping documents and on one bill of lading; Howell was listed on another bill of lading and on the certificate of origin; Tradax prepared the shipper's export declaration, but identified the shipper as Howell; Tradax paid the shipping and loading expenses and the brokerage fees, but sometimes did so under Howell's name.

Critical to this controversy, Howell listed the Bar Schwartz transaction as an account receivable on its books, with a corresponding and equivalent account payable to Tradax. Tradax documented the transaction on its books as a sale to Howell, but did not invoice Howell for a sale.

The rice was successfully, but not uneventfully, delivered to Bar Schwartz.[6] In due course, Howell sent an invoice to Bar Schwartz for the purchase price of the rice. On April 29, 1987, Bar Schwartz arranged for the letter of credit to be issued, naming Howell as beneficiary.

On June 18, 1987, Howell presented the letter of credit and the necessary supporting documents to First National. It was understood that Howell would transfer the proceeds to Tradax when the letter of credit matured, in May, 1988. But on April 4, 1988, before the maturity date, Howell filed for Chapter 11 bankruptcy. Upon the filing of the bankruptcy, First National came forward to claim its perfected security interest in Howell's accounts receivable. The Bar Schwartz letter of credit was swept into the bankruptcy.

Tradax brought this complaint before the bankruptcy court on May 9, 1988, asserting that Bar Schwartz's letter of credit was not one of Howell's accounts receivable and therefore was not subject to First National's security interest. Tradax alternatively argued that the letter of credit was subject to a constructive trust in favor of Tradax.

In an order, entered September 8, 1989, the bankruptcy court ruled that Tradax did have an equitable interest in the letter of credit and its proceeds as beneficiary of a constructive trust. The bankruptcy court then looked to the UCC as adopted in Arkansas to define First National's security interest in "all accounts receivable." Section §4-9-106 of the Arkansas Statutes defines "account" as "any right to payment for goods sold." The bankruptcy court ruled that because the letter of credit could be characterized as a "right to payment," First National had a perfected security interest in the letter of credit. The bankruptcy court, faced with two competing claims to the letter of credit, found that First National qualified as a bona fide purchaser for value and held an interest superior to Tradax's equitable interest.

Tradax appealed to the district court, which affirmed on April 16, 1990. On appeal, Tradax argued that the district court erred in ruling that the Bar Schwartz letter of credit was an "account" or evidence of a right to payment to Howell, that First National had a security interest in the letter of credit and that First National was entitled to prevail on general equitable principles.

II. Discussion

As the second reviewing court, we review the bankruptcy court's legal conclusions de novo and its factual findings under the clearly erroneous

---

6. A short time after the rice was loaded on a barge, Tradax determined that the ship which would carry the rice overseas was delayed. Tradax arranged a swap with Sunrice, another rice trading company, whereby the original barge-load was sold in exchange for a barge-load of rice available at a later date. The second load of rice was loaded aboard the ocean-going vessel on May 26, 1987.

standard. Wegner v. Grunewaldt, 821 F.2d 1317, 1320 (8th Cir. 1987). The parties, in this case, do not dispute the factual findings of the bankruptcy court. This case turns, instead, on the legal characterization of the Bar Schwartz letter of credit. As such, our review is de novo.

Both parties acknowledge that First National had a perfected security interest in Howell's accounts receivable. As the parties would frame the issue, if the letter of credit is an account receivable, First National is entitled to its proceeds; if not an account receivable, the asset goes to Tradax.

The court eschews the parties' categorical inquiry. A letter of credit is an instrument of commerce, which is sui generis.[7] Its unique character is reflected in the fact that Article 5 of the UCC is devoted to letters of credit. The court is disinclined to go beyond the UCC and decide this case on unnecessarily broad grounds. Analysis reveals that the court need not answer whether a letter of credit can ever constitute an account. It is clear that this particular letter of credit was never intended to be an account and was listed as such purely by happenstance.

In this court's view, the primary and relevant inquiry is whether or not First National's undisputed security interest can reach that particular line item in Howell's accounts receivable identified as the Bar Schwartz account. With this inquiry in mind, the court turns to the specific facts of this case.

Arkansas has adopted the UCC secured transactions and letters of credit provisions. Ark. Stat. Ann. §§4-9-101 to 4-9-507; 4-5-101 to 4-5-117. Under Arkansas Statutes, §4-9-203, a security interest cannot attach unless "the debtor has rights in the collateral." The courts below found that Howell had a legal interest in the Bar Schwartz account receivable, subject to Tradax's equitable interest. This court has a less expansive view of Howell's rights.

Howell's only claim to the Bar Schwartz account receivable is by reason of its arbitrarily having elected to record the Bar Schwartz letter of credit on its receivable ledger. Tradax had no opportunity to know of or protest this infelicitous listing. More critically, Tradax had no notice that Howell's accounts receivable were encumbered by First National's security interest. The lower courts determined, as matters of fact, that the only agreement

---

7. Letters of credit are means of guaranteeing payment for sales of goods. Here, the seller did not wish to deliver goods without assurance of payment; likewise the buyer did not want to pay prior to receiving the goods. The letter of credit resolved this difficulty by substituting a stable third party's, here a bank's, credit for that of the buyer. Upon receiving the letter of credit, the seller delivers the requested goods to a common carrier and obtains a payment-authorizing document in return. The seller presents the letter of credit and the required documentation to the issuing bank to collect payment. After honoring the letter of credit, the bank is entitled to reimbursement and a fee from the buyer. Upon reimbursement, the bank gives the bill of lading to the buyer who then can present it to the common carrier and receive the goods. See generally 2 J. White & R. Summers, Uniform Commercial Code §19-1 (3d ed. 1988) [now vol. 3, §26-1(a) (5th ed. 2008) — Eds.].

between Tradax and Howell was that Howell would allow Tradax to use its name on pertinent documents. Howell did not, and could not, claim any right in the Bar Schwartz account or the proceeds of the letter of credit, because the rice was always owned by Tradax.

Certainly Howell acquired physical possession of the letter of credit, but mere possession of such a document is insufficient to establish a right to collateral upon which to base a security interest. Rohweder v. Aberdeen Production Credit Assn., 765 F.2d 109 (8th Cir. 1985); Pontchartrain State Bank v. Poulson, 684 F.2d 704, 707 (10th Cir. 1982); Montco, Inc. v. Glatzer, 665 F.2d 36, 40 (2d Cir. 1981). Howell was involved in this transaction for the sole and limited purpose of serving as a conduit for Tradax's sale to Bar Schwartz.

This lawsuit, however, became inevitable when Howell mistakenly attempted to "book" the deal. The court finds this factual occurrence to be of no legal effect; the fact of booking this transaction as an account receivable did not make it an account receivable in law. Howell did not own and could not legitimately encumber any interest in the Bar Schwartz account, regardless of the bookkeeping procedure it chose.

Finally, the court declines to embrace the "equitable" theory referenced by the courts below. Each suggested that Tradax was a "culpable" party and was, perforce, responsible for the legal consequences here. Certainly, Tradax and Howell sought to hide the identity of the true seller from Bar Schwartz. But no legal consequences flow from this fact. Legal arrangements through undisclosed partners, agents, and proxies are not unknown in the marketplace. The court finds no reason, based solely on an undisclosed but legal arrangement, to require Tradax to pay twice, with no hope of recompense, for the same barge of rice by permitting First National to execute its security interest on the Bar Schwartz account. Moreover, while First National was an innocent third party in this transaction, First National has shown no detrimental reliance on Howell's accounting error.

III. Conclusion

For the foregoing reasons we reverse the judgment of the district court and remand the case for entry of judgment in favor of Tradax.

———

CHAPTER 4   ASSESSMENT: MULTIPLE CHOICE QUESTIONS

1. Bruce Banner gets a loan for his biotech business, putting up as collateral his precision scientific instruments. What category of collateral are the instruments?
   a. Instruments.
   b. Inventory.
   c. Equipment.

d. General intangibles.

e. All of the above

2. Banner gets his loan from Hector. The parties make an oral agreement, sealed with a handshake. Hector delivers the money. Banner promises that the instruments are collateral for the debt, although Banner will retain them and use them in the lab's work. If called on to testify, Banner would freely testify to the agreement. Is the security agreement effective to create a security interest? Meaning, for example, will it stand up if Banner goes into bankruptcy or another creditor gets a judgment against Banner?

a. Yes, because Banner does not deny the effectiveness of the agreement.

b. Yes, because Hector has performed and so may enforce the agreement.

c. Yes, if Banner can provide evidence that the money was delivered, such as an account statement.

d. No, because there was no agreement signed by Banner and Hector was not in possession of the collateral.

3. Pemulis Auto delivered a car to Lloyd under a Lease Agreement, which provided that Lloyd would own the car after making the required payments. Because such a transaction is in substance a secured sale on credit, Article 9 applies to the transaction. Does that mean that Pemulis Auto would have no effective security interest, because the parties signed a Lease Agreement, not a security agreement?

a. Pemulis Auto will not have an effective security interest, for lack of a signed security agreement.

b. Pemulis Auto has an effective security agreement, because the Lease Agreement will qualify as a security agreement.

c. Pemulis Auto will not have a security interest, because it did not provide value.

d. Pemulis Auto will not have a security interest, becauses Lloyd has no interest in the collateral.

4. Maximilian M. Miltzlaf signed a security agreement to put up his art collection as collateral and got a loan from Slippup Bank. Slippup Bank filed a UCC financing statement, but misspelled the debtor's name as "Maximilian M. Milztlaf." A search of the state's UCC records using its standard search logic under the debtor's correct name does not disclose the financing statement. Is the financing statement effective?

a. Yes. Even though the debtor's name was slightly misspelled, it was not seriously misleading.

b. No. The error is deemed seriously misleading, because a search using the correct name does not disclose the statement filed with the incorrect name.

c. It depends on whether other creditors had been misled by the inaccurate filing.

    d. It depends on whether a search with the incorrect name would disclose the financing statement filed under the correct name.

    e. Yes, as long as the collateral is described correctly. The debtor's name is not important.

5. Assume the financing statement is not effective. Does Slippup Bank have an enforceable security interest?

    a. No. The financing statement is what makes the security interest enforceable.

    b. No. Slippup Bank is an unsecured creditor.

    c. Yes. Slippup Bank has a security interest that is enforceable against Maximilian M. Milztlaf, but would probably lose its security interest if Milztlaf went into bankruptcy or another of Milztlaf's creditors got a judgment lien on the art collection.

    d. Yes. The security agreement is all that is necessary to give Slippup Bank rights in the art collection that will stand up against anyone else.

ANSWERS

1. *C* is the best answer. Instruments are not necessarily instruments. Rather, in classifying collateral, we look to the definitions in the UCC. "Instruments," under §9-102(47), are promissory notes, checks and the like. Here, the precision scientific instruments are goods (movable things, §9-102(44)). Goods has four sub-categories. The precision instruments are not inventory, because they are not held for sale, §9-102(48). They are not farm products, as §9-102(34) quickly confirms. They are not consumer goods, because Banner does not have them for personal, family or household use. §9-102(23). They must then fall into the residual category of goods, equipment. See §9-102(33). They are not remotely general intangibles, which is the residual category for things that do not fall into any of the other defined categories of collateral.

2. *D* is the best answer. Article 9 has a stricter writing requirement than contract law. Sales contracts, for example, may be enforced without a signed writing if the party admits the existence of the contract or if the goods have been accepted. §2-201. But an enforceable security agreement requires either a signed writing or that the creditor is in possession of the collateral. §9-203.

3. *B* is the best answer. To have an enforceable security agreement, the creditor must meet three requirements, under §9-203:

    — a signed security agreement or creditor in possession of the collateral by agreement;

    — value has been given;

    — debtor has rights in the collateral.

The Lease Agreement will qualify as a security agreement. Article 9 reaches out to cover all transactions that, in effect, create a security interest in personal property. Consistent with that, the definition of "security agreement" is forgiving, covering any agreement that has the effect of creating a security interest in personal property. §9-102(74). Pemulis Auto has given value — not money, but the car. Lloyd has rights in the car, which has been delivered by Pemulis Auto. All three requirements are met and so Pemulis Auto has an enforceable security interest. As later chapters will discuss, Pemulis Auto may find that it faces difficulties if it fails to perfect the security interest or if it does not follow Article 9's rules about enforcing the security interest.

4. *B* is the best answer. The key piece of information in a UCC financing statement is the debtor's name, contrary to D, because the records are principally searched using the debtor's name to see if the debtor's property is encumbered. A seriously misleading finance statement is not effective, even if no one was affected, contrary to C. For the debtor's name, the UCC provides a test of whether the error was seriously misleading: if a search using the right name discloses the financing statement filed under the incorrect name, then it was not seriously misleading. Even though the error was only switching two letters, it resulted in a search that did not disclose the statement with the incorrect name. The filing was seriously misleading and so ineffective, contrary to A. D puts the test backwards.

5. *C* is the best answer. As stated above, to have an enforceable security interest, the creditor needs to meet three requirements: (1) signed security agreement or collateral in possession; (2) value has been given; (3) debtor has rights in the collateral. Slippup Bank has met all three requirements. None of them requires that an effective financing statement has been filed. So Slippup Bank has an enforceable security interest (which also means that its security interest has "attached"). See §9-203.

What about that ineffective financing statement? A financing statement is not necessary for the security agreement to be enforceable *against the debtor*. But, as later chapters discuss, it may be necessary to make the security interest effective *against other claimants*. Filing a financing statement perfects the security interest. By filing, the creditor gives notice to others of its claim. If the creditor does not perfect, as we will see, it will likely lose to other claimants: Milztlaf's bankruptcy trustee, another creditor that attaches a judgment lien to the art collection, or a buyer of the art collection. Creditors file financing statements in order to retain priority in the collateral, even if the debtor goes into bankruptcy, if the collateral is attached by a judgment creditor, or if the collateral is sold.

CHAPTER 5

PERFECTION OF THE SECURITY INTEREST

We are all striving for perfection, of course, but in secured lending the term has a specialized meaning. A creditor's security interest in the debtor's collateral is "perfected" when the creditor has taken all the steps required by the law to give that creditor top-dog priority in that collateral. Later entities may make subsequent claims to the collateral (other creditors, the debtor's trustee in bankruptcy, buyers of the collateral, etc.), and the creditor wants its attorney to make sure that no steps have been missed and that creditor's interest will trump these other claimants. It's easy to make missteps here, missteps that conjure up the ugly word "malpractice." Learning the basics and making sure they are complied with time after time is very important. Lawyers fresh out of law school and familiar with this course will do fine, but as time passes errors may occur as the lawyer gets busy, delegates the duties to assistants, or life inevitably becomes more complicated. Keeping up vigilance here, year after year, will be difficult, but whoever said the practice of law is easy?

If a security interest is *perfected*, it is senior to most later creditor interests (especially that of the trustee in bankruptcy, should the debtor go bankrupt). Read §9-308 carefully. Note particularly that a security interest must first *attach* before perfection is possible. (If you think about it, this is an obvious requirement: A security interest must be effective between the debtor and the creditor before it has legal meaning as to other parties.)

The UCC's most common means of perfection is by having the secured party (the creditor) file a financing statement in the appropriate place. In fact, §9-310 presumes that the filing of a financing statement is the usual way of perfecting a security interest in the debtor's property. However, the Code does permit perfection in other ways too. Perfection of security interests in tangible collateral (goods, instruments, documents, and chattel paper) may be accomplished by the creditor's taking physical possession of the collateral (a common law *pledge*; see below). Further, for some types of collateral the security interest is *automatically* perfected without filing *or* possession; attachment is all that is required. For some goods, such as vehicles, a security interest usually must be perfected by having a notation made on the certificate of title. Finally, perfection for some types of collateral can be accomplished by achieving "control" over the collateral. The legal steps involved in all these sorts of perfection choices are considered next.

I. PERFECTION BY POSSESSION (PLEDGE)

If the collateral is in the physical possession of the creditor, the world at large is alerted to that creditor's possible interest in the property, and no other notice is therefore required. Obviously, only collateral having physical form can be possessed. Read §9-313 and its Official Comments 2, 3, and 4. The Code drafters did not attempt to define "possession," leaving that to the common law. Professors White and Summers comment that possession "is a notoriously plastic idea"; White & Summers §23-8(b) at 1207.

PROBLEM 45

Your client, Archibald Gracie, owns The White Star of England, a famous large diamond currently on display at the Astor Museum in New York. Molly Brown, a wealthy Colorado investor, has agreed to buy the diamond from Gracie, and she has made a substantial down payment, with an agreement to make three more payments before she gets possession. Gracie and Brown have signed the purchase agreement, which contains a clause granting him a security interest in his own diamond until she has made all the required payments. His question to you is this: Can he perfect a security interest in the diamond by simply notifying the Astor Museum of the sale and telling the museum to hold it for his benefit until she makes payment in full, thus creating an escrow arrangement in which possession is held by the escrow agent? See §9-313(c), (f), and (g).

Sometimes the collateral is so large that possession by the secured party is too awkward. In that case it may be possible to store the goods in a warehouse and get a negotiable warehouse receipt representing the goods. Such a receipt is regulated by Article 7 of the Uniform Commercial Code, where an important provision, §7-403(c), provides that the warehouse cannot surrender the goods unless the recipient turns over any outstanding warehouse receipt (a *document of title*—the same rule applies to negotiable bills of lading, another kind of document of title). Read §9-312(c). Sometimes, as in the next Problem, it is more convenient for the warehouse to come to the goods instead of vice versa, a practice called *field warehousing*.

PROBLEM 46

Kiddie Delight, Inc., a manufacturer of toys, wanted to borrow money and use its inventory of toys as collateral. It called up Fred's Field Warehouse Company, and Fred's came to the plant, put the inventory in a locked room, and posted a sign on the door saying "Contents of Room Under Control of Fred's Field Warehouse." Fred's then issued a negotiable warehouse receipt deliverable to the order of Kiddie Delight. Fred's hired Mort Menial, the Kiddie Delight janitor, as its local warehouse custodian (Mort was paid $1 a week by Fred's to mind the goods; he continued to receive his normal paycheck from Kiddie Delight). Kiddie Delight pledged the warehouse receipt (a *document*) to Mammon State Bank in return for a loan. Kiddie Delight went bankrupt shortly thereafter.

(a) By having possession of this document, did the bank have a perfected security interest in the inventory? See §9-312(c) and Official Comment 3 to §9-313.

(b) Assume the warehouse receipt is validly issued and effective. If the bank and Kiddie Delight signed a written security agreement covering the warehouse receipt and the inventory it represented and if the bank gave Kiddie Delight the money, does the bank have a perfected security interest in the warehouse receipt even *before* the bank gets possession of it? See §9-312(e) (this is called *temporary perfection*—see Official Comment 9).

(c) If Kiddie Delight (prior to bankruptcy) wanted to get the warehouse receipt back from the bank in order to present it to the warehouseman (Mort), get the goods, clean them, return them to the field warehouse, and get back the receipt for rehypothecation to the bank, will the bank lose its perfection if it turns the document over to the debtor? Read §9-312(f).

(d) If the bank loses its perfection, who would you advise it to sue? See §7-204(a).

PROBLEM 47

Octopus National Bank (ONB) made a loan to Pi Solutions, Inc., secured by Pi's patent on a solar-powered night light. ONB learned that it is unsettled whether a security interest is perfected by filing in the state UCC office or the federal patent and trademark office. ONB had a brainwave. Rather than filing, can ONB perfect with a pledge—taking possession of Pi's patent certificate? See In re Coldwave Systems, LLC, 368 B.R. 91 (Bankr. D. Mass. 2007).

PROBLEM 48

Karate, Inc., was a self-defense training school. It pledged 36 of the promissory notes given it by its customers to Nightflyer Finance Company in return for a loan. The parties signed a security agreement, and the finance company took possession of the notes. A month later, Karate, Inc.'s president, Arnold Sun, asked Nightflyer to let him have back one of the notes so that he could present it to the customer for payment (an Article 3 *presentment*). The finance company gave him the note on April 6. Sun put it in his desk at the school and forgot about it. On October 12 the karate school went bankrupt. Does the bank have a perfected security interest in any or all of the promissory notes? See §9-312(g) and (h). Could the finance company have protected itself by filing a financing statement as to the promissory notes? See §9-312(a).

NOTE

The primary use of §9-312(e) and (f) occurs in letter of credit transactions (UCC Article 5), wherein the issuing bank receives a bill of lading (a *document*) covering the goods and turns it over to the buyer (*debtor*) so the buyer can get the goods from the carrier, sell them, and reimburse the bank. During the 20-day period the bank's security interest in the document remains perfected even though the document is out of its possession. Under §5-118, a section added to Article 5 by the 1999 revision of Article 9, the issuer of a letter of credit will always have a security interest in bills of lading presented under the letter of credit until the issuer is reimbursed by its customer (the *applicant*).

II.   AUTOMATIC PERFECTION

Automatic perfection means that the secured party need only make sure that its security interest has *attached*, and perfection is thereby accomplished without the need for any further steps. The materials below explore the situations in which this occurs.

A. Purchase Money Security Interest in Consumer Goods

The various transactions qualifying for automatic perfection are listed in §9-309. The first of these we will study is the automatic perfection given to purchase money security interests in consumer goods; read §9-309(1). The reason for having an automatic perfection of purchase money security interests in consumer goods without requiring either filing or possession was partly historical (it had always been done that way) and partly practical. Consumer goods are unlikely to be used as collateral *twice*, so there are rarely any later creditors to protect. Filing costs money, and it is simply not worth it for merchants to file to perfect a security interest in every nickel and dime sale (note that there is no automatic perfection for motor vehicles—see §9-311(a)(2); security interests in them require definite steps for perfection, typically notation of the lien interest on the certificate of title once the vehicle leaves the dealer's inventory).

To qualify for automatic perfection under §9-309(1), the security interest in consumer goods must qualify as a *purchase money* interest, a term defined in §9-103. A purchase money security interest (PMSI) is granted to sellers or lenders whose willingness to extend credit permitted the debtor to acquire the collateral. Such creditors obviously have a superior equity in the collateral vis-à-vis other creditors, and the Code therefore frequently affords them special considerations.

PROBLEM 49

Bilko Siding, Inc., put aluminum siding on Mr. and Mrs. Brown's home. They signed a contract on August 4, giving the company a security interest in all their currently owned consumer goods plus those acquired in the future. On September 25, the Browns went to First Finance Company and borrowed $80 for the stated purpose of buying a sewing machine. They signed a security agreement with the finance company, granting it a security interest in the machine. First Finance did not file a financing statement. The Browns bought the machine on October 11. They filed for bankruptcy on October 12. Bilko, First Finance, and their trustee all claim the machine.

(a) Did Bilko's security interest attach to the sewing machine? See §9-204(b); In re Johnson, 1973 WL 21366 (Bankr. D. Neb. 1973) (creditor's security interest in "all consumer goods" held totally invalid because the bankruptcy judge found the after-acquired property clause overbroad, unconscionable, and unfair as it had an *in terrorem* effect on consumers). What did the bankruptcy judge in this last-cited opinion mean? And why, in the first place, would Bilko want a security interest in a used sewing machine (which, after all, has little resale value)?

(b) Was the loan agreement a *purchase money security interest* even though First Finance was a lender and not the seller of the machine? See §9-103(a)(2).

(c) Would it have been a purchase money security interest if the Browns had used the $80 to pay a liquor bill and had used $80 from their savings account to buy the sewing machine? How can finance companies protect themselves from the debtor's misuse of the funds advanced? See §3-110(d).

(d) Assuming the $80 was used for the announced purpose, who gets the sewing machine?

Congress thought it was outrageous to allow creditors to take a non-purchase money security interest in consumer goods that the consumer would otherwise want to claim as exempt from creditor process, so §522(f) of the Bankruptcy Code permits the debtor in bankruptcy to avoid such security interests. This has led to a much-litigated issue: If a purchase money transaction has later been renegotiated and either consolidated with other debts or new money loaned, does it retain its purchase money character so as to escape avoidance under Bankruptcy Code §522(f)? The next case illustrates the problem.

In re Short

United States Bankruptcy Court, Southern District of Illinois, 1994
170 B.R. 128

KENNETH J. MEYERS, Bankruptcy Judge.

Debtors Robert and Dawn Short seek to avoid the lien of American General Finance, Inc. ("American") as a nonpossessory, non-purchase money security interest impairing an exemption claimed by them in household goods. See 11 U.S.C. §522(f)(2). American objects that its lien is a purchase money security interest not subject to avoidance under §522(f)(2) and that its lien retained this status even though the original note granting such interest was consolidated with another obligation of the debtors, with the goods in question serving as collateral for the entire amount. The debtors respond that this refinancing destroyed the purchase money character of American's lien and that the lien, therefore, may be avoided under §522(f)(2).

The facts are undisputed. On June 20, 1992, the debtors entered into a retail installment contract with Anderson Warehouse Furniture for the purchase of bedroom furniture. Under the contract, no interest was charged for one year and no payments were due until June 20, 1993, at which time the entire balance of $2,880 became due. The contract, which granted a security interest in the bedroom furniture purchased by the debtors, was assigned to American on the date it was signed. The debtors made no payments under this contract.

On July 16, 1993, the debtors executed a note with American in which they consolidated the June 20 contract obligation with another note to American for $3,642.33 dated June 22, 1992. The July 16 note in the amount of $7,337.30 provided funds to pay off the June 20 and June 22 notes, with the remaining balance applied to pay credit life and disability insurance premiums. The July 16 note, providing for an interest rate of 21.90 percent, was to be paid in monthly installments, with the final payment due in July 1997.

A disclosure statement accompanying the note described the collateral for the July 16 note as a "continued purchase money interest" in the debtors' bedroom furniture and, on a separate line, listed numerous other recreational and household items owned by the debtors. There was no indication that these latter items served as collateral for the June 22 note or that American had a purchase money security interest in them.

The debtors made one payment under the July 16 note of $248.38 and a partial payment of $146. On January 4, 1994, the debtors filed their Chapter 7 bankruptcy petition. The debtors then moved to avoid American's lien on household goods, including the bedroom furniture, under §522(f)(2).

DISCUSSION

Section §522(f)(2) allows a debtor to avoid the fixing of a lien on property that would otherwise be exempt if such lien is a non-possessory, non-purchase money security interest.[1] The Bankruptcy Code does not define "purchase money security interest" or specify how a lien's purchase money status is affected by refinancing or consolidation with other debt. Reference must be had, therefore, to the state law definition of "purchase money security interest" in §9-107 of the Uniform Commercial Code. See Pristas v. Landaus of Plymouth, Inc. (In re Pristas), 742 F.2d 797, 800 (3d Cir. 1984).

---

1. Section 522(f)(2) provides in pertinent part:

(f) [T]he debtor may avoid the fixing of a lien on an interest of the debtor in property to the extent that such lien impairs an exemption to which the debtor would have been entitled . . . if such lien is —
    (2) a nonpossessory, nonpurchase-money security interest in any —
        (A) household furnishings . . . that are held primarily for the personal, family, or household use of the debtor. . . .

11 U.S.C. §522(f)(2).

That section provides:

> A security interest is a "purchase money security interest" *to the extent* that it is
>   (a) taken or retained by the seller of the collateral to secure all or part of its price; or
>   (b) taken by a person who by making advances or incurring an obligation gives value to enable the debtor to acquire rights in . . . collateral.

810 ILCS 5/9-107 (emphasis added).

Under this definition, a seller obtains a purchase money security interest by retaining a security interest in goods sold. A financing agency, such as American in the present case, obtains a purchase money security interest when it advances money to the seller and takes back an assignment of chattel paper. See Uniform Commercial Code, §9-107, cmt. 1 (1993); Raymond B. Check, The Transformation Rule Under §522 of the Bankruptcy Code of 1978, 84 Mich. L. Rev. 109, 126 n.104 (1985) (hereinafter Check, Transformation Rule).

In this case, American clearly had a purchase money security interest in the debtors' bedroom furniture when it accepted an assignment of the debtors' contract on these goods. Debtors contend that this interest was canceled when their original note of June 20 was consolidated with other indebtedness and the note was paid by renewal. American argues, however, that its purchase money lien survived despite this refinancing and that it retained a nonavoidable purchase money security interest in the debtors' bedroom furniture to the extent of the balance remaining on the original note for purchase of the collateral.

There is a split of authority among the circuits concerning whether a purchase money security interest is extinguished when the original purchase money loan is refinanced through renewal or consolidation with another obligation. One line of cases holds that a purchase money security interest is automatically "transformed" into a nonpurchase money interest when the proceeds of a renewal note are used to satisfy the original note. See Matthews v. Transamerica Financial Services (In re Matthews), 724 F.2d 798, 800 (9th Cir. 1984); Dominion Bank of Cumberlands v. Nuckolls, 780 F.2d 408, 413 (4th Cir. 1985); In re Keeton, 161 B.R. 410, 411 (Bankr. S.D. Ohio 1993); Hipps v. Landmark Financial Services of Georgia, Inc. (In re Hipps), 89 B.R. 264, 265 (Bankr. N.D. Ga. 1988); In re Faughn, 69 B.R. 18, 20-21 (Bankr. E.D. Mo. 1986). Because the collateral now secures an antecedent debt rather than a debt for purchase of the collateral or, in the case of a renewal note consolidating debt or advancing new funds, secures more than its purchase price, these courts hold that the resulting lien on the purchased goods no longer qualifies as a "purchase money security interest" under §9-107. Following such refinancing, then, the lien may be avoided in its entirety under §522(f)(2).

The second line of cases, rejecting the "all or nothing" approach of the transformation rule, holds that a lien may be partially purchase money and partially non-purchase money and that the purchase money aspect of a lien is not automatically destroyed by refinancing or consolidation with other debt. See Billings v. Avco Colorado Industrial Bank (In re Billings), 838 F.2d 405, 409 (10th Cir. 1988); Pristas, 742 F.2d at 801 (3d Cir. 1984); Geist v. Converse County Bank (In re Geist), 79 B.R. 939, 941 (D. Wyo. 1987); In re Hemingson, 84 B.R. 604 (Bankr. D. Minn. 1988); In re Parsley, 104 B.R. 72, 75 (Bankr. S.D. Ind. 1988). This view, referred to as the "dual status" rule, is premised on the language of §9-107, which provides that a lien is a purchase money security interest "to the extent" that it is taken to secure the purchase price of collateral. Accordingly, the purchase money security interest taken under the original note is preserved to the extent of the balance remaining unpaid on the original purchase money loan. See Russell v. Associates Financial Services Co. (In re Russell), 29 B.R. 270, 273-274 (Bankr. W.D. Okla. 1983).

Courts adopting the "dual status" rule note that it gives effect to the substance of the refinancing transaction.

> Though in form the original note is canceled, its balance is absorbed into the refinancing loan. To the extent of that balance, the purchase money security interest taken under the original note likewise survives, because what is owed on the original note is not eliminated[;] it is merely transferred to, and increased in amount by, another obligation. The refinancing changes the character of neither the balance due under the first loan nor the security interest taken under it.

Associates Finance v. Conn (In re Conn), 16 B.R. 454, 459 (Bankr. W.D. Ky. 1982); see *Russell*, 29 B.R. at 273.

The difficulty with the dual status rule lies in determining the extent of the purchase money interest remaining after refinancing. See *Pristas*, 742 F.2d at 801; Coomer v. Barclays American Financial, Inc. (In re Coomer), 8 B.R. 351, 353-354 (Bankr. E.D. Tenn. 1980). When a purchase money loan has been consolidated with non-purchase money debt and payments have ensued, some method of applying payments between the purchase money and non-purchase money portions of the refinanced loan is necessary so that the purchase money collateral secures only its own price and does not remain as collateral for the entire obligation. See Mulcahy v. Indianapolis Morris Plan (In re Mulcahy), 3 B.R. 454, 457 (Bankr. S.D. Ind. 1980). This problem has led some courts to find that purchase money status is forfeited if no method of allocation has been supplied, either by the parties' contract or by statute. See *Coomer*, 8 B.R. at 355; *Mulcahy*, 3 B.R. at 457; cf. *Pristas*, 742 at 802 (apportionment formula supplied by statute); Matter of Weigert, 145 B.R. 621, 623 (Bankr. D. Neb. 1991) (parties' agreement provided allocation formula). Other courts have adopted a judicial "first in, first out" method of allocation, under which payments are applied sequentially to purchase money debts in the order in which they were incurred. See In re Clark, 156 B.R. 693, 695 (Bankr. S.D. Fla. 1993); *Parsley,* 104 B.R. at 75; Matter of Weinbrenner, 53 B.R. 571, 579-580 (Bankr. W.D. Wis. 1985); *Conn,* 16 B.R. at 458; In re Gibson, 16 B.R. 257, 267-268 (Bankr. D. Kan. 1981); see generally Bernard A. Burk, Preserving the Purchase Money Status of Refinanced or Commingled Purchase Money Debt, 35 Stan. L. Rev. 1133, 1144-1146 (1983) (hereinafter Burk, Preserving Purchase Money Status).

Having considered the rationales for both the "automatic transformation" and "dual status" rules, this court finds that the dual status rule more closely adheres to the statutory language of §9-107 while effectuating the policy behind §522(f)(2). The "to the extent" language of §9-107 clearly contemplates that a lien may be partially purchase money and partially non-purchase money, depending on the circumstances of its creation. Thus, if a lender makes two separate loans—one for the purchase of goods, the other a cash advance—and retains a security interest in the purchased goods for both loans, the resulting lien is both purchase money (for the outstanding balance of the purchase money loan) and non-purchase money (for the amount remaining on the cash advance loan). No reason appears why the purchase money character of the first loan should disappear if the two loans are later consolidated, so long as the amounts attributable to the two loans may be separated. See Check, Transformation Rule, at 128.

Section 522(f)(2), moreover, with its distinction between purchase money and non-purchase money liens, was designed to permit debtors to avoid liens attached to household goods already owned by them rather than liens on collateral purchased with the money advanced. See *Russell,* at 274. Congress limited this avoidance option to non-purchase money interests in order to protect those lenders whose credit enabled the debtor to acquire the collateral in the first place. Check, Transformation Rule, at 127. When a purchase money loan is refinanced, the creditor is not committing the type of overreaching that §522(f)(2) aims to prevent, as the purchased goods remain as collateral for the loan. Thus, application of the dual status rule, with its recognition of the continued existence of the creditor's purchase money interest after refinancing, preserves the legislative balance between debtors' and creditors' rights in exempt property that is the purpose of §522(f)(2). See id.; In re Billings, 838 F.2d at 409-410.

Courts in the Seventh Circuit have not embraced either the transformation or the dual status rule but have, for the most part, taken a case by case approach which examines whether the debtor's obligation has been so changed by the refinanced loan that the resulting lien can no longer be characterized as a purchase money security interest. See In re Hatfield, 117 B.R. 387, 389-390 (Bankr. C.D. Ill. 1990) (quoting from In re Hills, No. 86-72037, slip op. at 4-5 (Bankr. C.D. Ill. July 29, 1987)); In re Gayhart, 33 B.R. 699, 700-701 (Bankr. N.D. Ill. 1983); Matter of Weinbrenner, 53 B.R. at 579-581; Johnson v. Richardson (Matter of Richardson), 47 B.R. 113, 117 (Bankr. W.D. Wis. 1985); but see In re Parsley, 104 B.R. at 75 (applying "dual status" rule). Under this approach, a refinanced loan is determined to be either a renewal of the original purchase money obligation, in which case the purchase money lien survives, or a novation, which extinguishes the purchase money character of the loan, depending upon the degree of change in terms and obligation between the two loans. See *Hatfield,* 117 B.R. at 390 ("the greater the degree of change in obligation . . . the more likely a novation will be found").

While the "middle of the road" approach of these courts lacks the certainty of a well-defined rule such as the transformation or dual status rule, this approach is not surprising given the diversity of fact situations presented in cases examining the purchase money character of refinanced loans. In the case of a simple refinancing that merely extends the repayment period of a loan—with a reduction in the amount of monthly payments and the same interest rate and security, strict application of the automatic transformation rule works an obvious injustice to the lender who has acted to benefit the borrower. See *Gayhart,* 33 B.R. at 700-701; *Hatfield,* 117 B.R. at 390. At the other end of the spectrum, when a purchase money loan is refinanced for new consideration and the second note involves different security and terms, this change may be seen to evidence the parties' intent to enter into a new obligation that cannot be characterized as a purchase money loan. See *Hills,* slip op. at 5 (refinanced note involving fresh advance of funds constituted a novation). Thus, courts that employ a case by case approach attempt to give effect to the parties' intent as derived from the facts of a particular transaction.

The facts of this case support a finding that American retained a purchase money lien on the debtors' bedroom furniture under either the dual status rule of the Tenth and Third Circuits or the case by case approach of bankruptcy courts in this circuit. As noted above, the problem under the dual status rule is allocating payments between the purchase money and non-purchase money aspects of a loan following consolidation in order to determine the extent to which the purchase money lien survives refinancing. The problem under the case by case approach is to determine whether the facts evidence the parties' intent to continue the purchase money character of the original loan.

In this case, the debtors had made no payments on the original purchase money loan of June 20 at the time they agreed to consolidate this obligation with another, non-purchase money note of June 22. Since the entire purchase price of the collateral remained unpaid, it is unlikely the parties intended to extinguish the debtors' obligation under the first note or to change its character. Rather, the purchase money note of June 20, a no-interest note with one annual payment, was essentially "extended" by the consolidation note of July 16 to allow for monthly payments at a commensurately high interest rate. Thus, the July 16 note merely enabled the debtors to pay the original purchase price of the bedroom furniture over a longer period of time. Despite the change in interest rate and repayment terms, the purchase money character of the loan had not become blurred by repeated refinancings, see Slay v. Pioneer Credit Co. (In re Slay), 8 B.R. 355, 358 (Bankr. E.D. Tenn. 1980) ("at some point the number of transactions between the lender and the debtor destroys any claim that the debt is part purchase money"), and the essential character of American's interest in the purchase money collateral remained intact.

The parties' intent to continue the purchase money character of American's lien following consolidation was specifically stated in the documentation for the July 16 note, in which the security was described as a "continued purchase money interest" in the debtors' bedroom furniture. Cf. In re Billings, 838 F.2d at 109 (loan document expressly stating intent to continue the purchase money security interest showed parties did not intend to extinguish the original debt and security interest). While such a statement would not be sufficient, of itself, to preserve purchase money status upon refinancing, it adds weight to the Court's conclusion that the parties considered the new note to be a continuation of the debtors' original purchase money obligation. This statement of intent distinguishes the present case from In re Hills, in which the court found a novation based on the fact that the parties' note consolidating a purchase money obligation with non-purchase money debt did not identify the purchased goods as collateral and stated that the creditor was "not being given a 'security interest in the goods or property being purchased.'" *Hills,* slip op. at 1. Based on the parties' express statement of intent in this case and the fact that no payments had been made on the original purchase money loan at the time of refinancing, the Court finds that the parties intended to continue the purchase money status of American's lien in the July 16 note consolidating debt.

The problem of determining the extent of American's purchase money lien following consolidation is complicated only slightly by the fact that the debtors made one monthly payment and a partial payment on the consolidated note before their bankruptcy filing. If the debtors had made no payments at all, the purchase money portion of the consolidated debt would be the amount owing on the purchase money debt at the time of the consolidation. See In re Slay, 8 B.R. at 358. The *Slay* court, noting the difficulty of apportioning payments between the purchase money and non-purchase money parts of a consolidated loan, ruled that normally a creditor's purchase money status is forfeited upon consolidation with non-purchase money debt. However, the court found an exception to this general rule based on the fact that the debtors in *Slay* had made no payments following consolidation. Id.

It would be ironic if the debtors' payments here of $248.38 and $146 on a note that included $2,880 in purchase money debt would cause American's lien to lose its purchase money status completely. Neither the parties' contract nor an applicable statute provides a method for allocating payments between the purchase money and non-purchase money portions of the consolidated debt. However, courts of equity are peculiarly suited to the task of allocating payments, see In re Weinbrenner, 53 B.R. at 580 (citing Luksus v. United Pacific Insurance Co., 452 F.2d 207, 209 (7th Cir. 1971)), and have, in other contexts, supplied an allocation method when the parties failed to do so. See Burk, Preserving Purchase Money Status, at 1160, 1163 n.107 (creditor's burden to prove security interest extends only to production of facts and documents necessary to application of tracing rule). Therefore, in the absence of contractual or legislative direction, the Court will allocate the debtors' payments to determine the amount still owing on the purchase money debt—and, hence, the extent of American's purchase money lien—following consolidation. See In re Conn, 16 B.R. at 458.

Under the "first in, first out" allocation method employed by most courts, payments are deemed applied to the oldest debts first, with the result that purchase money liens are paid off in the order in which the goods are purchased. See *Parsley,* 104 B.R. at 74; *Conn,* 16 B.R. at 458. Once the purchase price of an item has been paid, any security interest remaining in it becomes a nonpurchase money security interest and is avoidable under §522(f)(2). The purchase price includes the cost of the item and any financing charges and sales taxes attributable to that item. *Parsley*; see Burk, Preserving Purchase Money Status, at 1178 (charges that would be considered part of the purchase money obligation of the original sale are accorded similar status after refinancing). In this case, there were no financing charges on the June 20 purchase money loan, as it was interest-free for the one-year term of the loan. The $2,880 amount of the loan presumably included sales taxes on the purchase of the bedroom furniture. Accordingly, the debtors' payments of $248.38 and $146 will be applied to reduce the unpaid purchase price of $2,880, resulting in a continued purchase money lien on the bedroom furniture of $2,485.62. The debtors' motion to avoid lien is granted to the extent of American's remaining nonpurchase money lien on this furniture.

NOTES

1. Why would Congress have enacted §522(f), which permits the debtor to avoid non-possessory, non-purchase money security interests in certain

items? What policy is at work to restrict the use of such collateral in lending? Note that Bilko Siding, Inc., in the last Problem, attempted to do this. Because most used consumer goods have little resale value, why would creditors ever want the debtor to use them as collateral?

2. Both the Federal Trade Commission and the Federal Reserve Board have issued regulations forbidding creditors from taking non-possessory security interests in household goods unless they are purchase money security interests. See F.T.C. Trade Regulation Rule Concerning Credit Practices, 16 C.F.R. part 444.2(4), effective March 1, 1985; F.R.B. Reg. AA, 12 C.F.R. part 227, effective January 1, 1986. These rules should be in your statute book under the heading "FTC Credit Practices Rule."

3. The 1999 revision of Article 9 now provides that in non-consumer goods cases, the "dual status" rule prevails, and creates methods of allocating the payments so as to ascertain what portion of the purchase money debt survives. Read §9-103(e) through (g). But these rules do not obtain where the collateral is consumer goods, leaving cases like the one you have just read as arguably good law. Read §9-103(h) and its Official Comment 8. Why did the drafters not extend the statutory change to consumer goods? Surely the lenders here have typically done no evil and therefore ought not to lose their purchase money status in bankruptcy because of a technical misstep. Nonetheless, one of the major compromises made by the drafters of the 1999 Article 9 revision was to exempt consumer goods transactions from most of the Article 9 rules, leaving the resolution of these issues to other statutes or common law decisions.

PROBLEM 50

Facade Motors decided to buy an expensive Oriental rug for its main office. It selected one from the stock of Treasures of Persia, Inc., which let Facade Motors take the rug back to the office to try it out to see if it wanted to buy the rug. All of the equipment of Facade Motors was covered by a perfected floating lien in favor of Octopus National Bank. As soon as Facade gets possession of the rug (and before it makes up its corporate mind whether it wants to buy it), does the bank's lien attach? See §2-326(1) and (2). Facade Motors did decide to purchase the rug, so it signed a contract to do so with Treasures of Persia, Inc., making a down payment at the time it did so. To finance the rest of the installment payments, Facade Motors borrowed the necessary amount from Nightflyer Savings and Loan, giving it a security interest in the rug. Does Nightflyer's security interest qualify as the purchase money kind? See §9-103(a), its Official Comment 3, and the next case.

General Electric Capital Commercial Automotive Finance, Inc. v. Spartan Motors, Ltd.

New York Supreme Court, 1998
246 App. Div. 2d 41, 675 N.Y.S.2d 626

FRIEDMANN, J.

This appeal arises from a dispute between two automobile finance companies as to which had a superior security interest in two Mercedes-Benz cars—part of the inventory of the defendant Spartan Motors, Ltd. (hereinafter Spartan), a now-defunct car dealership. The issue presented is whether by advancing Spartan the funds to purchase the vehicles after Spartan itself had already paid for and received them, the defendant General Motors Acceptance Corporation (hereinafter GMAC) thereby acquired a purchase money security interest in the merchandise that could defeat a previously-perfected security interest in all of Spartan's inventory held by the plaintiff, General Electric Capital Commercial Automotive Finance, Inc. (hereinafter GECC). We conclude that under the circumstances presented here, GMAC has established that its post-purchase advance entitled it to a purchase money security interest in the disputed collateral such that its lien enjoyed priority over GECC's prior "dragnet" lien.

FACTS

On Sept. 28, 1983, a predecessor of GECC entered into an "Inventory Security Agreement" with Spartan in connection with its "floor plan" financing of the dealership's inventory. By assignment of that agreement, GECC acquired a blanket lien (otherwise known as a "dragnet" lien) on Spartan's inventory to secure a debt in excess of $1,000,000. "Inventory" was defined in the agreement as "[a]ll inventory, of whatever kind or nature, wherever located, now owned or hereafter acquired, and all returns, repossessions, exchanges, substitutions, replacements, attachments, parts, accessories and accessions thereto and thereof, and all other goods used or intended to be used in conjunction therewith, and all proceeds thereof (whether in the form of cash, instruments, chattel paper, general intangibles, accounts or otherwise)." This security agreement was duly filed in the Office of the Dutchess County Clerk and with the New York State Secretary of State.

On July 19, 1991, Spartan signed a new Wholesale Security Agreement with GMAC, in which the latter agreed to finance or "floor-plan" Spartan's inventory. According to its terms, Spartan covenanted, inter alia, as follows:

> In the course of our business, we acquire new and used cars, trucks and chassis ("Vehicles") from manufacturers or distributors. We desire you to finance the acquisition of such vehicles and *to pay the manufacturers or distributors therefor.*

We agree upon demand to pay to GMAC *the amount it advances or is obligated to advance to the manufacturer or distributor* for each vehicle with interest at the rate per annum designated by GMAC from time to time and then in force under the GMAC Wholesale Plan.

We also agree that to secure collectively the payment by us of *the amounts of all advances and obligations to advance made by GMAC to the manufacturer, distributor or other sellers,* and the interest due thereon, GMAC is hereby granted a security interest in the vehicles and the proceeds of sale thereof ("Collateral") as more fully described herein.

The collateral subject to this Wholesale Security Agreement is new vehicles held for sale or lease and used vehicles acquired from manufacturers or distributors and held for sale or lease. . . .

We understand that we may sell and lease the vehicles at retail in the ordinary course of business. We further agree that *as each vehicle is sold, or leased, we will faithfully and promptly remit to you the amount you advanced or have become obligated to advance on our behalf to the manufacturer, distributor or seller* (emphasis supplied).

It is not disputed that GMAC's security agreement was duly filed. In addition, by certified letter dated July 17, 1991, GMAC officially notified GECC of its competing security interest in Spartan's inventory, as follows:

This is to notify you that General Motors Acceptance Corporation holds or expects to acquire purchase money security interests in inventory collateral which will from time to time hereafter be delivered to Spartan Motors Ltd. of Poughkeepsie, New York, and in the proceeds thereof.

Such inventory collateral consists, or will consist, of the types of collateral described in a financing statement, a true copy of which is annexed hereto and made a part hereof.

On May 7, 1992, Spartan paid $121,500 of its own money to European Auto Wholesalers, Ltd. to acquire a 1992 600 SEL Mercedes Benz. Six days later, on May 13, 1992, GMAC reimbursed Spartan and the vehicle was placed on GMAC's floor plan.

On July 7, 1992, Spartan paid $120,000 of its own money to the same seller to acquire a second 1992 600 SEL Mercedes. Two days later, on July 9, 1992, GMAC reimbursed Spartan for that amount and placed the second vehicle on its floor plan. The two vehicles remained unsold in Spartan's showroom.

A few months later, on or about Oct. 2, 1992, GECC commenced this action against Spartan, seeking $1,180,999.98, representing money then due to GECC under its agreement with Spartan. Claims were also made against the principals of Spartan, upon their guarantees, as well as against GMAC and Mercedes-Benz of North America, Inc. (hereinafter MBNA), to determine lien priority in the collateral.

After commencement of the litigation, Spartan filed a bankruptcy petition and ceased doing business. GECC, GMAC, and MBNA took possession of and liquidated their respective collateral pursuant to a prior agreement between the parties. Among the assets appropriated and sold by GMAC were the two Mercedes-Benz automobiles, which were auctioned for $194,500.

Since commencing this action, GECC has apparently settled its claims against all of the defendants except GMAC, which it has accused of converting the two Mercedes-Benz vehicles in violation of GECC's antecedent security interest.

The court granted GECC's motion for summary judgment (and, upon reargument, adhered to its original determination), finding persuasive GECC's argument that a literal reading of GMAC's security agreement with Spartan, in conjunction with the wording of Uniform Commercial Code §9-107(b) [now §9-103(a)(2) — Eds.], required a holding that GMAC had a purchase money secured interest *only* to the extent that it paid funds *directly* to "manufacturers, distributors and sellers" of Spartan's inventory *in advance* of the transfer of the merchandise to the car dealership. The court reasoned that because "[n]owhere in the contracts of adhesion signed by Spartan with GMAC is there an obligation by GMAC to *reimburse* Spartan for funds used to purchase automobiles" (emphasis supplied), GECC's previously-perfected security interest in all of Spartan's inventory should prevail.

We now reverse and, upon searching the record, grant summary judgment to GMAC.

ANALYSIS

A perfected purchase money security interest provides an exception to the general first-in-time, first-in-right rule of conflicting security interests. Thus, a perfected purchase money security interest in inventory has priority over a conflicting prior security interest in the same inventory. . . . However, as the Supreme Court, Dutchess County observed, the purported purchase money security interest must fit within the Uniform Commercial Code definition to qualify for the exception.

Uniform Commercial Code §9-107 [now §9-103 — Eds.] defines a "purchase money security interest" as a security interest:

> (a) taken or retained by the seller of the collateral to secure all or part of its price; or
> (b) taken by a person who by making advances or incurring an obligation gives value to enable the debtor to acquire rights in or the use of collateral if such value is in fact so used.

The issue here is therefore whether GMAC's payment as reimbursement to Spartan after it had acquired the two Mercedes-Benz vehicles on two different occasions qualifies as an "advance" or "obligation" that enabled Spartan to purchase the cars, such that GMAC acquired a purchase money security interest in the vehicles. The arguments against finding a purchase money security interest under these circumstances are basically twofold: Firstly, of the few courts to construe Uniform Commercial Code §9-107(b), many have been reluctant to decide that a purchase money security interest has been created where, as here, title to and possession of the merchandise have passed to the debtor before the loan is advanced. Secondly, the literal wording of the agreement between GMAC and Spartan appears to accord GMAC purchase money secured status only when the finance company paid Spartan's "manufacturer, distributor or other seller" directly. As the supreme court noted, nothing in GMAC's contract with Spartan appears to contemplate any obligation on the part of the financier to "reimburse" the auto dealership for funds that the latter had already expended to purchase merchandise. These two interrelated arguments will be discussed seriatim.

(1)   WHETHER AFTER-ADVANCED FUNDS MAY QUALIFY FOR PURCHASE MONEY
      SECURITY STATUS UNDER UNIFORM COMMERCIAL CODE §9-107(b)

Research indicates that there is no judicial authority in New York construing the application of UCC §9-107(b) vel non, to circumstances such as those presented here. Indeed, there has been little judicial discussion in any jurisdiction of the applicability of UCC §9-107(b) to a creditor's subsequent reimbursement of a debtor for an antecedent purchase of collateral.

Accordingly, it is appropriate to examine the legislative history of UCC §9-107(b), to arrive, if possible, at the intent of the framers.

Professor Grant Gilmore, one of the original drafters of UCC Article 9 (see, MBank Alamo Natl. Assn. v. Raytheon Co., 886 F.2d 1449, 1459), has explained that UCC §9-107(b) was enacted at least in part to liberalize the rather rigid traditional rules, e.g., regarding the circumstances under which purchase money secured status could be obtained by a creditor who enables a debtor to acquire new inventory (see, Gilmore, The Purchase Money Priority, 76 Harv. L. Rev. 1333, at 1373 [1963]).

For example, whereas under pre-Code law a person who advanced the purchase price on a buyer's behalf directly to the seller would be found to have a purchase money interest in the items so acquired, no such security interest was guaranteed to the person advancing money to a buyer who then used the funds to pay for merchandise (see, e.g., Manlove v. Maggart, 111 Ind. App. 398, 41 N.E.2d 633; Hughbanks, Inc. v. Gourley, 12 Wash. 2d 44, 120 P.2d 523). Under UCC §9-107(b), however, if a financier can show both that his advance was made for the purpose of enabling the debtor to acquire the collateral and that it was in fact so used, he will be accorded purchase money secured status (Gilmore, The Purchase Money Priority, supra, at 1373).

Similarly, under pre-Code law the *sequence* of the transfers was dispositive. Indeed, as Professor Gilmore noted, even 9-107(b), on its face, seems
to assume "the sequence of loan first and acquisition second or . . . that
the loan and acquisition take place simultaneously." Where, for example,
"the buyer pays the price (or writes a check) on Monday and borrows that
amount from the secured party on Tuesday," the secured party is faced with
the obvious difficulty of satisfying both the "'to enable'" and the "'in fact so
used'" prongs of the statute (Gilmore, at 1374). However, under the Code,
"in . . . the hypothetical [case] just put a court could reasonably find that
the secured party had acquired a purchase money interest. If the loan transaction appears to be *closely allied* to the purchase transaction, that should
suffice. The evident intent of paragraph (b) is to free the purchase money
concept from artificial limitations; rigid adherence to particular formalities
and sequences should not be required" (Gilmore, at 1374, emphasis supplied; see also, 2 Gilmore, Security Interests in Personal Property, §29.2, at
782; Anderson, Uniform Commercial Code, §9-107:26, at 529; White and
Summers, Uniform Commercial Code, §33-5, at 325-326 [Practitioner's
4th ed.][2]).

If under UCC §9-107(b) neither the chronology of the financing nor the
configuration of the cash flow is, without more, dispositive (see, e.g., Clark,
The Law of Secured Transactions Under the Uniform Commercial Code,
§3.09[2][a]), how can we tell if a loan transaction is sufficiently "closely
allied" to a purchase transaction to qualify for purchase money status?

One factor that courts have considered is simple temporal proxim-
ity—that is, whether the value is given by the creditor "more or less contemporaneously with the debtor's acquisition of the property" (see, e.g.,
Matter of Brooks, 1980 WL 98467 [U.S. Bankr. Ct., D. Me.]). However, it
should be noted that early drafts of UCC §9-107 contained an additional
paragraph (c), which envisioned a purchase money interest to the extent
of value advanced for the purpose of financing new acquisitions within 10
days of the debtor's receiving possession of the new goods, *even though the
value was not in fact used to pay the price.* The paragraph was deleted according to the sponsors, because it extended the purchase money interest too
far (see, Gilmore, The Purchase Money Priority, supra, at 1374, n.97, citing
1956 Recommendations of the Editorial Board for the Uniform Commercial
Code §9-107). It appears, then, that mere closeness in time is but another
mechanical circumstance to be considered—a significant clue, but not one
dispositive of the relationship between the transactions.

The authorities are agreed that the critical inquiry, as in all contract matters, is into the intention of the parties (see, e.g., Township of Stambaugh
v. Ah-Ne-Pee Dimensional Hardwood, 841 F. Supp. 803; New West Fruit

---

2. [Now §33-4, at 331-334 (6th ed. 2010)—Eds.]

Corp. v. Coastal Berry Corp., 1 Cal. App. 4th 92, 1 Cal. Rptr. 2d 664, 668; see also, Anderson, Uniform Commercial Code, supra, at 529). "In determining whether a security interest exists, the intent of the parties controls, and that intent may best be determined by examining the language used and considering the conditions and circumstances confronting the parties when the contract was made" (Baldwin v. Hays Asphalt Constr., 20 Kan. App. 2d 853, 856, 893 P.2d 275). In assessing the relationship of the transactions, the test should be whether the availability of the loan was a factor in negotiating the sale, and/or whether the lender was committed at the time of the sale to advance the amount required to pay for the items purchased (see, Matter of Hooks, 40 B.R. 715 [U.S. Bankr. Ct., M.D. Ga.]; Anderson, Uniform Commercial Code, supra, at 529; Clark, The Law of Secured Transactions Under the Uniform Commercial Code, §3.09[2][a] [rev. ed. 1993]).

Applying these principles to the matter before us: (1) The record establishes that GMAC's reimbursements to Spartan following its two Mercedes-Benz purchases were only six and two days apart, respectively. (2) GECC does not dispute GMAC's contention that a post-purchase reimbursement arrangement was common in the trade, as well as routine in Spartan's course of dealing with GMAC and its other financers, depending upon the circumstances of the purchase. For example, GMAC employee Philip Canterino, who handled GMAC's account with Spartan, has averred without contradiction by GECC that although it was customary for GMAC to pre-pay a car manufacturer before it delivered new vehicles to Spartan's showroom, in a case of the sort at issue here — where the vehicles were difficult to obtain from the manufacturer but were readily available from a distributor — it was not uncommon for GMAC to reimburse Spartan after the cars had been delivered to Spartan's showroom, upon Spartan's presentation of proof of clear title. In the language of Uniform Commercial Code §9-107(b): GMAC was committed to give value to enable the car dealership to acquire rights in the collateral. The value so extended was intended to and in fact did enable Spartan to acquire the two Mercedes-Benzes, as GECC does not seriously suggest that without GMAC's backing Spartan could have afforded to purchase the expensive vehicles. Accordingly, the literal requirements of Uniform Commercial Code §9-107(b) are satisfied, notwithstanding the inverted purchase-loan chronology (see, e.g., Matter of McHenry, 71 B.R. 60 [U.S. Bankr. Ct., N.D. Ohio]; Thet Mah & Assocs. v. First Bank of N. Dakota, 336 N.W.2d 134 [Sup. Ct., N.D.]). Because GMAC's loans were "closely allied" with Spartan's inventory acquisitions, GMAC enjoys a purchase money security interest in the contested merchandise (see, e.g., Matter of Hooks, supra).

Concededly, in making assessments of this sort, courts have considered an important factor to be whether or not title had passed to the borrower before the loan was issued (see, e.g., DeKalb Bank v. Purdy, 205 Ill. App. 3d

62, 562 N.E.2d 1223 [purchase money status clear where title to cattle did not pass until creditor advanced payment]; Matter of Hooks, supra [creditor had purchase money security interest where legal ownership in cows was not transferred to the debtor until loan closed]). This is because, where the borrower already possesses all possible rights in the collateral, the value extended by the creditor looks more like a loan procured to satisfy a pre-existing debt than an advance "enabl[ing] the debtor to acquire rights in . . . the . . . collateral" (UCC 9-107[(b)]). However, it seems ill-advised to create an artificial rule premised upon this circumstance, as there will be cases where a purchase money arrangement will not be established even though title has not passed, and other cases, like the one before us, where the passing of title is irrelevant to the creditor's demonstration that the value he extended was closely allied to the purchase of the collateral. In this regard, it is worthy of note that the *Hooks* court, and to some degree the *DeKalb* court as well, treated the passage of title as merely one element to consider—albeit a significant one—in applying the "closely allied" test to arrive at the parties' intentions (see, e.g., Matter of Hooks, supra, at 340-341; DeKalb Bank v. Purdy, supra, at 1226-1227).

A classic case holding the opposite, North Platte State Bank v. Production Credit Assn. (189 Neb. 44, 200 N.W.2d 1), relied upon by GECC, is distinguishable for many reasons. There, the borrower took a loan from the plaintiff bank approximately one and one-half months after purchasing certain cattle, without informing the bank that the loan was intended for any particular purpose. The *North Platte* court noted that the debtor had merely borrowed money several weeks after acquiring title to and possession of a herd of cattle in order to discharge an antecedent debt. Although the "closely allied" test was not discussed by the *North Platte* court, which focussed instead on the pre-loan passage to the debtor of all rights in the collateral, the case is in fact an illustration of a failure to meet that test's requirement (see also, e.g., First Interstate Bank of Utah, N.A. v. I.R.S., 930 F.2d 1521; Valley Bank v. Estate of Rainsdon, 117 Idaho 1085, 793 P.2d 1257; ITT Commercial Finance Corp. v. Union Bank & Trust Co. of N. Vernon, 528 N.E.2d 1149 [Ind. App.]; Wade Credit Corp. v. Borg-Warner Acceptance Corp., 83 Or. App. 479, 732 P.2d 76; Matter of Manuel, 18 B.R. 403 [U.S. Bankr. Ct., D.S.C.]). In contrast to the matter before us, there was no pre-transaction meeting of the minds between debtor and creditor; the bank was not "obligated" to give value to enable the debtor to acquire rights in the collateral; and the purchase and loan transactions were not close in time, but were nearly two months apart. Put somewhat differently, in North Platte the availability of the loan was not a factor in the debtor's negotiation of the sale; and the plaintiff bank was not committed at the time of the sale to advance the amount required to pay for the items purchased.

In addition, the *North Platte* court's conclusion that the plaintiff had not acquired a purchase money interest in the debtor's collateral was reinforced

by the "even more fundamental" consideration that the plaintiff had
neglected to file its security interest within 10 days of the debtor's receiving
possession of the merchandise, as required by Uniform Commercial Code
§9-312(4) (North Platte State Bank v. Production Credit Assn., 189 Neb. 44,
200 N.W.2d 1, 6; see also, White and Summers, Uniform Commercial Code,
supra, at 326[3]). Here, in contrast, it is not disputed that GMAC timely filed
its purchase money security interest in Spartan's inventory, and that in July
1991 it notified GECC of that interest.

(2) WHETHER GMAC'S LIEN IS CIRCUMSCRIBED BY THE PRECISE LANGUAGE OF
     ITS AGREEMENT WITH SPARTAN

It is well established that the terms of a written security agreement may
be amplified by "other circumstances including course of dealing or usage
of trade or course of performance" (UCC 1-201[(3)]; see also, UCC 1-205,
2-208; New West Fruit Corp. v. Coastal Berry Corp., supra). Here, GECC
does not deny that, although the written terms of GMAC's contract with
Spartan *appeared* to contemplate a single method of inventory-financing
(i.e., GMAC's payment to Spartan's sellers in advance of the purchase transaction), *in fact* it was not at all unusual for the parties to pursue the same
end by somewhat different means (i.e., GMAC's post-transaction reimbursement to Spartan for its inventory purchases), as GMAC employee Canterino
repeatedly explained.

Generally, the express terms of an agreement and a differing course
of performance, course of dealing, and/or usage of trade "shall be construed whenever reasonable as consistent with each other" (UCC 1-205[(4)],
2-208[(2)]). Only when a consistent construction would be "unreasonable"
must express terms control over course of performance, and course of performance prevail over course of dealing and usage of trade. GMAC's election on some occasions to fund Spartan's floor-planning by reimbursing the
car dealership for its purchases can hardly be considered inconsistent with
its decision on other occasions to accomplish the same goal by following the
strict wording of the contract and pre-paying the supplier directly. Rather, it
is only reasonable to consider these two methods of financing to be entirely
compatible with one another.

In any event, it is well established that a written contract may be *modified* by the parties' post-agreement "course of performance" (UCC 2-208[(1)],
[(3)]; see, e.g., Farmers State Bank v. Farmland Foods, 225 Neb. 1, 402 N.W.2d
277; see also, Rose v. Spa Realty Assoc., 42 N.Y.2d 338, 343-344; Maynard Ct.
Owners Corp. v. Rentoulis, 235 A.D.2d 867; Indemnity Ins. Co. of N. Am.
v. Levine, 168 A.D.2d 323, 326; Recon Car Corp. of N.Y. v. Chrysler Corp.,

---

3. [Now at 334-335 (6th ed. 2010) — Eds.]

130 A.D.2d 725, 729). In this regard, GECC offered no rebuttal to the testimony and affidavit of GMAC's employee who had handled the financier's account with Spartan, to the effect that it was the custom in the trade, as well as in GMAC's course of dealing with Spartan and others, for the financier to reimburse the debtor following delivery of the merchandise to the debtor's showroom, and upon presentation by the debtor of proof of clear title.

There is no merit to GECC's suggestion that, because Spartan and GMAC had diverged in practice from the literal language of their contract, GECC lacked notice of the inventory covered by GMAC's security interest. . . .

CONCLUSION

Accordingly, the supreme court erred when it found that, having financed the two vehicles at issue here by way of reimbursements — "the very opposite of an advance" — GMAC did not acquire a purchase money security interest pursuant to Uniform Commercial Code 9-107(b). Rather, since GMAC has established — and GECC does not deny — that GMAC was "obligated" to give value to enable Spartan to acquire rights in the two Mercedes-Benzes, and the purchase and loan transactions were only days apart, it is clear that Spartan's purchase and GMAC's subsequent reimbursement were sufficiently "closely allied" to give GMAC a purchase money security interest in the subject vehicles. Under these circumstances, we conclude, upon searching the record, that GMAC is entitled to retain the proceeds of the sale of the two contested vehicles and to summary judgment against GECC (see, CPLR 3212[(b)]). . . .

B. Certain Accounts and Other Intangibles

Read §9-309(2) and Official Comment 4's first paragraph. The courts have split over whether the major test is "significant part" (a percentage test) or "casual or isolated transaction" (the Official Comment test). See White & Summers §23-7. A creditor is ill advised to rely on §9-309(2) and not file; it is simply too dangerous to take the chance that a court will find that the section applies. Grant Gilmore, one of the drafters of the original Article 9, concluded that the exemption was meant to protect assignees who don't normally take such assignments and are therefore unlikely to file. Under his test the assignee must be "both insignificant and ignorant." G. Gilmore, Security Interests in Personal Property §19.6 (1965). One court adopted his test and permitted the assignee to establish his "insignificance and ignorance" so as to have a perfected interest without filing, E. Turgeon Constr. Co. v. Elhatton Plumbing & Heating Co., 110 R.I. 303, 292 A.2d 230 (1972).

In re Wood

United States District Court, Western District of New York, 1986
67 Bankr. 321

TELESCA, J.

This appeal is from the order of the Bankruptcy Court holding that the security interest and the accounts assigned to the plaintiff, Edwin M. Larkin, by the debtors is unsecured due to the lack of perfection by filing under the Uniform Commercial Code. Specifically, the decision of the court below determined that the transaction in question did not fall within the exemptions from filing contained in UCC §9-302(1)(e).

The facts are relatively simple. Both the plaintiff and the defendant are practicing attorneys. They have had a continuing professional and personal relationship spanning a number of years. On or about March 15, 1977, Mr. Larkin loaned to his friend and attorney, Robert F. Wood, the sum of $10,000. The debtors executed a demand promissory note at that time including provision for the payment of interest. No payment was made on the note by either of the debtors for a period of five years. By letter agreement dated on or about June 3, 1982, the debtors agreed to pay to Mr. Larkin the sum of $1,000 within ten days of May 28, 1982, to be applied towards the payment of accrued interest. Subsequent payments would also be applied first to interest and then to reduction of the principal balance. In the agreement, the debtors also agreed to a limited assignment of the proceeds that might be due the debtors from two litigations in which the debtors were engaged. The litigations provided for contingency fee agreements between Mr. Wood and his clients. The assignment of the contingency proceeds contained restrictions on the assignee's right to disclose the existence of the assignment to any third parties, including the clients, or to participate in the prosecution of the underlying litigations or any settlement negotiations.

On September 9, 1983, the debtors filed voluntary petitions pursuant to Chapter 11 of the Bankruptcy Code. In this proceeding, the debtors seek to avoid the security interest of Larkin and the proceeds subsequently received by the debtors from the settlement of the litigations.

In reaching its decision, the Bankruptcy Court reviewed numerous court decisions relating to the interpretation of U.C.C. §9-302(1)(e) [now §9-309(2) — EDS.]. Relevant language is:

> (1) A financing statement must be filed to perfect all security interests except the following. . . .
>> (e) an assignment of accounts which does not alone or in conjunction with other assignments to the same assignee transfer a significant part of the outstanding accounts of the assignor; . . .

The official Comment 5 to the above section explains the policy as follows:

> The purpose of the subsection (1)(e) exemptions is to save from ex post facto invalidation casual or isolated assignments: some accounts receivable statutes have been so broadly drafted that all assignments, whatever their character or purpose, fall within their filing provisions. Under such statutes, many assignments which no one would think of filing might have been subject to invalidation. The subsection (1)(e) exemptions go to that type of assignment. Any person who regularly takes assignments of any debtor's accounts should file. . . .

After reviewing the cases and learned articles on the subject, the Bankruptcy Court concluded that the appropriate standard to be applied in interpreting UCC §9-302(1)(e) is a combination of both the "percentage test" and "casual and isolated transaction test." Both tests need to be reviewed in conjunction with all of the facts and circumstances involved in the relationship between the parties and the transactions in which they are engaged. See, generally, 85 A.L.R.3d at 1050, 1053-1054, 1062. See also, White and Summers, Uniform Commercial Code §23-8.[4]

No hard and fast rule interpreting UCC §9-302(1)(e) can be established in view of the unlimited variety of facts and circumstances present in private lending transactions. A standard utilizing either or both the percentage test and the casual and isolated transaction test ought to be employed. . . .

This court elects to follow the policy stated in In re B. Hollis Knight Company, 605 F.2d 397, 401 (8th Cir. 1979):

> Both of the policies underlying the two tests appear to be valid limitations on the scope of UCC §9-302(1)(e). The language of the section would not permit an assignee to escape the filing requirements if he received a large portion of an assignor's accounts whether or not the transaction was an isolated one.

Nor is it unfair to require a secured party who regularly takes such assignments to file, since the comments to UCC §9-302(1)(e) indicate that the section was designed as a narrow exception to the filing requirement—not applicable if the transaction was in the general course of commercial financing.

The Bankruptcy Court correctly determined that the burden of meeting each test is on the assignee. Miller v. Wells Fargo Bank Intl. Corp., 406 F. Supp. 452 (S.D.N.Y. 1975). The court then held that Larkin failed to meet his burden in either test.

---

4. [Now §23-78 (6th ed. 2010)—Eds.]

This court will not disturb the Bankruptcy Court's finding that the assignee Larkin failed to meet his burden to demonstrate the size of the assignment made by the debtor in this case in relation to the debtor's other outstanding accounts at the time of the assignment was not significant. However, in reviewing the application of the casual and isolated transaction test, the court below incorrectly held that by reason of the fact that Mr. Larkin was an attorney at law, he should be familiar with the importance of perfecting security interests by filing and that this imputed professional knowledge excluded him as one of the members of the class protected under UCC §9-302(1)(e). This was an erroneous interpretation of the casual and isolated transaction test and is not supported by any reported authority.

The casual and isolated transaction test requires the court to examine the circumstances surrounding the transaction, including the status of the assignee, to determine whether the assignment was, in fact, casual and isolated. Architectural Woods, Inc. v. State of Washington, 88 Wash. 2d 406, 562 P.2d 248 (1977). The underlying rationale behind the test is that it would not be unreasonable to require a secured creditor to file if he regularly takes assignments of a debtor's accounts, but it would be unreasonable if this was not a usual practice. However, the authorities are clear that where the assignee is regularly engaged in commercial financing and routinely accepts assignments of accounts, perfection by way of filing under the UCC is required regardless of the actual amount of the accounts assigned. In re B. Hollis Knight Co., supra.

In reviewing the reported authority, the distinguishing fact in determining whether or not the *status* of the assignee required filing for protection turned on whether or not the assignee was involved in commercial lending or regularly took assignment of accounts. The court, however, cited no authority for the stated proposition that attorneys who accept the security interest in an account are excluded from this exception to the filing requirement, nor has research revealed any. This court is unable to find any authority which characterizes attorneys as a group which are ineligible to engage in casual and isolated assignments of accounts under UCC §9-302(1)(e).

The record in this case clearly establishes that Larkin was not a commercial lender engaged in regularly accepting assignments from debtors. He made one loan to the debtors and subsequently obtained one assignment of the proceeds of two cases as collateral for the repayment of the loan. The record amply supports the conclusion that this was a casual and isolated transaction between two individuals who maintained a personal and professional relationship. That requires a finding that Larkin was not regularly engaged in the business of taking accounts, and therefore, he clearly falls within the exemption from filing under UCC §9-302(1)(e). It was an error for the Bankruptcy Court to hold otherwise. . . .

The Bankruptcy Court's holding that plaintiff's claim was unperfected and unsecured is reversed. Plaintiff had a perfected security interest in the two accounts as of June 4, 1982. This case is remanded to the Bankruptcy Court for proceedings not inconsistent with this opinion, including reconsideration of plaintiff's motion for contempt.

So Ordered.

_____

Now read all of §9-309, extending the same automatic perfection to the transfer of a number of types of intangible or quasi-intangible collateral.

PROBLEM 51

Octopus National Bank sold all the promissory notes it was holding in its vault to Last National Bank. Remember that the *sale* of promissory notes is an Article 9 transaction (with the seller being the "debtor" and the buyer the "secured party"—see §9-109(a)(3)). Must Last National file a financing statement or make sure it has possession in order to perfect its security interest in the notes? See §9-309(4).

The sale of debt is big business; there is a huge market for the transfer of payment obligations of all kinds. Often investors will create a trust to buy up debts from others (mortgages, promissory notes, accounts receivable, etc.), and then sell stock in this trust (the whole process is called *securitization*). Similarly, credit card companies can sell the credit card account receivables to others; banks making big loans can sell off parts thereof to other bankers (called a *loan-participation* agreement); and banks can extend loans to mortgage lenders, taking a security interest in the underlying mortgages (*mortgage warehousing*). The financial world is busy creating all sorts of new financing mechanisms and markets for the transfer of debt.

When debts are sold, they are sometimes transferred "with recourse," and sometimes "without recourse." The difference has to do with which party assumes the risk of non-collection. If the sale is "with recourse," then if the underlying obligors do not make full payment of the debts sold, the original seller must make up the deficiency. If the sale is "without recourse," then the buyer of the debt assumes both the risk that the debts won't be paid and gets any surplus if more is collected than the selling price.

It is important to appreciate this: The automatic perfection rules for the sale of some types of debt—§9-309(3) and (4)—apply only if a true *sale* is taking place. If the seller of the debt keeps any of the indicia of ownership, there is an argument that a "sale" has not taken place. In that case, automatic perfection will not work, and the so-called "buyer" must take the usual steps for perfection (possession, filing a financing statement) in order to prevail over other claimants to the obligations sold. If the transfer was "with recourse," it looks more like merely a loan than an outright sale, so the buyer is arguably not automatically perfected when its interest attaches. In doubtful cases, as always, the smart thing to do is to file a financing statement or take possession of the promissory notes and thus be assured of perfection. See White & Summers §23-7; In re Commercial Money Center, Inc., 350 B.R. 465 (B.A.P. 9th Cir. 2006) ($47 million worth of payment intangibles lost when the court deemed the transaction a loan rather than a sale and the buyer failed to perfect by filing).

PROBLEM 52

When Nightflyer Finance Company (NFC) loaned $20,000 to Portia Moot to enable her to expand her law practice, she gave the finance company a security interest in her accounts receivable (the monies her client owed her), which NFC promptly perfected by filing a financing statement in the appropriate place. One of these accounts has a surety, the mother of the client, who promised Portia that she would pay the debt if the client did not. What must NFC do to perfect its interest in the surety obligation of the mother? See §§9-102(a)(78), 9-102(a)(72), 9-203(f), and 9-308(d). Note that under the cited definitions, the same rule for automatic perfection extends to letters of credit that support the original transaction.

III. PERFECTION BY FILING

The basic supposition of §9-310 is that except for the transactions listed therein, the *filing* of a "financing statement" is the exclusive method of perfection of the creditor's security interest.

A. The Mechanics of Filing

Under the original version of Article 9, the filing rules were quite complicated and often required dual or sometimes even triple filing of financing statements in both local and statewide offices. This made some sense in the pre-computer age, when the state offices were hard to get to and the searches were often done manually by rifling through paper records. The UCC now mandates central filing (typically in the office of the Secretary of State) for almost all financing statements, with local county filing only for matters having to do with realty: minerals to be extracted from the earth, timber, or fixtures; see §9-501.

PROBLEM 53

Hamlet Corporation borrowed $100,000 from the Elsinore Finance Company and gave it a security interest in the corporation's equipment. The parties properly filled out a financing statement; W. Shakespeare was mentioned on the financing statement as the president of Hamlet Corporation. Elsinore gave the financing statement and the filing fee to a clerk at the Secretary of State's office. The clerk, Ophelia Nunnery, had just announced her intention to quit to her fellow office workers and was not paying attention to her job as she indexed the financing statement under "Shakespeare" instead of "Hamlet." One year later, another finance company loaned Hamlet Corporation more money, taking a security interest in the same equipment (the second finance company had checked the records and discovered nothing under "Hamlet Corp."). Since priority of creditors in this situation depends on order of filing (§9-322(a)(1)), did Elsinore "file" first, or did it bear the risk of clerical error? See §§9-516(a), 9-517 (and its Official Comment 2); In re Masters, 273 B.R. 773 (Bankr. E.D. Ark. 2002); In re Butler's Tire & Battery Co., 1975 WL 22897 (Bankr. D. Or. 1975), *aff'd on opinion below,* 1976 WL 23725 (D. Or. 1976) (creditor not protected where creditor's error caused filing official's mistake). Whichever creditor loses should sue the state for negligence. Some states have set aside a fund from the filing fees with which to pay judgments against the filing officer.

Where perfection depends not on filing a financing statement, but rather on having the security interest noted on the certificate of title, the rule may demand more of the creditor. See In re Hicks, 491 F.3d 1136(10th Cir. 2007) (creditor not perfected, where it properly filed Notice of Security Interest with certificate of title agency, but agency issued certificate of title that did not have notation of security interest).

NOTE

An attorney who files a financing statement should retain proof of what was filed, where it was filed, and when it was filed, in case people or computers in the UCC office misdirect or lose the financing statement. For online filings, the UCC office will typically return an electronic confirmation and a downloadable copy of the filing. The careful attorney will print out copies for the file, because those digital files may go astray over the years. All states now accept online filings. Paper filings are sometimes more convenient, such as when the creditor attaches documents. An increasing number of states now accept only online filings, although many accept attached files. For paper filings, always pay whatever extra amount is necessary to have duplicate copies of the financing statement made, stamped, and returned to you (or get an acknowledgment of the filed written record). See §9-523 for the procedure.

B.   Other Filings

A financing statement is effective for five years and then it lapses unless a continuation statement is filed (*public finance transactions*—defined in §9-102(a)(67), and *manufactured home transactions*—defined in §9-102(a)(53), are effective for 30 years). Read §9-515. The filing office is commanded by statute to keep records of lapsed financing statements for an additional one-year period; see §9-522. If the secured party *assigns* the security interest to another creditor, the two creditors may (it is not compulsory) file an assignment statement; read §9-514. If the debtor and secured party want to free some of the collateral from coverage under a filed financing statement, see the procedure provided for in §9-512.

PROBLEM 54

Octopus National Bank (ONB) had a security interest in the equipment of the Weekend Construction Company for which it filed a financing statement in the proper place on May 1, 2020. Antitrust National Bank (ANB) took a security interest in the same collateral and filed its financing statement on May 2, 2020, in the same place.

(a) How long is a financing statement effective? See §9-515(a).

(b) If ONB files a continuation statement on May 1, 2024, is its perfected position continued? See §§9-515(d), 9-510(c). Pre-revision decisions called this the problem of "premature renewal."

(c) If ONB never files a continuation statement at all, after May 1, 2025, does it nonetheless retain its priority over ANB (who, after all, always thought of itself as junior to ONB's prior filing and would get a windfall if it suddenly prevails)? See §9-515(c).

(d) If ONB fails to file a continuation statement in time, so that its perfection lapses, but a week later files another financing statement, is it still senior to ANB? See Signature Credit Partners, LLC v. Casaic Offset & Silkscreen, Inc., 2012 WL 1999494 (W.D. La. 2012) (no).

(e) Is an attorney who fails to file a continuation statement guilty of malpractice? See Barnes v. Turner, 278 Ga. 788, 606 S.E.2d 849 (Ga. 2004).

PROBLEM 55

When Portia Moot paid off her debt to Last National Bank, which had loaned her $3,000 to buy a computer for her law office (and had taken a purchase money security interest therein, for which it had duly filed a financing statement), she wanted the bank to clear up the records down at the filing office. Does she have this right? See §9-513. What can she do if they stiff-arm her? See §§9-509(d)(2), 9-625(b) and (e)(4).

One happy idea codified in the 1999 revision of Article 9 is called the *open drawer* concept of file searches. What this means is that later searchers are given absolutely everything related to the original financing statement (amendments, assignments, deletions, continuation statements, termination statements, etc.) when they do a search, so that they have complete information as to the current status of the filed transaction. Note that the definition of *financing statement* includes an original filing and *all related amendments*; §9-102(a)(39). Section 9-519(c) requires the filing office to index the filing under the debtor's name and the file number and associate all related filings to the original filing. Thus, when a later searcher requests the financing statement per §9-523(c), the entire file will be forthcoming. Section 9-522(a) requires the filing office to maintain all filings until at least one year after the filing has lapsed with respect to all secured parties of record; §9-519(g) prohibits the removal of a debtor's name from the index until one year after complete lapse. When you put all this together, you have the "open drawer" system where a "drawer" is created for each new financing statement into which all related filings are deposited. Everything stays in the searchable drawer until a year after lapse. That is not to say that everything in the drawer is legally effective. A valid termination might have been filed by all secured parties of record. But note that the effectiveness of the termination (or any other filing, for that matter) cannot be ascertained from the public record, as it needs to have been properly authorized to be effective. For a complete discussion of this and other issues related to the filing system, see Darrell W. Pierce, Revised Article 9 of the Uniform Commercial Code: Filing System Improvements and Their Rationale, 31 UCC L.J. 16 (1998).

The case that follows should cause you to tremble. The misstep involved caused the law firm's client to lose $1.5 billion!

In re Motors Liquidation Company

United States Court of Appeals, Second Circuit, 2015
777 F.3d 100

Per Curiam:

We assume familiarity with our prior certification opinion, *Official Committee of Unsecured Creditors of Motors Liquidation Co. v. JP Morgan Chase Bank, N.A.* (*In re Motors Liquidation Co.*), 755 F.3d 78 (2d Cir. 2014), and the resulting decision of the Delaware Supreme Court, *Official Committee of Unsecured Creditors of Motors Liquidation Co. v. JPMorgan Chase Bank, N.A.*, 103 A.3d 1010 (Del. Supr. 2014). We restate the most salient facts.

Background

In October 2001, General Motors entered into a synthetic lease financing transaction (the "Synthetic Lease"), by which it obtained approximately $300 million in financing from a syndicate of lenders including JPMorgan Chase Bank, N.A. ("JPMorgan"). General Motors' obligation to repay the Synthetic Lease was secured by liens on twelve pieces of real estate. JPMorgan served as administrative agent for the Synthetic Lease and was identified on the UCC-1 financing statements as the secured party of record.

Five years later, General Motors entered into a separate term loan facility (the "Term Loan"). The Term Loan was entirely unrelated to the Synthetic Lease and provided General Motors with approximately $1.5 billion in financing from a different syndicate of lenders. To secure the loan, the lenders took security interests in a large number of General Motors' assets, including all of General Motors' equipment and fixtures at forty-two facilities throughout the United States. JPMorgan again served as administrative agent and secured party of record for the Term Loan and caused the filing of twenty-eight UCC-1 financing statements around the country to perfect the lenders' security interests in the collateral. One such financing statement, the "Main Term Loan UCC-1," was filed with the Delaware Secretary of State and bore file number "6416808 4." It "covered, among other things, all of the equipment and fixtures at 42 GM facilities, [and] was by far the most important" of the financing statements filed in connection with the Term Loan. *Official Comm. of Unsecured Creditors of Motors Liquidation Co. v. JPMorgan Chase Bank, N.A.* (*In re Motors Liquidation Co.*), 486 B.R. 596, 603 n.6 (Bankr. S.D.N.Y. 2013).

In September 2008, as the Synthetic Lease was nearing maturity, General Motors contacted Mayer Brown LLP, its counsel responsible for the Synthetic Lease, and explained that it planned to repay the amount due. General Motors requested that Mayer Brown prepare the documents necessary for JPMorgan and the lenders to be repaid and to release the interests the lenders held in General Motors' property.

A Mayer Brown partner assigned the work to an associate and instructed him to prepare a closing checklist and drafts of the documents required to pay off the Synthetic Lease and to terminate the lenders' security interests in General Motors' property relating to the Synthetic Lease. One of the steps required to unwind the Synthetic Lease was to create a list of security interests held by General Motors' lenders that would need to be terminated. To prepare the list, the Mayer Brown associate asked a paralegal who was unfamiliar with the transaction or the purpose of the request to perform a search for UCC-1 financing statements that had been recorded against General Motors in Delaware. The paralegal's search identified three UCC-1s, numbered 2092532 5, 2092526 7, and 6416808 4. Neither the paralegal nor the associate realized that only the first two of the UCC-1s were related to the Synthetic Lease. The third, UCC-1 number 6416808 4, related instead to the Term Loan.

When Mayer Brown prepared a Closing Checklist of the actions required to unwind the Synthetic Lease, it identified the Main Term Loan UCC-1 for termination alongside the security interests that actually did need to be terminated. And when Mayer Brown prepared draft UCC-3 statements to terminate the three security interests identified in the Closing Checklist, it prepared a UCC-3 statement to terminate the Main Term Loan UCC-1 as well as those related to the Synthetic Lease.

No one at General Motors, Mayer Brown, JPMorgan, or its counsel, Simpson Thacher & Bartlett LLP, noticed the error, even though copies of the Closing Checklist and draft UCC-3 termination statements were sent to individuals at each organization for review. On October 30, 2008, General Motors repaid the amount due on the Synthetic Lease. All three UCC-3s were filed with the Delaware Secretary of State, including the UCC-3 that erroneously identified for termination the Main Term Loan UCC-1, which was entirely unrelated to the Synthetic Lease.

A. General Motors' Chapter 11 Bankruptcy Filing

The mistake went unnoticed until General Motors' bankruptcy in 2009. After General Motors filed for chapter 11 reorganization, JPMorgan informed the Committee of Unsecured Creditors (the "Committee") that a UCC-3 termination statement relating to the Term Loan had been inadvertently filed in October 2008. JPMorgan explained that it had intended to terminate only liens related to the Synthetic Lease and stated that the filing was therefore unauthorized and ineffective.

On July 31, 2009, the Committee commenced the underlying action against JPMorgan in the United States Bankruptcy Court for the Southern District of New York. The Committee sought a determination that, despite the error, the UCC-3 termination statement was effective to terminate the Term

Loan security interest and render JPMorgan an unsecured creditor on par with the other General Motors unsecured creditors. JPMorgan disagreed, reasoning that the UCC-3 termination statement was unauthorized and therefore ineffective because no one at JPMorgan, General Motors, or their law firms had intended that the Term Loan security interest be terminated. On cross-motions for summary judgment, the Bankruptcy Court concluded that the UCC-3 filing was unauthorized and therefore not effective to terminate the Term Loan security interest. *In re Motors Liquidation Co.,* 486 B.R. at 647-48.

B. Prior Certification Opinion

On appeal to this Court, the parties offered competing interpretations of UCC §9-509(d)(1), which provides that a UCC-3 termination statement is effective only if "the secured party of record authorizes the filing." JPMorgan reasoned that it cannot have "authorize[d] the filing" of the UCC-3 that identified the Main Term Loan UCC-1 for termination because JPMorgan neither intended to terminate the security interest nor instructed anyone else to do so on its behalf. In response, the Committee contended that focusing on the parties' goal misses the point. It interpreted UCC §9-509(d)(1) to require only that the secured lender authorize the act of filing a particular UCC-3 termination statement, not that the lender subjectively intend to terminate the particular security interest identified for termination on that UCC-3. The Committee further argued that even if JPMorgan never intentionally instructed anyone to terminate the Main Term Loan UCC-1, JPMorgan did literally "authorize[ ] the filing"—even if mistakenly—of a UCC-3 termination statement that had that effect.

In our prior certification opinion we recognized that this appeal presents two closely related questions. First, what precisely must a secured lender of record authorize for a UCC-3 termination statement to be effective: "Must the secured lender authorize the termination of the particular security interest that the UCC-3 identifies for termination, or is it enough that the secured lender authorize the act of filing a UCC-3 statement that has that effect?" *In re Motors Liquidation Co.,* 755 F.3d at 84. Second, "[d]id JPMorgan grant to Mayer Brown the relevant authority—that is, alternatively, authority either to terminate the Main Term Loan UCC-1 or to file the UCC-3 statement that identified that interest for termination?" *Id.*

Recognizing that the first question—what is it that the UCC requires a secured lender to authorize—seemed likely to recur and presented a significant issue of Delaware state law, we certified to the Delaware Supreme Court the following question:

> Under UCC Article 9, as adopted into Delaware law by Del. Code Ann. tit. 6, art. 9, for a UCC-3 termination statement to effectively extinguish the perfected nature of a UCC-1 financing statement, is it enough that the secured

lender review and knowingly approve for filing a UCC-3 purporting to extinguish the perfected security interest, or must the secured lender intend to terminate the particular security interest that is listed on the UCC-3?

Id. at 86. The second question—whether JPMorgan granted the relevant authority—we reserved for ourselves, explaining that "[t]he Delaware Supreme Court's clarification as to the sense in which a secured party of record must authorize a UCC-3 filing will enable us to address . . . whether JPMorgan in fact provided that authorization." *Id.* at 86-87.

C. The Delaware Supreme Court's Answer

In a speedy and thorough reply, the Delaware Supreme Court answered the certified question, explaining that if the secured party of record authorizes the filing of a UCC-3 termination statement, then that filing is effective regardless of whether the secured party subjectively intends or understands the effect of that filing:

> [F]or a termination statement to become effective under §9-509 and thus to have the effect specified in §9-513 of the Delaware UCC, it is enough that the secured party authorizes the filing to be made, which is all that §9-510 requires. The Delaware UCC contains no requirement that a secured party that authorizes a filing subjectively intends or otherwise understands the effect of the plain terms of its own filing.

Official Comm. of Unsecured Creditors of Motors Liquidation Co., 103 A.3d at 1017-18. That conclusion, explained the court, follows both from the unambiguous terms of the UCC and from sound policy considerations:

> JPMorgan's argument that a filing is only effective if the authorizing party understands the filing's substantive terms and intends their effect is contrary to §9-509, which only requires that "the secured party of record authorize [ ] the filing." . . .
>
> Even if the statute were ambiguous, we would be reluctant to embrace JPMorgan's proposition. Before a secured party authorizes the filing of a termination statement, it ought to review the statement carefully and understand which security interests it is releasing and why. . . . If parties could be relieved from the legal consequences of their mistaken filings, they would have little incentive to ensure the accuracy of the information contained in their UCC filings.

Id. at 1014-16 (first alteration in original) (footnote omitted).

DISCUSSION

The Delaware Supreme Court has explained the sense in which a secured party must "authorize[ ] the filing" of a UCC-3 termination statement. What remains is to answer the question we reserved for ourselves in our prior certification opinion: Did JPMorgan authorize the filing of the UCC-3 termination statement that mistakenly identified for termination the Main Term Loan UCC-1?

In JPMorgan's view, it never instructed anyone to file the UCC-3 in question, and the termination statement was therefore unauthorized and ineffective. JPMorgan reasons that it authorized General Motors only to terminate security interests related to the Synthetic Lease; that it instructed Simpson Thacher and Mayer Brown only to take actions to accomplish that objective; and that therefore Mayer Brown must have exceeded the scope of its authority when it filed the UCC-3 purporting to terminate the Main Term Loan UCC-1.

JPMorgan's and General Motors' aims throughout the Synthetic Lease transaction were clear: General Motors would repay the Synthetic Lease, and JPMorgan would terminate its related UCC-1 security interests in General Motors' properties. The Synthetic Lease Termination Agreement provided that, upon General Motors' repayment of the amount due under the Synthetic Lease, General Motors would be authorized "to file a termination of any existing Financing Statement relating to the Properties [of the Synthetic Lease]." J.A. 2151. And, to represent its interests in the transaction, JPMorgan relied on Simpson Thacher, its counsel for matters related to the Synthetic Lease. No one at JPMorgan, Simpson Thacher, General Motors, or Mayer Brown took action intending to affect the Term Loan.

What JPMorgan intended to accomplish, however, is a distinct question from what actions it authorized to be taken on its behalf. Mayer Brown prepared a Closing Checklist, draft UCC-3 termination statements, and an Escrow Agreement, all aimed at unwinding the Synthetic Lease but tainted by one crucial error: The documents included a UCC-3 termination statement that erroneously identified for termination a security interest related not to the Synthetic Lease but to the Term Loan. The critical question in this case is whether JPMorgan "authorize[d] [Mayer Brown] to file" that termination statement.

After Mayer Brown prepared the Closing Checklist and draft UCC-3 termination statements, copies were sent for review to a Managing Director at JPMorgan who supervised the Synthetic Lease payoff and who had signed the Term Loan documents on JPMorgan's behalf. Mayer Brown also sent copies of the Closing Checklist and draft UCC-3 termination statements to JPMorgan's counsel, Simpson Thacher, to ensure that the parties to the transaction agreed as to the documents required to complete the Synthetic Lease payoff transaction. Neither directly nor through its counsel did JPMorgan express any concerns about the draft UCC-3 termination statements or about the Closing Checklist. A Simpson Thacher attorney responded simply as follows: "Nice job on the documents. My only comment, unless I am missing something, is that all references to JPMorgan Chase Bank, as

Administrative Agent for the Investors should not include the reference 'for the Investors.' "J.A. 921.

After preparing the closing documents and circulating them for review, Mayer Brown drafted an Escrow Agreement that instructed the parties' escrow agent how to proceed with the closing. Among other things, the Escrow Agreement specified that the parties would deliver to the escrow agent the set of three UCC-3 termination statements (individually identified by UCC-1 financing statement file number) that would be filed to terminate the security interests that General Motors' Synthetic Lease lenders held in its properties. The Escrow Agreement provided that once General Motors repaid the amount due on the Synthetic Lease, the escrow agent would forward copies of the UCC-3 termination statements to General Motors' counsel for filing. When Mayer Brown e-mailed a draft of the Escrow Agreement to JPMorgan's counsel for review, the same Simpson Thacher attorney responded that "it was fine" and signed the agreement.

From these facts it is clear that although JPMorgan never intended to terminate the Main Term Loan UCC-1, it authorized the filing of a UCC-3 termination statement that had that effect. "Actual authority . . . is created by a principal's manifestation to an agent that, as reasonably understood by the agent, expresses the principal's assent that the agent take action on the principal's behalf." Restatement (Third) of Agency §3.01 (2006); *accord Demarco v. Edens,* 390 F.2d 836, 844 (2d Cir. 1968). JPMorgan and Simpson Thacher's repeated manifestations to Mayer Brown show that JPMorgan and its counsel knew that, upon the closing of the Synthetic Lease transaction, Mayer Brown was going to file the termination statement that identified the Main Term Loan UCC-1 for termination and that JPMorgan reviewed and assented to the filing of that statement. Nothing more is needed.

CONCLUSION

For the foregoing reasons, we REVERSE the Bankruptcy Court's grant of summary judgment for the Defendant and REMAND with instructions to the Bankruptcy Court to enter partial summary judgment for the Plaintiff as to the termination of the Main Term Loan UCC-1.

This decision caused a sensation not so much for its legal result, which seems clearly right, but for the astounding amount of money that was lost over a clerical error. Would the law firm have to reimburse its client, in your judgment, for the money lost? What if it doesn't have that much money? How can your law firm—future attorney—avoid this sort of misstep? How much malpractice insurance should you buy when you start your practice?

PROBLEM 56

When attorney Sam Ambulance handled a divorce for a client, he incurred the wrath of her ex-husband, Andrew Anarchist, president of the Freeman Common Law Movement, a group that did not recognize the authority of the state or federal government. The irate ex-spouse filed 42 phony financing statements in the public records to show that all of Sam's assets were security for various nonexistent loans in favor of Anarchist, the secured party of record. What can Sam do to clear up these clouds on his title to his property (which the common law would have regarded as defamation)? See §§9-513, its Official Comment 3, 9-518, its Official Comment 2, and 9-625(b) and (e)(3) and (4); United States v. Orrego, 2004 WL 1447954 (E.D.N.Y. 2004).

Prison inmates frequently file fraudulent UCC-1 financing statements against prosecutors and prison officials. Some penitentiaries have declared UCC materials contraband, and confiscated them after lockdowns and searches. See Monroe v. Beard, 536 F.3d 198 (3d Cir. 2008) (addressing First Amendment issues of inmates' access to legal materials).

Recent years have seen an increase in bogus UCC-1 filings for such purposes as harassment and fraud. See National Association of Secretaries of State, State Strategies to Subvert Fraudulent Uniform Commercial Code (UCC) Filings (updated April 2013). In response, some states have enacted procedures to allow filing offices to refuse or remove unauthorized filings. Some states permit expedited court procedures to expunge such filings. Making a bogus filing is now a crime in many states. See People v. Cratty, 2013 WL 967803 (Mich. Ct. App. 2013) (upholding conviction for making fraudulent filings against judges, lawyers, and court officers involved in home foreclosure case).

IV. PERFECTION BY CONTROL

In addition to the possibility of filing a financing statement, for certain types of collateral the secured party may achieve perfection of the security interest by gaining control over the collateral. Section 9-314(a) provides that a "security interest in investment property, deposit accounts, letter-of-credit rights, or electronic chattel paper may be perfected by control of the collateral under Section 9-104, 9-105, 9-106, or 9-107." *Control* generally means that the secured party has taken the steps described in these sections, so it is obvious to anyone investigating the state of the collateral that the secured party has rights therein. We will investigate perfection by control when we take up the issue of priority in Chapter 7.

CHAPTER 5   ASSESSMENT: MULTIPLE CHOICE QUESTIONS

1. Ataturk Gallery offered to put up an Old Master painting, *Portrait of a Merchant*, as collateral to get a loan from Beaux Finance. Ataturk Gallery, however, was reluctant to allow Beaux Finance to file a UCC financing statement to perfect the security interest, regarding such a filing as déclassé. The parties agreed that Beaux Finance would perfect its security interest by possession of the painting, but Ataturk Gallery also wished to continue displaying the painting in its gallery. So the parties decided that the security agreement would provide that Ataturk Gallery was in possession of the painting as the agent for Beaux Finance. Would that be effective to perfect the security interest?
   a. No. A creditor cannot perfect by possession if the creditor simply leaves the debtor in possession of the collateral.
   b. Yes. Beaux Finance would be in possession, through its agent, Ataturk Gallery.
   c. No filing is necessary to perfect, because a painting is consumer goods.
   d. No filing is necessary to perfect, because the transaction is a purchase money security interest.

2. Miyazaki borrowed money from Beaux Finance to purchase a painting, *The Howl*, for his home, signing an agreement making the painting itself collateral for the debt. Beaux Finance did not bother filing a financing statement. Does Beaux Finance have a perfected security interest?
   a. No, because it did not file a financing statement.
   b. Yes, because it has constructive possession through the debtor, Miyazaki.
   c. Yes, because the security interest in this transaction will perfect without filing or possession by the creditor.
   d. No, because an expensive painting is not consumer goods.
   e. No. Beaux Finance was not the seller, so the transaction is not a purchase money transaction.

3. Beaux Finance had a painting as collateral in yet another transaction. Khan Biologics purchased *Triple Helix* from Ataturk Gallery, borrowing the funds from Beaux Finance and signing a security agreement. Once again, Beaux Finance did not file a UCC-1 financing statement. Is the security interest perfected?
   a. Yes, because it is a purchase money security interest.
   b. No, because the painting is not consumer goods.

    c. No, because Ataturk Gallery did not sign the security agreement.

    d. No, because paintings are certificate of title goods.

4. After a year or so, Beaux Finance realizes its error with respect to the Khan Biologics loan. Fortunately, during that time, nothing has happened that would give someone else priority over Beaux Finances' security interest. As later chapters discuss, Beaux Finance could have lost its unperfected security interest if Khan Biologics filed bankruptcy, or sold the painting, or was subject to a judgment lien. Breathing a sigh of relief, Beaux Finance filed a financing statement on September 1, 2017. To retain its perfected status, when should it file a continuation statement?

    a. A continuation statement is not necessary here. A continuation statement is only necessary where the debtor continues to acquire new collateral, such as with a security interest in all the debtor's inventory or accounts.

    b. Immediately, to ensure no lapse occurs.

    c. After five years from the date of the loan.

    d. Within the last six months of five years from the date of filing the financing statement.

5. Suppose that Beaux Finance fails to file a continuation statement. What practical effect would it have, when the financing statement expires?

    a. The debt would be cancelled and Beaux Finance would be left with nothing.

    b. The debt would become an unsecured debt, meaning Khan Biologics would still owe the money but Beaux Finance would no longer have the painting as collateral.

    c. Beaux Finance would still have a security interest in the painting, but it would be unperfected.

    d. No effect whatsoever.

ANSWERS

1. *A* is the best answer. A creditor can perfect a security interest without filing a financing statement, if the creditor is in possession of the collateral. Possession is a flexible concept. The first case many students encounter in law school is *Pierson v. Post*, on whether possession of a fox was secured by giving chase to it or by actually killing it. Article 9 does not define "possession," and some courts have recognized constructive possession through an agent. But courts would not consider the creditor to be in possession here, because such a rule would make filing unnecessary. Creditors could simply always agree that the debtor is in possession on their behalf. Creditors would not need to file, and other creditors would

not receive the notice that filing provides, one of the key aspects of the Article 9 system.

The other answers review an important rule. A creditor perfects without filing, with a purchase money security interest in consumer goods. But that rule does not apply here, because the transaction is not a purchase money security interest (Ataturk Gallery already owns the painting and is not borrowing to acquire it) and is not consumer goods (Ataturk Gallery has the painting for business purposes, not as consumer goods). C and D are therefore incorrect.

2. *C* is the best answer. A creditor generally needs to file or possess to perfect the security interest, but there are a good number of exceptions. This question illustrates one of the most common: a security interest will perfect without filing for a purchase money security interest in consumer goods. A purchase money creditor may be either a vendor (who sells the collateral) or a lender (who funds the purchase), contrary to E. Consumer goods are any goods acquired for personal, family or household purposes, even luxury goods, contrary to D.

3. *B* is the best answer. This variation emphasizes a key distinction. A security interest perfects automatically in a purchase money security interest *in consumer goods*. The collateral here is not consumer goods, rather a painting acquired by a business, which would be inventory (probably not in this case) or equipment. Students (and sometimes lawyers) often learn the rule for purchase money security interests in consumer goods and apply it too broadly, to every purchase money security interest that they spot. C and D are quite off base. Only the debtor need sign the security interest, and Ataturk Gallery is not even a party to the loan transaction. No filing is necessary, or even effective, for goods like cars that require a notation on the certificate of title for perfection. But no state has paintings as certificate of title goods, contrary to D.

4. *D* is the best answer. A financing statement will expire after five years after filing, unless a timely continuation statement is filed. That rule applies whether there is after-acquired collateral or not, contrary to A. But the drafters wanted to prevent creditors from filing continuation statements right after financing statements were filed, which would lead to zombie financing statements that were effective long after the loan had been paid. A continuation statement is effective only if filed within "six months before the expiration of the five-year period," §9-515(c), contrary to B. Beaux Finance must remind itself to file anywhere between 4 ½ to 5 years after the date of filing (not the date of the loan, the second inaccuracy in C).

5. *C* is the best answer, reminding us of the difference between a perfected and unperfected security interest. The financing statement serves to perfect the security interest. If it becomes unperfected, that does not negate

the security interest, rather makes it unperfected. Beaux Finance could still enforce the security interest (take possession of the painting and sell it) if Khan Biologics defaulted on the debt. But if a third party claimed an interest in the painting (a bankruptcy trustee, buyer of the painting, or rival creditor), Beaux Finance would likely lose that priority contest, as later chapters will discuss. Beaux Finance, if it allowed the financing statement to expire, should file a new one and become perfected again.

CHAPTER 6
MULTISTATE TRANSACTIONS

A secured transactions lawyer's life would be easier if all Article 9 matters took place in one state, but that world doesn't exist. Instead the debtor and the creditor may live in different jurisdictions while the collateral is in a third. Which state's law controls and what happens if things change: after the deal is done the debtor moves to another state or the collateral is transferred there? In this chapter these issues and more are our area of study.

I. GENERAL CHOICE OF LAW RULES

Section 1-301 includes the Code's general choice of law provision. It permits *party autonomy,* so that those involved in the transaction may agree to be bound by the law of any state or nation bearing a "reasonable relation" to the transaction.[1] Article 9 has its own overriding conflicts provisions,

---

1. The 2001 revision of Article 1 changed this standard (which was in the original §1-105), to allow the parties to choose the law of *any* jurisdiction, even one with no obvious relationship to the transaction. After every adopting state rejected the change and retained the original language of old §1-105, the drafters returned to the original standard in the present version of §1-301.

chiefly §9-301, and when Article 9 dominates the problem, this section is controlling. The original Article 9 rules had very complicated choice of law provisions. The law of the state where the collateral was located generally governed. But a debtor may have collateral in many states. Some collateral moves from state to state. Intangible collateral does not have a location. So there had to be special rules for all those cases.

Things are much simplified in the 1999 revision, which primarily adopts a *domicile* approach and looks to the law of the *debtor's location* as the state in which the steps for perfection need to be taken. See §9-301(1). However, if the collateral has physical form, the law of the jurisdiction in which the collateral is located will govern issues involving priority and other Article 9 matters; §9-301(1) and (3). So, the secured party looks to the jurisdiction in which the debtor is located as the *place* of perfection but the jurisdiction of the collateral's physical location to resolve *questions* of perfection or priority as to that collateral.

All 50 states (as well as the District of Columbia, the Commonwealth of Puerto Rico, Guam, and the U.S. Virgin Islands, along with an increasing number of Native American tribes) have adopted the Uniform Commercial Code. The rules are often the same in all relevant jurisdictions, so courts need not decide which jurisdiction's law governs. But choice of law becomes an issue where jurisdictions have non-uniform variations. In addition, every jurisdiction has a different rule for where the financing statement should be filed.

PROBLEM 57

Mary Bush lived in a home she owned in Cheyenne, Wyoming but she also wanted to buy a large sailboat in Cleveland, Ohio and planned to keep the boat there after the purchase for use in her charter fishing business. Ohio law provides that whenever a buyer has paid more than 75 percent of a debt secured by a boat, the creditor's security interest automatically is stripped from the boat. Wyoming has no such rule. If a creditor loans Mary money to buy the sailboat and takes a security interest in it, where should the creditor file the financing statement? When Mary has paid 75 percent of the debt, will the creditor's security interest still be attached to the boat?

Sections 9-301 through 9-306 have some special choice of law rules for certain kinds of collateral: minerals to be extracted from the ground (§9-301(4)), agricultural liens (§9-302), goods covered by a certificate of title (§9-303, considered in detail below), deposit accounts (§9-304), investment property (§9-305), and letter of credit rights (§9-306). The provisions of these sections generally choose the law where these types of collateral are located to resolve the relevant issues.

PROBLEM 58

Peripatetic Corporation was organized under the laws of the State of Delaware but has its large retail store outlet in New Jersey. Further, the corporation was really a husband-and-wife type of business, and they did all the corporate paperwork at their home in Baltimore, Maryland (where they also kept the corporate records). Their corporate stationery used their home address. When the corporation borrows money against its accounts receivable, in which state should the financing statement be filed? See §9-307(b) and (e). If the corporation was registered and had its only place of business in the Republic of Jahala, a Pacific island nation, where should the financing statement be filed? See §9-307(c).

Section 9-307(a) gives some guidance as to where a debtor's place of business is located, and the courts have developed a number of tests for this issue (still applicable where the debtor is not a registered organization). In re Mimshell Fabrics, Ltd., 491 F.2d 21 (2d Cir. 1974) (principal place is "frequent and notorious" to "probable potential creditors"); In re Carmichael Enters., 334 F. Supp. 94 (N.D. Ga. 1971) (the "factual" principal place of business). See also this oft-quoted passage from In re McQuaide, 5 U.C.C. Rep. Serv. 802, 806-807 (Ref. Bankr., D. Vt. 1968):

> "Place of business" is defined in 48 C.J. 1213 §3 as an agency, an office; a place actually occupied, either continually or at regular periods, by a person or his clerks, or those in his employment; a place devoted by the proprietor to the carrying on of some form of trade or commerce; a place where people generally congregate for the purpose of carrying on some sort of traffic, or where people are invited or expected to come to engage in some sort of mercantile transaction; a place where a calling for the purpose of gain or profit is conducted; a place where business is carried on by persons under their control and on their own account; some particular locality, appropriated exclusively to a local business, such as a farm, store, shop, or dwelling place; that specific place within a city or town at which a person transacts business. *An occasional use or occupation of a place for business purposes is not sufficient to constitute it as a place of business.* (Emphasis in original.)

Under §9-307(c), if the debtor is located abroad, the creditor files in that jurisdiction only if it has the equivalent of Article 9, a system for filing non-possessory security interests in public records. Otherwise the creditor files in the District of Columbia. Most jurisdictions do not have a filing system equivalent to Article 9. See Dayka & Hackett, LLC v. Del Monte Fresh Produce N.A., Inc., 2012 WL 234142 (Ariz. App. 2012); Arnold S. Rosenberg, Where to File Against Non-U.S. Debtors: Applying U.C.C. §9-307(c) [Rev.] to Foreign Filing, Recording and Registration Systems, 39 UCC L.J. 109

(2006). Some countries have systems similar to Article 9, or even copied from Article 9. Albania, for example, modeled its secured transactions law on that of Saskatchewan, which in turn was modeled on Article 9. Other formerly communist countries have adopted a version of Article 9 as part of reforming their legal system for a market economy. Other countries follow a wide range of approaches. The 1804 Napoleonic Code, the basis for many civil law legal systems, "eliminated all nonpossessory security interests in movables, ironically out of the drafters' despair at ever being able to design an effective registration system." Id. That approach persists in some civil law jurisdictions, although others have been driven by commercial practices to adopt registration systems for personal property used as collateral.

NOTE

For perfectly obvious reasons, when in doubt, file everywhere.

PROBLEM 59

Factory, Factory & Money is a legal partnership that has its only place of business in Chicago, Illinois where Octopus National Bank, which has a security interest in the accounts receivable of the firm, had filed its financing statement. If the law firm makes a permanent move to Washington, D.C., on January 1, 2021, does the bank lose its perfection or does it have a grace period in which to refile in the new jurisdiction? Read §9-316(a). If the law firm *merges* with a law firm in D.C. with the new D.C. firm assuming all the debts of the former one, is the time period the same? See §9-316(a)(3). Is the creditor protected as to collateral debtor acquires between the move or merger and during the applicable time period? See §9-316(h) and (i)[2]?

PROBLEM 60

Suppose that Factory, Factory & Money, the Chicago law firm in the last Problem, had two creditors before its permanent move to D.C., each of which had a perfected security interest in the firm's accounts receivable—Octopus National Bank, which had filed its financing statement first, and Last National Bank, which had filed second, both creditors filing in Chicago early in the year 2016. When the move occurred on January 1, 2017, Last National promptly refiled in D.C. before the end of March of that year, but Octopus National was careless and didn't realize that the firm had moved until that September.

---

2. These two provisions were added in the 2010 revisions to Article 9.

If Octopus National Bank files in D.C. in September, will it retain its priority over Last National? See §9-316(b) and its Official Comment 3. Note the definitions of *purchase* and *purchaser* in §1-201(b)(29) and (30).

II. CERTIFICATES OF TITLE

Grant Gilmore, one of the principal drafters of the original version of Article 9, wrote a famous treatise on its meaning, Security Interests in Personal Property (1965). In his treatise he had this to say about automobile financing:

> The automobile, in addition to its potentialities as an instrument of destruction and an agent of social change, has been one of the great sources of law in the twentieth century. As the most expensive chattel ever to come into general use, it generated novel methods of secured financing. Its unique mobility, combined with the high resale value of used cars, made theft both easy and profitable.
>
> From a legal point of view there is nothing interesting in the situation where *A*, a thief, steals *B*'s car and sells it to *C*: *A*, if apprehended, will go to jail and *C*, if found, can be forced to return the car to *B*. However, the fact that most automobile purchases are financed under some kind of security device has led to a refined version of automobile theft which is legally much more interesting than the crude business of smash and grab. Under the refined version, *A* buys a car, making the smallest possible down payment and executing a chattel mortgage, a conditional sale contract or an Article 9 security agreement for the balance in favor of *B*. *A*, representing the car to be free from liens, now sells it to *C*, who buys it, we may assume, in good faith and without actual knowledge of *B*'s interest. *C* is typically a used car dealer, so that a further complication is introduced when *C* resells to *D*, who also buys in good faith and without notice. *A*'s behavior is criminal and legally uninteresting; if caught, he will and should go to jail. The sales to *C* and *D*, however, begin to be worth thinking about since *A*, who is a criminal, albeit a refined one, is also in some sense an owner of the car, with some kind of title to it, and our legal system has always sharply distinguished between the lot of the good faith purchaser from a thief without title (who gets nothing) and that of the good faith purchaser from a person with a defective title (who may get perfect title, despite the intervening fraud or crime).

Section 20.1, at 550-551. For the protected status of a good faith purchaser buying from someone with voidable title, read §2-403(1) (and remember that *purchaser* is broadly defined in Article 1 to include any voluntary transferee — creditors as well as buyers).

PROBLEM 61

Lyle Saylor was a trucker who lived and worked in the State of Michigan. When his old rig wore out and he decided to buy a completely new truck, he went to Pennsylvania and purchased a truck on credit from Ringer Truck City. Because the State of Indiana charged a great deal less for licenses and other registration fees, Saylor told the dealership that he lived in Indiana and that the truck would be domiciled there. He gave Ringer Truck City the address of his sister, who did live in Indiana. Indiana law requires that lien interests be noted on the certificate of title, a step that Ringer Truck City duly took when it procured the Indiana certificate. When Saylor went bankrupt a year later, the trustee in bankruptcy argued that Ringer Truck City was unperfected because it had not gotten a *Michigan* certificate of title and had its lien interest noted thereon, as Michigan law required. Ringer Truck City argued that it was entitled to believe the debtor when he told the company that he lived in Indiana. How should this come out? See §9-303(a); In re Stanley, 249 B.R. 509 (D. Kan. 2000).

Metzger v. Americredit Financial Services, Inc.

Court of Appeals of Georgia, 2005
273 Ga. App. 453, 615 S.E.2d 120

BERNES, Judge.

Theresa Metzger appeals from an order entered by the Superior Court of Clayton County granting partial summary judgment to Americredit Financial Services, Inc. on her claim for conversion based on the alleged wrongful repossession of her vehicle. Metzger contends that the Superior Court erred by failing to conclude that she took her vehicle free of Americredit's security interest under the special good faith purchaser rule for goods covered by a certificate of title set forth in OCGA §11-9-337(1). We agree and reverse.

The underlying facts are not in dispute. On or about October 1, 2002, Americredit repossessed a 1997 Ford Taurus from Metzger, who had purchased the vehicle from a used car dealership in March of 2002. Metzger did not realize that Americredit had a prior lien on the vehicle or that it had been repossessed. As a result, she reported the vehicle as stolen to the police.

Metzger later learned that Americredit had obtained a security interest in the vehicle in 1998, when the company financed James Strong's purchase of the vehicle in the State of New York. The New York certificate of title issued to Strong reflected Americredit's security interest in the vehicle.

Strong later moved from New York to Georgia and submitted a "MV1Z" application form, along with the existing title and the required fee, to the

Cobb County tag agent for the Georgia Department of Motor Vehicles ("DMV") in order to convert the existing New York certificate of title to a Georgia one. The DMV processed the application, but as a result of a clerical data entry error, the DMV issued a Georgia certificate of title that did not reflect Americredit's security interest in the vehicle.

Strong later transferred the vehicle to an automobile dealer owner, and the vehicle thereafter passed through a non-dealer owner and additional dealer owners before Metzger purchased it in March of 2002. None of the subsequent Georgia certificates of title issued for the vehicle in connection with these transfers reflected Americredit's security interest.

After Metzger purchased the vehicle and registered it with the DMV, Americredit, having finally located the vehicle, repossessed it from Metzger's residence and sold it at auction. Once she learned from the police department that her vehicle had been repossessed rather than stolen, Metzger filed suit against Americredit in the Superior Court of Clayton County. She contended that Americredit wrongfully repossessed her vehicle and kept her personal belongings contained therein, and, as a consequence, should be held liable for conversion, negligence, deceptive trade practices, breach of the peace, breach of good faith, racketeering, unjust enrichment, and breach of sale.

Metzger subsequently filed a motion seeking partial summary judgment on her claim of conversion. Americredit filed its response and a cross motion for summary judgment on all of Metzger's claims. The Superior Court denied Metzger's motion for partial summary judgment and granted summary judgment in favor of Americredit on Metzger's conversion claim only. The Superior Court concluded that Americredit had a perfected security interest in the vehicle that it could enforce against Metzger. Metzger now appeals from that order.

"When reviewing the grant or denial of a motion for summary judgment, this Court conducts a de novo review of the law and the evidence. . . ." (Citation and punctuation omitted.) Osman v. Olde Plantation Apartments on Montreal, LLC, 270 Ga. App. 627, 607 S.E.2d 236 (2004). In order to establish a claim for conversion, "the complaining party must show (1) title to the property or the right of possession, (2) actual possession in the other party, (3) demand for return of the property, and (4) refusal by the other party to return the property." (Citation omitted.) Johnson v. First Union Nat. Bank, 255 Ga. App. 819, 823(4), 567 S.E.2d 44 (2002). The sole issue regarding Metzger's conversion claim is whether Metzger had the exclusive right of possession to the vehicle, making Americredit's seizure unlawful, or whether Americredit's security interest instead empowered it to practice self-help and repossess the vehicle from Metzger. See, e.g., Fulton v. Anchor Savings Bank, FSB, 215 Ga. App. 456, 468(5), 452 S.E.2d 208 (1994). Because the material facts are undisputed, resolution of this issue turns on our interpretation of the applicable statutory framework.

"[I]n construing [Georgia statutes], we apply the fundamental rules of statutory construction that require us to construe a statute according to its terms, to give words their plain and ordinary meaning, and to avoid a construction that makes some language mere surplusage." (Citation omitted.) Slakman v. Continental Cas. Co., 277 Ga. 189, 191, 587 S.E.2d 24 (2003). See also City of Atlanta v. Yusen Air & Sea Svc. Holdings, Inc., 263 Ga. App. 82, 84(1), 587 S.E.2d 230 (2003). With these rules in mind, we turn to the Motor Vehicle Certificate of Title Act, OCGA §40-3-1 et seq. (the "Act"), which provides the exclusive procedure for perfecting a security interest in a motor vehicle in Georgia. Staley v. Phelan Finance Corp. of Columbus, 116 Ga. App. 1, 1-2, 156 S.E.2d 201 (1967).

Under the Act, a security interest in a motor vehicle is perfected, at the latest, on the date when the application documents for obtaining a certificate of title are delivered to the DMV or local tag agent, so long as the application documents properly reflect the existence of the security interest:

> (b)(1) A security interest is perfected by delivery to the commissioner or to the county tag agent of the county in which the seller is located, of the county in which the sale takes place, of the county in which the vehicle is delivered, or of the county wherein the vehicle owner resides, of the required fee and:
>
> (A) The existing certificate of title, if any, and an application for a certificate of title containing the name and address of the holder of a security interest; or
>
> (B) A notice of security interest on forms prescribed by the commissioner.

Perfection occurs on that date, irrespective of whether the certificate of title subsequently issued by the DMV fails to reflect the security interest:

> (b)(2) The security interest is perfected as of the time of its creation if the initial delivery of the application or notice to the commissioner or local tag agent is completed within 20 days thereafter, regardless of any subsequent rejection of the application or notice for errors; otherwise, as of the date of the delivery to the commissioner or local tag agent. The local tag agent shall issue a receipt or other evidence of the date of filing of such application or notice. When the security interest is perfected as provided for in this subsection, it shall constitute notice to everybody of the security interest of the holder.

OCGA §40-3-50(b). "Compliance with the filing requirements of the Act has the effect of imputing constructive notice to all who may subsequently acquire an interest in or lien against the property." (Citation and punctuation omitted.) Cobb Center Pawn & Jewelry Brokers, Inc. v. Gordon, 242 Ga. App. 73, 75(2), 529 S.E.2d 138 (2000).

Based on this statutory language and case law, it might appear that because Strong delivered proper application forms reflecting Americredit's security interest to the Cobb County tag agent, Americredit could enforce its security interest against Metzger, who under OCGA §40-3-50(b)(2) would have constructive notice of the security interest despite the clerical error contained in the Georgia certificate of title that was later issued. However, OCGA §40-3-50 contains three statutory exceptions:

> (a) *Except as provided in Code Sections 11-9-303, 11-9-316, and 11-9-337,* the security interest in a vehicle of the type for which a certificate of title is required shall be perfected and shall be valid against subsequent creditors of the owner, subsequent transferees, and the holders of security interests and liens on the vehicle by compliance with this chapter.

(Emphasis supplied.) OCGA §40-3-50(a).

Significantly, one of those exceptions, OCGA §11-9-337, states:

> If, *while a security interest in goods is perfected by any method under the law of another jurisdiction,* this state issues a certificate of title that does not show that the goods are subject to the security interest or contain a statement that they may be subject to security interests not shown on the certificate:
>
> *(1) A buyer of the goods, other than a person in the business of selling goods of that kind, takes free of the security interest if the buyer gives value and receives delivery of the goods after issuance of the certificate and without knowledge of the security interest. . . .*

(Emphasis supplied.) OCGA §11-9-337(1). An explanation of this provision is set forth in Comment 2 to Uniform Commercial Code §9-337:

> This section affords protection to certain good-faith purchasers for value who are likely to have relied on a "clean" certificate of title, i.e., one that neither shows that the goods are subject to a particular security interest nor contains a statement that they may be subject to security interests not shown on the certificate. Under this section, a buyer can take free of, and the holder of a conflicting security interest can acquire priority over, a security interest that is perfected by any method under the law of another jurisdiction. . . .

UCC §9-337 cmt. 2.

In the present case, the undisputed evidence of record shows that the six requirements of the statutory exception contained in OCGA §11-9-337(1) have been met. First, the parties agree that, at the time that Strong filed his application for a Georgia certificate of title with the Cobb County tag agent, Americredit had previously perfected its security interest in the vehicle under New York law, and the security interest remained perfected. Second, the certificate of title issued by the DMV to Strong failed to show that the vehicle was subject to a security interest. Third, Metzger is not a person in the business of selling automobiles. Fourth, Metzger gave value for the vehicle. Fifth, Metzger received delivery of the vehicle after issuance of the Georgia certificate of title by the DMV erroneously omitting reference to Americredit's security interest. Sixth and finally, Metzger was without knowledge of the security interest that Americredit held in the vehicle. Thus, Metzger was entitled to invoke OCGA §11-9-337(1). It necessarily follows that Metzger took the vehicle free of Americredit's security interest.

However, Americredit contends that two additional statutes found in Georgia's Uniform Commercial Code, OCGA §§11-9-303 and 11-9-316, indicate that Metzger took the vehicle subject to the security interest. Based on these two statutes, Americredit argues that the special good faith purchaser rule set forth in OCGA §11-9-337(1) has no application in this case, because its perfected security interest in Metzger's vehicle was no longer governed by New York law once the proper application documents and required fee for a Georgia certificate of title were submitted to the Georgia DMV by James Strong. Thus, in Americredit's view, OCGA §11-9-337(1) does not apply under the circumstances here because the erroneous Georgia certificate of title was not issued "while" its security interest in the vehicle was perfected "under the law of another jurisdiction."

Americredit's statutory argument is based on a strained reading of the interplay between OCGA §§11-9-303, 11-9-316(d) and (e), and 11-9-337. OCGA §11-9-303, entitled "Law governing perfection and priority of security interests in goods covered by a certificate of title," is a choice of law provision, as its title suggests. OCGA §11-9-303(b) provides that:

> Goods become covered by a certificate of title when a valid application for the certificate of title and the applicable fee are delivered to the appropriate authority. Goods cease to be covered by a certificate of title at the earlier of the time the certificate of title ceases to be effective under the law of the issuing jurisdiction or the time the goods become covered subsequently by a certificate of title issued by another jurisdiction.

Section 11-9-303(c) then provides that "[t]he local law of the jurisdiction under whose certificate of title the goods are covered governs perfection." These provisions indicate that even when a security interest in goods has been perfected in another state, Georgia law determines perfection and priority issues once the goods become "covered" by a Georgia certificate of title, which occurs when a valid application and fee are submitted to the Georgia DMV.

Once it becomes clear that Georgia law governs because the goods are covered by a Georgia certificate of title, the next question is whether the security interest previously perfected in another state remains perfected. That issue is addressed by OCGA §11-9-316, entitled "Continued perfection of security interest following change in governing law," specifically subsections (d) and (e), which deal with certificates of title. These subsections set forth the general rules for when a security interest perfected in another state remains perfected in Georgia, once the goods are "covered" by a Georgia certificate of title.

"A statute must be construed in relation to other statutes of which it is a part, and all statutes relating to the same subject-matter, briefly called statutes in pari materia, are construed together, and harmonized wherever possible, so as to ascertain the legislative intendment and give effect thereto." (Punctuation omitted.) City of Buchanan v. Pope, 222 Ga. App. 716, 717(1), 476 S.E.2d 53 (1996). When read in pari materia with OCGA §11-9-303 and 11-9-316(d) and (e), OCGA §11-9-337(1) gives protection to a good faith purchaser for value who is not "in the business of selling goods of that kind," when there is continued perfection of the security interest under OCGA §11-9-316(d) and (e), but the Georgia certificate of title fails to reflect the security interest. Consequently, in the present case, although Americredit's security interest in the vehicle remained perfected at the time that Metzger purchased the vehicle, that security interest could not be enforced as against Metzger, a good faith purchaser as that term is defined in OCGA §11-9-337(1), since the security interest was not properly reflected on the Georgia certificate of title.

Furthermore, "a specific statute will prevail over a general statute, absent any indication of a contrary legislative intent, to resolve any inconsistency between them." (Punctuation and emphasis omitted.) Hooks v. Cobb Center Pawn & Jewelry Brokers, 241 Ga. App. 305, 309(6), 527 S.E.2d 566 (1999). OCGA §11-9-316(d) and (e) are general statutory provisions addressing continued perfection of an out-of-state security interest once goods become covered by a Georgia certificate of title. In contrast, OCGA §11-9-337(1) sets forth a more specific rule addressing what occurs in the unique circumstance where the Georgia certificate of title that covers the goods erroneously fails to reflect the security interest originally perfected in another state. Because OCGA §11-9-337(1) is the more specific statute, it controls, even if there were a perceived inconsistency between the various statutory provisions. Accordingly, Americredit's statutory interpretation argument is unavailing. . . .

For these reasons, we reverse the partial grant of summary judgment in favor of Americredit. We remand to the superior court to enter summary judgment in favor of Metzger on her conversion claim.

PROBLEM 62

When Nick Dunne bought his wife Amy a new car, he financed it through Flynn Bank, which made sure its security interest in the car was noted on the certificate of title that Missouri issued with her name as the record owner. Before the loan was paid off Amy forged a letter to the Missouri Department of Motor Vehicles supposedly from Flynn Bank stating that the loan had been repaid, after which the State issued her a new certificate of title showing no lien on the vehicle. Amy then left her husband, moved to New York, and sold the car to Desi Collings, an old boyfriend who knew nothing about the car's history. He obtained a clean certificate of title from the State of New York. When Flynn Bank discovered what was going on it tracked the car down and repossessed it in New York. When Collings pointed to the UCC provisions you have just studied the bank replied that it's a basic rule of law that a thief cannot pass good title. How does this come out? See Mercedes-Benz Financial v. Powell, 2014 WL 3844013 (Mich. App. 2014).

PROBLEM 63

May 10, Holly Tourist, a resident of Dallas, Texas, bought a new car on credit while on vacation in Norman, Oklahoma, from Norman Car Sales, Inc., (NCS). Oklahoma law required lien interests to be noted on the certificate of title as a condition of perfection, which NCS did on May 12. On May 14, Holly drove the car to Dallas, and that same day she re-registered the car there and received a Texas certificate. Somehow she was able to do this without surrendering the Oklahoma certificate (though Texas law apparently required her to turn in the old certificate before a new one should have been issued). Texas required lien interests to be noted on the certificate of title as a condition of perfection, but the Texas certificate showed no liens of any kind thereon. On May 26, Holly sold the car to her neighbor, William Innocent, who paid full value therefor without knowledge of NCS's interest. On May 28, learning of the sale to William, NCS arranged for the car to be repossessed from in front of his house. Assuming that her resale of the car was a "default" so as to entitle NCS to repossess, decide which of them is entitled to the car. See §§9-303 and its Official Comment 6, 9-316(d) and (e) and its Official Comment 5, and 9-337 and its Official Comment. Note that §9-337 favors non-business buyers; a used car lot buying an out-of-state vehicle is not entitled to the same protection. Why would the drafters have made this distinction?

PROBLEM 64

Joseph Armstrong bought a yacht in his home state that did not use certificates of title for boats and that required filing for perfection in such collateral, a step that the financing bank, Octopus National Bank (ONB), duly took. Armstrong then moved to a state that required all security interests on boats to be noted on certificates of title issued by that state, but he never took the time to get such a certificate. Does ONB's perfection in the second state last as long as its filed financing statement is still effective or for only four months? See §9-316(b)(2). Suppose that the opposite situation occurs: Armstrong starts in a title state and ONB's interest is duly noted on that state's certificate. Armstrong moves to a state that has no certificates of title at all for boats, ONB never files there, and Armstrong never re-registers the yacht. Now what result? See §9-303 and its Official Comment.

CHAPTER 6   ASSESSMENT: MULTIPLE CHOICE QUESTIONS

1. Clark lives in Gardiner, Montana. She runs tours into Yellowstone National Park, Wyoming using equipment that she leaves in Yellowstone. Her business office is in Driggs, Idaho. Old Faithful Finance signed her up to a line of credit, secured by her equipment. To perfect the security interest, where must Old Faithful Finance file its financing statement?
   a. Montana, the location of the debtor's residence.
   b. Wyoming, the location of the debtor's business activities.
   c. Idaho, the location of the debtor's principal office.
   d. Wyoming, the location of the collateral.
   e. None of the above.

2. Old Faithful Finance will also make a loan to Lewis to purchase some pricey kayaks, for Lewis's use as a hobby in Yellowstone. Lewis lives and works as a park ranger in Yellowstone and has a post-office box in Idaho, used for eBay sales of collectibles. To perfect the security interest in the kayaks, where should Old Faithful Finance file its financing statement?
   a. Montana, the location of the debtor's residence.
   b. Wyoming, the location of the debtor's business activities.
   c. Idaho, the location of the debtor's principal office.
   d. Wyoming, the location of the collateral.
   e. None of the above.

3. Another Gardiner resident, Floyd, is the sole shareholder of a small corporation, Discovery Corps, which does construction in Montana and Wyoming. Discovery Corps is incorporated in Delaware. The business office is in Montana. If Old Faithful Finance makes Discovery Corps a loan secured by its equipment, where is it necessary for Old Faithful Finance to file its financing statement, to perfect its security interest?
   a. Montana, the location of the debtor's residence.
   b. Delaware, the location of the debtor.
   c. Montana and Wyoming, the location of the debtor's business activities.
   d. Montana, the location of the debtor's principal office.

e. Montana and Wyoming, the location of the collateral.

f. None of the above.

4. Hadfield Explorers, a Canadian corporation, has an office in Montana and does business at drilling sites in Wyoming, Montana, and Idaho. Hadfield Explorers has its chief executive office and most of its operations in the province of Alberta, Canada. When Old Faithful Finance lends to Hadfield Explorers taking a security interest in its equipment and accounts, where should it file the financing statement?

a. In Alberta, if Alberta has the equivalent of an Article 9 filing system; otherwise in Washington, D.C.

b. Montana, the location of its US office.

c. Wyoming, Montana, and Idado, the locations of its US property.

d. Wyoming, Montana, and Idado, the locations of its US places of business.

5. Garcia, a trucker living in Gardiner, put up her sixteen-wheeler as collateral for a loan from Old Faithful. Garcia should have registered her truck in Montana, but has a valid certificate of title issued by Illinois. If Old Faithful, not realizing that Garcia lives in Montana, had itself listed on the Illinois certificate of title, would that perfect its security interest?

a. No, because the certificate of title would not count, as coming from the wrong state.

b. No, because the notation would not put Garcia's Montana creditors on notice.

c. Yes, because if a certificate of title is issued, then it governs perfection in the vehicle.

d. No notation is necessary, because the security interest perfects automatically.

ANSWERS

1. *A* is the best answer. The present version of Article 9 takes the simplest approach to determining governing law for filing the financing statement. Traditional property law would call for filing in the state where the property is located. But a debtor may have collateral in multiple states, collateral may move from state to state, and some collateral has no location, if it is intangible rights like accounts. The present version of Article 9 shifted from using the location of the collateral to the location of the debtor, to simplify things. It then defines the location of the debtor in ways likely to give a single place to file. An individual is located at the individual's principal residence, which tends to remain relatively stable over time.

2. *E* is the best answer. This question reminds us that sometimes it is not necessary to file, and so, not necessary to figure out where to file. This transaction is a purchase money security interest in consumer goods, so the security interest perfects without filing. No filing is necessary to perfect the security interest, making E the best answer. Note that, although it is not necessary to file in order to be perfected, the creditor may file for other reasons, such as to have priority over a buyer of the consumer goods (as the next chapter discusses), in which case the creditor should file in the state of the debtor's residence, Montana.

3. *B* is the best answer. Contrary to A, the debtor here is Discovery Corps, the corporation, not the individual that owns the corporation's shares, Floyd. Article 9 takes the clearest approach possible for corporations: a corporation is located in the state where it is organized. Discovery Corps is a Delaware corporation, so Old Faithful Finance should file its financing statement in Delaware. This approach makes life simpler for creditors. Under the previous version of Article 9, the creditor would have to identify all states where the debtor had collateral and file in each state, and also figure out where to file for intangible collateral, and continue to keep track in case collateral changed jurisdictions. Now the creditor need simply check the Secretary of State's office for the relevant state to confirm that the debtor is incorporated there (and this also helps get the debtor's name correct on the financing statement, because the debtor's name is the name on its incorporation documents).

4. *A* is the best answer. If the debtor is located in a foreign jurisdiction, then the filing statement must be filed there—if the jurisdiction has the functional equivalent of the Article 9 filing system. As it happens, Canada does have such a system, so Alberta would be the place to file. Civil law jurisdictions (which include most jurisdictions in the world) do not, and for those transactions the filing would be in the District of Columbia.

5. *C* is the best answer. For certificate of title goods such as vehicles, perfection must be achieved by making a notation on the certificate of title, not filing a financing statement. Since vehicles already have a system for making public record of claims to ownership, Article 9 simply has a creditor use that system to give notice of the security interest in the vehicle. Article 9 again takes the simplest approach. If a certificate of title has issued, that state's law governs, even "if there is no other relationship between the jurisdiction under whose certificate of title the goods are covered and the goods or the debtor." §9-303(a),(c). The Illinois certificate of title governs.

CHAPTER 7
PRIORITY

When the secured party files its financing statement it is with the hope that its legal rights in the collateral will prevail over other parties. It is the job of the lawyer to make sure that that hope is fulfilled, or at least that the client is aware of what other interests might trump a perfected security interest. The attorney must know those risks well, and this chapter explores possible problems (the collateral is sold, other creditors file a financing statement, the debtor files for bankruptcy, the debtor merges with another entity, etc.) and highlights what can be done to lessen their effects.

I. SIMPLE DISPUTES

When the debtor's financial situation collapses, the creditors all scramble to seize the debtor's assets. The legal issue of *priority* decides which creditor gets what. A basic priority provision is §9-317, which lists the parties prevailing over an *unperfected* security interest (one that has attached but that the creditor has failed to take the steps required for perfection). Read it and work through these Problems.

PROBLEM 65

Epstein's Bookstore borrowed $10,000 from Octopus National Bank (ONB), signing a security agreement giving the bank a floating lien over the store's inventory. ONB, due to negligence, never got around to filing the financing statement. Martin's Travel Service was an unpaid creditor of the bookstore that sued on the debt and recovered a judgment against the store. It then had the sheriff levy on the inventory. ONB learned of this and calls you, ONB's attorney. Does ONB or Martin's Travel Service get paid first when the inventory is sold? See §9-317(a)(2), and the definition of *lien creditor* in §9-102(a)(52). Compare United States v. Cox, 2008 WL 2397615 (W.D.N.C. 2008). If, instead of a judgment creditor seizing the goods, Epstein's Bookstore had filed a bankruptcy petition while ONB's lien was still unperfected, what result? What result if, instead, Epstein's Bookstore had sold the inventory to a good faith buyer? See §9-317(b).

PROBLEM 66

Coke Travel Agency used its accounts receivable as collateral for a loan from the Mansfield State Bank, but the bank failed to file the financing statement that Coke Travel Agency had authorized because the bank's attorney lost the statement in the maze of papers on her desk. Six months later, Coke Travel Agency needed another loan and applied for one from the Bentham National Bank, which searched the files, discovered that there were no financing statements recorded for Coke Travel Agency as debtor, and took a security interest in the agency's accounts receivable. Bentham National Bank did file a financing statement in the proper place. Which bank has the superior interest in the collateral? See §9-322(a)(2) and Official Comment 3 to §9-317.

The major Article 9 priority section is §9-322(a)(1), which you should read after you finish this paragraph. Use it to resolve the Problems that follow.

PROBLEM 67

Jay Eastriver ran a clothing store and needed money. He went to two banks, the First National Bank and the Second State Bank, and asked each to loan him money using his inventory as collateral. They each made him sign a security agreement. First National Bank filed its financing statement first, on September 25, but did not loan Eastriver any money (nor did it make any commitment to do so) until November 10. On October 2, Second State both loaned Eastriver the money and filed its financing statement. Eastriver paid neither bank. Answer these questions:

(a) Did both banks have a perfected security interest, assuming they filed in the proper place? That is, is it possible for two creditors to have perfected security interests in the same collateral?

(b) Remembering that attachment is a prerequisite to perfection, §9-308, and that attachment cannot occur until the creditor gives value, decide which bank has the superior right to the inventory. See Example 1 in Official Comment 4 to §9-322.

(c) If either bank had *knowledge* of the transaction between Eastriver and the other bank at the time it perfected, does that affect its priority? See St. Paul Mercury Ins. Co. v. Merchants & Marine Bank, 882 So. 2d 766 (Miss. 2004).

(d) Suppose First National Bank had filed its financing statement *before* the debtor signed its security agreement. Subsequently, Second National Bank filed an authorized financing statement to perfect its security interest in the same collateral. Next, the debtor signed a security agreement with First National Bank, which counted on the existing financing statement to perfect its interest in the identical collateral. Which bank would have priority? See Official Comment 4 to §9-322 (the third paragraph; In re Adoni Group, Inc., 530 B.R. 592 Bankr. S.D.N.Y. 2015).

PROBLEM 68

When First National Bank took a perfected security interest in the inventory of Jay Eastriver's clothing store, the security agreement provided that the inventory would secure not only the current loan "but all future advances of whatever kind." Six months later, First National loaned Eastriver an additional $10,000 and had him sign a new promissory note for that amount. Do the existing filed financing statement and security agreement need to be altered in any way, or are they sufficient as is to protect the bank? See §9-204(c) and its Official Comment 5.

Assume that after First National made Eastriver the first loan and filed its financing statement, he then borrowed more money from Second State Bank, using the same inventory as collateral, and this lender also filed a financing statement in the correct place. Eastriver then paid off the loan to First National completely, but the bank never filed a termination statement. A month later, First National loaned Eastriver more money. The parties signed a new security agreement, but no new financing statement was filed. First National's attorney reasoned that the earlier financing statement would protect the later loan's priority, even though this loan was not contemplated when the first financing statement was filed. Is this right? Second State would prefer that the court rule that the first financing statement was "spent" when the underlying debt was paid off, and could not be used to give a top priority to a later uncontemplated loan. See §9-323(a) and its Official Comment 3, Example 1, and Official Comment 2 to §9-502. Often a security agreement will have in it a clause stating that the collateral protects not only this loan, but all future advances as well; see §9-204(c). If such a future advances clause had *not* been in the original security agreement that Eastriver signed with First National, does that affect the answer at all? See In re K&P Logging, Inc., 272 B.R. 867 (Bankr. D.S.C. 2001); Korea Trade Ins. Corp. v. Neema Clothing, Ltd., 2015 WL 363569 (S.D. N.Y. 2015) (financing statement mentioning the amount of the original loan protected loans made later in excess of that amount).

PROBLEM 69

Phillip Philately pledged his valuable stamp collection to the Collectors National Bank (CNB) in return for a loan (he gave CNB an oral security interest in the collateral; no financing statement was filed). The bank put the stamp collection in its vault. Philately later borrowed money from his father, Filbert Philately, and gave him a signed security agreement in the same stamp collection. The father filed a financing statement in the proper place. Answer these questions:

(a) Who has priority between CNB and the father?

(b) If Phillip goes to the bank and takes the collection home so that he can add new stamps but does then return it, does the answer change? At common law the pledgee could return the collateral to the pledgor for a "temporary and limited purpose" without losing its perfection. See G. Gilmore §14.5. Has this doctrine survived the enactment of the Code? See §9-313(d). Is §9-312(f) relevant?

(c) If CNB makes Phillip sign a security agreement and then turns the collection over to him but never files a financing statement, who wins? See §9-308(c). What should CNB have done?

Section 9-204(c) broadly authorizes future advance clauses in the security agreement. Does it also give the drafters' imprimatur to the so-called "dragnet clause," a clause purporting to expand the security interest to cover unrelated obligations owed by the debtor to the creditor? Professor Gilmore thought not and, in §35.6 of his treatise, proposed that the courts develop a test based on the intention of the parties and a requirement that the later obligation be "related," "similar," or "of the same class" as the original transaction. Under prior versions of Article 9, the courts often followed this recommendation — see the case below. Is it still good law? See Official Comment 5 to §9-204.

PROBLEM 70

Howard "Red" Poll decided to go into the cattle business and borrowed $65,000 from the Brangus National Bank to finance part of the purchase of the initial herd. Poll signed a security agreement using the cattle as collateral for this "and all other obligations now or hereafter owed to the bank." A financing statement covering this transaction was filed in the appropriate place. Two years later, Poll received a charge card from the same bank and used it to finance a trip to Australia to look over cattle ranching there. When he failed to pay the credit card bill, the bank repossessed the cattle (even though his payments on the cattle purchase loan were current). Did the bank's security interest in the cattle encompass the credit card obligation? Would it make a difference if he had gone to Australia in search of the perfect wave for surfing? See In re Johnson, 9 B.R. 713 (Ref. Bankr., M.D. Tenn. 1981) (consumer goods held not to secure future advances of a business nature in spite of dragnet clause); Kimbell Foods, Inc. v. Republic Natl. Bank, 401 F. Supp. 316 (N.D. Tex. 1975) ("The true intention of the parties is really the sole and controlling factor in determining whether future advances were covered by the original agreement . . . [or] would have to be reperfected."); John Miller Supply Co. v. Western State Bank, 55 Wis. 2d 385, 199 N.W.2d 161 (1972) (adopts the Gilmore tests); Note, Future Advances Financing Under the UCC: Curbing the Abuses of the Dragnet Clause, 34 U. Pitt. L. Rev. 691 (1973).

In re Zaochney

United States District Court, Alaska, Bankruptcy Division, 2011
2011 WL 6148727

MEMORANDUM ON MOTION TO VALUE SECURITY INTEREST

DONALD MACDONALD IV, Bankruptcy Judge.

The debtor filed a motion to value the security interest of Alaska USA Federal Credit Union in a 2008 Chevrolet Impala. Alaska USA contends that the Impala is encumbered by a purchase money lien as well as by sums due on a credit card, through dragnet clauses found in its loan documentation. The debtor alleges that the dragnet clauses are unenforceable. I agree with Alaska USA and find the dragnet clauses valid. The debtor's motion will be granted, in part. Alaska USA's secured claim is valued at $12,950.00. However, the vehicle is collateral for both the debtor's car loan and her credit line loan.

The debtor signed a two-page credit line loan agreement with Alaska USA on September 12, 2009. On the first page, above the debtor's signature, the agreement had bold headings for a series of 11 paragraphs. One paragraph, headed "Cross-Collateralization," states:

> Collateral pledged as security for other loans I have now or in the future with
> Credit Union will also be security for this agreement. This cross-collateral

provision does not apply to my principal dwelling or household goods pledged as security for other loans.

The debtor says she signed this agreement because employees at Alaska USA told her it was a one-time offer to obtain credit at a favorable rate. She alleges that there was no discussion of the cross-collateral provision when she signed the agreement. She says personnel at the credit union also told her during this visit that she could obtain a car loan.

Ten days after receiving the credit line, the debtor purchased a car from Alaska Sales and Service. She financed the purchase through Alaska USA. The retail installment sales contract provided that the "Seller intends to assign this contract to Alaska USA Federal Credit Union." The sales contract had a large box in the lower right hand corner with Alaska USA's logo. It stated: "Questions?" and listed Alaska USA's P.O. Box and two separate phone numbers. In her supporting memorandum, the debtor confirms that she knew, at the time she made the purchase, that the financing would be through Alaska USA.

On the front page of the sale contract, above the box containing the debtor's signature, is a provision regarding a security interest. It states:

> Security Interest. You are giving a security interest in the goods or Property Being Purchased as described above. As permitted by law the goods or Property Being Purchased secures other obligations now or hereafter owed by you to the Creditor and other Collateral held by the Creditor, including funds on deposit with the Creditor, secures this Contract (see reverse side under Security).

The reverse side of the sales contract contains a paragraph in fine print labeled "*Security.*" It provides, in part:

> As provided by law, the Collateral for this contract secures other obligations you owe now or later to the Creditor, and other Collateral the Creditor presently holds or later obtains, also secures this contract. This cross-collateralization provision does not cover or extend to your principal dwelling or household goods pledged as security for other loans.

The debtor filed for chapter 7 relief on August 4, 2011. The only creditor listed on Schedules D and F is Alaska USA. The debtor lists two secured debts owed to the credit union: a mortgage on a residence for $220,000.00 and her obligation on the 2008 Chevrolet Impala of $12,000.00. She also lists two unsecured debts owed to the credit union: a deficiency balance of $4,836.22 on a repossessed 2005 Chevrolet Trailblazer and $5,000.00 for her credit line.

The debtor sought to reaffirm her car loan. Alaska USA places a value of $12,950.00 on the vehicle and the debtor does not dispute this. Alaska

USA contends the vehicle secures not only the balance due on the Impala, $11,097.87, but also roughly $1,852.13 of the outstanding balance on the credit line. The debtor disagrees. She contends the Impala is collateral only for the vehicle loan.

In *Alaska Fur Gallery*,[1] I found a cross-collateralization clause in a commercial contract to be valid and enforceable. I went on to state:

> My conclusion here is limited to commercial transactions. Consumer debtors are held to a less stringent standard than commercial debtors. In a consumer transaction, courts may still look to the "true intent" of the parties. Other considerations, such as good faith, overreaching or unconscionability, might also alter the outcome. These are issues left for another day.

According to the debtor, that day has arrived and this court must now strike down the cross-collateral provisions found in the Alaska USA loan documents. I respectfully decline to do so for a number of reasons.

The debtor argues that the Alaska Supreme Court's decision, Lundgren v. National Bank of Alaska,[2] applies here. *Lundgren* involved a dragnet clause in a second deed of trust against commercial real property. The court found that such clauses deserved strict scrutiny, and adopted guidelines for determining whether these clauses could be enforced. However, the court also indicated that UCC policy considerations were not relevant to its determination of the impact of the dragnet clause in the deed of trust.

Lundgren is distinguishable from this case. No deed of trust is involved. While courts in other jurisdictions have applied a *Lundgren*-type analysis to UCC transactions, the Alaska Supreme Court has not. Additionally, *Lundgren* was decided prior to the nationwide adoption of amendments to the UCC in 2001. AS 45.29.204 was amended effective July 1, 2001, fourteen years after the *Lundgren* decision was issued. AS 45.29.204(c) permits a security agreement to "provide that collateral secures . . . future advances or other value, whether or not the advances or value are given pursuant to the commitment." The Official Comment to U.C.C. §9-204, the corresponding subsection of the Uniform Commercial Code, indicates that *Lundgren*'s dragnet rationale is inapplicable to UCC cases. The Comment states:

> **Future Advances; Obligations Secured.** Under subsection (c) collateral may secure future as well as past or present advances if the security agreement so provides. This is in line with the policy of this Article toward security interests in after-acquired property under subsection (a). Indeed, the parties are free to agree that a security interest secures any obligations whatsoever.

---

1. Alaska Fur Gallery v. First National Bank Alaska (In re Alaska Fur Gallery, Inc.), 457 B.R. 764 (Bankr. D. Alaska 2011).
  2. 756 P.2d 270 (Alaska 1987).

Determining the obligations secured by collateral is solely a matter of construing the parties' agreement under applicable law. *This Article rejects the holdings of cases decided under former Article 9 that applied other tests, such as whether a future advance or other subsequently incurred obligation was of the same or a similar type or class as earlier advances and obligations secured by the collateral.*

To support her position here, the debtor has cited cases that preceded the 2001 amendments to the UCC. Those cases applied an analysis similar to the one adopted in *Lundgren*. In a recent memorandum disposition, the Ninth Circuit BAP indicated that such cases have been superceded by the adoption of U.C.C. §9-204.[3] However, the BAP remanded that case for determination of certain factual issues pertaining to enforceability of the cross-collateralization clause. These issues included whether applying the clause would be unconscionable or violate the duty of good faith under the U.C.C.

In a few published decisions issued after the UCC amendments, courts have declined to enforce a cross-collateralization clause on facts distinguishable from the ones found here. In In re Keeton,[4] the bankruptcy court found that a dragnet clause in a loan taken out by joint debtors and secured by a vehicle did not operate to secure the credit card liability of just one of the debtors. The court's rationale was that, where the loan defined "debtor" to mean both of the debtors, there was no indication that the parties intended the vehicle to secure the separate and individual obligations of just one of the debtor[s]. Similarly, in First National Bank of Izard County v. Garner,[5] an Arkansas appellate court declined to apply a dragnet clause in a loan taken out by three debtors, secured by real property and a tractor, so that it would encompass a subsequent loan taken out by just one of the debtors individually. The court found that the subsequent loan was entirely unrelated to the first loan and could not have been within the contemplation of the parties at the time the first loan was taken out. Finally, in Wooding v. Cinfed Employees Federal Credit Union,[6] the court found that the debtor's credit card debt was not secured by a vehicle that was collateral for an earlier loan. The court found there was no meeting of the minds with respect to the cross-collateralization provisions found in the loan documents because the credit card application signed by the debtor provided only for a security interest in her accounts and there was no evidence that the debtor had received the underlying credit card agreement. Further, the loan documents were ambiguous and there was nothing in them to indicate that the vehicle would secure the credit card account as well.

3. Frontier Fin. Credit Union v. Dumlao (In re Dumlao), 2011 WL 4501402 at 5 (9th Cir. B.A.P. Aug. 5, 2011) (mem. disposition).
4. 2008 WL 686938 (Bankr. M.D. Ala. Mar. 10, 2008).
5. 167 S.W.3d 664 (Ark. App. 2004).
6. 171 Ohio App. 3d 665, 872 N.E.2d 959 (Ohio App. 1 Dist. 2007).

In other cases decided subsequent to the amendment of the UCC, courts have enforced cross-collateralization provisions in a consumer context, with the result that credit lines or deficiency balances were secured by the debtor's vehicle.[7] One court did so in spite of finding that the loans were adhesion contracts.[8] Another court stated that a debtor's failure to read the loan documentation was an inadequate defense to the enforcement of these provisions.[9]

Here, the loan documents signed by the debtor plainly state that collateral pledged for one loan will secure other existing or future loans extended by the credit union. The dragnet provisions are not embedded in fine print and are in simple English. Although I did indicate, in *Alaska Fur Gallery,* that different standards for interpreting a dragnet clause might be applied in consumer transactions, a debtor must provide the court with something more than a citation to *Lundgren* and the assertion of an adhesion contract. The debtor here has not submitted any evidence that the "true intent" of the parties was anything other than as set forth in the documents. Nor has she submitted any evidence of bad faith, overreaching or unconscionability.

I conclude that the dragnet clauses found in the debtor's loan documents with Alaska USA are valid and enforceable. The debtor's vehicle is valued at $12,950.00. Because Alaska USA is owed less than this, $11,097.87, on the vehicle loan, it wants to use the balance of the equity in the vehicle to secure roughly $1,852.13 of the outstanding balance on the debtor's credit line. It may do so under the terms of the loan documents. The debtor's motion to value security interest is granted, in part. Alaska USA's secured claim is valued at $12,950.00.

An order and judgment will be entered consistent with this memorandum.

PROBLEM 71

Aware of difficulties with cross-collateralization clauses, rancher Howard Poll was always careful to keep his consumer obligations (from his Visa card, using the objects purchased as collateral) with a different bank than the one that financed his ranching operations (with a traditional loan, using his cattle as collateral). Each bank had him sign security agreements that provided that the collateral nominated for each debt would also protect "any and all debts,

---

7. See In re Hobart, 452 B.R. 789 (Bankr. D. Idaho 2011); In re Shemwell, 378 B.R. 166 (Bankr. W.D. Ky. 2007); In re Nagata, 2006 WL 2131318 (Bankr. D. Hawaii Jul. 20, 2006); In re Watson, 286 B.R. 594 (Bankr. D.N.J. 2002)

8. *Watson,* 286 B.R. at 602-603.

9. *Hobart,* 452 B.R. at 801 n.29.

now existing or after-acquired" owed to the same creditor. Howard was therefore distressed to learn that when the two banks merged, the new bank's loan
officer now insisted that his cattle also protect the debts he owed on his Visa
card. Is that right?

II. PURCHASE MONEY SECURITY INTERESTS

A.   The Basic Rule

The seller who extends credit to the buyer or the lender who advances
the money to enable the buyer to purchase the collateral has a special equity
in it in the eyes of the law. If the parties sign a security agreement, the seller/
lender gets a *purchase money security interest* (PMSI). Read §9-103. Even though
the goods become subject to an existing security interest when they come
into the buyer's possession, the PMSI is given priority. This is true in spite of
the fact that the PMSI is later in time to earlier perfected interests. Where
the collateral is consumer goods, no further steps are required for a PMSI
therein to prevail over prior or later interests. See §9-309(1). All other PMSIs
must be perfected during a 20-day "grace period" following the buyer's possession of the goods in order to take advantage of a relation-back of priority
to that date. Read §§9-317(e) and 9-324(a) carefully. Section 9-324(b) has a
special rule for PMSIs taken in goods that are to become part of the buyer's
inventory, and §9-324(d) has a similar one for a PMSI in *livestock,* but we'll
defer consideration of those rules for a few pages.

PROBLEM 72

When Paramount Homes finished building "Utopia, Ltd.," its newest
fancy apartment complex, it had to furnish the clubhouse, so it sent its construction manager, Bill Gilbert, to Sophy's Interiors, a furniture store, where he
made $2,000 worth of credit purchases and signed a security agreement on
behalf of Paramount Homes in favor of the seller. The agreement was signed
on June 8; the goods were delivered that same day. Bill failed to mention
that all his employer's equipment was designated as collateral on an existing
security agreement and financing statement in favor of Sullivan National Bank.
This agreement contained an "after-acquired property" clause, which stated
that later similar collateral coming into the buyer's estate would automatically
fall under the bank's security interest. (See §9-204(a).) The policy of Sophy's
Interiors was not to file financing statements for its credit furniture sales.

(a) Why might it have such a policy? Is it wise here?

(b) On June 10, which creditor will have priority in the furniture? On June 30?

In re Wild West World, L.L.C., Debtor

United States Bankruptcy Court for the District of Kansas, 2008
2008 WL 4642266

Robert E. Nugent, United States Chief Bankruptcy Judge.

Memorandum Opinion

On November 17, 2005 debtor [Wild West World] entered into a purchase agreement with Larson to purchase the Ride for $190,000. Pursuant to the express terms of the purchase agreement, Texas law governs the construction and enforcement of the purchase agreement. Paragraph 5 of the Terms and Conditions of the purchase agreement provides:

> 5.1 Title to the goods shall remain with the Seller until Seller actually receives payment in full for the goods, unless otherwise expressly provided in the terms appearing on the face of this Contract.
>
> 5.2 Seller shall retain a security interest on the goods sold on credit to Buyer, including all rides sold to Buyer, all parts, attachments and additions thereto now or hereafter acquired and all replacements and substitutions therefore and all proceeds from the sale of such rides, including accounts receivable, until paid in full by Buyer (the "Ride"). Seller may file any financing statements or their equivalent in any jurisdiction at any time it deems necessary to maintain its interest, with or without the signature of Buyer; Buyer agrees to execute any financing statements and any amendments thereto required by Seller and hereby specifically authorizes Seller to file such statements with its signature.

The undisputed practice in the amusement ride industry is that title to a ride does not pass until the ride has been paid in full. Pursuant to the purchase agreement, delivery of the Ride to debtor was scheduled for November 15, 2006 and the Ride was actually delivered no later than March 5, 2007. Larson filed its financing statement on the Ride with the Kansas Secretary of State's office on June 8, 2007. Larson filed a proof of claim in this bankruptcy for the unpaid balance on the Ride in the amount of $164,824.

First National loaned over $6 million to debtor for the construction of the Wild West World amusement park. In conjunction with the construction loan, debtor and First National entered into a commercial security agreement in which debtor granted a blanket security interest in debtor's property. First National filed its financing statement with the Kansas Secretary of

State on March 24, 2006 perfecting a security interest in all business assets of the debtor. First National's lien secures a claim of $6,507,871.

During the pendency of this bankruptcy, the Ride was liquidated and debtor holds net proceeds of $85,800, plus accrued interest. The prevailing party in this adversary will be entitled to these sale proceeds.

ANALYSIS AND CONCLUSIONS OF LAW

A. SELLER'S RESERVATION OF TITLE AND UCC §2-401

Larson asserts that notwithstanding its delivery of the Ride to debtor in March 2007, it reserved title to the Ride pursuant to the explicit terms of the purchase agreement and industry practice and that title to the Ride did not pass to debtor until the Ride was paid in full. Larson therefore reasons that debtor had no interest in the Ride to which a security interest (including First National's) could attach and therefore, its ownership interest in the Ride is superior to First National.

First National counters that §2-401 of the Uniform Commercial Code limits a seller's ability to reserve title once the seller has delivered the goods to the buyer. It relies upon In re Samuels & Co. First National contends that once the goods are delivered, the effect of reserving title is to give the seller a security interest in the goods delivered. It further argues that since Larson did not timely perfect its purchase money security interest, Larson's interest in the Ride is inferior to First National's interest.

The parties disagree on the interpretation of §2-401. The pertinent parts of the UCC text of §2-401 titled "Passing of Title; Reservation for Security; Limited Application of This Section," states:

> Each provision of this Article with regard to the rights, obligations, and remedies of the seller, the buyer, purchasers, or other third parties applies irrespective of title to the goods except where the provision refers to such title. Insofar as situations are not covered by the other provisions of this Article and matters concerning title become material, the following rules apply:
>
> (1) Title to goods cannot pass under a contract for sale prior to their identification to the contract (Section 2-501), and unless otherwise explicitly agreed, the buyer acquires by their identification a special property as limited by this Act. *Any retention or reservation by the seller of the title (property) in goods shipped or delivered to the buyer is limited in effect to a reservation of a security interest. Subject to these provisions and to Article 9,* title to goods passes from the seller to the buyer in any manner and on any conditions explicitly agreed on by the parties.

Texas' version of §2-401, while containing lettered paragraphs rather than numbered paragraphs, is identical to the UCC official text. For ease of reference, the Court will simply reference §2-401 in this opinion.

The Court has carefully reviewed the parties' case authorities and concludes that *Samuels,* cited by First National, is a correct interpretation of the law. Although *Samuels* involved an unpaid seller's reclamation claim vis-à-vis the buyer's creditor claiming a security interest in after-acquired property, that factual distinction has no bearing on the outcome of the case at bar. The pertinent legal conclusion in *Samuels* applicable here is that the interest of an unpaid seller in goods already delivered to a buyer is subordinate to the interest of the holder of a perfected security interest in those same goods. That legal conclusion is based upon the Fifth Circuit Court of Appeals' interpretation of UCC §2-401. As the Fifth Circuit observed:

> However, the U.C.C. specifically limits the seller's ability to reserve title once he has voluntarily surrendered possession to the buyer: "Any retention or reservation by the seller of the title (property) in goods shipped or delivered to the buyer is limited in effect to a reservation of a security interest." §2.401(a).

Samuels holds that this limitation applies whether the sale is a cash sale or a credit sale. The *Samuels* court went on to address the perceived unfairness to the unpaid seller.

> Any seeming unfairness to [sellers] resulting from the Code's operation is illusory, for the sellers could have protected their interests, even as against [a third party's] prior perfected interest, if they had merely complied with the U.C.C.'s purchase-money provisions. [Citations omitted.] The Code favors purchase-money financing, and encourages it by granting to a seller of goods the power to defeat prior liens. The seller at most need only (1) file a financing statement and (2) notify the prior secured party of its interest before delivery of the new inventory. The procedure is not unduly complex or cumbersome. But whether cumbersome or not, a [seller] who chooses to ignore its provisions takes a calculated risk that a loss will result.
>
> In the instant case [sellers] did not utilize §9.312's purchase-money provision. The sellers never perfected. Thus, in a competition with a perfected secured party they are subordinated, and in this case, lose the whole of their interests. [citations omitted].

Numerous other courts across the country are in accord with *Samuels* and interpret §2-401 in a like fashion. Section 2-401(1) negates the ability to delay passage of title beyond delivery. Any express agreement of the parties or reservation of title in the seller is limited by §2-401(1). Moreover, §2-401(1) cannot be varied by custom and usage in the trade, course of dealing, or agreement.

The Court rejects Larson's argument that because it has expressly reserved title until full payment under the purchase agreement, it avoids the operation of §2-401(1). Larson seizes upon the "unless otherwise explicitly agreed" language in the first sentence and the "title . . . passes . . . in any manner and on any conditions explicitly agreed on by the parties" language in the third sentence of §2-401(1). However, it ignores the prefatory language in the statute: "*Subject to these provisions* and to Article 9, title to goods passes from the seller to the buyer in any manner and on any conditions explicitly agreed on by the parties." It could not be any clearer to this Court that the ability to expressly agree on when title passes to the buyer is *subject to* the second sentence of §2-401(1). The limiting operation of reservation of title found in the second sentence of §2-401(1) is triggered by delivery. Delivery of the goods is the key. It is only when the seller has delivered the goods to the buyer that a seller's express reservation of title is limited to retention of a security interest. If there has been no delivery, the express reservation of title may be enforced.

The Court therefore concludes that Larson is an unpaid credit seller of the Ride to debtor. Larson's reservation of title until the Ride was paid in full, by both the express terms of the purchase order and by industry custom and practice, is negated and limited by operation of §2-401(1). Because Larson voluntarily delivered the Ride to debtor prior to payment in full, Larson retained only a security interest in the Ride.

B.   PRIORITY BETWEEN LARSON AND FIRST NATIONAL — UCC §9-322 AND §9-324

Having concluded that Larson retained only a security interest in the Ride, the Court next determines priority between the two competing security interests in the Ride — Larson versus First National.

The general rule of priority between parties claiming a perfected security interest in the same property is "the first-to-file." This general rule is set forth in Kan. Stat. Ann. §84-9-322(a)(1) (2007 Supp.). Likewise, a perfected security interest takes priority over an unperfected security interest in the same collateral.

Kan. Stat. Ann. §84-9-324(a) (2007 Supp.) provides an exception to the general priority rules and creates a special priority for purchase money security interests. It elevates the holder of a purchase money security interest over a perfected non-purchase money security interest in the same collateral, provided the purchase money creditor perfects its security interest within twenty days of delivery of the collateral to the debtor. This special priority rule for purchase money security interests applies even if the non-purchase money security interest was perfected by filing prior to the purchase money security interest.

Here, there is no dispute that Larson held a purchase money security interest in the Ride. The uncontroverted facts establish that the debtor received possession of the Ride no later than March 5, 2007, when Larson delivered the Ride to debtor. Thus, Larson had until March 25, 2007 in which to file its financing statement to perfect its purchase money security interest in the Ride and obtain special priority status under §84-9-324(a). The uncontroverted facts further establish that Larson did not perfect its purchase money security interest in the Ride until June 8, 2007, outside the 20-day period from delivery. Accordingly, Larson is not entitled to special priority over First National as the holder of a purchase money security interest.

This means that the Court must fall back to the general priority rules in §84-9-322(a)(1) to determine the priority between Larson and First National. The undisputed facts establish that First National perfected its blanket security interest by filing a financing statement on all of debtor's "business assets" (including the Ride) on March 24, 2006. Since Larson did not perfect its security interest in the Ride until filing its financing statement on June 8, 2007, First National was the "first-to-file" and its security interest is prior to Larson's.

By failing to timely perfect its purchase money security interest after delivery of the Ride, Larson finds itself in the same unfortunate position as the unpaid seller in *Samuels*. Larson failed to avail itself of the special priority and protection afforded holders of purchase money security interests and must suffer the loss. . . .

CONCLUSION

Pursuant to UCC §2-401(1)'s limiting operation, Larson's reservation of title to the Ride that it sold and voluntarily delivered to debtor effected only a reservation of a security interest in the Ride. As the first to file its financing statement on the Ride, First National's perfected security interest in the Ride is prior to and superior to Larson's competing perfected security interest under Kan. Stat. Ann. §84-9-322(a)(1). Because Larson failed to perfect its security interest within 20 days of delivery of the Ride to debtor, it is not entitled to special priority as the holder of a perfected purchase money security interest in the Ride under Kan. Stat. Ann. §84-9-324(a). Accordingly, First National has priority to the Ride proceeds and is entitled to summary judgment on its claim against Larson for the amount of the Ride proceeds, together with accrued interest thereon. A Judgment on Decision shall issue this day.

SO ORDERED.

PROBLEM 73

Video Wonder, an electronics store, had granted a floating lien over its inventory and equipment to Last National Bank, which perfected its security interest by filing a financing statement in the appropriate place. Needing a guard dog for the store, Video Wonder's manager responded to an ad in the newspaper placed by Agatha Shaw, who was selling her beloved German shepherd, Fang. She had bought him for protection when he was but a pup, but he had proven too much for her, having seriously injured a meter-reader and two mail carriers. She checked out the store carefully before agreeing to sell Video Wonder the dog, saying she wanted a good home for Fang. He cost the store $1,200. The manager agreed to send her $100 a month until the dog was paid for, at which time she agreed in writing to sign over Fang's papers. Ms. Shaw and the manager agreed that the store would not get any title to Fang until all the payments had been made. Fang proved to be a fine watchdog for the store, but when Video Wonder stopped making payments to all creditors two months later, Last National Bank seized all of the store's assets, including Fang. Agatha Shaw is upset. She calls you, her attorney. Is there any hope for her? Can she argue that the bank's security interest only attached to Video Wonder's equity in the dog, or that until Video Wonder had paid the entire debt, it had no property interest to which the bank's floating lien could attach? See ITT Indus. Credit Co. v. Regan, 487 So. 2d 1047 (Fla. 1986); First Natl. Bank v. Quintana, 733 P.2d 858 (N.M. 1987).

PROBLEM 74

Hart Farm Equipment leased a construction backhoe to Farmer Bean for a six-month period with the understanding that Farmer Bean would be given the option to purchase the backhoe at any time during that period, and, in fact, the lease at one point called this a "sale on approval." Farmer Bean's equipment was already subject to a perfected floating lien in favor of Octopus National Bank. Three months after the delivery of the backhoe, Farmer Bean agreed to buy the backhoe, and Hart Farm Equipment filed its financing statement the next day, claiming its purchase money security interest. Who wins in the priority battle between Hart Farm Equipment and Octopus National Bank? See §2-326(2); Official Comment 3 to §9-324.

PROBLEM 75

Danica Entropy traded in her SUV for a hybrid Maxwell Demon at Cash For Clunkers, Inc., at a time when she still owed Cash For Clunkers $15,000 on the SUV, which is now worth $10,000. To finance this transaction, Danica borrowed $25,000, secured by the Maxwell Demon, from Octopus National Bank, which made her a hybrid loan of $20,000 to pay the price of the new Maxwell Demon and $5,000 to pay off her "negative equity" in the old SUV. Does Octopus National Bank have a purchase money security interest for the full amount? See the following case.

In the Matter of Faith Ann Peaslee and Others

Court of Appeals of New York, 2009
13 N.Y.3d 75, 913 N.E.2d 387

PIGOTT, J.

The United States Court of Appeals for the Second Circuit, by certified question, asks us to decide whether "the portion of an automobile retail installment sale attributable to a trade-in vehicle's 'negative equity' [is] a part of the 'purchase-money obligation' arising from the purchase of a new car, as defined under New York's U.C.C.?" (547 F.3d 177, 186 [2d Cir. 2008].) We find that it is.

I.

On August 28, 2004, Faith Ann Peaslee entered into a retail installment contract for the purchase of a 2004 Pontiac Grand Am. As part of the transaction, Peaslee traded in her vehicle, which had a negative trade-in value, or negative equity, of $5,980.[10] That amount was rolled into the financing of her new car along with other charges, resulting in financing totaling $23,180. The lien against the trade-in was paid off by the dealer, and the dealer's security interest in the new vehicle was assigned to GMAC, LLC.

Nearly two years after purchasing her new vehicle, Peaslee filed for chapter 13 bankruptcy and a trustee was appointed to handle the estate. As part of her bankruptcy plan, Peaslee proposed that she retain possession of the vehicle and that, pursuant to United States Bankruptcy Code (11 U.S.C.) §506(a)(1),[11] GMAC's secured claim would be reduced to $10,950, representing the alleged retail value of the vehicle. Under Peaslee's proposal, the remaining amount owed to GMAC, $6,954.95, would be treated as an unsecured claim.

GMAC objected to this characterization of its claim and argued that, pursuant to the "hanging paragraph" set forth in Bankruptcy Code §1325(a), it was entitled to have the entire $17,904.95 treated as a secured claim. The "hanging paragraph," which was enacted as part of the Bankruptcy Abuse Prevention and Consumer Protection Act of 2005, states, in pertinent part, that

---

10. In automobile industry parlance, "negative equity" occurs when the trade-in vehicle is subject to a lien that exceeds the vehicle's value.

11. This provision states, in pertinent part, that

"[a]n allowed claim of a creditor secured by a lien on property in which the estate has an interest . . . is a secured claim to the extent of the value of such creditor's interest in the estate's interest in such property . . . and is an unsecured claim to the extent that the value of such creditor's interest . . . is less than the amount of such allowed claim."

"[f]or purposes of paragraph (5), [Bankruptcy Code] section 506 shall not apply to a claim described in that paragraph if the creditor has a purchase money security interest securing the debt that is the subject of the claim, the debt was incurred within the 910-day [sic] preceding the date of the filing of the petition, and the collateral for that debt consists of a motor vehicle (as defined in section 30102 of title 49) acquired for the personal use of the debtor" (emphasis supplied).

The trustee moved to have the Bankruptcy Court determine that GMAC had a secured claim of $10,950 and only an unsecured claim for the balance. The Bankruptcy Court did just that, and held that the term "purchase money security interest" (PMSI), as set forth in New York's Uniform Commercial Code, did not include negative equity (358 B.R. 545, 558 [Bkrtcy. W.D.N.Y. 2006]). The United States District Court for the Western District of New York reached the opposite conclusion (373 B.R. 252, 258-261 [Bkrtcy. W.D.N.Y. 2007]). The Second Circuit, noting that Congress failed to provide a definition of purchase-money security interest either in the hanging paragraph or elsewhere, concluded "that state law governs the definition of PMSI in the hanging paragraph" and certified to us the question of whether the New York Uniform Commercial Code considers that portion of a retail installment sale attributable to the negative equity of a trade-in vehicle to be part of the purchase-money obligation arising from the sale of a new car (547 F.3d 177, 184, 186 [2008]).

For the reasons that follow, we answer the question in the affirmative.

II.

"A security interest in goods is a purchase-money security interest . . . to the extent that the goods are purchase-money collateral with respect to that security interest" (UCC 9-103[(b)][(1)]). Purchase-money collateral is defined as "goods or software that secures a purchase-money obligation incurred with respect to that collateral" (UCC 9-103[(a)][(1)]). A purchase-money obligation is "an obligation of an obligor incurred as all or part of the price of the collateral or for value given to enable the debtor to acquire rights in or the use of the collateral if the value is in fact so used" (UCC 9-103[(a)][(2)] [emphasis supplied]). The UCC therefore establishes two ways that a purchase-money obligation may arise: (1) where the obligor—the debtor—incurs an obligation as all or part of the "price" of the collateral, or (2) where "value" is given to enable the debtor to acquire the collateral. We conclude that the "negative equity" here fits within either definition.

III.

Addressing "price" first, although that term is not defined by New York's UCC, the expansive examples given in an official comment concerning what items constitute the "price of the collateral" indicate that the term "price" should be afforded a broad interpretation. Specifically, with respect to a purchase-money obligation,

> "'price' of collateral or the 'value given to enable' includes obligations for expenses incurred in connection with acquiring rights in the collateral, sales taxes, duties, finance charges, interest, freight charges, costs of storage in transit, demurrage, administrative charges, expenses of collection and enforcement, attorney's fees, and other similar obligations" (UCC 9-103, Comment 3 [emphasis supplied]).

The list of examples in Comment 3 that clarify "price" is representative, not exhaustive, and cannot be read to limit those "other similar obligations" to the 10 items preceding that term, all of which are clearly either transaction costs and/or components of price. Indeed, the phrase "and other similar obligations" intimates that "price" under New York's UCC is broad enough to encompass negative equity financing. For instance, just as "finance charges" and "interest" constitute obligations that are paid over and above the vehicle's actual cost (such charges being incurred as part of the overall financing of the vehicle), negative equity is likewise part of the overall price of a new vehicle. Moreover, negative equity constitutes an obligation that fits comfortably within the "other similar obligations" language in Comment 3, particularly in regard to automobile sales because the negative equity from the trade-in is often "rolled in" as part of the overall price of the newer vehicle to facilitate the transaction. It follows, then, that under New York's UCC negative equity constitutes "an obligation . . . incurred as all or part of the price of the collateral."

This broad interpretation of the term "price" to include negative equity furthers New York's policy that the UCC "be liberally construed and applied to promote its underlying purposes and policies," including "the continued expansion of commercial practices through custom, usage and agreement of the parties" [[UCC §1-305]). After all, the parties to the instant transaction agreed that the negative equity from the older vehicle would be "rolled-in" as part of the purchase price of the newer vehicle, not an uncommon practice in the realm of automobile sales (see In re Graupner, 537 F.3d 1295, 1303 [11th Cir. 2008]), thereby furthering the policy of facilitating commercial transactions. Indeed, to exclude negative equity as part of the "price" would serve to hinder commercial practices rather than facilitate them.

Additionally, and not inconsequentially, New York has defined "price" in its Motor Vehicle Retail Installment Sales Act (MVRISA) to include negative equity (see Personal Property Law §301[(6)]). Under the MVRISA, "cash sale price" can "include the unpaid balance of any amount financed under an outstanding motor vehicle loan agreement or motor vehicle retail installment contract or the unpaid portion of the early termination obligation under an outstanding motor vehicle retail lease agreement" (id.).

IV.

Turning to "value given," we likewise disagree with the trustee's contention that negative equity is not related to the acquisition of collateral because it is merely a payoff of an antecedent debt such that it cannot be deemed "value given to enable the debtor to acquire rights in or the use of the collateral if the value is in fact so used" (UCC 9-103[(a)][(2)]).

By paying off the outstanding debt on the trade-in, a lender is giving "value" to the debtor in order to allow, or "enable," the debtor to purchase, or "acquire rights in," the vehicle (see In re Price, 562 F.3d 618, 625 [4th Cir. 2009]). When a lender finances the purchase of a new vehicle and a portion of that financing pays off the negative equity owed on the trade-in (i.e., "the value is in fact so used" [UCC 9-103(a)(2)]), that loan constitutes a purchase-money obligation of the buyer, the purchased vehicle constitutes purchase-money collateral, and the security interest obtained by the lender is a PMSI.

V.

Finally, Comment 3 instructs that the existence of a PMSI also "requires a close nexus between the acquisition of collateral and the secured obligation" (UCC 9-103, Comment 3); and that requirement has plainly been met here. Without a payoff of the trade-in debt, the buyer will generally not be able to consummate the purchase of the newer car, and the financing of the negative equity is thus integral to the completion of the sale (see generally Graupner, 537 F.3d at 1302).

Here, Peaslee's debt to GMAC was incurred at the time of the trade-in, under the same retail installment contract and for the same purpose of purchasing the Grand Am. Simply put, the financing of the negative equity was "inextricably linked to the financing of the new car" (In re Petrocci, 370 B.R. 489, 499 [Bkrtcy. N.D.N.Y. 2007]), thereby satisfying the "close nexus" requirement under the New York UCC.

Accordingly, the certified question should be answered in the affirmative.

NOTE

This question about whether financing "negative equity" in a car loan eliminates the status of the financing creditor as the holder of a "purchase money security interest" has primarily arisen in bankruptcy cases, as the above case indicates. All of the federal Circuits eventually agreed that such a creditor does get acquire a PMSI, until the Ninth Circuit broke ranks, and, over a strong dissent, denied such status if negative equity is part of the loan; see In re Penrod, 636 F.3d 1175 (9th Cir. 2011). Eventually the United States Supreme Court will have to settle the issue since it has the final say as to the meaning of the Bankruptcy Code.

B. Inventory and Livestock

The inventory financier will have a perfected interest in existing and after-acquired inventory, in effect a floating lien over the mass of changing goods available for sale by the debtor to others. If the debtor buys new inventory and gives the seller a purchase money security interest therein, the original financier is seriously hurt if (a) it does not know of the purchase money interest but instead thinks *all* the inventory is collateral in which it has priority, and (b) the purchase money interest is held to prevail over the already perfected interest in after-acquired inventory. To protect the first creditor, §9-324(b) provides a notification procedure that the purchase money secured creditor must follow in order to take the normal priority. See White & Summers §25-4(c); G. Gilmore §29.3.

PROBLEM 76

The Merchants Credit Association held a perfected security interest in the inventory of Harold's Clothing Store. Harold went to a fashion showing in New York and contracted to buy $4,000 worth of new clothes for resale; the seller was to be Madame Belinda's Fashions, Inc., which took a purchase money security interest in the clothes on December 10, the date of sale. Madame Belinda herself wrote the Merchants Credit Association on December 11 and informed the credit manager of the sale. He protested but did nothing. Madame Belinda filed on December 11; the goods were delivered to the store on December 12.

(a) Who has priority?

(b) Would your answer change if Madame Belinda's notice wasn't received until December 13?

(c) If the notice was received on December 11, as above, is it sufficient to permit Madame Belinda to keep selling goods to Harold for an indefinite period thereafter or only for this one transaction? See §9-324(b)(3); T. Gluck & Co., Inc. v. Craig Drake Mfg., Inc., 2013 N.Y. Misc. LEXIS 2384 (N.Y. Sup. Ct. 2013).

How does it help the creditor with the prior perfected interest in the inventory to get notice if that creditor still ends up junior to the purchase money creditor? The Code drafters decided that if the prior creditor has notice, it can take whatever steps are called for to protect its interest. The creditor may not care that the debtor is encumbering the inventory with PMSIs believing that the inventory will sell for enough to make all the creditors happy. Or, if the creditor does care, it can call the loan (or forcefully explain to the debtor the folly of continuing to subordinate the creditor's security interest by such purchases). In any event, alerted by the §9-324(b) notice as to what is going on, the prior creditor must watch out for itself and cannot complain if the purchase money creditor prevails as to the inventory covered by the notice.

Kunkel v. Sprague National Bank

United States Court of Appeals, Eighth Circuit, 1997
128 F.3d 636

JOHN R. GIBSON, Circuit Judge.

In this appeal two creditors, Hoxie Feeders, Inc., and Sprague National Bank, both claim first priority security interests in the same cattle. The district court affirmed the bankruptcy court's summary judgment for Hoxie holding that Hoxie's purchase money security interest had priority over Sprague's earlier security interest in the cattle. Kunkel v. Sprague Nat'l Bank, 198 B.R. 734, 735 (D. Minn. 1996). As an alternative holding for Hoxie, the district court held that Sprague did not have a security interest in the cattle because the debtor lacked "rights in the collateral," as required by the Uniform Commercial Code. Id. at 739. On appeal, Sprague alleges that the district court erred in interpreting and applying various provisions of the UCC governing sales and secured transactions. We reverse the district court's holding that Sprague did not have a security interest in the cattle but affirm its judgment for Hoxie because Hoxie's security interest is senior to Sprague's security interest.

Beginning in 1990, Sprague made a number of loans to John and Dorothy Morken pursuant to certain loan agreements and promissory notes. The Morkens executed a security agreement in favor of Sprague covering their inventory, farm products, equipment, and accounts receivable presently owned or thereafter acquired. Sprague filed with the Kansas Secretary of State a UCC-1 financing statement regarding the collateral located in Kansas. Sprague contends that the Morkens' debt to Sprague currently exceeds $1.9 million.

Hoxie is in the business of financing and selling cattle and operating a feedlot near Hoxie, Kansas. In five transactions between February and April 1994, John Morken purchased interests in approximately 1900 head of cattle from Hoxie. Hoxie financed Morken's cattle purchases. For each transaction, Morken executed a loan agreement and promissory note in favor of Hoxie and a security agreement granting Hoxie a purchase money security interest (PMSI) in the cattle, which were identified by lot number when the documents were executed. In addition, Hoxie was paid $100 per head by either Morken or a company in which he owned an interest. The invoices for the cattle transactions recited that the cattle were shipped to Morken, Hoxie, or both.

Hoxie did not file a UCC-1 financing statement with the Kansas Secretary of State but instead perfected its security interest by taking possession of the cattle pursuant to feedlot agreements between Morken and Hoxie. The feedlot agreements stated that the cattle belonged to "the Party of the First Part," meaning Morken, and acknowledged that Morken had delivered the cattle to Hoxie, although Morken never had physical possession of the cattle. Under the feedlot agreements, the cattle were to remain on Hoxie's feedlot for purposes of care and feeding. The feedlot and loan agreements authorized Hoxie to sell the cattle in its own name for slaughter, to receive direct payment from the packing house, and to deduct the feeding and purchase expenses from the sale proceeds and then remit the balance to Morken. Hoxie's general manager acknowledged, however, that he needed Morken's authority to sell the cattle, and that Morken determined at what price the cattle would be sold. The loan agreements recited that Morken bore all risk as to the profit or loss generated by feeding and selling the cattle.

On June 10, 1994, Morken and his wife filed a Chapter 11 bankruptcy case under Title 11 of the United States Bankruptcy Code. After the bankruptcy case was commenced, Hoxie sold the cattle to Iowa Beef Processors for slaughter. After deducting amounts owed to Hoxie for the care and feeding of the cattle, approximately $550,000 in sale proceeds remained. It is these funds which are subject of competing claims by Sprague and Hoxie.

After the cattle sales, the Morkens' bankruptcy trustee commenced an adversary proceeding in the bankruptcy court to determine which party—Sprague or Hoxie—was entitled to the net sale proceeds. Hoxie and the trustee subsequently reached a settlement. Hoxie and Sprague filed cross-motions for summary judgment regarding entitlement to the funds.

The bankruptcy court granted Hoxie's motion for summary judgment and denied Sprague's motion. It held that both Sprague and Hoxie had perfected security interests in the cattle but Hoxie's interest had first priority under the Kansas UCC, Kan. Stat. Ann. §84-9-312(3) [now §9-324(b) —Eds.]. This UCC provision gives "superpriority" to a creditor with a PMSI in inventory if certain conditions are met, including the requirement that the creditor must send a specified notification to any competing secured party. The competing secured party must receive the notification within five years before the debtor receives possession of the inventory. Although Sprague [*sic*—Hoxie] did not send its statutory notification to Hoxie [*sic*—Sprague] until March 1995, long after the cattle had been sold and slaughtered and the adversary proceeding commenced, the bankruptcy court held that the timing of the notification was nevertheless sufficient because "the Debtor never obtained possession and never will."

Sprague appealed to the district court, which affirmed the bankruptcy court's summary judgment in favor of Hoxie. The district court held that a creditor that has perfected its security interest in inventory through possession, rather than by filing, is not required to provide notification of its PMSI to competing secured creditors to attain "superpriority." According to the district court, the "superpriority" provision presumes that the creditor perfected by filing and that the debtor has possession of the inventory. The court concluded that this presumption was strong evidence that the notification requirement did not apply to a PMSI creditor that perfects by possession. 198 B.R. at 737-738.

As an alternative holding, the district court ruled that Sprague did not even have a security interest in the cattle because delivery of the cattle to Morken had not been completed and, therefore, no "present sale" had occurred. The court explained:

> Under Kansas law, a delivery may be completed although the goods remain in the possession of the seller if the seller's possession "is as an agent or at the request of the buyer under an agreement to store or care for the property, *and nothing further remains to be done by either party to complete the sale.*" Lakeview Gardens, Inc. v. Kansas, 221 Kan. 211, 557 P.2d 1286, 1290-91 (1976) (emphasis added). Here, something further was required, payment to Hoxie under the loan agreement.

Id. at 739. Because the transactions were not a "present sale," the court reasoned that Morken did not have "rights in the collateral," as required by the Kansas UCC, Kan. Stat. Ann. §84-9-203(1)(c), to convey a security interest in the cattle to Sprague. Morken's interest in the cattle was only a "remedial" interest against Hoxie; such an interest was inadequate to support Morken's alleged grant of a security interest to Sprague. Id. at 739-740.

I.

. . . The issues on appeal are: (a) did Sprague have a perfected security interest in the cattle?; (b) did Hoxie have a "super-priority" purchase money security interest which had priority over Sprague's interest in the cattle?; and (c) was Hoxie entitled to the proceeds from the sale of the cattle to IBP?

II.

The district court held that Sprague did not have a security interest in the cattle because Morken did not have "rights in the collateral" sufficient for a security interest to attach. We reverse on this issue.

Under the UCC, a security interest is not enforceable against the debtor or third parties, and does not attach, unless and until the following three requirements are met: (a) either the secured party has possession of the collateral by agreement with the debtor (as is the case here) or the debtor has signed a security agreement; (b) value has been given; and (c) "the debtor has rights in the collateral." Kan. Stat. Ann. §84-9-203(1). Only the last requirement is at issue in this case.

The phrase "rights in the collateral" is not defined in the UCC. "If the debtor owns the collateral outright, it is obvious that the security interest may attach. . . ." B. Clark, The Law of Secured Transactions Under the Uniform Commercial Code ¶2.04[1], at 2-43 (Rev. ed. 1993). It is also well settled, however, that "rights in the collateral" may be an interest less than outright ownership, but must be more than the mere right of possession. See id.; see also 4 J. White & R. Summers, Uniform Commercial Code 126 (4th ed. 1995) ("It follows that almost any 'rights in the collateral' will suffice under 9-203."). The concept of "title" is not determinative. See Kan. Stat. Ann. §84-9-202. "An agreement to purchase can give rise to sufficient rights in the debtor to allow a security interest to attach, regardless of whether the debtor has technically obtained title to the property." United States v. Ables, 739 F. Supp. 1439, 1444 (D. Kan. 1990). Courts consider factors such as the extent of the debtor's control over the property and whether the debtor bears the risk of ownership. See, e.g., Kinetics Tech. Intl. Corp. v. Fourth Natl. Bank, 705 F.2d 396, 399 (10th Cir. 1983) (debtor's control); Chambersburg Trust Co. v. Eichelberger, 588 A.2d 549, 552-553 (Pa. Super. Ct. 1991) (debtor had risk of ownership). The debtor need not have possession in order to pledge the property; the UCC expressly contemplates that the secured party may retain possession of the collateral. See Kan. Stat. Ann. §84-9-305 [now §9-313 — Eds.].

The district court looked to Article 2 of the UCC, which governs sales, to determine whether Morken had "rights in the collateral." It was appropriate to consider Article 2 principles. "In many cases the secured creditor may turn to Article 2 of the UCC to measure the debtor's 'rights' with respect to collateral." Kan. Stat. Ann. §84-9-203 Kan. cmt. (1996). The district court erred, however, in its interpretation of Article 2 and its conclusion that the cattle transactions did not bestow Morken with "rights in the collateral." As will be seen, the cattle were sold and delivered by Hoxie to Morken and Morken thus acquired "rights in the collateral."

A "sale" is the passing of title from buyer to seller for a price. Kan. Stat. Ann. §84-2-106(1). Where delivery of the goods is made without moving the goods, title passes from buyer to seller at the time parties contracted if the goods are identified at that time. Id. §84-2-401(3)(b). When identification occurs, the buyer acquires a "special property" and, importantly, any title interest retained by the seller is limited to the reservation of a security interest. Id. §84-2-401(1). Physical receipt of the goods by the debtor is not necessary; rather, a sale may take place if the goods are constructively delivered to the buyer through delivery to the buyer's agent or bailee. "Delivery is not required for a 'sale' to take place, and the buyer does not even need any right to possession of the goods in question." B. Clark, The Law of Secured Transactions ¶3.04[2], at 3-48.

In this case, the cattle were identified in the invoices and other transaction documents, and the parties agreed that delivery would be made to Morken by delivering the cattle to Hoxie at its feedlot. The feedlot agreements recited that the cattle belonged to Morken. Morken solely bore the risk that the venture would not generate a profit. Hoxie became a bailee of the cattle because it took "delivery of property for some particular purpose on an express or implied contract that after the purpose has been fulfilled the property will be returned to the bailor, or dealt with as he directs." M. Bruenger & Co., Inc. v. Dodge City Truck Stop, Inc., 675 P.2d 864, 868 (Kan. 1984) (quoting 8 C.J.S. Bailments §1). Even though Hoxie had the right to deduct the costs of purchasing and caring for the cattle from the sale proceeds, the parties viewed Morken as owner of the cattle, and Morken determined when cattle would be sold and at what price. In sum, Morken became the owner of an interest in the cattle, and Hoxie's interest in the cattle was therefore limited to that of a bailee and secured party.

In similar circumstances, other courts have held that the debtor acquired "rights in the collateral" even though the debtor received only constructive delivery of the cattle to a feedlot. See, e.g., The Cooperative Fin. Assn., Inc. v. B & J Cattle Co., 937 P.2d 915, 917, 920-921 (Colo. Ct. App. 1997) (debtor acquired rights when cattle were delivered to a third party feedlot; secured creditor prevailed over unpaid cattle seller); O'Brien v. Chandler, 765 P.2d 1165, 1168-1169 (N.M. 1988) (same); see also The Hong Kong & Shanghai Banking Corp. v. HFH USA Corp., 805 F. Supp. 133, 142-143 (W.D.N.Y. 1992) (physical possession of the collateral is not necessary for the debtor to have rights).

Hoxie contends that the sale transactions were not completed because it had the right to stop delivery of the cattle upon discovering Morken's insolvency. See Kan. Stat. Ann. §84-2-702. Hoxie lost its Article 2 right to stop delivery, however, when the cattle were constructively delivered to Morken and Hoxie acknowledged to Morken in the feedlot agreements and other transaction documents that Morken had purchased the cattle and Hoxie was holding them for Morken for feeding and sale purposes. See id. §84-2-705(2)(b); see also Abilene Natl. Bank v. Fina Supply, Inc. (In re Brio Petroleum, Inc.), 800 F.2d 469, 472 (5th Cir. 1986) ("the Code makes clear that a seller's right to stop goods in transit may continue after delivery and until the buyer is in actual, physical or constructive possession of them"); Ramco Steel, Inc. v. Kesler (In re Murdock Mach. & Engr. Co.), 620 F.2d 767, 773 (10th Cir. 1980) (same).

Moreover, in some circumstances, the debtor can transfer greater rights in the collateral to a third party than the debtor himself holds. Thus, "[a] person with voidable title has power to transfer a good title to a good faith purchaser for value." Kan. Stat. Ann. §84-2-403(1). "Purchase" includes taking an interest in property by mortgage, pledge, or lien. Id. §84-1-201(32). Therefore, a secured party such as Sprague can be a "good faith purchaser" which can acquire an interest in the collateral greater than the interest of the debtor, Morken, and superior to the interest of an unpaid seller such as Hoxie. The leading case on this point is Stowers v. Mahon (In re Samuels & Co., Inc.), 526 F.2d 1238 (5th Cir.) (en banc) (per curiam), *cert. denied,* 429 U.S. 834 (1976), pitting a creditor with a security interest in the debtor's cattle against the unpaid seller of the cattle. The court held that the secured creditor's interest was superior to the unpaid seller's interest under UCC §2-403 which "gives good faith purchasers of even fraudulent buyers-transferors greater rights than the defrauded seller can assert." Id. at 1242. As to whether the debtor had "rights in the collateral," the court reasoned that the UCC's priority scheme of elevating a "good faith purchaser" over an unpaid seller necessarily requires that the debtor had "rights in the collateral" even though it had not paid for the cattle:

> The existence of an Article Nine interest presupposes the debtor's having rights in the collateral sufficient to permit attachment, §9-204(a). Therefore, since a defaulting cash buyer has the power to transfer a security interest to a lien creditor, including an Article Nine secured party, the buyer's rights in the property, however marginal, must be sufficient to allow attachment of a lien.

Id. at 1243. Thus, the debtor had "rights in the collateral," even though it had not paid the seller for those cattle.

In summary, when the dust had settled after each of the five cattle transactions: (a) a sale had occurred; (b) Hoxie had constructively delivered the cattle to Morken and had possession of the cattle on Morken's behalf; (c) Morken had title to and owned the cattle; (d) the only interest retained by Hoxie in the cattle was a security interest and interest as bailee; (e) Hoxie's UCC Article 2 remedy of refusing to deliver the cattle had been cut off; and (f) Morken had "rights in the collateral" sufficient for Sprague's security interest to attach. Accordingly, we hold that Sprague had a perfected security interest in the cattle and reverse the district court on this issue.

III.

Having determined that Sprague held a perfected security interest in the cattle, we now turn to the priority dispute between the two secured creditors, Sprague and Hoxie. We hold that Hoxie attained purchase money security interest "superpriority" under the Kansas UCC, Kan. Stat. Ann. §84-9-312(3), and has priority over Sprague's interest.

Section 9-312 of the UCC sets forth rules for determining priorities among conflicting security interests in the same collateral. See Kan. Stat. Ann. §84-9-312. The general priority scheme is that the first creditor to perfect its security interest beats later perfected security interests. See Kan. Stat. Ann. §84-9-312(5)(a). There is an important exception to this "first-to-perfect" rule for a purchase money security interest. A PMSI in inventory has "superpriority" over an earlier perfected interest if: (a) the PMSI is perfected at the time the debtor receives possession of the inventory; (b) the PMSI creditor gives written notification to all holders of competing security interests which had UCC-1 financing statements on file when the PMSI creditor filed its UCC-1; (c) the competing secured creditor receives the notification within five years before the debtor receives possession of the inventory; and (d) the notification states "that the person giving the notice has or expects to acquire a purchase money security interest in inventory of the debtor, describing such inventory by item or type." Id. §84-9-312(3).

Sprague contends that the §84-9-312(3)'s "superpriority" status cannot be attained by a creditor that has perfected its security interest in inventory by possession, rather than by filing a UCC-1 financing statement. It emphasizes language in this UCC section and its commentary that refers to perfection by filing and the debtor receiving possession of the inventory. See Kan. Stat. Ann. §84-9-312(3) & Official UCC cmt. 3. We observe, however, that there is no language expressly excluding a creditor that has perfected by possession from taking advantage of this UCC section. More importantly, there is no sound policy reason to distinguish between perfection by filing and possession, and to provide the former, but not the latter, the opportunity to attain "superpriority." The common law of pledge—perfection by possession—predates, and was incorporated by, the UCC. In addition, pre-UCC law afforded special priority to purchase money security interests, and this has been carried over into the UCC. See B. Clark, The Law of Secured Transactions ¶3.09[1], at 3-100 ("the purchase money priority . . . breaks up what would otherwise be a complete monopoly on the debtor's collateral"). Thus, the UCC, as it stands today, does not reflect any intent to penalize a PMSI creditor by depriving it of the opportunity to attain "superpriority" simply because of its means of perfection.

We believe that there is a more logical explanation for UCC §9-312(3)'s contemplation that a creditor with a security interest in inventory would likely perfect by filing rather than possession. Inventory are goods "held for immediate or ultimate sale." Kan. Stat. Ann. §84-9-109 [now §9-102(a)(48) —Eds.] & Official UCC cmt. 3. The debtor typically needs its inventory to run its business and is not in a position to allow a third party, such as its lender, to possess the inventory. Therefore, the situation here—in which the creditor has possession of the inventory—will arise only rarely. The fact that the "superpriority" provision of §84-9-312(3) does not expressly refer to perfection by possession does not establish that its scope is limited to perfection by filing. The UCC was not drafted to address every possible factual situation, but, rather, was "intentionally designed to allow room to grow," Kan. Stat. Ann. §84-1-102 Kan. cmt. 1 (1996), and to accommodate the "expansion of commercial practices." Id. Official UCC cmt. 1.

Having concluded that it was possible for Hoxie to use §84-9-312(3) to attain "superpriority," we must now decide whether it did so by fulfilling the statutory requirements. The only requirement at issue here is the timing of Hoxie's PMSI notice, which was received after the cattle were sold and slaughtered and this litigation was commenced. We believe that this issue turns on the meaning of "possession" in the context of §84-9-312(3). As explained above, the UCC treats constructive possession as analogous to actual possession in certain circumstances. If Morken's constructive possession triggered the notification requirement, then Hoxie's notification was untimely because Sprague received the notification after Morken received constructive possession of the cattle. On the other hand, if "possession" is limited to actual possession, Hoxie's notice was timely because Sprague received it before Morken could ever receive actual possession.

Professor Grant Gilmore, the primary drafter of UCC Article 9, provides guidance on the meaning of "receives possession" in §84-9-312(3). Professor Gilmore's treatise Security Interests in Personal Property has been described as "an invaluable source of legislative intent because he is the fountainhead in this area." B. Clark, The Law of Secured Transactions ¶1.01[2][c], at 1-8. In that treatise, Professor Gilmore states that "'[r]eceives possession' is evidently meant to refer to the moment when the goods are physically delivered at the debtor's place of business—not to the possibility of the debtor's acquiring rights in the goods at an earlier point by identification or appropriation to the contract or by shipment under a term under which the debtor bears the risk." II G. Gilmore, Security Interests in Personal Property §29.3, at 787 (1965). In light of Professor Gilmore's comments, we interpret UCC §9-312(3)'s notification requirement to be triggered by actual possession of the inventory by the debtor. Because Sprague received Hoxie's notification within five years before Morken could have received actual possession, that notification was timely.

Sprague complains that the purpose of §84-9-312(3) is frustrated by granting "superpriority" to a PMSI without requiring pre-perfection notification to prior filed secured creditors. It contends that debtors on the brink of insolvency will now have the motive to create "secret liens" to the detriment of prior perfected secured creditors. The notification requirement, however, was not intended to allow other secured creditors veto power over the extension of new credit because the notification does not have to be given before the PMSI is acquired. The notification is required to state "that the person giving the notice *has* or expects to acquire a purchase money security interest in inventory of the debtor, describing such inventory by item or type." Kan. Stat. Ann. §84-9-312(3)(d) (emphasis added). Thus, the PMSI creditor can wait to notify competing secured creditors after it has acquired and perfected its security interest. The Official UCC Comment explains that the notification protects the inventory financier from making additional advances to the debtor in the mistaken belief that it is secured by inventory which, in fact, has been financed by a third party with a PMSI in that inventory. If the inventory financier "has received notification, he will presumably not make an advance; if he has not received notification (or if the other interest does not qualify as a purchase money interest), any advance he may make will have priority." Kan. Stat. Ann. §84-9-312 & Official UCC cmt. 3.

Our holding is consistent with this purpose in the context of this case. Sprague did not extend further credit in reliance on the cattle serving as its collateral; in fact, Sprague had not made any loans to Morken since at least a year before Morken acquired an interest in these particular cattle. We stop short, however, of holding, as did the district court, that a PMSI creditor that perfects by possession of inventory does not ever have to send a statutory notification. It is not necessary to reach that issue because Hoxie timely sent its statutory notification. A different fact pattern in another case might justify a different conclusion. See Scallop Petroleum Co. v. Banque Trad-Credit Lyonnais, 690 F. Supp. 184, 192 (S.D.N.Y. 1988) (PMSI creditor was required to send notification even though debtor never had possession of the inventory). . . .

[The court also concluded that Hoxie prevailed as to the proceeds of the sale.]

In conclusion, we reverse the district court's holding that Sprague did not have a security interest in the cattle, but affirm its judgment that Hoxie's security interest has priority over Sprague's security interest.

This case should continue to be good law even after the 1999 revision was adopted. Official Comment 5 to §9-324 states that if "the debtor never receives possession, the five-year period never begins, and the purchase-money security interest has priority even if notification is not given."

The revised version of Article 9 extends the superpriority procedure for gaining a PMSI security interest in inventory to a PMSI in the debtor's livestock (see §9-324(d)), and, in Appendix II to the 1999 revision, gives the states the option to use the same procedure for creditors taking a PMSI in the debtor's future crops (there called a *production money security interest*).

PROBLEM 77

Hans Racing Equipment bought much of its inventory from Standard Auto Wholesales, Inc., which always took a purchase money security interest in the goods sold to Hans and which filed a financing statement on the same day. Hans also borrowed money from the Matching Dishes National Bank (MDNB) to finance the purchase of inventory from wholesalers, part of which was used to pay off Standard Auto. MDNB filed a financing statement, claiming a security interest in Hans's inventory. On March 28, Hans contracted to buy $3,000 in goods from Standard, making a down payment of $1,500 and giving Standard a purchase money security interest in the goods for the rest. On that same day, he borrowed the $1,500 down payment from MDNB and also gave the bank a purchase money security interest in the same goods. Both creditors knew of the other, so they both sent written notice to each other. The goods were delivered to Hans on April 2. Which creditor has priority? See §9-324(g) and its Official Comment 13 (termed by some, "vendor beats lender").

Similar problems arise, of course, with consignments. Even true consignors hoping to prevail over perfected interests in the inventory of the consignee must follow a notification procedure of this type. See §9-103(d) and Example 3 in Official Comment 3 of §9-319.

PROBLEM 78

Barbara Shipek was pleased and flattered when Tim Isle, owner of Isle's Fine Art Works, asked her if he could exhibit and sell some of her pottery. She gave him five of her favorite pieces. The next day she took a party of friends down to the store to see the display and was astounded to learn that Octopus National Bank (ONB), which had a perfected floating lien on the store's inventory, had foreclosed and seized everything in the store, including Barb's pottery. Can ONB do this to her? Murphy v. Southtrust Bank of Ala., 611 So. 2d 269 (Ala. 1992).

III.   *CONTROL AND PRIORITY*

The 1999 revision of Article 9 created the idea of *control* as a means of perfection. White & Summers explain the basic concept best by telling us that "'control' is to intangibles as 'possession' is to goods"; White & Summers §23-4. Taking the steps for control, described below, gives the world some notice at least that the creditor has legal rights in the intangible property that must be respected.

A. *Control over Investment Property*

The 1994 version of Article 8, concerning investment securities, dealt not only with traditional stocks and bonds represented by actual pieces of paper (*certificated securities;* see §8-102(a)(4)), and similar rights against the issuing corporation that are merely registered in a computer at that corporation (*uncertificated securities;* see §8-102(a)(18)), but also with the widespread practice of holding securities in an account with a stockbroker, with the investor's rights reflected merely by a bookkeeping entry in the stockbroker's records (called a *securities entitlement;* see §8-102(a)(17)).[12] Article 9 lumps all these methods of holding securities, along with similar rights in commodity contracts and accounts, and names them *investment property.* Read §9-102(a)(49).

How is a security interest taken in investment property? There are two ways: the filing of a financing statement and/or the taking of *control* over the investment property, with the latter trumping the former (that is, a secured party who has control has priority over one who has merely filed; see §9-328(1)). *Control* is defined in §8-106, with similar rules for commodity contracts in §9-106(b). Generally, one has control over a certificated security by taking delivery of it along with any necessary indorsements; §§8-106(a), (b), and 8-301(a). The same is true of uncertificated securities (see §8-106(c)), only here *delivery* is artificially defined in §8-301(b) as making sure that the secured party is registered as the stock owner in the records of the issuing corporation. In the context of indirect holding, *control* requires that the secured party take steps to make sure that it can reach the rights of the debtor in the event that it needs to foreclose, as is illustrated in the following Problem.

PROBLEM 79

Mr. Goldbury instructed his stockbroker, Bing, Bong & Bell (BB&B) to buy 100 shares of Utopia, Ltd., stock and place it in his account at BB&B. Bing, Bong & Bell bought the shares and kept them in the account it held at Clearing Corporation but marked its records to indicate that Mr. Goldbury was really the owner of this number of shares of the stock. In this case, Article 8 would deem Mr. Goldbury an *entitlement holder* who has a *securities entitlement* in

---

12. The stockbroker may not itself have possession of the actual certificates either, but may only have rights to an account it carries with a clearing corporation or bank, where the actual certificates are physically located. In this case the broker has a security entitlement in the latter account, and its rights pass through to its investor free of the claims of most creditors of either upper-tiered party; see §8-503(a).

a *security account* with a *securities intermediary;* see §8-102, which defines all these terms (*securities account* is in §8-501(a)). Mr. Goldbury went to Octopus National Bank (ONB) and asked to borrow money using the above 100 shares as collateral. You are the counsel for ONB and are in charge of making sure that the bank's security interest is perfected, which means getting "control" over the securities entitlement. Look at §8-106(d) and its Official Comment 4, and advise the bank. Which of the possible methods is the safest for your client?

Then answer these two questions:

(a) If another creditor also gets control over the rights to the 100 shares, which has priority? See §9-328(2).

(b) If Mr. Goldbury borrows money from BB&B after ONB has control and grants BB&B a security interest in all stocks held in his account with them, is BB&B's security interest superior to ONB's? See §9-328(3) and Official Comment 4, Example 5.

For all these issues of control and perfection of security interests in investment property, the Official Comments to both §§8-106 and 9-328 contain a wealth of information, including Examples aplenty, to which you are referred in the event of an actual legal dispute.

B. Control over Deposit Accounts

Similar rules govern the use of bank accounts as collateral. Prior to the 1999 revision of Article 9, it was unclear whether a bank account could stand as collateral for debts owed to anyone other than the bank in which the account was maintained (and, subject to non-uniform amendments, the prior version of Article 9 excluded deposit accounts from its scope). The revision allows a perfected security interest in such accounts by a creditor obtaining control over the account. Consumer accounts may not be used as collateral for consumer debts (though they could be so used for non-consumer debts); see White & Summers §22-9.

PROBLEM 80

Computer World, Inc., desires to borrow money from Investment Bank of America, which will grant it a revolving line of credit, secured in part by the bank account that Computer World maintains at Last National Bank. You are the attorney for Investment Bank of America. Advise the bank how it can perfect its security interest in this bank account and which of the methods of control specified in §9-104 would be the safest form of security. If Computer

World later borrows money from Last National Bank and grants the bank a security interest in the account carried there, would Last National have priority over your client? See §9-327(3) and (4).

C.   *Control over Letters of Credit Rights*

Letters of credit (the subject of Article 5 of the Uniform Commercial Code) are an increasingly popular means of financing various transactions. If one party does not trust the other to make payment at an agreed upon time, that party may require that the payment be made directly by a bank of good repute. If this is done, the bank that is persuaded to do so will issue a letter of credit to the person to whom payment is to be made (called the *beneficiary*) specifying the circumstances under which the bank will honor drafts drawn on it by that person. The other party to the transaction who persuades the bank to issue the letter of credit (the bank's customer) is called the *applicant*. The beneficiary may use its rights under the letter of credit as collateral for a different loan with a different creditor, who will then want to perfect its security interest in the rights represented by the letter of credit.

PROBLEM 81

Computer World agreed to sell 10,000 computers to Football University for the sum of $25,000, with Football University agreeing to obtain a letter of credit for this amount in favor of the seller. Shortly thereafter Computer World received a letter of credit from Octopus National Bank (ONB) naming Computer World as the beneficiary and stating that it would honor drafts drawn on the bank in favor of Computer World for the amount of $25,000 on presentation of an invoice showing shipment of the computers to the university by September 25 of that year. Computer World comes to you, its attorney, in February of the same year with the following problem. It needs to borrow $10,000 from some lender in order to finance the construction of the computers by the required deadline. It wants to use the letter of credit as collateral for this loan. How can the new lender obtain a perfected interest in the rights represented by the letter of credit? See §9-107. When Computer World asked ONB if it would agree to an assignment of the proceeds of the letter of credit to Computer World's lender, the bank not only refused but pointed to clauses in the letter of credit that provided a number of things: (1) the right of Computer World to draw drafts on the bank was not transferable; and (2) the letter of credit specifically forbade the beneficiary (Computer World) the right to make an assignment of the proceeds of the letter of credit and *voided* the letter of credit if the beneficiary made such an assignment without the bank's consent.

What can Computer World tell potential lenders who might be willing to loan it money if the letter of credit rights could be used as collateral? Remember, as you read the cited sections that follow, that the obligation from Football University to Computer World is an *account*. See §§5-114, 9-308(d), 9-102(a)(78), 9-409, and the latter's Official Comments.

IV. BUYERS

Section 9-201(a) states what White & Summers called Article 9's "Golden Rule" (White & Summers §24-12 (3d ed. 1998)):

Except as otherwise provided by the Uniform Commercial Code, a security agreement is effective according to its terms between the parties, against purchasers of the collateral and against creditors.

Section 9-320(a) is one of the sections that fit in the "except" language of §9-201; so is §9-317(b), which lists other buyers who win out over the *unperfected* secured party in some circumstances. A corollary to §9-201's "Golden Rule" is §9-315(a)(1):

(a) Except as otherwise provided in this article and in Section 2-403(2):
(1) a security interest or agricultural lien continues in collateral notwithstanding sale, lease, license, exchange, or other disposition thereof unless the secured party authorized the disposition free of the security interest or agricultural lien; . . .

PROBLEM 82

Betty Consumer bought a television set from Distortion TV, Inc., a retail store. A month later, Distortion went bankrupt, and a minor functionary from the Octopus National Bank (ONB) showed up on her stoop and asked her to turn over the set. He explained that ONB held a perfected security interest in all of Distortion's inventory and that since Distortion had not paid off its debts to ONB, the bank was repossessing.

(a) What should Ms. Consumer tell the bank's flunky? See §9-320(a).

(b) Would it matter if she had known that ONB had a perfected security interest in Distortion's inventory? See White & Summers §25-8(b); Official Comment 3 to §9-320.

(c) Would it matter if she bought at a "Liquidation Sale" and was informed by the store's owner that the store planned to file a bankruptcy petition the following week? See In re Fritz-Mair Mfg. Co., 16 Bankr. 417 (Bankr. N.D. Tex. 1982).

(d) What if Ms. Consumer had put the TV on "layaway" and had paid 50 percent of the price but permitted Distortion to keep the TV (she signed a contract obligating herself to pay the balance), and then the store filed for bankruptcy? Read §2-502 and its Official Comments. The Bankruptcy Code also offers such consumers some relief in §507(a)(7), which gives layaway buyers a priority payment up to the amount of $2,775 per individual.

International Harvester Co. v. Glendenning

Texas Supreme Court, 1974
505 S.W.2d 320

WILLIAMS, C.J.

This appeal is from a take nothing judgment in a suit to recover damages for wrongful conversion of three tractors.

International Harvester Company and International Harvester Credit Corporation (both hereinafter referred to as International) brought this action against Don Glendenning in which it was alleged that International was the holder of a duly perfected security interest in three new International Harvester tractors; that such security agreements had been executed in favor of International by Jack L. Barnes, doing business as Barnes Equipment Company, an International Harvester dealer; that Barnes and Glendenning had entered into a fraudulent conspiracy wherein Glendenning had wrongfully purchased the three tractors from Barnes; that Glendenning was not a buyer in the ordinary course of business; that he did not act in a commercially reasonable manner and did not act honestly, therefore taking the tractors subject to International's security interest. It was further alleged that Barnes and Glendenning had wrongfully conspired to convert the ownership of the tractors and to deprive International, by fraud and deceit, of its ownership of the tractors by virtue of their security interest therein in that (1) Glendenning acquiesced in falsifying a retail order form so that it was made to indicate receipt of $16,000 in cash and the trade-in of two used tractors allegedly worth a total of $8,700, while in fact both Glendenning and Barnes knew that Glendenning had only paid the sum of $16,000 in cash, a sum far below the market value of the tractors; (2) Glendenning, in the furtherance of the conspiracy and unlawful conversion, represented to a representative of International that he, Glendenning, had, in fact, traded certain used tractors to Barnes, which was untrue; and (3) Glendenning removed the new tractors in which International had a security interest to the State of Louisiana where he sold the same and converted the proceeds to his own use and benefit. International sought damages in the sum of

$24,049.99 which was alleged to be the reasonable value of the tractors on the date of conversion.

Glendenning answered by a general denial and with the special defense to the effect that he purchased the tractors in the ordinary course of business and that such purchase was made in good faith and without any knowledge of any security interest held by International. The court submitted the case to the jury on one special issue:

> Do you find from a preponderance of the evidence that on the time and occasion in question, the defendant, Don Glendenning, was a buyer in the ordinary course of business?

In connection with this issue the court instructed the jury that the term "buyer in ordinary course of business" means "a person who in good faith and without knowledge that the sale to him is in violation of the ownership rights or security interest of the third party in the goods buys in the ordinary course from a person in the business of selling goods of that kind."

The court instructed the jury that the term "good faith" means "honesty in fact in the conduct or transaction concerned."

The jury answered the special issue "Yes." . . .

[The court quoted §§9-307(1) (the predecessor to §9-320(a)), 1-201(b)(9), and 1-201(b)(19) and noted that "whether a sale is in the ordinary course of business is a mixed question of law and fact."]

The material testimony presented to the court and jury may be summarized, as follows:

At the time of the trial of this case appellee Glendenning was a farmer in Collin County. He described himself as being not only a farmer but a trader. He said that he frequently traded tractors and other farm equipment as well as anything else from which he could make a profit. He has had almost twenty years' experience in the business of buying and selling farm tractors. In the early 1950s he owned an International Harvester dealership in Frisco, Collin County, Texas. From 1956 to 1960 he was a salesman for International Harvester. After leaving International he began trading farm equipment of his own, using some of the implements on his own farm and holding others strictly for resale. For many years he had been familiar with International Harvester's custom of "floor-planning" tractors and other farm equipment. By this plan International would supply tractors and other equipment to the dealers who, in turn, would give International a note and security agreement to protect International in its investment. When a dealer sold a piece of equipment from the floor he would pay International the amount due. He also testified that he knew that when used tractors were taken as trade-ins by International Harvester dealers such used tractors were also mortgaged or covered by the security agreement to International. He admitted that

International Harvester always kept close tabs to see what was wrong with the used tractors and that International always wanted to know what its dealers traded for in connection with new equipment sales. Glendenning acknowledged that any false information contained on a retail order form would provide incorrect information concerning the transactions to International Harvester, or any other lender.

Glendenning said that he had known Jack L. Barnes, an International Harvester dealer, for two or three years and during that time he had bought several tractors from him. In the early part of July 1971 Barnes, and Joe Willard, another friend, came to his home in Collin County and talked to him about buying some tractors. He said that Barnes had eight tractors to sell but that he was only interested in buying three of the machines. Barnes described the tractors and told Glendenning that he wanted $18,500 for the three. Glendenning declined that offer but told Barnes that he would give $16,000 cash for the three. Barnes accepted the offer.

At the time of this transaction Glendenning knew that the three tractors were reasonably worth $22,500. Willard went to Vernon, Texas, and got the tractors and delivered them to Mr. Glendenning's home. Glendenning asked Willard to bring him a bill of sale when he returned with the tractors. Willard received from Barnes an instrument entitled "Retail Order Form" dated July 5, 1971, which recited that Glendenning had purchased from Barnes three tractors for the total price of $24,700 with a cash payment of $16,000 leaving a balance of $8,700. The instrument recited that Glendenning had traded in four tractors with values totaling $8,700 so that the total consideration of $24,700 was shown to have been paid.

Glendenning said that the next day Barnes came to his home to get payment for the tractors. At that time Glendenning requested a "bill of sale" and he watched Barnes fill in another retail order form similar to the one that he had obtained from Willard the day before. This order form stated that Glendenning had traded in four tractors worth $8,700 in addition to payment of $16,000 in cash making a total purchase of $24,700. After Barnes had completed filling out this form and signed the same Glendenning said that he put his signature on the instrument also. He then gave Barnes $16,000.

Concerning the contents of the retail order form Glendenning said that at the time Barnes filled in the blanks indicating that Glendenning was trading in four tractors he knew that he was not trading anything and that he did not question Barnes about the trade-in information contained in the form. He admitted that he did not ask Barnes whether the tractors which he purchased were free and clear nor did he call International to determine whether or not such company had a mortgage on the tractors. Glendenning admitted that he knew that the information contained in the printed form concerning trade-ins and total consideration for the sale of the three new tractors was false; that he knew of this falsification when he signed the order form; and that he also knew that such falsification would mislead any creditors relying on the document such as a dealer, a manufacturer or a bank lending money with the equipment as collateral. He admitted that at the time of the transaction in question Barnes was probably "trying to come out even" or that he did it to make his books balance. Glendenning admitted that he was suspicious of the manner in which Barnes prepared the order form and confessed that his actions amounted to dishonesty. He said that to his knowledge he had never before signed an order form with false trade-ins. He admitted that such action was "unusual."

A few days after the transaction a Mr. McKinney, collection manager for International Harvester Company, and a representative of International Harvester Credit Corporation, telephoned Glendenning concerning the transaction in question. In that conversation Glendenning told McKinney that he had traded four tractors to Barnes in addition to paying $16,000 cash for the three new International tractors. Glendenning testified that he knew that he had lied to Mr. McKinney concerning the trade-ins and that such oral misrepresentation or lie was dishonest.

After receiving the tractors Glendenning removed them to a barn near Alexandria, Louisiana, although it was his usual practice to place equipment on his own premises or at another dealer's place of business. He subsequently sold the three tractors in Louisiana.

As a part of his direct examination Glendenning testified that he considered the deal to be a purchase of three tractors for $16,000; that he had no side agreement with Barnes; that he thought he was making a good deal; and that he was acting in good faith.

At the very beginning of this trial appellee Glendenning confessed the validity of appellant's cause of action against him based upon fraud, conspiracy and conversion, but sought to evade legal liability by assuming, pursuant to Tex. R. Civ. P. 266, the burden of going forward and establishing his sole defense that he was a buyer in ordinary course of business within the meaning of §9.307(a) (1968). This assumption carried with it the additional burden of establishing by competent evidence that Glendenning acted in good faith and without knowledge that the sale to him was in violation of the ownership rights or security interest of a third party. Good faith, as the court correctly charged the jury, means honesty in fact in the conduct or transaction concerned. In an effort to establish this affirmative defense and thereby evade liability, appellee Glendenning testified on direct examination with the broad conclusory statement that he had acted in good faith. However, this subjective and conclusory statement was immediately annihilated by factual evidence falling from the lips of Glendenning himself.

Appellee Glendenning's own testimony immediately removes him from the category of an innocent Collin County farmer who seeks to purchase one or more tractors in the ordinary course of business. By his own testimony he has had many years of experience as a tractor dealer, a salesman and one of the most active traders of farm equipment in Collin County. Based upon this experience he is knowledgeable in the very nature of business done by International by "floor-planning" its equipment. With all of this knowledge and information in his possession he purchased the equipment for considerably less than its value, made no investigation of International's security interest, acquiesced in the falsification of the retail order form showing non-existent trade-ins, and misrepresented the particulars of the transaction to International's representative by stating that there were, in fact, trade-ins. He confesses that his actions were dishonest.

Thus it is evident to us that Glendenning's own testimony, which is the only material testimony offered, is entirely devoid of honesty in fact and completely negates his contention that he was a buyer in the ordinary course of business within the meaning of the Texas Business & Commerce Code.

While we have been unable to find any Texas authorities decided under this specific provision of the Business & Commerce Code a recent Uniform Commercial Code release notes that the good faith requirement was added "to make it clear that one who buys dishonestly is not within the definition. The 'without knowledge' addition spells out one important type of dishonesty." UCC Release No. 27-1973, 6 Bender's Uniform Commercial Code Service §1-201 at 1-29 (1965).

The complete picture revealed by all of the material testimony in this case reveals a definite pattern of lies, deceit, dishonesty and bad faith. We find no competent evidence in this record to support the jury's answer to the special issue submitted and therefore the same should have been set aside and disregarded by the trial court. . . .

————————

Even where the Code is silent about a "good faith" requirement, §1-304 imposes one. There is a growing body of UCC law that says that good faith is a condition precedent to any protection under the statute. "Bad faith," a phrase not defined in the Code, can alter the usual Article 9 priorities. See Limor Diamonds, Inc. v. D'Oro by Christopher Michael, Inc., 558 F. Supp. 709 (S.D.N.Y. 1983).

PROBLEM 83

Deering Milliken was a textile manufacturer. It routinely sold textiles on credit to Mill Fabrics, a firm that finished the textiles into dyed and patterned fabrics. It was Mill Fabrics' practice to resell the fabrics to Tanbro Fabrics, a wholesaler. While the textiles were still in Deering's warehouse, Mill Fabrics contracted to buy them from Deering, signing a security agreement to that effect and giving Deering a financing statement, which it duly filed. In turn, Mill Fabrics sold the textiles to Tanbro, which paid Mill Fabrics for them, but delayed taking delivery for a few weeks, so that the fabrics remained in Deering's possession. Deals of this kind were common in the textile industry, and all parties knew of the others' interest. Unfortunately, Mill Fabrics became insolvent and never paid Deering for the textiles, and Deering therefore refused to deliver them to Tanbro. The latter sued. Who should prevail? See §9-320(e) and its Official Comment 8.

In re Western Iowa Limestone, Inc.

United States Court of Appeals, Eighth Circuit, 2008
538 F.3d 858

HANSEN, Circuit Judge.

I.

Western Iowa Limestone, Inc. (WIL) owned several quarries throughout Iowa, and it began marketing agricultural lime as a by-product of its operations in 2004. It marketed the ag lime through six fertilizer and chemical dealers, who resold the ag lime at retail. In January 2005, one of WIL's dealers, Independent Inputs, LLC, purchased 5,000 tons of ag lime from WIL, and in February 2005, two other dealers, Paul Leinen and Leinen, Inc. (collectively "Leinen" and hereinafter, together with Independent Inputs, referred to as "Dealers"), purchased a total of 13,400 tons of ag lime. The Dealers paid for the ag lime at the time of the purchases, and each of the bills of sale noted that the ag lime would remain at the quarry until the Dealers sold the ag lime to their ultimate customers. This arrangement was beneficial to WIL, which also provided trucking services. WIL maintained its ag lime in a single fungible pile on its premises. The ag lime that the Dealers purchased likewise remained in the fungible pile until resold to their customers and removed from the premises.

WIL filed a petition under Chapter 11 of the Bankruptcy Code on December 12, 2005. At that time, Independent Inputs had resold and removed 416 tons of ag lime from WIL's premises, and Leinen had removed 1,406 tons. United Bank of Iowa is WIL's largest secured creditor, and it had a security interest in all of WIL's assets, including its inventory, accounts receivable, and proceeds, to secure a $6 million loan. The ag lime remaining on WIL's premises was sold in the bankruptcy proceedings as part of its inventory, and the Dealers filed a joint objection to the proposed distributions from the sale of the inventory, claiming priority over United Bank as buyers in the ordinary course of business (BIOC) to the extent of the value of the ag lime they had purchased but had not yet removed from WIL's premises. Independent Inputs' claim was for $35,522, and Leinen's claims were for $89,508.

The bankruptcy court initially determined that the Dealers failed to establish BIOC status under Iowa law because they did not take physical possession of the ag lime or have a right to recover the goods under Article 2 of the Iowa Uniform Commercial Code (Iowa UCC) as required by Iowa Code §554.1201(9). On a motion to alter or amend, the bankruptcy court reversed itself, concluding that the Dealers had taken constructive possession of the ag lime and had satisfied the requirements for BIOC status under §554.1201(9). United Bank appealed, and the BAP reversed, concluding that the Dealers did not constructively possess the ag lime under Iowa law for purposes of a priority contest between a secured creditor and a purchaser. Because the BAP concluded that the Dealers did not have constructive possession of the ag lime, it avoided the separate issue of whether constructive possession satisfies the requirement of "tak[ing] possession" contained in §554.1201(9). The Dealers appeal from the BAP's decision.

II. . . .

Under Iowa's UCC law, "a buyer in ordinary course of business . . . takes free of a security interest created by the buyer's seller, even if the security interest is perfected and the buyer knows of its existence." Iowa Code §554.9320(1). Thus, the Dealers take free of United Bank's prior security interest if they meet the definition of a BIOC. "Buyer in ordinary course of business" is defined by the Iowa UCC as

> a person that buys goods in good faith, without knowledge that the sale violates the rights of another person in the goods, and in the ordinary course from a person . . . in the business of selling goods of that kind. A person buys goods in the ordinary course if the sale to the person comports with the usual or customary practices in the kind of business in which the seller is engaged or with the seller's own usual or customary practices. . . . Only a buyer that takes possession of the goods or has a right to recover the goods from the seller under Article 2 may be a buyer in ordinary course of business. "Buyer in ordinary course of business" does not include a person that acquires goods in a transfer in bulk or as security for or in total or partial satisfaction of a money debt.

Iowa Code §554.1201(9).

Relevant to this appeal, BIOC status requires that the sale comport with the usual or customary practices for the kind of business involved and that the buyer take possession of the goods. (The Dealers do not claim that they had a right to recover under Article 2.) We begin with the central issue of this case—that is, whether a buyer who purchases fungible goods from a seller but leaves the goods at the seller's premises satisfies the requirement that the buyer "take[] possession of the goods." Id. We must determine whether constructive possession is within the meaning of the statute, and if so, whether the circumstances of this case amount to constructive possession sufficient to confer BIOC status.

The penultimate sentence of the definition of a BIOC requires that the buyer either "take[] possession" or "ha[ve] a right to recover the goods from the seller under Article 2." Id. The requirement was added to the Uniform Commercial Code (UCC) in 1999, and the Iowa legislature adopted the revised UCC provision verbatim in 2000. The term "possession" is not defined in the Iowa UCC, and §554.1201(9) does not elaborate on what is meant by "tak[ing] possession." Iowa courts "determine legislative intent from the words chosen by the legislature. . . . Absent a statutory definition or an established meaning in the law, words in the statute are given their ordinary and common meaning by considering the context within which they are used." City of Waterloo v. Bainbridge, 749 N.W.2d 245, 248 (Iowa 2008) (internal marks omitted). Iowa courts look beyond the statute's express terms only when the language is ambiguous. "A statute . . . is ambiguous if reasonable minds could differ or be uncertain as to the meaning of the statute." Id. Language that is "plain, clear, and susceptible to only one meaning" is unambiguous. Id.

Section 554.1201(9) refers only to "possession," not to "physical possession" or "constructive possession." In the context of §554.1201(9), both physical possession and constructive possession are plausible meanings of the bare term "possession," and we conclude that the term is ambiguous as used in §554.1201(9). See First Nat'l Bank in Lenox v. Lamoni Livestock Sales Co., 417 N.W.2d 443, 447 (Iowa 1987) ("'Ambiguity in the word *possession* dates from the introduction into the law of the concept of *constructive possession.*'" (quoting Jacobson v. Aetna Cas. & Sur. Co., 233 Minn. 383, 46 N.W.2d 868, 871 (Minn. 1951)). We therefore apply the rules of statutory interpretation to ascertain the Iowa legislature's intent in requiring a buyer to take possession before being considered a BIOC.

In interpreting a statute, the Supreme Court of Iowa looks to the common law to construe undefined terms. See *Lamoni Livestock Sales,* 417 N.W. 2d at 447-48; S & S, Inc. v. Meyer, 478 N.W.2d 857, 860 (Iowa Ct. App. 1991) ("Unless displaced by the UCC, . . . the common law supplement[s] its provisions."). In *Lamoni Livestock Sales,* the court interpreted the term "possession" in the context of comment 4 to Iowa UCC §554.9109, which distinguished between the characterization of goods as farm products or inventory depending on whether the goods were "in the possession of a debtor engaged in farming operations" or had "come[] into the possession of a marketing agency."

Iowa Code §554.9109, cmt. 4 (1987). The court relied on the concept of constructive possession to hold that livestock in the physical possession of a sale barn (or marketing agency) was nonetheless constructively possessed by the farmer who placed the livestock with the sale barn because the farmer retained ownership of the livestock. *Lamoni Livestock Sales,* 417 N.W.2d at 448. The Supreme Court of Iowa noted that possession is not defined in the UCC and looked to property law concepts for an analogy. Id. at 447-48; see also Iowa Code §554.9313, cmt. 3 (recognizing that "possession" is not defined and "adopt[ing] the general concept as it developed under former Article 9," which applied the principles of agency).

There is no reason to believe without some explicit indication that Iowa courts would construe the undefined term "possession" to include constructive possession in some sections of the Iowa UCC and not in others. See Iowa Code §554.1103(2) ("Unless displaced by the particular provisions of this chapter [referring to the Iowa UCC], the principles of law and equity, including the law of . . . principal and agent . . . supplement its provisions."). Where the Iowa legislature intended to supplant the common law in the UCC, it specifically provided so. For example, in defining "control" for purposes of a certificated security in §554.8106, the comments specify that control has a particularized meaning and is not to be interpreted by reference to other bodies of law. See Iowa Code §554.8106 cmt. 7. The comment provides that "[i]n particular, the requirements for 'possession' derived from the common law of pledge are not to be used as a basis for interpreting subsection (c)(2) or (d)(2)" of §554.8106. Id. Rather, "[t]hose provisions are designed to supplant the [common law] concepts of 'constructive possession' and the like." Id. This comment recognizes that the Iowa legislature intended courts to look to the common law to interpret undefined terms contained in the Iowa UCC, and that under the common law of Iowa, possession includes constructive possession.

The transfer of possessory rights as between the buyer and the seller is a logical point at which to sever the security interest held by the seller's lender when the seller sells its goods in the ordinary course of its business. See U.C.C. §1-201, cmt. 9 ("The penultimate sentence prevents a buyer that does not have the right to possession as against the seller from being a buyer in ordinary course of business."); 9 William D. Hawkland, Richard A. Lord, Charles C. Lewis, & Frederick H. Miller, Hawkland UCC Series Art. 9 Appendix (Part II) (2008) (suggesting that under the "amendment, a buyer will become a [BIOC] when the buyer becomes entitled to a possession remedy"). Construing possession to include constructive possession is consistent with this demarcation and with the purpose of the BIOC status. If §554.1201(9) required physical possession to the exclusion of constructive possession, then a buyer who completed a sales transaction and placed goods with a bailee would not be considered a BIOC, but would continue to be subject to the lender's security interest. In this scenario, as between the buyer and the seller, the seller has no authority for regaining possession of the goods from the bailee, and the buyer clearly has the superior possessory interest as compared to the seller. Further, at this point, the lender is secured by the proceeds of the sale and no longer needs the security provided by the goods themselves. See GMAC Bus. Credit, L.L.C. v. Ford Motor Co. (In re H.S.A. II, Inc.), 271 B.R. 534, 541 (Bankr. E.D. Mich. 2002) ("[T]he reason that a security interest does not continue in collateral that is sold to a buyer in ordinary course is that the security interest continues in the proceeds, thus protecting the secured creditor."); see also 4 White & Summers—Uniform Commercial Code §33-8(b) ("Normally a lender with a security interest in inventory intends the debtor to be able to sell the inventory free and clear.").

In this situation, we see no reason for the buyer not to receive the inventory free of the lender's security interest even though the buyer took constructive rather than physical possession of the goods. The outcome should not differ based on whether the bailee is a third party or is the seller, where, as here, the buyer completes the sales transaction, the buyer takes delivery of the goods at the seller's premises, and the buyer and the seller explicitly agree that the seller will hold the goods for the buyer, such that the buyer constructively possesses the goods. See Kunkel v. Sprague Nat'l Bank, 128 F.3d 636, 643 (8th Cir. 1997) (applying Kansas law and holding that under the UCC, a seller loses its Article 2 right to stop delivery when the goods are constructively delivered to the buyer via a bailee, even when the bailee is the seller); see also Havens Steel Co. v. Commerce Bank, N.A. (In re Havens Steel Co.), 317 B.R. 75, 87 (Bankr. W.D. Mo. 2004) (holding that constructive possession satisfies the "take possession" requirement under Missouri's UCC §1-201(9)). We hold that "possession" as used in Iowa UCC §554.1201(9) includes constructive possession.

Having determined that the requirement in Iowa UCC §554.1201(9) may be met through constructive possession, we turn to the separate issue of whether the Dealers satisfied the requirements of constructive possession under Iowa law. The bankruptcy court concluded that the Dealers had constructive possession of the ag lime, but the BAP disagreed. According to the BAP, under Iowa law a buyer has constructive possession of goods held by the seller only if the buyer takes "some visible and apparent step to inform the world of the change in possession from the [seller] to the [buyer]." In re W. Ia. Limestone, Inc., 375 B.R. at 525-26 (discussing Boothby & Co. v. Brown, 40 Iowa 104, 1874 WL 609 (1874); McAfee v. Busby, 69 Iowa 328, 28 N.W. 623 (Iowa 1886)). The Dealers assert that adoption of the UCC in the 1960s by the Iowa legislature rendered these cases inapplicable, and that more recent cases support their position that they could take constructive possession of the ag lime without notice to the secured creditor.

"[u]nless otherwise explicitly agreed where delivery is to be made without moving the goods, if the goods are at the time of contracting already identified and no documents are to be delivered, title passes at the time and place of contracting"); Sam & Mac, Inc. v. Treat, 783 N.E.2d 760, 764 (Ind. Ct. App. 2003) (explaining that title (and with it a possessory interest) passes from seller to buyer at the time and place the seller delivers the goods as agreed by the parties). Notably, this occurred in January and February of 2005, and each of the Dealers, without restriction, removed portions of the ag lime from WIL's premises as it was resold to the Dealers' customers.

United Bank argues only that it had no notice of the sale of the inventory. Because notice is not a requirement for constructive possession under Iowa law, the BAP erred in concluding that constructive possession required notice to the world. We hold that the Dealers constructively possessed the ag lime left at WIL's quarry based on the completed sale, the identification of the ag lime to the contract, and the agreement in the bill of sale between the Dealers and WIL that the ag lime would remain on WIL's premises until resold. See In re Havens Steel Co., 317 B.R. 75 at 87 (holding that the buyer's "possessory rights, arising from [its] payment for and title to the steel, were sufficiently strong to imbue [the buyer] with constructive possession of the steel, in the context of [Missouri UCC] §1-201," where the steel was identified to the contract but held at the seller's warehouse).

Finally, United Bank argues that even if the Dealers took possession of the ag lime, they still are not entitled to BIOC status because the sales of ag lime were not conducted in a manner that was customary in WIL's business or in the industry. See §554.1201(9) (to qualify as a BIOC "the sale [must] . . . comport[] with the usual or customary practices in the kind of business in which the seller is engaged or with the seller's own usual or customary practices"). In the bankruptcy court proceedings, United Bank asserted that it was unusual for customers to prepay the ag lime contracts and to leave the ag lime on the quarry's premises. The bankruptcy court found that although WIL was new to the business of processing and selling ag lime through dealers, the sales to the Dealers were conducted in a manner that was "a usual and customary practice in the industry." (Add. at 36.)

We conclude that the bankruptcy court's finding is not clearly erroneous. The evidence in the record consists primarily of contradictory affidavits filed by Gary Hopp, President and owner with his wife, Dianna, of WIL, and by Pete Horne, acting CFO and a director of WIL. Mr. Hopp attested that most customers bought ag lime on credit and took immediate delivery, although a few customers prepaid their ag lime contracts and left the ag lime on the quarry's premises in early 2005. Mr. Horne attested that Dianna and Gary Hopp directed him to develop a product development and marketing plan for the ag lime that was being produced as the by-product of a large asphalt project in late 2004; that he developed a plan to market the ag lime through exclusive dealerships; and that prepaid contracts became the normal custom for WIL as a result of the newly developed marketing plan. He also attested that it was standard practice in the agricultural fertilizer business to conduct business in a similar manner. Faced with the contradictory affidavits, the bankruptcy court credited Mr. Horne's affidavit and found the transactions at issue to be usual and customary in the industry. This finding was further supported by the affidavits of Doug Welsh and Robert Bryant, who were also dealers of ag lime for WIL and who, like the Dealers here, paid for the ag lime in full and left the lime on WIL's premises until sold to their customers. There being no other evidence in the record about the customary practices in the ag lime business, we cannot say that the bankruptcy court clearly erred in crediting one affidavit over the other. See Dixon v. Crete Med. Clinic, P.C., 498 F.3d 837, 847 (8th Cir. 2007) ("Where there are two permissible views of the evidence, the factfinder's choice between them cannot be clearly erroneous.") (internal marks omitted).

III.

Because the Dealers satisfied the requirements of being buyers in the ordinary course of business under Iowa Code §554.1201(9), we reverse the decision of the BAP and affirm the September 26, 2006, order of the bankruptcy court.

There is quite a list of qualifications (culled from §9-320(a) and §1-201's definition of "buyer in the ordinary course of business") that a buyer must meet to purchase free of a prior security interest in the purchased property:

(1) He/she must be a buyer in the ordinary course of the seller's business (i.e., buying the seller's inventory in the routine way),

(2) who does not buy in bulk (that is, does not buy an entire inventoried business) and does not take the interest as security for or in total or partial satisfaction of a preexisting debt (that is, the buyer must give some form of "new" value),

(3) who buys from one in the business of selling goods of that kind (that is, cars from a car dealer, i.e., inventory),

(4) who buys in good faith and without knowledge that this purchase is in violation of others' ownership rights or security interests, and

(5) who does not buy farm products from a person engaged in farming operations,

(6) the seller's creditor must part with possession (the issue in the above Problem), and

(7) the competing security interest must be one "created by the buyer's seller."

PROBLEM 84

Octopus National Bank (ONB) had a perfected security interest in all cars on Smiles Motors' lot. Smiles owed $5,000 in past due insurance premiums to its insurance agent, Howard Teeth, who showed up one morning to buy a new car from Smiles. The president of Smiles first gave Howard a check for $5,000, but Howard endorsed it back over to Smiles when he saw a new car he wanted to buy. Is Howard a §1-201(b)(9) "buyer in the ordinary course of business" so as to take free of ONB's security interest? See Chrysler Credit Corp. v. Malone, 502 S.W.2d 910 (Tex. Civ. App. 1973). If Howard then sold the car, would Howard be liable to ONB for conversion? See In re TXNB Internal Case, 483 F.3d 292 (5th Cir. 2007).

PROBLEM 85

Arthur Greenbaum bought a new car on credit from Lorri's Car City, which took a purchase money security interest in the vehicle, perfecting same by notation of its lien interest on the certificate of title, as required by state law. Arthur was a used car dealer by profession, but he had purchased the car for his own private use. Nonetheless, he frequently parked the car on his lot, and one day sold it for cash to Ann Matheson, a customer in search of a good used car. Arthur did not mention to her that it was his personal car. When everyone learned what had happened, Ann sued Lorri's Car City, demanding that it release the title. What result? See Blue Ridge Bank and Trust Co. v. Hart, 152 S.W.3d 420 (Mo. App. 2005).

PROBLEM 86

Wonder Spa, Inc. pledged 50 of its promissory notes to the Conservative State Bank and Trust Company (CSBTC) in return for a loan. The bank took possession of the notes. The spa asked to have ten of the notes back for presentment to the makers for payment, and the bank duly turned over the notes, which Wonder Spa sold (*discounted*) to Octopus National Bank (ONB), a bona fide purchaser without knowledge of CSBTC's interest. This resale was in direct violation of the spa's agreement with CSBTC. Which bank is entitled to the instruments? Read §§9-312(g) and 9-331. Is ONB one of the parties protected by §9-331? See §§3-302 and 3-305.

Subsection (b) to §9-320 appears at first glance to apply to more situations than it really fits. It is meant to cover only a rare transaction: a sale of *consumer goods* by a *consumer* to a *consumer.* This is because the language of the statute clearly requires that the seller have acquired the goods for personal, family, or household purposes (i.e., "consumer goods"), and that the buyer is buying them for the same purposes. White & Summers §25-8(d); Balon v. Cadillac Auto. Co., 113 N.H. 108, 303 A.2d 194 (1973); Everett Natl. Bank v. Deschuiteneer, 109 N.H. 112, 244 A.2d 196 (1968). In such a sale the buyer takes free of the seller's creditor's security interest only if the buyer is both ignorant of it *and* if there is no financing statement on file.

PROBLEM 87

Andy Audio bought a stereo receiver on credit from Voice of Japan, Inc., an electronics store, giving it a purchase money security interest in the receiver. Voice of Japan did not file a financing statement. Six months later, when Andy still owed Voice of Japan $300, he held a garage sale and sold the receiver to Nancy Neighbor for $200 cash. If Andy stops making payments to Voice of Japan, can it repossess the receiver from Nancy? See §9-320(b) and its Official Comment 5.

NOTE

Even though a purchase money security interest in consumer goods is automatically perfected on attachment, per §9-309(1), the above Problem is meant to suggest the wisdom of filing a financing statement in big-ticket consumer transactions (such as the sale of a yacht or a famous painting) lest the creditor suffer the same fate as Voice of Japan when the consumer sells the collateral to another consumer.

PROBLEM 88

The Repossession Finance Company had a perfected (filed) security interest in the equipment of White Truck Ice Cream (WTIC), Inc. (the company sold ice cream from trucks that traveled through the city's neighborhoods). Though technically a corporation, WTIC was in actuality a family business, and Bill White-Truck himself frequently drove one of the trucks. One day while making his rounds, Bill met Frank Family, a consumer who asked about buying an ice cream–making machine for his family. Bill promptly sold him one of the machines the company owned, for which Frank paid cash. When WTIC failed to make its payments, the finance company lived up to its name and repossessed all equipment. When Frank refused to turn over the ice cream machine, Repossession sued him for conversion (a tort that does not require *scienter* or guilty knowledge for its commission). Answer these questions:

(a) Does he lose? Compare §§9-201, 9-401(b), and 9-315(a)(1) and Production Credit Assn. v. Nowatzski, 90 Wis. 2d 344, 280 N.W.2d 118 (1979); Bell Fin. Cmty. Credit Union v. Nagy, 862 N.E.2d 726 (Ind. Ct. App. 2007).

(b) Would we get a different result if the bank's interest were unperfected at the time of the sale? See §9-317(b).

(c) Would we get a different result if the bank knew and approved of the sale? Compare §9-315(a)(1); RFC Capital Corp. v. EarthLink, Inc., 2004 WL 2980402 (Ohio App. 2004).

PROBLEM 89

Paul Pop was a rock singer to whom Octopus National Bank (ONB) loaned $8,000 so he could buy stereo equipment for his road show. On April 2, Paul purchased the equipment, and on April 10, ONB filed its financing statement in the proper place. However, in the interim, on April 8, Paul sold the equipment to Used Stereo Heaven, which bought with no knowledge of the bank's purchase money security interest. Does ONB or Used Stereo Heaven have the superior claim to the equipment? Compare §§2-403, 9-201, and 9-317(e).

PROBLEM 90

When Farmer Bean borrowed a large amount of money from Farmers' Friend Financing Company (FFFC), he was required to sign a security agreement by which he promised not to sell the crop that was the collateral for the loan without the written consent of FFFC. Nonetheless, every year he sold the crop to the same buyer and remitted the proceeds to FFFC without getting its written consent. Does the buyer take free of the security interest of the secured party under §9-320(a)? If FFFC never protested what was going on year after year as the security agreement was violated, can it be said to have *waived* its security interest? Can a security interest be waived? See §9-315(a)(1) and the following famous case.

Clovis National Bank v. Thomas

New Mexico Supreme Court, 1967
77 N.M. 554, 425 P.2d 726

OMAN, J.

This is a suit by plaintiff-appellant for alleged conversion of cattle by defendant-appellee. The parties operate their respective businesses in

Clovis, Curry County, New Mexico, and will be referred to as plaintiff and defendant.

In its capacity as a bank, plaintiff, on March 27, 1963, loaned the sum of $8,800 to a Mr. W.D. Bunch. To evidence and secure the indebtedness he gave plaintiff a promissory note and a security agreement by which he granted a security interest in about 46 head of cattle belonging to him and branded "W D Bar." On April 11, 1963, a further security agreement, granting a security interest in 102 head of cattle, was given by him to plaintiff as additional security for the loan of March 27, and as security for additional loans to be made to him by plaintiff from time to time.

On July 29, 1963, he deposited $3,507 with plaintiff. This money represented proceeds from the sale by him of 35 head of cattle covered by the security agreements. $3,300 of this amount was applied by plaintiff on the indebtedness then owing by him.

On October 29, 1963, he deposited with plaintiff the sum of $5,613.17, the total amount of which was applied to his indebtedness, and which amount represented proceeds from the sale by him of 56 head of cattle covered by the security agreements. This deposit consisted of two checks given by defendant, who is a licensed commission house and market agency and as such handled the sale of the cattle for him.

Plaintiff admitted to being aware that Mr. Bunch was making sales of cattle covered by the security agreements.

In about September 1963, he made application to plaintiff for an additional loan with which to purchase additional cattle and with which to carry his cattle through the winter. An investigation was made by plaintiff during September, to determine the feasibility of granting this additional loan. Plaintiff approved the loan, and cattle were acquired by him and paid for by drafts drawn on plaintiff. By November 12, 1963, the additional cattle had been acquired.

On November 12, a new note in the principal amount of $21,500 and a new security agreement covering 283 head of cattle branded W D Bar were given by him to plaintiff to evidence and secure his then indebtedness. This indebtedness in the amount of $21,500 represented $2,007.67 still owing on the original note of March 27, $2,743.10 credited to his checking account on November 12, and amounts loaned or advanced to him during the intervening period. The security agreement was duly recorded in both Curry and Quay counties and in part provided:

DEBTOR FURTHER REPRESENTS, WARRANTS, AND AGREES THAT: . . .
   Without the prior written consent of Secured Party, Debtor will not sell,
   . . . or otherwise dispose of the collateral. . . .

Thereafter, cattle covered by the November 12 security agreement were consigned to defendant by Mr. Bunch for sale on his behalf at public auction. The plaintiff had no actual knowledge of these sales and had not given any express consent to Mr. Bunch to make the sales. He remitted no part of the proceeds from these sales to the plaintiff for application on his indebtedness. The sales were of 45 head of cattle on February 20, 1964, 95 head on May 14, 1964, and one head on May 21, 1964. The total value of these cattle was $16,450.34, and plaintiff sought recovery from defendant of this amount under the first cause of action of its complaint.

Mr. Bunch has a son by the name of William D. Bunch, Jr., also known as Bill Bunch, Jr., who will be referred to either by name or as the son. The son was the owner of a brand referred to as "Swastika K." Some time prior to July 15, 1964, at least 90 head of cattle were acquired by either Mr. Bunch or his son and were branded Swastika K. There was some evidence tending to show that these cattle, at least to some extent, were actually property of the father. No security agreement was ever given by either the father or the son by which a security interest in cattle branded Swastika K was granted to the plaintiff, unless in some way it can be held that they were covered by the security agreement of November 12.

On July 15, 1964, plaintiff requested that Mr. Bunch sell the remainder of his cattle, including the Swastika K cattle. On the following day, 90 head of Swastika K cattle were trucked to defendant's place of business for sale and were carried on the defendant's records as belonging to Bill Bunch, Jr. Plaintiff knew the cattle were at defendant's place of business to be sold and told defendant that plaintiff claimed some interest in the cattle. Defendant was not told the nature or extent of the claimed interest of plaintiff in these cattle.

The cattle were sold on July 16. Plaintiff was aware of the sale and advised defendant that it would be "nice" if the check in payment for these cattle could be made payable to one or both of the Bunches and to the plaintiff. At no time did the plaintiff demand payment or request that defendant not make payment to Bill Bunch, Jr.

Bill Bunch, Jr., consulted the local brand inspector and solicited his aid in securing payment from the defendant. The brand inspector advised defendant that the Swastika K brand was recorded in the name of Bill Bunch, Jr., and that insofar as the Cattle Sanitary Board was concerned, payment could be made to him.

An attorney also called defendant on behalf of Bill Bunch, Jr., concerning payment for the cattle, and demand was made by Bill Bunch, Jr., upon defendant to pay him the proceeds from the sale of the cattle. This the defendant did on July 22. This payment was in the amount of $7,777.84, which is the amount of plaintiff's claim against defendant under the second cause of action.

On this same date, plaintiff filed suit against W.D. Bunch and William D. Bunch, Jr., wherein plaintiff sought to recover from the father on the note of November 12, and sought to recover from the son the said sum of $7,777.84. In this proceeding plaintiff filed an affidavit in support of an application for a writ of garnishment, wherein it was asserted that the defendant was indebted to William D. Bunch, Jr. No claim was made that the proceeds from the sale belonged to plaintiff, but rather plaintiff asserted that the proceeds belonged to William D. Bunch, Jr., and, as already stated, tried to reach these proceeds by garnishment, which came too late. The present suit was then filed against defendant on August 31, 1964.

The plaintiff asserts thirteen separate points relied upon for reversal. However, the ultimate conclusions upon which the judgment for defendant rests are (1) the plaintiff consented to the sales of W D Bar cattle covered by the security agreement of November 12, and thus waived any possessory rights it may have had in these cattle, and (2) the plaintiff had no perfected security interest in the Swastika K cattle, and failed to prove an unperfected security interest in these cattle of which defendant had knowledge.

Insofar as the sales of the W D Bar cattle are concerned, the trial court found plaintiff, as a matter of common practice, usage and procedure, permitted Mr. Bunch to sell cattle covered by the security agreements of March 27 and April 11, and consented to receipt of the sale proceeds by Mr. Bunch. It also found that plaintiff, by common practice, custom, usage and procedure, permitted and consented to the sales of W D Bar cattle covered by the security agreement of November 12, and permitted and consented to the receipt by Mr. Bunch of the proceeds from these sales.

The trial court concluded that plaintiff had permitted, acquiesced in, and consented to these sales; that by its conduct, plaintiff had waived any possessory rights it may have had in and to these cattle; that defendant did not wrongfully convert cattle in which plaintiff had an enforceable security interest; and that defendant was not responsible for the debtor's failure to remit the proceeds of the sales to plaintiff.

We agree with the findings and conclusions of trial court. Insofar as consent and waiver on behalf of plaintiff are concerned, in addition to the facts recited above, the plaintiff's officers testified that it was the custom and practice of plaintiff to permit a debtor, who has given cattle as collateral, to retain possession and to sell the collateral without ever obtaining prior written consent of plaintiff, and that at no time in its dealings with Mr. Bunch between the time of the making of the note on November 12, 1963, and the sale of cattle on May 21, 1964, did plaintiff demand of him that he obtain prior written consent before making a sale.

It is true there was some testimony that the collateral was not released from the lien until the debtor actually delivered the proceeds of the sale to plaintiff, but, as testified to by one of the plaintiff's officers, the debtor never contacts the plaintiff and secures permission to make a sale, but the sale is made and plaintiff relies upon the debtor to bring the proceeds to plaintiff to be applied on the indebtedness. This practice is followed because 99% of the people with whom plaintiff deals are honest and take care of their obligations.

The general rule of liability of an auctioneer, who sells, in behalf of his principal, property subject to a mortgage lien, is stated as follows in the annotation at 96 A.L.R.2d 208, 212 (1964):

> According to the overwhelming weight of authority, an auctioneer who sells property on behalf of a principal who has not title thereto, or who holds the property subject to a mortgage or other lien, or who for other reasons has no right to sell such property, is personally liable to the true owner or mortgagee for conversion regardless of whether he had knowledge, actual or constructive, of the principal's lack of title or want of authority to sell, in the absence of facts creating an estoppel or showing acquiescence or consent on the part of the true owner or mortgagee. . . .

The trial court, in addition to holding plaintiff had consented to and acquiesced in the sales and had waived his possessory rights in the cattle, concluded plaintiff was estopped from recovery by reason of its conduct. The plaintiff and the amicus curiae have both made strong attacks on this conclusion. We are inclined to agree that the essential elements of an estoppel are lacking. We do not, however, predicate our decision upon estoppel, but rather upon consent and waiver.

The plaintiff, if not expressly consenting to the questioned sales, certainly impliedly acquiesced in and consented thereto. It not only permitted Mr. Bunch, but permitted all its other debtors who granted security interests in cattle, to retain possession of the cattle and to sell the same from time to time as the debtor chose, and it relied upon the honesty of each debtor to bring in the proceeds from his sales to be applied on his indebtedness.

Plaintiff was fully aware of its right to require its written authority to sell or otherwise dispose of the collateral, but it elected to waive this right. Waiver is the intentional abandonment or relinquishment of a known right. Smith v. New York Life Ins. Co., 26 N.M. 408, 193 Pac. 67; Miller v. Phoenix Assur. Co. Ltd., 52 N.M. 68, 191 P.2d 993.

In Farmers' Natl. Bank v. Missouri Livestock Comm. Co., 53 F.2d 991 (8th Cir. 1931), suit was brought by the holder of chattel mortgages for alleged conversion of cattle by a livestock commission house. Although the facts are dissimilar from those of the present case, that case does stand for the principle that consent may be established by implication arising from a course of conduct as well as by express words, and that consent to a sale operates as a waiver of the lien or security interest. See also Moffet Bros. & Andrews Comm. Co. v. Kent, 5 S.W.2d 395 (Mo. 1928).

In First Natl. Bank & Trust Co. v. Stock Yards Loan Co., 65 F.2d 226 (8th Cir. 1933), the effect of a course of conduct on the part of a mortgagee, such as was followed by the mortgagee in that case and such as was followed by plaintiff in the present case, was stated to be:

> . . . When a mortgagee under a chattel mortgage allows the mortgagor to retain possession of the property and to sell the same at will, the mortgagee waives his lien, and this is true whether the purchaser knew of the existence of the chattel mortgage or not.

The fact that plaintiff may have intended that the proceeds from the sales of cattle covered by the security agreements should be remitted to plaintiff by Mr. Bunch for application on his indebtedness did not change the waiver. When plaintiff consented to the sales and the collection of the proceeds of the sales by him, it lost its security interest in the collateral and was then looking to him personally for payment. . . .

The collateral here in question—livestock, falls within the classification of "farm products," and these products are expressly excluded from the classifications of "equipment" and "inventory." Section 9-109(3), N.M.S.A. 1953. By excluding "farm products" from the classifications of "equipment" and "inventory," and by expressly providing in §9-307(1) [now §9-320(a)—EDS.], N.M.S.A. 1953, that a buyer in the ordinary course of business of farm products from a person engaged in farming operations does not take free of a security interest created by the seller, the draftsmen of the code apparently intended "to freeze the agricultural mortgagee into the special status he has achieved under the pre-code case law." 2 Gilmore, Security Interests in Personal Property 714 (1965).

It would only seem logical and consistent that if the buyer from one engaged in farming operations takes subject to the security interest, then the selling agent is subject to the rights of the secured party in the collateral. This is consistent with the foregoing cited authorities. See also United States v. Union Livestock Sales Co., 298 F.2d 755 (4th Cir. 1962); United States v. Matthews, 244 F.2d 626 (9th Cir. 1957).

Section 9-306(2) [now §9-315(a)(1)—EDS.], N.M.S.A. 1953 provides:

> Except where this article otherwise provides, a security interest continues in collateral notwithstanding sale, exchange or other disposition thereof by the debtor unless his action was authorized by the secured party in the security agreement or otherwise, and also continues in any identifiable proceeds including collections received by the debtor.

No section of the code provides otherwise as to farm products. Thus, the holder of the security interest in farm products has the same protection under the code which he had under the pre-code law, and the cattle broker is still liable to the secured party for conversion of the collateral. United States v. Sommerville, 211 F. Supp. 543 (W.D. Pa. 1962), *aff'd on other grounds,* 324 F.2d 712 (3d Cir. 1963), *cert. denied,* 376 U.S. 909 (1964). See also 2 Gilmore, Security Interests in Personal Property 715 (1965).

Also, under the code the secured party may consent to the sale of the collateral, and thereby waive his rights in the same. See Official Comment No. 3, §9-306, and Official Comment No. 2, §9-307 [in the 1999 revision, see Official Comment 2 to §9-315, second paragraph—EDS.]. There being no particular provision of the Code which displaces the law of waiver, and particularly waiver by implied acquiescence or consent, the code provisions are supplemented thereby. Section 1-103, N.M.S.A. 1953. The defendant cannot be held liable for a conversion of the W D Bar cattle, because plaintiff consented to and acquiesced on the sales thereof, and thereby waived its rights in this collateral. . . .

It follows from what has been stated that the judgment should be affirmed. It is so ordered.

CHAVEZ, C.J., and NOBLE and COMPTON, JJ., concur. CARMODY, J. (dissenting). [Omitted.][13]

NOTE

This case and the waiver issue it presents have an uneasy history. The difficulty is created by the rule in §9-320(a) that a buyer in the ordinary course from one selling farm products does not take free of the secured party's interest in the products sold. Why would the Code drafters have done this? The answer lies in the special deference always shown to farmers as debtors.

The importance of farming to our society has created any number of rules favoring agricultural borrowers. It is crucial that financial institutions be encouraged to loan money to farmers, and §9-320(a) is an example of a statute that reflects this policy. If the lenders can follow the collateral into the hands of an innocent buyer, they are more secure and therefore more likely to make the original loan to the farmer. In truth, a farmer's sale of the annual crop is more like an Article 6 *bulk sale* (the sale of a large part of the inventory) than the typical retail sale that §9-320(a) usually covers, so the buyer from a farmer ought to be more careful to make sure that everything is squared with the farmer's lender. On the other hand, §9-320(a) catches all buyers, even auctioneers and commission merchants, and involves them in policing the relationship between the farmer and the bank, and these buyers bitterly resented fulfilling this function.

---

13. The New Mexico legislature responded by amending the UCC to provide that course of dealing or trade usage could not have the effect of waiving a security interest in farm products. The court did not consider the proper definitions in §1-303; had it, would the result have changed? Compare Official Comment 2 to §1-303 with §1-303(f).

Where the bank was aware that the farmer was routinely ignoring the security agreement's requirement of written consent, the courts were, like in the *Clovis* case, especially likely to find a waiver of the security interest. Later courts generally (though not always) followed *Clovis*. See the case law summary in Anon, Inc. v. Farmers Prod. Credit Assn., 446 N.E.2d 656 (Ind. App. 1983). Some courts developed a "conditional consent" test whereby the waiver was ineffective unless the condition under which it was made (typically payment of the proceeds to the secured party) was complied with. See, e.g., Baker Prod. Credit Assn. v. Long Creek Meat Co., 97 Ore. 1372, 513 P.2d 1129 (1973). Other courts, noting that the bank's "waiver" was really nothing more than the acceptance of a *fait accompli* ("I sold the collateral even though I said I wouldn't; here's the money."), did not permit such a "course of dealing" to override the express selling prohibition of the security agreement. See §1-205(4); Wabasso St. Bank v. Caldwell Packing Co., 251 N.W.2d 321 (Minn. 1976).[14] For the position of revised Article 9 on this issue, see Official Comment 2, second paragraph, to §9-315. Courts are more likely to find a waiver of the security interest in the *collateral* than they are to find a waiver of the right to *proceeds* of the sale, and those are two different issues; see discussion in Peoples Trust & Sav. Bank v. Security Sav. Bank, 815 N.W.2d 744 (Iowa 2012).

The answer of many states to the sale of farm products was to enact a statute creating a system whereby a buyer would take free of the security interest of the farmer's creditor if the buyer first jumped through certain hoops. These statutes proved to be the model for a federal statute that has now replaced them and has completely preempted the farm products exclusion in UCC §9-320(a), §1324 of the Food Security Act of 1985 (hereinafter FSA), 7 U.S.C. §1631. (This statute is in your statute book.) The FSA contemplates the following schema: The security agreement between the farmer and the bank requires the farmer to furnish the bank with a list of prospective buyers of the farm products (see §1631(h)(1)), and the farmer agrees not to sell to anyone else unless the farmer notifies the bank in writing at least seven days before the sale (§1631(h)(2)). The bank then sends a direct notice to the listed buyers informing them of any payment instructions the bank wants to impose; the notice must contain the details mentioned in §1631(e)(1)(A). If the buyers follow the payment instructions, they take free of the bank's security interest (§1631(d) and (e)). In addition to the above, the state may establish a central filing system for the registration of financing statements covering farm

---

14. One other matter: Fair or not, it is the rule that no agent of the United States government has actual or apparent authority to waive the government's security interests. United States v. Hughes, 340 F. Supp. 539 (N.D. Miss. 1972). Where the federal government is the farmer's creditor, the courts are quick to find conversion despite the buyer's lack of knowledge; FDIC v. Bowles Livestock Commn. Co., 739 F. Supp. 1364 (D. Neb. 1990). For an informative discussion of the meaning of conversion in Article 9, see Mammoth Cave Prod. Credit Assn. v. Oldham, 569 S.W.2d 833 (Tenn. App. 1977).

products.[15] Buyers then register with the central filing office, which regularly sends them a list of the relevant financing statements concerning the types of farm products they wish to buy. Or the central filing office will respond to buyers' inquiries within 24 hours as to the existence of any financing statements covering farm products they wish to purchase; §1631(c)(2). If the buyers then obtain either a release or a waiver from the secured parties (or follow their instructions as to payments), the buyers take free of the security interests in the farm products. See White & Summers §25-9.

PROBLEM 91

Farmer Bean borrowed money from Octopus National Bank (ONB), which had him sign a security agreement covering his crops. The security agreement forbade him the right to sell his crops without the written consent of the bank. It also required him to give the bank a list of potential buyers of the crop. Farmer Bean did so. The list was of the five buyers to whom he had sold his crop (or parts thereof) in the past. The bank sent a written notice complying with §1631(e)(1) to each of the listed buyers, telling them that all payments for Farmer Bean's crops should be by check made payable to ONB. One buyer not on the list was Rural Silo, Inc., a grain merchant that contracted to buy all of Farmer Bean's 2016 wheat crop. Rural Silo knew that Farmer Bean had borrowed money from ONB and that ONB had filed a financing statement to perfect its security interest (the state had not created an FSA central filing system). It bought the crop from Farmer Bean and paid him cash for it at his request. Is Rural Silo, which after all knew all about ONB's security interest, a *buyer in the ordinary course* as defined in §1631(c)(1)? See Lisco State Bank v. McCombs Ranches, Inc., 752 F. Supp. 329 (D. Neb. 1990); Ashburn Bank v. Farr, 206 Ga. App. 517, 426 S.E.2d 63 (1992). Does Rural Silo take free of the bank's security interest? See §1631(d). Does the bank have any other remedy here? See §1631(h)(3).

---

15. Nineteen states have central filing systems; see the list at http://www.gipsa.usda.gov/Lawsandregs/cleartitle.html. The financing statement to be filed in the central filing system must be more detailed than the usual one filed under the UCC. See §1631(c)(4) for the definition of effective financing statement, which must include, among other things, the Social Security number of the debtor, the amount of farm products covered, and their location. See Sanford, The Reborn Farm Products Exception Under the Food Security Act of 1985, 20 UCC L.J. 3 (1987). The central filing system indexes these financing statements by four different categories, including *crop year*. See §1631(c)(2). "Attorneys for agricultural lenders have recently found themselves pondering such questions as: What is the 'crop year' of a pig?" Reiley, State Law Responses to the Federal Food Security Act, 20 UCC L.J. 260 (1988). The regulations adopted pursuant to the Act have shed some light on this and other mysteries; see 9 C.F.R. §205.107 (*crop year* of an animal is the year in which it is born or acquired).

Farm Credit Bank of St. Paul v. F&A Dairy

Wisconsin Court of Appeals, 1991
165 Wis. 2d 360, 477 N.W.2d 357

CANE, J.

F&A Dairy (the dairy) appeals a judgment in favor of Farm Credit Bank of St. Paul for conversion of secured farm property. The dairy raises four issues on appeal: (1) The trial court erred by basing its decision on §9-307, in contravention of 7 U.S.C. §1631 (1988), which the dairy claims preempts state law; (2) the dairy took free and clear of the bank's security interest because the bank did not meet the notice requirements of §1631; (3) the bank was not in possession or entitled to immediate possession of the secured property and, thus, could not maintain an action for conversion; and (4) the trial court's decision was unfair, inequitable and contrary to the policy behind §1631. . . .

John and Barbara Bonneprise own and operate a dairy farm. The Bonneprises borrowed $300,000 from Farm Credit Bank of St. Paul. As collateral for the loan, the bank obtained and perfected a security interest covering the Bonneprises' milk and all accounts arising from the sale or other disposition of their milk and milk products. The Bonneprises were selling milk to Land O' Lakes Dairy. In return for waiver of its lien, the bank executed an assignment with Land O' Lakes and the Bonneprises whereby Land O' Lakes would pay the bank $4,333 per month from the Bonneprises' milk proceeds.

In August 1988, the Bonneprises switched dairies and began selling their milk to F&A Dairy. After the bank received no payment in August, it found out that the Bonneprises had switched dairies. The Bonneprises refused to make an assignment directing the dairy to make payments to the bank. By letter dated August 22, 1988, the bank notified the dairy of its previous assignment with Land O' Lakes and demanded payments of $4,333 in accordance with the assignment. Also, the bank enclosed a copy of the assignment, a product lien notification statement and a copy of its financing statement filed in accordance with the UCC. Four days later the bank notified the dairy of its perfected security interest in the Bonneprises' milk and all accounts arising from the sale or other disposition of their milk and milk products and enclosed a copy of the security agreement.

The dairy refused to pay the bank $4,333 per month for milk sales during August, September, October and November.[16] The reasons it gave for not paying the bank were that there was no assignment between the bank, the Bonneprises and the dairy, and that John Bonneprise directed it to pay him and not the bank. Each of these months' sales to the dairy exceeded $4,333.

---

16. The milk sales from December 1988 and following are not in issue because they were placed in escrow.

The trial court found that the bank had an effective perfected security interest covering the sale of the Bonneprises' milk to the dairy. It also found that the Bonneprises defaulted on their payments to the bank in August 1988, and, therefore, the bank was entitled to immediate possession of the secured property. The trial court concluded that the dairy bought the Bonneprises' milk subject to the bank's security interest under §1631 because the bank met the §1631 notice requirements. It further concluded that the dairy was guilty of converting the sum of $4,333 per month during September, October, November, and December (constituting proceeds from the August, September, October, and November milk sales), totaling $17,332. The trial court entered judgment in the amount plus 5% interest from the date of conversion to the date of judgment, and costs.

PREEMPTION

[The court concluded that 7 U.S.C. §1631 (Food Security Act) preempted what is now §9-320(a).]

APPLICATION OF 7 U.S.C. §1631

Next, we address whether the dairy purchased the Bonneprises' milk subject to or free of the bank's security interest, under §1631. The application of a statute to a particular set of facts is a question of law that we review de novo. Cleaver v. DOR, 158 Wis. 2d 734, 738, 463 N.W.2d 349, 351 (1990).

Section 1631(d) provides that a buyer of farm products takes free of a security interest except as provided in §1631(e). Subsection 1631(e) provides in part:

> (e) Purchases subject to security interest
> A buyer of farm products takes subject to a security interest created by the seller if—
> (1)(A) within 1 year before the sale of the farm products, the buyer has received from the secured party . . . written notice of the security interest organized according to farm products that—
> (i) is an original or reproduced copy thereof;
> (ii) contains,
> (I) the name and address of the secured party;
> (II) the name and address of the person indebted to the secured party;
> (III) the social security number of the debtor . . . ;
> (IV) a description of the farm products subject to the security interest created by the debtor . . . ; and . . .
> (V) [contains] any payment obligations imposed on the buyer by the secured party as conditions for waiver or release of the security interest; and
> (B) the buyer has failed to perform the payment obligations. . . .
> (Footnote omitted.)

If the bank has met the §1631(e) notice requirements, including notice of any payment obligation, and the dairy failed to perform the payment obligations, it purchased the milk from the Bonneprises subject to the bank's security interest.

Here, the bank sent letters and documents to the dairy containing a copy of the security agreement creating the security interest in the milk and accounts from its sale, the bank's name and address, the Bonneprises' names and address, John Bonneprise's social security number and a reasonable description of the secured property and where it was located. It also demanded the monthly sum of $4,333.

The dairy argues that the bank did not meet the "payment obligation" notice requirement because its payment obligation was ambiguous. We disagree. Under its perfected security interest and by giving proper notice under §1631(e), the bank was entitled to receive all proceeds from the sale of the Bonneprises' milk, not merely the payment amount of $4,333. See Miracle Feeds, Inc. v. Attica Dairy Farm, 129 Wis. 2d 377, 385 N.W.2d 208 (Ct. App. 1986). The requirement of giving notice of "any payment obligations" is merely to allow the bank, if it wishes, to accept a lesser amount of milk sale proceeds and to waive its lien for the balance of the proceeds. The bank's documents and letters sent to the dairy provide sufficient notice that it had a lien on the Bonneprises' milk and proceeds from its sale, and that it demanded payment of $4,333 per month as a waiver of its lien.

The dairy also argues that the bank's payment obligation notice required an assignment from the Bonneprises directing it to pay a specific amount to the bank because the lien notification statement sent to the dairy referred to such an assignment. It further argues that because there was no such assignment, the notice requirements of §1631(e) are not met and it therefore takes free of the bank's security interest.

Subsection (e) does not require an assignment to be filed with the buyer. Although the bank's lien notification statement arguably requires such an assignment, the lack of an assignment does not allow the dairy to take free of the bank's security interest. If we were to view only the lien notification statement without an assignment, arguably the bank would be entitled to all proceeds from the milk sales because there would be no payment obligation for waiver of its lien. However, reviewing the correspondence and documents sent to the dairy, the only reasonable construction is that the bank was demanding payment of $4,333 per month in lieu of receiving the Bonneprises' milk and all proceeds arising from its sale. Thus, we hold that the bank adequately informed the dairy of "any payment obligations . . . as conditions for waiver" under §1631(e).

Section 1631(e) requires that the notice be given within one year before the sale of the farm products. The bank's notice was given in late August. The Bonneprises began selling their milk to the dairy earlier in August. Thus, the notice was given before the September, October, and November sales, but not before the August sales. Consequently, we hold that the bank's notice was timely only as to the September, October, and November milk sales, covering the October, November, and December proceeds. We therefore reverse that portion of the judgment pertaining to the August milk sales and September proceeds.

In addition to proper notice, §1631(e) requires that the buyer failed to perform the payment obligations of the secured party. At no time did the dairy make a payment of $4,333, or any other amount, to the bank. Thus, we conclude that the dairy, having proper notice of the bank's security interest and payment obligations as conditions for waiver for the September, October, and November milk sales, failed to comply with those payment obligations. Consequently, the bank met all the requirements of §1631(e), and the dairy takes subject to the bank's security interest.

CONVERSION

Next, the dairy contends that the bank cannot succeed on its action for conversion because it was not in possession or entitled to immediate possession of the secured property, and because it did not allege in the complaint that the Bonneprises defaulted on their loan. The issue of whether a particular set of facts fulfill a particular legal standard is a question of law that we review de novo. State v. Trudeau, 139 Wis. 2d 91, 103, 408 N.W.2d 337, 342 (1987). An action for conversion is the proper means for a secured party to enforce its security interest against a transferee. United States v. Fullpail Cattle Sales, 640 F. Supp. 976, 980 (E.D. Wis. 1986) (applying state law). Conversion is the wrongful or unauthorized exercise of dominion or control over a chattel. PCA v. Equity Coop Livestock Sales Assn., 82 Wis. 2d 5, 10, 261 N.W.2d 127, 129 (1978). A plaintiff in a conversion action must prove that he was in possession of or entitled to immediate possession of the chattel that was converted. Id.

The bank did not receive the August payment from the Bonneprises' milk sales. Thus, as of August, the Bonneprises were in default on their payments and, under §9-503 [now §9-609—EDS.], the bank had the right to immediate possession of the secured property. The bank established that the Bonneprises had defaulted on their required payments from August through December. Thus, we conclude that the bank was entitled to immediate possession of the Bonneprises' milk proceeds, and the dairy wrongly exercised control over them by not giving the required proceeds to the bank. . . .

Because we conclude that 7 U.S.C. §1631 preempts §9-307, and §1631 applies to the facts in this case, we need not consider the dairy's argument that the trial court's decision was contrary to equity, fairness and the policy behind §1631. Therefore, we hold that the bank is entitled to recover the proceeds from milk sales in September, October, and November, plus interest. The matter is therefore remanded to the trial court to modify the judgment consistent with this opinion.

By the Court—Judgment affirmed in part; reversed in part and cause remanded with directions. No costs to either party.

PROBLEM 92

Mr. and Mrs. Halyard purchased a large sailboat with money borrowed from the Boilerplate National Bank (BNB), which took a security interest therein and promptly filed a financing statement in the proper place. The Halyards sold the boat to Oil Slick Boat Sales, Inc., a used boat concern, telling Oil Slick of the bank's interest and of the necessity of making monthly payments to the bank. Oil Slick turned around and resold the boat to Mr. and Mrs. Blink, innocent people who paid full value for the boat believing Oil Slick had clear title. When BNB did not receive its usual monthly payment, it investigated, found the boat, and repossessed it. Has the Blinks' property been converted, or don't they fit into §9-320(a)? What does "created by the buyer's seller" mean in §9-320(a)? See White & Summers §25-8(b). Does Article 2's "entrusting" rule, §2-403, help the Blinks? What is §2-403's relationship with Article 9? See White & Summers §25-8(c); Conseco Finance Servicing Corp. v. Lee, 2004 WL 1243417 (Tex. App. 2004). The "created by the buyer's seller" language will often cause trouble for buyers buying goods from a used merchandise dealer. Why would the drafters have favored the original creditor in this situation over a buyer in the ordinary course? If the Blinks lose this lawsuit, whom should they sue, and what is their theory? See §2-312. Can Oil Slick use the same theory against the Halyards?

V. LEASES

In resolving the Problems that follow, it should be noted that according to §2A-103(1)(j) (defining *lease*): "Unless the context clearly indicates otherwise, the term includes a sublease."

PROBLEM 93

The Highbid Construction Company gave a security interest to Octopus National Bank (ONB) in all of its construction equipment "now owned or after-acquired." ONB filed a financing statement in the proper place. Two years later, Highbid was in the middle of an enormous construction project at Football University when a number of its key employees quit, leaving it very short-staffed. To avoid breach of contract, it became necessary to farm out the project to someone else, though Highbid had never done this before. The president of Highbid reached an agreement with Newcomer Construction Company, one of its subcontractors on the Football University job, by which Highbid would lease all of its construction equipment to Newcomer for the length of the Football University project so that Newcomer could finish the job for Highbid. Use the rules of Article 2A to answer the following question: Is the lessee subject to ONB's existing security interest in the equipment? See §§2A-307, 2A-103(1)(o), 9-321(c).

PROBLEM 94

When the Football University project was completed, the lease described in the last Problem ended, and the machinery was returned by the lessee to Highbid Construction Company. Things were going so well for Highbid that it was able to pay off all of its loans in full and free all of its assets from the security interests that had encumbered them. Highbid's lawyer advised the company that for both tax and accounting reasons it would be better if Highbid leased the new grading machine that it had recently purchased rather than owning it outright. To accomplish this, Highbid's attorney worked out a deal by which Octopus National Bank (ONB) would purchase the grading machine from Highbid and then lease it back to Highbid. The term of the lease was exactly equal to the useful life of the grading machine.

Two months after this arrangement had come into being, Highbid's president absconded with the company's liquid assets, leaving the company in bad financial shape and needing to borrow some money. ONB refused to advance further funds, so Highbid looked elsewhere. The new president of Highbid went to Antitrust National Bank (ANB) and sought a loan, offering the grading machine as collateral. He was able to produce a bill of sale showing that Highbid had purchased the grading machine a mere three months ago when it was involved in the Football University contract. He did not tell ANB about the subsequent sale and leaseback arrangement that Highbid had with ONB. After ANB checked the public records and found no evidence of a security interest in the grading machine, it had Highbid sign the necessary Article 9 documents and a promissory note, loaned the money, and filed its financing statement in the appropriate place.

When Highbid defaulted on its lease payments, ONB repossessed the grading machine, at which point ANB claimed the superior interest therein. ANB's attorney argued that ONB was a party to fraud in that the sale and leaseback helped Highbid create the false appearance of assets.

How does this come out? See §§2A-307, 2A-308(3), and 1-203, and compare §2-402(2) in Article 2. Would you reach the same result if the lease agreement between Highbid and ONB provided the lessee with a right of termination at any time?

VI.   ARTICLE 2 CLAIMANTS

PROBLEM 95

Jack Gladhand was a traveling salesman dealing in many kinds of office supplies. He needed new luggage to carry his samples and bought a set from Alligator Fashions, which reserved a security interest therein and filed a financing statement. A month later, in the middle of a hot sales deal, Jack sold all of his samples and the luggage to Mark Impulse, a compulsive buyer. Jack told Mark (who paid cash for the goods) that the luggage was genuine alligator (a lie—he knew it was lizard). When Mark discovered the truth, he revoked his acceptance of the goods pursuant to §2-608 and claimed a security interest in the goods. Read §2-711(3). On learning of Jack's resale to Mark and of the latter's revocation of acceptance, Alligator Fashions decided to call the loan and repossess the luggage. Who is entitled to the luggage? See §9-110.

The rights of an unpaid seller are governed by both Article 2 and Article 9. If the seller gets a security agreement covering the item sold, a purchase money security interest (§9-103) arises, and Article 9 handles the priority in §9-324(a) and (b). If the seller extends credit to the buyer but fails to reserve a security interest, §2-702 applies. Finally, if the buyer gets the goods and pays with a check that is then dishonored (NSF—not sufficient funds), the seller's rights are governed by §§2-403, 2-507, and 2-511 (which you should now read), not by §2-702.

PROBLEM 96

Guy Baldwin was a successful author who decided to self-publish his latest book and market it directly to retailers. He received an order for 200 copies from Cowskin Book Chain, and he shipped off the books immediately, along with an invoice for their price. Two days later, he learned that Cowskin was hopelessly insolvent and unable to pay any creditors. What can he do? See §2-702. Suppose that two weeks before he shipped the books, Cowskin had sent him a letter lying about its financial condition; now how long does he have to make his reclamation demand? If he gets the books back, can he sue Cowskin for the wasted shipping costs? See §2-702(3). If Cowskin's inventory was subject to a perfected security interest in favor of a bank, which thereby had a floating lien on the inventory, could he still reclaim the books? See §§2-702(3) and 2-403(1); In re Nitram, Inc., 323 B.R. 792 (Bankr. M.D. Fla. 2005). Note that the definition of a *purchaser* in §1-201(b)(29) and (30) includes any voluntary transferee, which would encompass secured parties. What should Baldwin have done? See §9-324(b).

If, in the last Problem, the buyer had filed a bankruptcy petition shortly before receiving the books, Bankruptcy Code §546(c) might allow him to recover the books from the bankruptcy trustee:

> (1) Except as provided in subsection (d) of this section and in section 507(c), and subject to the prior rights of a holder of a security interest in such goods or the proceeds thereof, the rights and powers of the trustee under sections 544(a), 545, 547, and 549 are subject to the right of a seller of goods that has sold goods to the debtor, in the ordinary course of such seller's business, to reclaim such goods if the debtor has received such goods while insolvent, within 45 days before the date of the commencement of a case under this title, but such seller may not reclaim such goods unless such seller demands in writing reclamation of such goods —
>
> (A) not later than 45 days after the date of receipt of such goods by the debtor; or
>
> (B) not later than 20 days after the date of commencement of the case, if the 45-day period expires after the commencement of the case.
>
> (2) If a seller of goods fails to provide notice in the manner described in paragraph (1), the seller still may assert the rights contained in section 503(b)(9).

In re Arlco, Inc.

United States Bankruptcy Court, Southern District of New York, 1999
239 B.R. 261

ARTHUR J. GONZALEZ, Bankruptcy Judge.

On June 6, 1997, Arley Corporation ("Arley") and Home Fashions Outlet, Inc. ("Home Fashions" and together with Arley, the "Debtors") each filed a petition under chapter 11 of title 11 of the United States Code (the "Bankruptcy Code"). Arley was engaged in the business of manufacturing, importing, and wholesaling home furnishings, window coverings, bedcoverings, and linens which were sold to retailers, one of which was Home Fashions, Arley's wholly-owned subsidiary. Home Fashions operated retail outlet stores in Massachusetts and California. In addition, the Debtors maintained business and corporate offices, a showroom, and a design facility in New York. They also maintained business offices in Massachusetts and manufacturing facilities in Massachusetts, North Carolina, South Carolina, and California.

On September 15, 1997, pursuant to 11 U.S.C. §363, the Court approved an asset purchase agreement for the sale of substantially all of the Debtors' assets as a going concern. The asset purchase agreement included a requirement that the Debtors change their corporate names contemporaneously with the closing of the sale transaction. Thus, Arley changed its name to Arlco, Inc. and Home Fashions changed its name to HFO, Inc. On August 6, 1998, the Debtors chapter 11 cases were converted to chapter 7. Thereafter, Robert Fisher, Esq. was appointed as chapter 7 trustee (the "Trustee").

Galey & Lord, Inc. ("Galey") is a fabric manufacturer. Prior to the filing of the Debtors' petitions, Galey, in its ordinary course of business, sold textile goods on credit to Arley. On May 16, 1997, Galey sent a letter to Arley by fax, overnight courier, and certified mail (the "May 16th Letter") demanding that Arley return the merchandise it "received during the applicable periods referred to in [§2-702 of the Uniform Commercial Code]" and notifying Arley that "all goods subject to [Galey's] right of reclamation should be protected and segregated by [Arley] and are not to be used for any purpose whatsoever." Subsequently, on May 21, 1997, Galey sent the Debtor an additional notice detailing each invoice issued to Arley within the 10-day period prior to May 16, 1997 for the goods allegedly subject to reclamation. Since early 1995, CIT Group/Business Credit Inc. ("CIT") has held a perfected security interest in substantially all Arley's assets, including accounts receivable and inventory.

On June 9, 1997, prior to the sale of the Debtors' assets, Galey commenced an adversary proceeding against Arley seeking reclamation of the textile goods referred to in the May 16th Letter. On June 11, 1997, Galey filed an Amended Complaint. Currently before the Court are motions for summary judgment filed by Galey and by the Trustee, respectively.

In its summary judgment motion, Galey maintains that it has complied with all the statutory requirements for establishing a valid claim for reclamation. The Trustee refutes Galey's contention and opposes entry of summary judgment in favor of Galey. Rather, the Trustee maintains that his arguments support entry of summary judgment in Arley's favor. The three principal reasons advanced by the Trustee in opposition to Galey's motion and in support of his own motion are that 1) the reclamation notice was legally deficient, 2) Galey failed to prove what goods Arley still had on hand when Galey made its demand, and 3) Galey's right to reclamation is subject to CIT's perfected security interest. In addition, Arley contends that there are factual disputes that preclude entry of summary judgment in favor of Galey.

DISCUSSION

The purpose of 11 U.S.C. §546(c) is to recognize any right to reclamation that a seller may have under applicable nonbankruptcy law. In re Victory Markets Inc., 212 B.R. 738, 741 (Bankr. N.D.N.Y. 1997). Section 546(c) does not create a new, independent right to reclamation but merely affords the seller an opportunity, with certain limitations, to avail itself of any reclamation right it may have under nonbankruptcy law. Id.; Toshiba America, Inc. v. Video King of Illinois, Inc. (In re Video King of Illinois, Inc.), 100 B.R. 1008, 1013 (Bankr. N.D. Ill. 1989). Pursuant to §546(c), a seller may reclaim goods it has sold to an insolvent debtor if it establishes:

(1) that it has a statutory or common law right to reclaim the goods;
(2) that the goods were sold in the ordinary course of the seller's business;
(3) that the debtor was insolvent at the time the goods were received; and
(4) that it made a written demand for reclamation within the statutory time limit after the debtor received the goods.

Victory Markets, 212 B.R. at 741. The reclaiming seller has the burden of establishing each element of §546(c) by a preponderance of the evidence. *Victory Markets*, 212 B.R. at 741. Thus, in addition to establishing the requirements necessary to obtain reclamation under common law or any statutory right for such relief, the seller seeking reclamation under §546(c) must prove that it sold the goods in the ordinary course of business and it made a written demand within ten days of the receipt of the goods. Pester Refining Co. v. Ethyl Corp. (In re Pester Refining Co.), 964 F.2d 842, 845 (8th Cir. 1992). Moreover, Bankruptcy Code §546(c) limits the definition of insolvency to that found in 11 U.S.C. §101(31). *Video King*, 100 B.R. at 1013.

In addition, to be subject to reclamation, goods must be identifiable and cannot have been processed into other products. Party Packing Corporation v. Rosenberg (In re Landy Beef Co., Inc.), 30 B.R. 19, 21 (Bankr. D. Mass. 1983). It has also been noted that "an implicit requirement of a §546(c) reclamation claim is that the debtor must possess the goods when the reclamation demand is made." Flav-O-Rich, Inc. v. Rawson Food Service, Inc. (In re Rawson Food Service, Inc.), 846 F.2d 1343, 1344 (11th Cir. 1988). . . . However, it is not clear "whether possession is an element under §546(c) of the Bankruptcy Code or in establishing an independent right of reclamation under nonbankruptcy law to be recognized under §546(c)." *Video King*, 100 B.R. at 1014. Logic dictates that, if not possession, the debtor should at least have control over the goods if it is to be required to return them. For the same reason, if the goods are not identifiable, the debtor could not identify or extract the goods to return them to the reclaiming seller. The issue concerning control of the goods or the identifiable nature of the goods would be relevant whether or not the reclaiming seller is seeking the goods in a bankruptcy context. Thus, it appears that these elements are requirements under the "independent right of reclamation under nonbankruptcy law." *Video King*, 100 B.R. at 1014.

Section 546(c) also affords the bankruptcy court broad discretion to substitute an administrative claim or lien in place of the right to reclaim. *Pester*, 964 F.2d at 845. This discretion gives the court needed flexibility and permits it to recognize the reclaiming creditor's rights while allowing the debtor the opportunity to retain the goods in order to facilitate the reorganization effort. Id.

Uniform Commercial Code ("U.C.C.") §2-702, as enacted in various jurisdictions, ordinarily forms the statutory right upon which sellers base their reclamation demand. Thus, as previously noted, the reclaiming seller must establish the requirements of the relevant U.C.C. section and remains subject to its limitations. Pursuant to U.C.C. §2-702(3), the seller's right to reclamation is "subject to" the rights of a good faith purchaser from the buyer. *Pester*, 964 F.2d at 844. . . . That the right of a reclaiming creditor is subordinate to that of a good faith purchaser does not automatically extinguish the reclamation right. *Pester*, 964 F.2d at 846. Rather, the reclaiming creditor is "relegated to some less commanding station." *Leeds*, 141 B.R. at 268.

Most courts have treated "a holder of a prior perfected, floating lien on inventory . . . as a good faith purchaser with rights superior to those of a reclaiming seller." See *Victory Markets*, 212 B.R. at 742 [many citations omitted]. Galey argues that the courts that have found parties with secured interests in inventory to be good faith purchasers have merely referred to the definitions of good faith purchaser under the U.C.C. §1-201(19), (32), and (33). Galey contends that because U.C.C. §2-702(3) refers to the reclaiming seller's interest as being subject to the interest of a good faith purchaser "under this Article," only parties acquiring their interests under Article 2 of the U.C.C. are the type of good faith purchasers encompassed within the protection of U.C.C. §2-702(3). Therefore, Galey contends that parties acquiring security interests under Article 9 of the U.C.C. are not included. Galey also points to the Seventh Circuit decision in In re Reliable Drug Stores, Inc., where the court, in dicta, noted that there was room for debate as to whether a party with a security interest qualified as a good faith purchaser. 70 F.3d 948, 949 (7th Cir. 1995).

U.C.C. §2-702(3) provides that the right to reclamation is "subject to the rights of a buyer in ordinary course or other good faith purchaser under this Article (Section 2-403)." However, neither U.C.C. §2-403 nor any other section in Article 2 defines "good faith purchaser." U.C.C. §2-403 is entitled "Power to Transfer; Good Faith Purchase of Goods; Entrusting" and concerns the power certain parties have to transfer goods and the rights of certain parties who acquire those goods. While the section makes reference to these various parties, it does not define who they are. In fact, the only definition provided in U.C.C. §2-403 is of the term "entrusting." To derive the definition of "good faith purchaser," reference must be made to several subsections of U.C.C. §1-201, which provides general definitions applicable to the entire U.C.C. First, "good faith" is defined as "honesty in fact in the conduct or transaction concerned." U.C.C. §1-201(19). This is further refined when dealing with a merchant because U.C.C. §2-103(1)(b) requires the "observance of reasonable commercial standards of fair dealing in the trade." A "purchaser" is defined as one "who takes by purchase," U.C.C. §1-201(33), and "purchase" is defined to include "taking by sale, discount, negotiation, mortgage, pledge, lien, issue or re-issue, gift or any other voluntary transaction creating an interest in property." U.C.C. §1-201(32). Thus, the definition of purchaser is broad enough to include an Article 9 secured party, which then qualifies as a purchaser under U.C.C. §2-403. See *Samuels & Co.*, 526 F.2d at 1242. The reference in U.C.C. §2-702(3) to "the rights of a buyer in ordinary course or other good faith purchaser under this Article (Section 2-403)" does not mean to imply that reclaiming sellers are only subject to interests acquired under Article 2. Rather, the focus is on the rights of the listed parties under Article 2. Under this reading, the purpose for the reference to U.C.C. §2-403 is clear. U.C.C. §2-403 provides, in part, that "[a] person with voidable title has power to transfer a good title to a good faith purchaser for value." As included in the U.C.C. §1-201(44) definition, "value" is considered to be given for rights if they are acquired "as security for or in total or partial satisfaction of a pre-existing claim." Thus, under Article 2—specifically U.C.C. §2-403—the party who qualifies as a "good faith purchaser" as defined under U.C.C. §1-201 and gives "value," as defined in U.C.C. §1-201(44), acquires greater rights than the party transferring the goods to it had. Therefore, U.C.C. §2-403 gives a transferor, even one who has acquired goods wrongfully, the power to transfer the goods "to a Code-defined 'good faith purchaser.'" *Samuels & Co.*, 526 F.2d at 1242. Thus, in the instant case, if CIT qualifies as a good faith purchaser pursuant to U.C.C. §1-201 and gave value pursuant to U.C.C. §1-201(44), then pursuant to U.C.C. §2-403, even if Arley had voidable title to the goods, it could transfer good title under Article 2 to CIT. Further, if CIT obtained the goods in this manner, the demand of a reclaiming seller is subject to CIT's interest. U.C.C. §2-702(3). . . .

Galey also directs the Court's attention to dicta in *Reliable Drug*, 70 F.3d at 949-50, where the court noted that, although there was substantial case law holding that properly perfected lienholders were good faith purchasers, legal scholars debated the issue. The *Reliable Drug* court observed that one view was that "[U.C.C. §2-702(2)] gives a vendor the rights of a purchase-money security holder for 10 days, and the purchase-money lender undoubtedly beats a creditor with a security interest in after-acquired inventory." Id. at 950 (citing Thomas A. Jackson & Ellen Ash Peters, Quest for Uncertainty:

A Proposal for Flexible Resolution of Inherent Conflicts Between Article 2 and Article 9 of the Uniform Commercial Code, 87 Yale L.J. 907, 965-70 (1977-78)). The law review article is premised on the view that a party with a security interest should only be considered a good faith purchaser for value if it has suffered detrimental reliance by extending new value. The authors of the article acknowledge that a prior secured lender with an after-acquired property interest "meets the apparently literal requirements of a good faith purchaser for value." 87 Yale L.J. at 965. Nevertheless, they argue that the "open-ended" language of U.C.C. §2-403, a comment to the section, and "the pervasive weighing of equities in Article 2" should "justify relying on [a] more flexible approach." 87 Yale L.J. at 966, 968.

However, if the language of a statute is plain, the court's role "is to enforce it according to its terms." U.S. v. Ron Pair Enterprises, Inc., 489 U.S. 235, 241, 109 S. Ct. 1026, 1030, 103 L. Ed. 2d 290 (1989). The Uniform Commercial Code includes "value" as being given for goods if they are acquired "as security for or in total or partial satisfaction of a pre-existing claim." U.C.C. §1-201(44). The state legislature is the appropriate forum to address the issue of whether or not the statute should be amended to allow a reclaiming seller priority against a prior secured lender with an after-acquired property interest who has not advanced new funding. However, this Court is required to interpret the statute as written and, based on our earlier analysis of the relevant sections of the Uniform Commercial Code as currently drafted, a creditor with a security interest in after-acquired property who acted in good faith and for value, which includes acquiring rights "as security for or in total or partial satisfaction of a pre-existing claim," U.C.C. §1-201(44), is a good faith purchaser to whose claim that of a reclaiming seller is subject.

The Court now turns to whether CIT acted in good faith. The U.C.C. definition of good faith is "honesty in fact," U.C.C. §1-201(19), which "for Article Two purposes, is 'expressly defined as . . . reasonable commercial standards of fair dealing.'" *Samuels & Co.*, 526 F.2d 1238 (5th Cir. 1976) (citing U.C.C. §§1-201, Comment 19; 2-103(a)(2)).

Galey argues that a determination as to CIT's good faith cannot be made on summary judgment because there is a factual issue as to CIT's good faith. However, Galey has not challenged the validity of the lien nor has it asserted that there was any misconduct by CIT. Neither has it alleged that CIT acted in bad faith in its dealings with Arley. Rather, Galey argues that CIT was aware that Arley was having financial problems and stopped advancing funds to Arley without informing Galey of its decision. Therefore it appears that Galey's argument is that Arley was aware that other creditors would be impacted by its decision to stop funding Arley.

However, the secured creditor with a floating lien remains a good faith purchaser even if it terminates funding with knowledge that sums are owed to third parties, as long as the decision concerning the funding was commercially reasonable. *Samuels,* 526 F.2d at 1244. There is no allegation that the contract obligated CIT to advance any additional funds. The "honesty in fact" element does not require a secured creditor to continue to fund a business with enormous debt and continuous losses. Id.; Mitsubishi Consumer Electronics America, Inc. v. Steinberg's, Inc. (In re Steinberg's, Inc.), 226 B.R. 8, 11 (Bankr. S.D. Ohio 1998). Rather, a decision to stop funding such an enterprise is "clearly reasonable." *Samuels,* 526 F.2d at 1244. An entity that advances funds secured by a valid lien on all the borrower's assets is a good faith purchaser absent a showing of misconduct by the secured creditor. Pillsbury Co. v. FCX, Inc. (In re FCX, Inc.), 62 B.R. 315, 320 (Bankr. E.D.N.C. 1986). The burden is on the reclaiming seller to show misconduct by the secured creditor. *FCX, Inc.,* 62 B.R. at 322. Some courts have framed the issue as an absence of bad faith. *Victory Markets,* 212 B.R. at 742 (citing cases). Others as the secured creditor's lack of good faith. *Steinberg's Inc.,* 226 B.R. at 11 (citing cases). Under any formulation, the reclaiming seller bears the burden of proof under §546(c). Id.; *Victory Markets,* 212 B.R. at 741. . . .

Galey's conclusory assertions concerning the absence of good faith by CIT are not sufficient to create the fair doubt required to show that the issue is genuine. Galey makes no allegation of misconduct by CIT in its negotiations with Arley or in its compliance with the terms of the financing agreement with Arley. CIT has not set forth any basis upon which to question CIT's good faith. Thus, there is no genuine issue of material fact concerning whether CIT acted in good faith. Moreover, there is no factual dispute on the issue of whether CIT gave value and qualifies as a good faith purchaser for value, pursuant to the Code's definitions of the various terms. Therefore, the Court grants summary judgment on the issue and finds that CIT qualifies as a good faith purchaser for value.

As previously noted, while a seller's right to reclamation is subject to the rights of a good faith purchaser, the reclamation right is not automatically extinguished. Relying on this principle, Galey argues that, pursuant to §546, it is entitled to either an administrative claim or lien in lieu of its right to reclamation. Galey maintains that if it is denied this relief, its claim effectively is extinguished by the presence of a good faith purchaser. Further, Galey contends that because there will be surplus collateral once CIT has been paid in full, that collateral should be used to pay Galey's reclamation claim and it should get its administrative claim or lien on that surplus.

The Trustee counters that it is not arguing that a reclaiming seller's claim is extinguished. Rather, the Trustee argues that when the goods subject to a reclamation demand are liquidated and the proceeds are used to pay the secured creditor's claim, the reclaiming seller's subordinated right is rendered valueless. The Trustee maintains that once the secured creditor is paid in full, the reclaiming seller is only entitled to reclamation when the surplus collateral remaining consists of the very goods sold by the reclaiming seller or the traceable proceeds from those goods.

Courts differ on the treatment to be afforded reclaiming sellers subject to the superior rights of good faith purchasers. Some courts have awarded a reclaiming seller, who otherwise meets the criteria to qualify as a reclaiming seller but is subject to a superior claim, an administrative claim or replacement lien for the full amount of the goods sought to be reclaimed. *Sunstate Dairy,* 145 B.R. at 345-46; In re Diversified Food Service Distributors, Inc., 130 B.R. 427, 430 (Bankr. S.D.N.Y. 1991). However, the majority view appears to be some method of assuring that the reclaiming seller only receive what it would have received outside of the bankruptcy context after the superior claim was satisfied. *Pester,* 964 F.2d at 847; *Leeds,* 141 B.R. at 269; *Blinn,* 164 B.R. at 448; *Victory Markets,* 212 B.R. at 744. Thus, it is only when the reclaiming seller's goods or traceable proceeds from those goods are in excess of the value of the superior claimant's claim that the reclaiming seller will be allowed either to reclaim the goods or receive an administrative claim or lien in an amount equal to the goods that remain after the superior claim has been paid. . . .

Thus, while the reclaiming seller's claim is not automatically extinguished, the reclaiming seller is also not automatically granted an administrative claim or lien in the full amount sought when it is subject to the rights of the good faith purchaser. *Victory Markets,* 212 B.R. at 743. Rather, the reclaiming seller's right to reclaim depends on the value of the excess goods remaining once the secured creditor's claim is paid or released. Id.

As the bankruptcy filing does not enhance the reclaiming seller's rights, the Court should determine what would have happened to the reclaiming seller's claim in a nonbankruptcy context. The parties concede that under state law the secured creditor would have the option of proceeding against any of its collateral. Therefore, the secured creditor may choose to foreclose on the goods sold by the reclaiming seller if these goods can be readily liquidated. When the secured claim, or a portion of it, is paid out of the goods sought to be reclaimed, the right to reclaim is rendered valueless. *Pester,* 964 F.2d at 847. Thus, "in the non-bankruptcy context, the secured creditor's decision with respect to its security interest in the goods will determine the value of the seller's right to reclaim." *Pester,* 964 F.2d at 847. Here, following the Debtors' filing, CIT decided not to seek relief from the Court to pursue those remedies available to it to secure the immediate liquidation of all the Debtors' assets. Rather, it supported the Debtors' efforts to sell its inventory including any Galey goods in the ordinary course of its business. As a result, all of the goods which Galey sought to reclaim were sold and the proceeds used to pay CIT. Moreover, even after CIT received payment from the sale of the goods, there was still a balance due it. Thus, Galey's reclamation claim was rendered valueless. . . .

Finally, because this Court finds that Galey is not entitled to an administrative claim or replacement lien in as much as any right to reclamation it might have was subject to CIT's security interest and was rendered valueless by CIT's interest, it is unnecessary for the Court to reach the issue of whether Galey otherwise complied with all the requirements for a right to reclamation.

CONCLUSION

CIT, as the holder of a perfected security interest in substantially all Arley's assets including accounts receivable and inventory, is a good faith purchaser for value. Galey's interest as a reclaiming seller in the goods it sold Arley is subject to CIT's rights as a good faith purchaser. Galey's reclamation claim was rendered valueless because the proceeds from the disposition of the Galey goods were used to pay CIT's secured claim. Therefore, the value of any right Galey has to an administrative claim or replacement lien, pursuant to §546, is zero. . . .

The Trustee is to settle an Order consistent with this Memorandum Decision.

QUESTION

What could the seller have done in this situation in order to prevail over the floating lien that CIT had on the buyer's inventory? See §9-324(b).

PROBLEM 97

Octopus National Bank (ONB) held a perfected security interest in all the cattle owned by Family Farms of Iowa, Inc. (a mom-and-pop operation). When it became obvious that the farm was failing financially, ONB decided to pull the plug. Before it did so, it wanted to make sure that the cattle were well-fed, so the ONB officer in charge of loan management called Cow Chow, Inc., and encouraged it to make another delivery of cattle feed to Family Farms, even though it had not been paid for its last two deliveries. ONB did not mention that it was about to foreclose on the fattened cattle, which it did as soon as they had consumed most of the new delivery (for which Cow Chow billed Family Farms in the amount of $10,000). Cow Chow was an unsecured creditor, which ONB well knew. Is ONB required to give Cow Chow any of the money it realizes from the foreclosure sale? See §§1-103 and 1-304; Ninth Dist. Prod. Credit Assn. v. Ed Duggan, Inc., 821 P.2d 788 (Colo. 1991); see also

Feresi v. The Livery, LLC, 2014 WL 7530260 (Cal. App. 2014) (breach of fiduciary duty destroys perfected security interest).

VII. STATUTORY LIEN HOLDERS

Just as the buyer in the ordinary course of business is a favorite of the law, those doing repairs in the ordinary course of business are frequently given priority over previously perfected consensual security interests. Read §9-333 and its Official Comments.

PROBLEM 98

The Repossession Finance Company (RFC) had a perfected security interest in Hattie Mobile's car (RFC's lien was noted on the certificate of title as required by state law). The car broke down on the interstate one day, and Hattie had it towed to Mike's Greasepit Garage, where it was repaired. State law gave a possessory artisan's lien to repairpersons. The garage told Hattie it was claiming such a lien, but when she pleaded with the manager, he let her drive the car to work after she assured him that she would return the car to the garage for storage every night (fortunately, she lived across the street). Repossession found out about this practice and, deeming itself insecure (§1-309), accelerated the amount due and repossessed the car from the parking lot in front of Hattie's place of business.

(a) Which creditor has the superior interest in the car under §9-333? Forrest Cate Ford v. Fryar, 62 Tenn. App. 572, 465 S.W.2d 882 (1970).

(b) If the car had been in Mike's possession when the conflict arose, would it matter under §9-333 that the finance company never gave its consent to the repairs? See Williamsport Natl. Bank v. Shrey, 612 A.2d 1081 (Pa. Super. 1992); Annot., 69 A.L.R.3d 1162.

(c) Once Mike's released the car to Hattie, did its lien reattach whenever she returned it to the garage? See M&I W. State Bank v. Wilson, 172 Wis. 2d 357, 493 N.W.2d 387 (Ct. App. 1992).

If the garage's charges are unconscionably high, does the lien still prevail? See §1-304; G. Gilmore §33.5, at 888: "To be entitled to priority under [§9-333] the lienor must have furnished services or materials 'in the ordinary course of his business.' This limitation should be read as tantamount to a requirement of good faith. . . . Section [9-333] is designed to protect the honest lienor and not the crook."

VIII.   FIXTURES

Article 9 of necessity had to make special rules for the creation and perfection of a *fixture*—the legal bugaboo that hangs in limbo somewhere between chattel mobility and realty attachment. See, e.g., §9-109(a) ("[T]his Article applies . . . to: (1) any transaction . . . that creates a security interest in personal property *or fixtures.* . . .") and §9-501(a)(1)(B) (directing that fixture filings be made in the real property records).

The Code has only the most limited definition of *fixtures:* "'Fixtures' means goods that have become so related to particular real property that an interest in them arises under real property law," §9-102(a)(41), and "A security interest does not exist under this article in ordinary building materials incorporated into an improvement on land," §9-334(a). Obviously pre-Code state law defining *fixtures* is very important. State law tests range from a pure *annexation* test (measured by the difficulty of removal) to an "intention of the parties" test (for which the leading case is Teaff v. Hewitt, 1 Ohio St. 511 (1853)). Moreover, some courts have developed different categories of fixtures. *Trade fixtures* are items of personal property necessary to the conduct of the tenant's business but not permanently affixed to the realty. They remain the tenant's and may be removed when the tenancy ends. Generally, the UCC courts treat a trade fixture as equipment and not as a true fixture, In re Factory Homes Corp., 333 F. Supp. 126 (W.D. Ark. 1971), though the wide-awake lawyer will advise dual filings. A similar idea is the *assembled industrial plant* doctrine, which has it that all items connected with the operation of a going business are fixtures (primarily a Pennsylvania way of thinking; for the doctrine's clash with the UCC, see In re Griffin, 182 B.R. 8 (Bankr. M.D. Pa. 1995)). For general treatise discussions of the meaning of *fixture,* see 8 Powell on Real Property §57 (Michael Allan Wolf ed., 2014); 5 Thompson on Real Property §46 (David A. Thomas ed., 2d ed., 2007); Friedman on Contracts & Conveyances of Real Property §3A:5 (James C. Smith ed., 7th ed. 2011);

George v. Commercial Credit Corp.

United States Court of Appeals, Seventh Circuit, 1971
440 F.2d 551

DUFFY, J.

This is an appeal from an order of the District Court affirming the decision of a Referee in Bankruptcy and sustaining a secured creditor's interest in a mobile home.

The question before us for decision is whether appellee's real estate mortgage on his mobile home may prevail against the trustee's claimed interest.

The referee and the District Court upheld the appellee's claim finding that the mobile home had become a fixture under Wisconsin law. The trustee argues that the mobile home was not a fixture, in fact, and secondly, that the law of fixtures does not apply to security interests in mobile homes.

Dale Wallace Foskett owned five acres of land in Jefferson County, Wisconsin. On December 6, 1968, he purchased a Marshfield Mobile Home, No. 9090, from Highway Mobile Home Sales, Inc. He signed an installment contract and paid $880 on the purchase price of $8,800. Added was a sales tax and interest covering a ten-year period.

Sometime in December 1968, Foskett executed a real estate mortgage to Highway Mobile Home Sales, Inc. The mortgage recites the sum of $14,227.70 and described the real estate in metes and bounds. The mortgage was assigned to Commercial Credit Corporation, the respondent-appellee herein.

The mobile home here in question could not move under its own power. It was delivered to Foskett's real property by Mobile Sales. This mobile home was never again operated on or over the highways as a motor vehicle.

The mobile home here in question was 68 feet in length, 14 feet in width and 12 feet in height. It contained six rooms and weighed 15,000 pounds.

The bankrupt owned no other home and he and his wife occupied the mobile home continuously from December 6, 1968, until forced to vacate same by order of the Trustee in Bankruptcy.

The home was set on cinder blocks three courses high. It was connected with a well. It was hooked up to a septic tank. It also was connected with electric power lines.

The bankrupt never applied for a certificate of title from the Wisconsin Motor Vehicle Department. However, he did apply for a home owner's insurance policy and he asked the seller to remove the wheels from his home. He also applied for a building permit and was told he had to construct a permanent foundation for the home. The permit was granted upon condition that the foundation be constructed within one year. However, within that period, the petition for bankruptcy was filed.

The issue before us can be thus stated: Commercial Credit Corporation argues that the mobile home was a fixture under applicable law and is not personalty. The trustee insists that the mobile home was and still is a "motor vehicle" and is personalty.

The mobile homes industry has grown rapidly in the last few years. There has been a great demand for relatively inexpensive housing by middle income families. In Wisconsin, a distinction is now recognized between mobile homes (those used as homes) and motor homes (those often used as vehicles).

In the recent case of Beaulieu v. Minnehoma Insurance Co., 44 Wis. 2d 437, 171 N.W.2d 348 (1969), the Wisconsin Supreme Court pointed out the unique character of mobile homes: "As indicated by the plaintiff, a mobile home has a dual nature. It is designed as a house; yet, unlike a house, it is also capable of being easily transported. In the instant case, it was employed solely as an economical means of housing. It was never moved, nor was moving contemplated at the time the insurance coverage was procured." (44 Wis. 2d at 439).

We look to state law to determine the applicable standards for determining when personalty becomes affixed to real property.

The Wisconsin law on the question is found in Auto Acceptance and Loan Corp. v. Kelm, 18 Wis. 2d 178, 118 N.W.2d 175 (1962) where the Wisconsin Supreme Court reaffirmed its decision in Standard Oil Co. v. LaCrosse Super Auto Service, Inc., 217 Wis. 237, 258 N.W. 791 (1935). That case held that the three tests for determining whether facilities remain personalty or are to be considered part of the realty are (1) actual physical annexation to the realty; (2) application or adaption to the use or purpose to which the realty is devoted; and (3) intention of the person making annexation to make a permanent accession to the freehold.

In the *Standard Oil Company* case, supra, the court pointed out that "physical annexation" is relatively unimportant and "intention" of the parties is the principal consideration.

In Premonstratensian Fathers v. Badger Mutual Insurance Co., 46 Wis. 2d 362, 175 N.W.2d 237 (1970), the court reaffirmed its adherence to the three-fold test saying, (46 Wis. 2d at p.367) "It is the application of these tests to the facts of a particular case which will lead to a determination of whether or not an article, otherwise considered personal property, constitutes a common-law fixture, and hence takes on the nature of real property."

Viewed in light of these Wisconsin tests, the finding of the referee and the District Court that this mobile home had become a fixture must clearly stand. The bankrupt's actual intention pointed definitely toward affixing the mobile home to the land as a permanent residence, as seen in his application for a building permit (which, by law, required him to erect a concrete slab as a permanent foundation within one year), his purchase of a homeowner's insurance policy, and his requests made to the seller to have the wheels of the home removed. Moreover, the home was clearly adapted to use as the permanent residence of the bankrupt and was never moved off of his five-acre plot.

The fact that it may have been physically possible for this mobile home to have been more securely attached to the ground should not alter our position. Physical attachment did occur by means of cinder blocks and a "C" clamp, while connections for electricity, sewage and natural gas were provided as well. Finally, we note that the very size and difficulty in transporting this mobile home further highlight the fact that this was a vehicle which was intended primarily to be placed in one position for a long period of time and to be used as an intended permanent home. . . .

Our reading of the Wisconsin Statutes is thus consistent with other statutory and common law provisions dealing with the fixture situation, such as §9-334 of the Uniform Commercial Code which takes care to state that the Code does *not* prevent creation of encumbrances upon fixtures or real estate pursuant to the law applicable to real estate. (See also 4A Collier on Bankruptcy, §70.20 pp.283-295.)

In view of our holding that this particular mobile home had become a fixture under Wisconsin law and that the law of fixtures may, by law, be applied to mobile homes in that state, the judgment of the District must be and is Affirmed.

NOTE

See White & Summers §25-5(a). Then there is this oft-quoted passage from Strain v. Green, 25 Wash. 2d 692, 695, 172 P.2d 216, 218 (1946):

> [W]e will not undertake to write a Treatise on the law of fixtures. Every lawyer knows that cases can be found in this field that will support any position that the facts of his particular case require him to take. . . . [T]here is a wilderness of authority. . . . Fixture cases are so conflicting that it would be profitless . . . to review . . . them.

PROBLEM 99

As stated above, in differentiating among goods (subject to UCC filing), fixtures (subject to UCC and realty filing), and ordinary building materials (subject only to realty filing), courts look to three tests: (1) actual physical annexation to the realty, (2) application or adaption to the use or purpose to which the realty is devoted, and (3) intention of the person making annexation to make a permanent accession to the freehold. Decide how each of the following would be characterized:

1. The furnace that heats the building and water;
2. The pipes that carry the hot water through the walls;
3. A couch that has been sitting in the living room for 20 years;
4. A lavish designer bathtub, handcrafted and carefully set in the corner; see In re Ryan, 360 B.R. 50 (Bankr. W.D.N.Y. 2007).
5. Security cameras, tracks, wiring, and equipment for wireless Internet access; see In re Marble Cliff Crossing Apartments, LLC, 484 B.R. 175 (Bankr. S.D. Ohio 2012).

In theory, your basic property course taught you to tell fixtures from non-fixtures with more refinement. Our main concern is resolution of priority disputes between those who have a security interest in the fixture and those who have or acquire an interest in the realty to which the collateral is affixed. Read §9-334 carefully, and then consider these Problems.

PROBLEM 100

Monopoly Railway went to Octopus National Bank (ONB) and asked to borrow money, using as part of the collateral its extensive network of railroad track (rails and ties), which winds through 12 western states. ONB consults you. The track is installed in a total of 117 counties. Must it file a financing statement in each one? See §§9-501(b) and 9-102(a)(81).

PROBLEM 101

Simon Mustache decided to erect an apartment building on a vacant lot he owned, so he borrowed $4 million from Construction State Bank (CSB), to which he mortgaged the real estate "and all appurtenances or things affixed thereto, now present or after-acquired." Simon and CSB signed the mortgage, which contained a legal description of the realty, and the mortgage was filed in the real property recorder's office. Is the mortgage effective as a financing statement? See §9-502(c). During construction of the apartment building, Simon Mustache bought a furnace on credit from Blast Home Supplies, giving Blast a security interest in the furnace that described the real estate. Where should Blast file its financing statement? See §9-501. Is there a technical sentence that needs to be in this financing statement? See §9-502(b)(2). Why would the drafters have added such a requirement? Even if Blast files a proper financing statement in the right place before the furnace is installed, will Blast prevail over CSB? See §9-334(d) and (h), and Official Comment 11. If CSB's interest is not perfected, will Blast prevail? See §9-334(e)(1). What can Blast do to ensure itself of priority? See §§9-334(f)(1), 9-339.

PROBLEM 102

Would your answer to the last Problem's priority disputes change if the object in question were a refrigerator? What if it were a computer that Simon purchased for use in his office (which is located in the apartment building)? (Note: some states would consider the computer a *fixture* under the *industrial plant* doctrine; see the discussion above.) See §9-334(e)(2) and (f)(2), and Official Comment 8.

Lewiston Bottled Gas Co. v. Key Bank of Maine

Maine Supreme Judicial Court, 1992
601 A.2d 91

CLIFFORD, J.

Plaintiff Lewiston Bottled Gas Company (LBG) appeals from an order of summary judgment entered by the Superior Court (Androscoggin County, Perkins, J.) in favor of defendant Key Bank of Maine in this declaratory judgment action brought to determine the rights of the parties with respect to ninety heating and air-conditioning units installed in the Grand Beach Inn at Old Orchard Beach. We agree with the Superior Court that Key Bank's mortgage gives it priority over LBG's purchase money security interest in the units and we affirm the judgment.

In July 1986, Key Bank loaned $2,580,000 to William J. DiBiase, Jr. The loan was secured by a mortgage on the real estate owned by DiBiase located on East Grand Avenue in Old Orchard Beach. The mortgage, which covered after-acquired fixtures, was properly recorded in the York County Registry of Deeds. On June 10, 1987, DiBiase incorporated Grand Beach Inn., Inc. (Grand Beach) for the purpose of constructing and operating the Grand Beach Inn on DiBiase's East Grand Avenue property. DiBiase was the president and sole shareholder of Grand Beach and at all relevant times was the owner of the property.

On June 15, 1987, Grand Beach contracted to purchase ninety heating and air-conditioning units from LBG. The contract provided that the units would remain the personal property of Grand Beach notwithstanding their attachment to the real property. On June 16, Grand Beach granted to LBG a purchase money security interest in the ninety units. Financing statements disclosing the security interest and identifying the debtor as "Grand Beach Inn, Inc., William J. DiBiase, Jr., President" and describing the real estate upon which the units were located as "Grand Beach Inn, East Grand Avenue, Old Orchard Beach, ME 04064" were filed with the Secretary of State and also recorded in the York County Registry of Deeds. In each place, they were indexed under the name "Grand Beach Inn, Inc." Nothing, however, was indexed under DiBiase's name. In September and October 1987, the units were installed in the exterior walls of each room in the Inn.

On June 29, 1987, Key Bank made a second loan to DiBiase secured by a second mortgage on the same property, also covering after-acquired fixtures and also properly recorded. The title search undertaken by Key Bank in the York County Registry of Deeds prior to the execution of the mortgage failed to disclose the financing statement and the existence of LBG's security interest in the units because LBG's financing statement was indexed under the name "Grand Beach" even though DiBiase was the record owner of the property at the time.

In May 1989, Key Bank foreclosed on both its mortgages. LBG was not joined as a party-in-interest because Key Bank was unaware of LBG's interest in the units until after the foreclosure was commenced. The parties agreed to allow the foreclosure to proceed and to litigate the issue of title to the heating and air-conditioning units later. Key Bank was the successful bidder at the foreclosure sale. LBG then filed the present complaint against Key Bank seeking a declaratory judgment that its purchase money security interest in the units had priority over the interest of Key Bank. The Superior Court granted summary judgment to Key Bank concluding that the heating and air-conditioning units were fixtures and that Key Bank's properly recorded mortgages had priority over LBG's unperfected security interest. This appeal followed. . . .

II. Units as Fixtures

11 M.R.S.A. §9-313(1)(a) [the predecessor to §9-334—Eds.] (1964 & Supp. 1991) provides that "[g]oods are 'fixtures' when they become so related to particular real estate that an interest in them arises under real estate law." That interest arises when the property is (1) physically annexed to the real estate, (2) adapted to the use to which the real estate is put, that is, the personal and real property are united in the carrying out of a common purpose, and (3) annexed with the intent to make it part of the realty. Boothbay Harbor Condominiums, Inc. v. Department of Transp., 382 A.2d 848, 854 (Me. 1978) (citing Bangor-Hydro Elec. Co. v. Johnson, 226 A.2d 371, 378 (Me. 1967)).

The evidence compels a conclusion that, under the first prong of the three-part fixture test, the units were physically annexed to the real estate. The heating and air-conditioning units were installed when the Inn was under construction and are part of the walls of the building. The units are attached by bolts and although they could be removed, their removal would create a large hole in the walls of each room. See Roderick v. Sanborn, 106 Me. 159, 162, 76 A. 263 (1909) (property need not be permanently fastened to realty to be physically annexed).

As to the second prong of the test, it is undisputed that the units, although they are catalogue items and not specially made for the Grand Beach Inn, were adapted to the use of the real estate as the Grand Beach Inn. The real estate was designed and built as an inn to accommodate overnight guests. The heating and air-conditioning units help create a livable atmosphere for those guests by providing heat and cooling to the rooms. The personal and real property, therefore, are united in the carrying out of a common enterprise. See *Bangor-Hydro,* 226 A.2d at 376. The fact that the units are catalogue items, and not custom-made, does not preclude them from being fixtures.

The intent of the person annexing the personal property to the real estate is the third and most important of the three prongs of the fixture test. *Bangor-Hydro,* 226 A.2d at 377. LBG contends that summary judgment was improperly granted to Key Bank because the agreements between DiBiase and LBG granted to LBG a purchase money security interest in the units and expressly stated that the units would remain personal property and therefore demonstrated DiBiase's intent that the units remain personal property. We disagree.

In determining the intent of the parties as to whether a chattel annexed to real estate becomes a fixture, it is not the hidden subjective intent of the person making the annexation that must be considered but rather "the intention which the law deduces from such external facts as the structure and mode of attachment, the purpose and use for which the annexation has been made and the relation and use of the party making it." *Bangor-Hydro,* 226 A.2d at 378. The agreement DiBiase made with LBG to have the heating and air-conditioning units remain personal property cannot be considered against Key Bank on the fixtures issue because Key Bank was not a party to those agreements and was unaware of them. Vorsec Co. v. Gilkey, 132 Me. 311, 314, 170 A. 722 (1934); Gaunt v. Allen Lane Co., 128 Me. 41, 46, 145 A. 255 (1929).

The objective manifestation of intent in this case, as evidenced by the physical annexation of the units to the walls of the building and their adaptation to the use of the real estate as an inn, leaves no genuine dispute that the units are fixtures and part of the Grand Beach Inn real estate.

III.   LBG's Failure to Perfect Its Security Interest

Because the heating and air-conditioning units were fixtures and part of the real estate, they became subject to Key Bank's mortgages pursuant to §9-313. Key Bank's first mortgage takes priority over LBG's security interest in the units unless LBG's security interest falls within one of the exceptions found in §9-313. 11 M.R.S.A. §9-313(7) (Supp. 1991). The only relevant exception in this case is §9-313(4)(a) [now §9-334(d) — Eds.], which states:

> (4) A perfected security interest in fixtures has priority over the conflicting interest of an encumbrancer or owner of the real estate where:
> (a) The security interest is a purchase money security interest, the interest of the encumbrancer or owner arises before the goods become fixtures, the security interest is perfected by a fixture filing before the goods become fixtures or within 10 days thereafter, and the debtor has an interest of record in the real estate or is in possession of the real estate.

The security interest of LBG was a purchase money security interest. 11 M.R.S.A §9-107 (1964). The record clearly demonstrates, however, that it was not properly perfected and does not otherwise come within any recognized exception that would give it priority over Key Bank's first mortgage.

A security interest is perfected when it has attached and all of the applicable steps required for perfection have been taken. 11 M.R.S.A. §9-303(1)(1964). To perfect a security interest in a fixture, the secured party must file a "fixture filing." "A 'fixture filing' is the filing in the office where a mortgage on the real estate would be filed or recorded of a financing statement covering goods which are or are to become fixtures and conforming to the requirements of section 9-402, subsection (5)." 11 M.R.S.A. §9-313(1)(b) (Supp. 1991). Section 9-402(5) (Supp. 1991) requires that, in addition to the general requirements for financing statements set forth in §9-402(1) (the name and signature of the debtor, the name and address of the secured party and a description of the collateral), the fixture filing must contain a description of the real estate and, if the debtor does not have an interest of record in the real estate, "the financing statement must show *the name of a record owner.*" 11 M.R.S.A. §9-402(5) (emphasis added).

In this case, LBG's financing statement was correctly filed in the York County Registry of Deeds, identified the debtor as "Grand Beach Inn, Inc., William J. DiBiase, Jr., President," and contained a description of the real estate that we assume is adequate. Because it failed to identify DiBiase as the record owner of the property, however, the financing statement does not comply with §9-402(5).

As a general rule, a financing statement is sufficient if, in all the circumstances, the filing would give a title searcher sufficient notice to justify placing a duty upon the searcher to make further inquiry concerning the possible lien. In the Matters of Reeco Elec. Co., 415 F. Supp. 238, 240 (D. Me. 1976). In this case, the financing statement was indexed under "Grand Beach Inn, Inc." A title searcher would not be expected to check the index for "Grand Beach Inn, Inc." at a time when the property is owned by DiBiase. Because LBG failed to perfect its security interest in the heating and air-conditioning units pursuant to §9-402(5), the rights of Key Bank as mortgage holder of the real estate to which the units are affixed take priority over LBG's unperfected security interest.

The entry is: Judgment affirmed.

All concurring.

PROBLEM 103

Simon Mustache (of the last Problem) failed to pay his attorney, Susan Mean, so she sued him, recovered judgment, and levied on the apartment building and its contents. Will Simon's creditors holding security interests in the fixtures prevail if they have perfected by fixture filings? See §9-334(e)(3). What if those creditors filed financing statements in all the correct places *except* the real estate records? See Official Comment 9 to §9-334; In re Allen, 221 B.R. 232 (Bankr. S.D. Ill. 1998).

PROBLEM 104

After the building was complete, Tuesday Tenant moved in. Not liking the refrigerator Simon had installed, she had him remove it, and she bought another refrigerator on time from Easy Credit Department Store, which reserved a security interest therein but never filed a financing statement. Assume state real property laws permit Construction State Bank's after-acquired property mortgage to reach fixtures installed by lessees. (If they do not, Easy Credit will always prevail. See §9-334(f)(2).) Will Easy Credit be entitled to priority if it is forced to repossess? See §9-334(e)(2)(C) and Official Comment 8, third paragraph.

PROBLEM 105

Assume Tuesday (last Problem) bought a trash compactor on credit from Easy Credit Department Store and had her kitchen area remodeled to accommodate it. It was installed on May 5. Easy Credit comes to you on May 7. Is it entitled to automatic perfection of its security interest in consumer goods here? See Official Comment 3 (last sentence) to §9-309. Suppose it has a financing statement indicating the debtor is Tuesday. Should the statement contain Simon Mustache's name too? Why? See §9-502(b)(4). Will Easy Credit prevail over CSB if it files on May 10? See §9-334(d). Will it prevail over Simon's landlord's lien?

PROBLEM 106

Assume that Blast Home Supplies held a perfected security interest in Simon's furnace and that this interest was entitled to priority over CSB, the real estate mortgagee. If Simon defaults on his payments, what liability does Blast have to CSB if removal (repossession) of the furnace will do $1,000 damage to the building's structure and if to replace it Simon (or CSB) will have to spend $8,000? See §9-604 and its Official Comment 2. What are CSB's rights? See the last sentence of §9-604(d). Is Blast liable to Simon for the damage to the building caused by the furnace's removal?

contract . . . [and] *the security interest allows Sears to repossess the merchandise*" in the event the Capers did not make payments as agreed. (Emphasis added.)

Summary judgment in favor of plaintiff is affirmed.

NOTE

Professor Shanker appears to have prevailed on this issue because revised Article 9 has very different rules for repossessing fixture creditors in §9-604, and Official Comment 3 to that section specifically states that it was meant to overrule the case you have just read. But what does that mean in the context of the facts of the case? What could Sears do if §9-604 had been the law when the case was decided? See Timothy R. Zinnecker, The Default Provisions of Revised Article 9 of the Uniform Commercial Code: Part I, 54 Bus. Law. 1113, 1124-1128 (1999).

It should also be noted that a creditor who is repossessing a fixture is bound by all the usual repossession rules that we will study in Chapter 10 (and therefore cannot breach the peace; see §9-609, for example).

PROBLEM 107

Farmer Bean had filed a mortgage on his home in favor of Rural State Bank. The mortgage stated that it extended to the realty and all things "growing on, or attached thereto, now in existence or in the future." When Farmer Bean borrowed money to plant this year's crop, he gave a security interest in the crop to Seeds, Inc., the purchase money lender. If the latter files its financing statement in the appropriate place, will it prevail over Rural State's mortgage lien? See §9-334(i), and its Official Comment 12.

PROBLEM 108

When Farmer Bean bought a doublewide trailer from Traveling Homes, Inc., for $100,000, he had it towed to a vacant lot on his farm with police protection en route and large WIDE LOAD signs attached. That was the only trip the doublewide made in its life. It was then placed on a foundation that had been built on the vacant lot, attached to various utilities for electricity and water, and Farmer Bean built a fancy deck that he extended out the front door of the trailer. If you are the attorney representing the bank that loaned Farmer Bean the money to buy the doublewide, what steps should be taken to perfect its purchase money security interest in the collateral: a real estate mortgage? a fixture filing under Article 9 of the Uniform Commercial Code? or notation of the bank's interest on a certificate of title issued for the doublewide? See §9-334(e)(4); compare In re Kroskie, 315 F.3d 644 (6th Cir. 2003) (certificate of title controls), with In re Gregory, 316 B.R. 82 (Bankr. W.D. Mich. 2004) (real property laws trump Article 9 rules); White & Summers §25-5(b)(5); Mark R. Koontz, Manufactured Homes Under U.C.C. Revised Article 9: A New Conflict Between Certificates of Title and Financing Statements, 80 N.C. L. Rev. 1829 (2002).

IX. ACCESSIONS AND COMMINGLING

When goods are affixed to other goods (as opposed to realty), an *accession* occurs, and the rights of the creditors are regulated by §9-335. A similar problem arises when goods are so combined with other goods (eggs in a cake mix, for example) that they cannot be recovered. See §9-336 on *commingling*. Article 9's contribution to the solution to these problems can only be completely understood in light of centuries of property law development. A lawyer embroiled in litigation should review the basic common law rules. See 2 Thompson on Real Property §13.04(g)(6) (David A. Thomas ed., 3d ed., 2014)

PROBLEM 109

When Jane Witherspoon filed her bankruptcy petition she was living in a manufactured home that was in no way attached to the realty on which it sat. In the bankruptcy proceeding Life-Master Financing Company claimed a security interest in the home and all accessions pursuant to a security agreement. The accessions were not separately listed in the security agreement, but LifeMaster argued they included a porch Jane had had installed, as well as storm windows, a heater, carpeting, a built-in dishwasher, a replacement bathtub, a refrigerator, a stove, one air conditioner unit for the bedroom window, smoke detectors, and drapes. Which of these items, in your opinion, are accessions and which are not? See §9-335(d) and its Official Comment 7; In re Eaddy, 2016 WL 745277 (Bankr. D. S.C. 2016).

X. FEDERAL PRIORITIES FOR DEBTS AND TAXES

A. The Federal Priority Statute

Most of the federal statutes concerning secured transactions are registration acts only and say little or nothing about priorities in the collateral.

There are two major exceptions: the general federal priority statute, 31 U.S.C. §3713, and the Federal Tax Lien Act, which is part of the Internal Revenue Code (§§6321 to 6323).

The federal priority statute (enacted originally in 1797!) is a broadly worded grant of pre-bankruptcy priority for *all* federal claims (no matter how they arise: as tax matters, contract debts, federal insurance loans, guaranties, etc.), so these claims are paid first when a debtor becomes insolvent. It is a truism that governments, when making laws, always protect themselves before others.

> *Priority of Government Claims 31 U.S.C. §3713*
>
> (a)(1) A claim of the United States Government shall be paid first when —
>
> (A) a person indebted to the Government is insolvent and —
>
> (i) the debtor without enough property to pay all debts makes a voluntary assignment of property;
>
> (ii) property of the debtor, if absent, is attached; or
>
> (iii) the act of bankruptcy is committed; or
>
> (B) the estate of a deceased debtor, in the custody of the executor or administrator, is not enough to pay all debts of the debtor.
>
> (2) This section does not apply to a case under title 11 [bankruptcy].
>
> (b) A representative of a person or an estate (except a trustee acting under title 11) paying any part of a debt of the person or estate before paying a claim of the Government is liable to the extent of the payment for unpaid claims of the Government.

The statute makes no exceptions to absolute federal priority, but the courts have subordinated the federal claim to an earlier lien (judicial, statutory, and consensual) if the lien is *choate*, a word dating back to 1534 and meaning "complete or perfected." The United States Supreme Court, in a maddening series of cases, has refused to clarify the current meaning of *choate*, so it is difficult to predict when an earlier perfected lien will be sufficiently choate to prevail over the federal debt. Lower federal courts have held that most security interests perfected under Article 9 are sufficiently choate to come ahead of the United States' claim. Pine Builders, Inc. v. United States, 413 F. Supp. 77 (E.D. Va. 1976). There is general agreement, however, that a security arrangement claiming a floating lien on after-acquired property or claiming a priority for future advances is inchoate and inferior to the federal claim. G. Gilmore §40.5. It is clear that if the Federal Tax Lien Act, discussed next, applies to a dispute then it and not the Federal Priority Statute resolves the issues involved. It should also be noted that the Bankruptcy Code provides that federal tax debts get all sorts of special treatment in a bankruptcy proceeding, including surviving an individual debtor's discharge (as to income tax debts owed for the last three years); 11 U.S.C. §523(a)(1).

B. Tax Liens — Basic Priority

A federal tax lien arises on *assessment* and covers all of the taxpayer's property, real or personal, presently owned or after-acquired. It is a secret lien, because it may happen that no one knows of the assessment except the IRS, but the tax lien nevertheless binds the property, and the government wins out over all parties claiming an interest in the property except those listed in §6323(a): "any purchaser, holder of a security interest, mechanic's lienor, or judgment creditor." To prevail over such persons, the federal tax lien must be *filed* in the place designated under state law (which is almost always the state's Secretary of State Article 9 filing system). See I.R.C. §6323(f).

C. Tax Liens and After-Acquired Property

PROBLEM 110

Octopus National Bank (ONB) had a perfected security interest in the inventory, accounts receivable, instruments, and chattel paper of an automobile dealership named Smiles Motors, to which the bank made periodic loans. Smiles Motors failed to pay its federal taxes, and the IRS filed a tax lien in the proper place on October 1. On the first days of November and December new shipments of cars arrived at Smiles's lot, and all during the year Smiles continued to sell cars on credit, generating chattel paper and accounts receivable. Does the filing of the tax lien cut off ONB's floating lien in whole or in part? Is this issue in any way affected by the bank's knowledge of the tax lien filing?

The answer to this Problem is that §6323(c) of the Internal Revenue Code expressly permits *commercial financing security* (defined at the end of the section) to fall under an existing perfected security arrangement and take priority over a filed federal tax lien if the new collateral is acquired by the taxpayer-debtor in the 45 days following the tax lien filing. The statute, like most of the tax code, is written in almost impenetrable language, but that is what it means. While §6323(c)(2)(A) requires that the loan has to be made without knowledge of the tax lien filing, the lender's later discovery of the tax lien filing in no way affects the priority of its floating lien during the 45-day period; see Treas. Reg. §301.6323(c)-1(d) (1976). Section 6323(c) reads:

(c) Protection for certain commercial transactions financing agreements, etc.

(1) *In general.* To the extent provided in this subsection, even though notice of a lien imposed by section 6321 has been filed, such lien shall not be valid with respect to a security interest which came into existence after tax lien filing but which —

(A) is in qualified property covered by the terms of a written agreement entered into before tax lien filing and constituting —

(i) a commercial transactions financing agreement,

(ii) a real property construction or improvement financing agreement, or

(iii) an obligatory disbursement agreement, and —

(B) is protected under local law against a judgment lien arising, as of the time of tax lien filing, out of an unsecured obligation.

(2) *Commercial transactions financing agreement.* For purposes of this subsection —

(A) Definition: The term "commercial transactions financing agreement" means an agreement (entered into by a person in the course of his trade or business) —

(i) to make loans to the taxpayer to be secured by commercial financing security acquired by the taxpayer in the ordinary course of his trade or business, or

(ii) to purchase commercial financing security, (other than inventory) acquired by the taxpayer in the ordinary course of his trade or business; but such an agreement shall be treated as coming within the term only to the extent that such loan or purchase is made before the 46th day of tax lien filing or (if earlier) before the lender or purchaser had actual notice or knowledge of such tax lien filing.

(B) Limitation on qualified property. The term "qualified property," when used with respect to a commercial transactions financing agreement, includes only commercial financing security acquired by the taxpayer before the 46th day after the date of tax lien filing.

(C) Commercial financing security defined. The term "commercial financing security" means (i) paper of a kind ordinarily arising in commercial transactions, (ii) accounts receivable, (iii) mortgages on real property, and (iv) inventory.

To take advantage of this 45-day period, Uniform Commercial Code §9-323(b) also creates a similar 45-day rule in which advances made by a perfected Article 9 creditor prevail over the intervening interest of a judicial lien creditor.[17]

17. Similarly, §9-323(d) creates a 45-day period that protects non-ordinary course buyers from future advances made with knowledge of the purchase or more than 45 days after the purchase. There is an identical rule for leases in §9-323(f). All of this will be explored in Problem 112.

Plymouth Savings Bank v. U.S. I.R.S.

United States Court of Appeals, First Circuit, 1999
187 F.3d 203

CUDAHY, Senior Circuit Judge.

Jordan Hospital ("Hospital") owed Shirley Dionne ("Dionne") $75,000. Dionne, in turn, was indebted to the Plymouth Savings Bank ("Bank") and the Internal Revenue Service ("IRS"), both of which held valid liens on the money the Hospital owed Dionne. The Hospital deposited the money with the district court, and we must now decide who is entitled to it. The problem is simply to determine which of the two liens has priority. We hold that the Bank's lien may trump the IRS's and therefore reverse the district court's grant of summary judgment in favor of the IRS.

Most of the facts are not in dispute. Dionne owned and operated the Greenlawn Nursing Home, a 47-bed state-licensed facility. On September 22, 1993 and apparently before extending credit, the Bank filed a financing statement with the state of Massachusetts describing and giving notice of its security interest in Greenlawn and other assets of Dionne. On April 13, 1994, Dionne executed an $85,000 promissory note in favor of the Bank. As security for the loan, Dionne granted the Bank a security interest in all of her tangible and intangible personal property individually, as well as in her capacity as a sole proprietor doing business as Greenlawn. Paragraph 2 of the agreement specifically granted the Bank: all cash and non-cash proceeds resulting or arising from the rendering of services by Dionne; all general intangibles including proceeds of other collateral; and all inventory, receivables, contract rights or other personal property of Dionne. On or about December 1, 1994, Dionne defaulted on her $85,000 obligation to the Bank, leaving some $65,465 unpaid.

Dionne's financial troubles did not end there. She failed to make Federal Insurance Contribution Act, 26 U.S.C. §3101, et seq. (FICA), payments of $19,639 for the second quarter of 1994. The IRS assessed liability on September 19, 1994 and filed a federal tax lien in the district court on December 19. Dionne again failed to make FICA payments of $62,767 for the fourth quarter of 1994. Liability was assessed on February 2, 1995 and a lien was filed on February 14.

On March 31, 1995, Dionne signed a contract in which she agreed to help the Hospital obtain a license to operate a skilled nursing facility in exchange for $300,000, payable in three installments. Dionne would receive $25,000 when she signed a letter of intent, $200,000 when Massachusetts approved a license and the final $75,000 two years after the license-approval date. With Dionne's assistance, by mid-May 1995 the Hospital had received approval for its license and had paid Dionne the first two installments, totaling $225,000. (In practical effect, it appears that Dionne transferred her

Greenlawn license to the Hospital.) The Hospital never paid Dionne the $75,000 balance.

The Bank sued the Hospital in Massachusetts state court to recover the unpaid balance of its loan to Dionne. Considering cross-motions for summary judgment, the state court ruled for the Bank. It found that, pursuant to the contract between Dionne and the Hospital, the $75,000 constituted cash proceeds arising from the rendering of personal services by Dionne. Because the security agreement between the Bank and Dionne expressly covered "proceeds" of services, the court held that the Bank had a secured interest in the money. The court rejected the Bank's argument that the security interest attached to the nursing home license or to proceeds of the transfer of that license. Instead of awarding the $75,000 to the Bank, however, the court directed the Bank to bring a declaratory judgment action to determine whether its interest in the money had priority over that of other lien-holders.

Ever diligent, the Bank brought such an action—this one—which the IRS subsequently removed to the district court. The Hospital, content to let the Bank and the IRS do battle, deposited the $75,000 with the district court and exited from the action. The Bank and the IRS filed cross-motions for summary judgment, each asserting that its lien trumped the other's. The court sided with the IRS. The Bank's right to recover as against the government depended on when Dionne had performed the services required by the contract, the district court stated. And, although the record on the timing of Dionne's performance was sparse, the court determined that it was undisputed that she had not helped the Hospital secure approval of a nursing home license within the 45 days following the tax lien filing as required by the Federal Tax Lien Act, 26 U.S.C. §§6321, 6323(c) (FTLA). See Dis. Ct. Mem. Op. & Order at 18-19. Accordingly, the district court held that the IRs's two liens were superior to the Bank's lien. The Bank appeals this decision, and we review de novo the district court's grant of summary judgment in favor of the government. . . .

When an individual fails to pay her taxes after a demand has been made, the FTLA grants the United States a lien "upon all property and rights to property, whether real or personal, belonging to such person." 26 U.S.C. §6321. The lien also attaches to property acquired by the delinquent taxpayer after the initial imposition of the lien. See, e.g., Glass City Bank v. United States, 326 U.S. 265, 267, 66 S. Ct. 108, 90 L. Ed. 56 (1945). Section 6323 of the FTLA, however, gives certain commercial liens priority over federal tax liens. Pursuant to §6323(a) and as defined in §6323(h), for example, tax liens are subordinate to security interests in a taxpayer's property that is "in existence" before the government files notice of the tax lien. (Subsection 6323(f) details the filing requirements.) And §6323(c) extends the priority of these prior security interests to certain "qualified property" that the taxpayer acquires even after the government has filed a notice of the tax lien. The scope of this safe harbor for after-acquired property under §6323(c) is at issue here. Mindful that we are entering "the tortured meanderings of federal tax lien law, intersected now by the somewhat smoother byway of the Uniform Commercial Code [UCC]," Texas Oil & Gas Corp. v. United States, 466 F.2d 1040, 1043 (5th Cir. 1972), we lay out the pertinent provisions with as much specificity as we can apply.

To fall within §6323(c)'s safe harbor for after-acquired property, a security interest must be in "qualified property covered by the terms of a written agreement entered into before tax lien filing," including "commercial transactions financing agreement[s]." 26 U.S.C. §6323(c)(1)(A)(i). The security interest must also be superior, under local law, to a judgment lien arising out of an unsecured obligation. See id. at §6323(c)(1)(B). A "commercial transactions financing agreement" is defined as "an agreement (entered into by a person in the course of his trade or business) . . . to make loans to the taxpayer to be secured by commercial financing security acquired by the taxpayer in the ordinary course of his trade or business," id. at §6323(c)(2)(A)(i), and must be entered into within 45 days of the date of the tax lien filing. See id. at §6323(c)(2)(A). "Commercial financing security" can include, among other things, "paper of a kind ordinarily arising in commercial transactions" and "accounts receivable," id. at §6323(c)(2)(C), and it must be "acquired by the taxpayer before the 46th day after the date of tax lien filing." Id. at §6323(c)(2)(B).

The relevant Treasury regulations include still more definitions. "Paper of a kind ordinarily arising in commercial transactions" means "any written document customarily used in commercial transactions," and includes "paper giving contract rights." 26 C.F.R. §301.6323(c)-1(c)(1). For purposes of the FTLA, a "contract right" is "any right to payment under a contract not yet earned by performance and not evidenced by an instrument or chattel paper." Id. at §301.6323(c)-1(c)(2)(i). "An account receivable is any right to payment for goods sold or leased or for services rendered which is not evidenced by an instrument or chattel paper." Id. at §301.6323(c)-1(c)(2)(ii).

Because Dionne signed the personal service contract with the Hospital exactly 45 days after the IRS filed notice of the second tax lien (February 14-March 31),[18] the fighting issue is whether by so doing she "acquired" rights to the $75,000, the money the Hospital owed Dionne and deposited with the district court. See 26 U.S.C. §6323(c)(2)(B). If, by signing the contract, Dionne acquired rights to the money, then the Bank's lien trumps the IRS's. For, if that is the case, it is undisputed that the Dionne-Hospital

---

18. The Bank does not claim that its lien should take priority over the first tax lien, filed on December 19, 1994. The duel here is between only the second tax lien (filed on February 14, 1995, and covering FICA payments of $62,767 for the fourth quarter of 1994) and the Bank's lien.

contract is commercial financing security within §6323(c)(2)(C) and that the Dionne-Bank agreement is a commercial transactions financing agreement within §6323(c)(1)(A)(i) & (c)(2). In this scenario, the Bank's security interest is in qualified property, and the $75,000 would fall within the safe harbor for after-acquired property. On the other hand, if Dionne did not acquire the rights to the money when she signed the contract, the IRS's lien takes priority.

The Treasury Department (of which the IRS is a part) has provided an answer. Recall that the potential qualified property here is the contract between Dionne and the Hospital, which granted Dionne certain rights to payments when she performed certain services. Before the 46th day after the tax lien was filed (that is, before April 1, 1995), if Dionne had acquired anything, she could only have acquired a contract right, not an account receivable, because she had yet to perform any services. See 26 C.F.R. §301.6323(c)-1(c)(2)(i) & (ii). The regulations provide that a "contract right . . . is acquired by a taxpayer when the contract is made." Id. at §301.6323(c)-1(d). So, Dionne acquired the right to be paid for services to be rendered in the future at the time she entered into that contract. In statutory terms, the commercial transactions financing agreement (the Dionne-Bank agreement), which was entered into well before the tax lien filing, covers the Bank's loan (the $85,000) to the taxpayer (Dionne). The loan in turn was secured by commercial financing security (the Dionne-Hospital contract). The Dionne-Hospital contract conferred contract rights (the right to be paid $75,000 two years after Massachusetts approved a nursing home license for the Hospital) and was acquired by the taxpayer within 45 days of the tax lien filing. See 26 U.S.C. §6323(c)(2)(A) & (B). The contract, and the rights (even if conditional) under it, are therefore qualified property covered by the Bank's security interest and protected by §6323(c)'s safe harbor.

Of course, the Bank is interested in the money, not the contract right. The regulations again point the way. "Proceeds" are "whatever is received when collateral is sold, exchanged, or collected." 26 C.F.R. §301.6323(c)-1(d). The regulations further provide: "Identifiable proceeds, which arise from the collection or disposition of qualified property by the taxpayer, are considered to be acquired at the time such qualified property is acquired if the secured party has a continuously perfected security interest in the proceeds under local law." Id. Recall that the commercial financing security (the Dionne-Hospital contract and the rights under it) is simply collateral for the loan (the Bank's $85,000 loan to Dionne). So, where the collateral is a contract giving contract rights, the proceeds of those rights, like the rights themselves, are considered to have been acquired at the time the contract was made. This is so even though the right to proceeds under the contract does not become unconditional until the contract is performed. Pursuant to the Treasury regulations, the conditional right to the proceeds relates back to the time the contract was formed and executed. Therefore, Dionne acquired the rights to the proceeds of the contract right on March 31, 1995, exactly 45 days from the date of the tax lien filing.

In this case, however, the proceeds of the contract right are simply an account receivable, the right to payment of $75,000 for services rendered by Dionne. See 26 C.F.R. §301.6323(c)-1(c)(2)(ii). And herein lies the rub. The IRS argues that, pursuant to the regulations, a taxpayer acquires an account receivable "at the time, and to the extent, a right to payment is earned by performance." Echoing the district court, the IRS correctly points out that Dionne did not earn a right to payment before the 45 days. See Appellee's Br. at 18. But the contract and the rights under it, rather than the account receivable, are the qualified property at issue here, and the regulations provide that the proceeds of qualified property are deemed to be acquired at the time the qualified property is acquired. The regulations do not distinguish between forms of proceeds. Well then, the IRS parries, the account receivable cannot be "proceeds" because the contract was not "sold, exchanged, or collected." See 26 C.F.R. §301.6323(c)-1(d). Had Dionne sold the contract, the IRS says, the Bank's lien would reach the proceeds of that sale; but performance (rendering the services) does not amount to a sale. See Appellee's Br. at 18. This ingenious quibble is unconvincing. Dionne's rendering of the contracted-for services effectively "exchanged" her contract right, converting it into an account receivable. See 26 C.F.R. §301.6323(c)-1(d). The IRS has given us no good reason, nor can we find any basis in commercial reality, to distinguish between a "sale" or an "exchange" and a conversion by performance for this purpose. In fact, performance would seem to be necessary for the production of proceeds even if there were a sale or exchange of the contract. We therefore conclude that the account receivable, the right to the $75,000, is the proceeds of the contract right.

To this, the IRS responds by complaining that we have expanded too far §6323(c)'s safe harbor for after-acquired property. It cites legislative history which it claims suggests that Congress intended §6323(c)'s protections to extend only to property that was collected within 45 days of the tax lien filing. See Appellee's Br. at 17 (citing S. Rep. No. 1708, 89th Cong., 2d Sess. (1966), at 2, 8). We find this argument unpersuasive. As an initial matter, this Senate Report does not directly address commercial financing secured by contract rights, the precise issue here. The Report does indicate, however, that the FTLA was "an attempt to conform the lien provisions of the internal revenue laws to the concepts developed in [the UCC]." S. Rep. No. 1708, 89th Cong., 2d Sess., at 2. The Treasury regulations reflect this intent by providing definitions for FTLA terms that closely track UCC definitions of like terms. For example, the FTLA definitions of "contract right" and "account receivable" match the pre-1972 revision definitions of "contract" and "account," compare, e.g., 26 C.F.R. §301.6323(c)-1(c)(i) & (ii) with Mass. Gen. Laws Ann. ch. 106, §9-106 (West 1998) (Official Reasons for 1972 Changes), and the two definitions of the term "proceeds" are almost identical, compare 26 C.F.R. §301.6323(c)-1(d) with Mass. Gen. Laws Ann. ch. 106, §9-306(a) (West 1988) [now §9-102(a)(64) — EDS.] (defining "proceeds" as "whatever is received upon the sale, exchange, collection or other disposition of collateral or proceeds"). Our conclusion that the Bank's security interest in the contract rights covers the proceeds of those rights — even if the proceeds are accounts receivable — is compatible with still other provisions of the UCC. See, e.g., Mass. Gen. Laws Ann. ch. 106, §9-306(2) (West 1980) [now §9-315 — EDS.] (providing that security interests extend to the proceeds of all secured property). In all events, whatever Congress intended, the regulations make it clear that, so long as the contract was entered into within 45 days of the tax lien filing, the rights under that contract and all of the proceeds of those rights fall within §6323(c)'s protective bounds.

This conclusion can hardly come as a surprise to the IRS. The IRS has advanced the same arguments which it uses here in cases analogous to this one, and has lost each time (except, of course, below). See Bremen Bank & Trust Co. v. United States, 131 F.3d 1259 (8th Cir. 1997); State Bank of Fraser v. United States, 861 F.2d 954 (6th Cir. 1988); In re National Fin. Alternatives, Inc., 96 B.R. 844 (Bkrtcy. N.D. Ill. 1989). Each of these cases, like this one, turned neither on a clever interpretation of the FTLA nor on a thorough scouring of the Congressional records in an attempt to divine intent, but instead on a plain reading of the regulations. It is that simple: the regulations governing §6323(c) say that contract rights and the proceeds thereof are acquired at the time the parties enter into the contract. It matters not that the proceeds of that contract right might be accounts receivable because the regulations do not distinguish among different kinds of proceeds. The IRS, which promulgates these regulations, has had ample opportunity to rewrite them to better suit its desired interpretation of the statute. (Congress, of course, might yet disagree.) To our knowledge, it has made no such effort. . . .

Because we find that the Bank's lien may trump the IRS's, we REVERSE the district court's grant of summary judgment in favor of the IRS. The case is REMANDED to the district court for proceedings consistent with this opinion.

PROBLEM 111

Six months after the IRS filed a tax lien against her, Charlene McGee bought a fire extinguisher system for her horse stables. She purchased the system on credit from King Protection Enterprises, which reserved a purchase money security interest in itself and perfected it. Is the IRS's lien superior to King's purchase money security interest? See Rev. Rul. 68-57, 26 C.F.R. §301.6321-1; In re Specialty Contracting & Supply, Inc., 140 Bankr. 922 (Bankr. N.D. Ga. 1992).

D.   Tax Liens and Future Advances

After the filing of the tax lien, the taxpayer's financing creditor may make a new loan, expecting it to be secured by an existing perfected interest in the collateral listed in the security agreement. If the secured party is aware of the filed tax lien, it almost certainly will refuse to make the advance, but if the lien is undiscovered and the advance is given, which has priority—the IRS or the lender?

Section 6323(d) of the Internal Revenue Code gives protection to future advances made without knowledge of the tax lien in the 45 days after its filing if the advance is collateralized by a perfected security interest in existing property of the taxpayer, such as equipment. It provides:

> (d) 45-day period for making disbursements.
> —Even though notice of a lien imposed by section 6321 has been filed, such lien shall not be valid with respect to a security interest which came into existence after tax lien filing by reason of disbursements made before the 46th day after the date of tax lien filing, or (if earlier) before the person making such disbursements had actual notice or knowledge of tax lien filing, but only if such security interest
>> (1) is in property (A) subject, at the time of tax lien filing, to the lien imposed by section 6321, and (B) covered by the terms of a written agreement entered into before tax lien filing, and
>> (2) is protected under local law against a judgment lien arising, as of the time of tax lien filing, out of an unsecured obligation.

PROBLEM 112

Marie Medici owned a hat factory. She financed her business through a series of loans from the Richelieu State Bank pursuant to an agreement by which she gave the bank a security interest in all of the factory's equipment, and the bank agreed to loan her money from time to time "as it thinks prudent." A financing statement covering the equipment was filed in the proper place. On August 1, she owed the bank $1,500 (having paid back most of the prior loans). The equipment consisted of two machines: the Habsburg Hat Blocker (worth $7,000) and the Huguenot Felt Press (worth $5,000). On that date, the United States filed a federal tax lien against all of Medici's property. On August 31, the bank loaned her another $10,000. Answer these questions:

(a) Assuming the bank did not know of the tax lien on August 31, does the bank or the United States have priority in the equipment, and to what amount? See I.R.C. §6323(d). What if the bank did know?

(b) Assume there is no tax lien, but on August 15 Louis Dupes paid Medici $5,000 cash for the Huguenot Felt Press, and on August 31 the bank loaned her the $10,000. Does the purchase cut off the bank's security interest? Does it matter whether or not the bank knew of the sale prior to the August 31 loan? See §§9-323(d) and (e), 9-102(a)(69).

(c) Instead of buying the machine, as in the last paragraph, assume that Dupes is another creditor of Medici. On August 15, he levied execution on the felt press pursuant to a judgment. If he did this with full knowledge of the bank's security interest and if with notice of his levy the bank still loans Medici the $10,000 on August 31, does Dupes or the Richelieu State Bank have the superior interest in the felt press as to the future advance? See §9-323(b). If the bank did not know of the levy by Dupes on August 15 but loaned Medici an additional $5,000 on October 15, who would have priority as to this advance?

CHAPTER 7   ASSESSMENT: MULTIPLE CHOICE QUESTIONS

1. Jin-Qua loaned $200,000 to Noble House, a Tennessee business which was in a financial jam. The parties signed an effective security agreement, granting Jin-Qua a security interest in Noble House's inventory, equipment, and accounts. Jin-Qua was not in the business of asset-based lending and did not know to file a UCC-1 financing statement. Eighteen months later, with its debts greater than its assets, Noble House filed bankruptcy. The debt to Jin-Qua was $222,000, including interest. The collateral was worth about $400,000. Will Jin-Qua's collateral ensure that Jin-Qua is paid?
   a. Yes, because Jin-Qua has an effective security interest.
   b. No, Jin-Qua will, in effect, lose its right to the collateral and be just another unsecured creditor in the bankruptcy.
   c. Yes, because there is no showing that the failure to file a financing statement induced other creditors to lend to Noble House, so they cannot show any reliance injury.
   d. Yes, because Jin-Qua can file a financing statement and become perfected, with priority over other claimants to the collateral.

2. On January 1, Baker Long Distance negotiated a line of credit from Kimetto Finance, signing a security agreement putting up its inventory and accounts as collateral. Kimetto Finance quickly filed its financing statement on that day, but dallied in actually handing over funds. It had

no obligations under the agreement to lend. Frustrated, Baker Long Distance signed an agreement with Mutai Bank on February 1, likewise giving a security interest in its inventory and accounts. Mutai Bank the same day filed its financing statement and loaned $200,000. A few weeks later, on March 1, Baker Long Distance borrowed $250,000 under its line of credit with Kimetto Finance. About a year later, Baker Long Distance refused demands by both lenders to repay. Its business setbacks meant the collateral was worth only about $200,000. Which lender has priority in the collateral?

   a. Kimetto Finance, because it filed before Mutai Bank filed or otherwise perfected.

   b. Mutai Bank, because it loaned first.

   c. Mutai Bank, because it perfected first.

   d. The lenders would share pro rata, having the same status as perfected secured creditors.

3. Khufu Construction got a construction project loan from Luxor Bank, secured by Khufu's state-of-the-art equipment. Luxor duly perfected its security interest by filing a financing statement covering Khufu Construction's "equipment, now-owned or after-acquired." A few months later, Khufu Construction purchased a Seismic Earthmover excavator on credit from Normous Machines, who duly filed its own financing statement the day after delivery. If Khufu Construction runs into problems, which creditor will have priority in the Seismic Earthmover?

   a. Luxor Bank, because it was first to file or perfect.

   b. Luxor Bank, because it perfected first.

   c. Normous Machines, because it has a perfected purchase money security interest.

   d. Luxor Bank, because Normous Machines has a purchase money security interest, but the collateral is not consumer goods.

   e. Luxor Bank, because Normous Machines did not file before delivering the collateral.

4. Khufu Construction, short of cash, sold the Seismic Earthmover to Great Wall Construction, who paid the market price for such a machine, in good faith, with no knowledge of the security interests of Normous Machines and Luxor Bank. Does Great Wall Construction take the machine free of the creditors' security interests?

   a. Yes, because it paid market price in good faith without notice.

   b. Yes, because it was not a party to the security agreements creating the security interests.

   c. No. The security interest generally remains with the collateral when sold, and none of the exceptions to that rule applies here.

   d. Yes. If the collateral is sold, the creditor lose its security interest but is entitled to claim the money received as its collateral.

5. Selassie Gallery gets a much-need loan to fund operating expenses from Nile Bank. Selassie Gallery signs an agreement making its inventory of art collateral for the debt, and promising not to sell any artwork without permission from Nile Bank. Shortly thereafter, Selassie Bank sells a painting to Moulson in a typical art gallery transaction. Does Moulson take the painting subject to Nile Bank's security interest?

   a. Yes, because the sale violated the security agreement.
   b. Yes, because a security interest continues in collateral despite sale.
   c. No, because Moulson is protected as a buyer in the ordinary course of business.
   d. No, because a good faith buyer takes free of a security interest.

ANSWERS

1. *B* is the best answer. This question illustrates how UCC Article 9 sets the basic structure for finance in the United States. Someone who makes a loan or sells goods or services on credit, may do so unsecured or secured. An unsecured creditor merely has a legally enforceable promise of payment. If the debtor has no assets to enforce that promise against, the unsecured creditor may be out of luck. A secured creditor has a claim on specific property of the debtor to get paid. To maintain its rights against not just the debtor, but other claimants to the collateral, the secured creditor must put the world on notice by perfecting the security interest, such as by filing a UCC-1 financing statement.

   A secured creditor that fails to perfect, as did Jin-Qua, will likely lose a priority contest to a bankruptcy trustee, or a perfected creditor, or a purchaser of the collateral. See §9-317. Someone who becomes a lien creditor takes priority over an unperfected security interest. §9-317. Lien creditors include judgment creditors who have attached the collateral and, most importantly, a bankruptcy trustee as of the moment the bankruptcy petition is filed. §9-102(52). Once the lien creditor has established priority, it retains it over a subsequently perfected security interest. §9-317. By these rules, Article 9, for most personal property collateral, draws the line between secured and unsecured creditors.

   To put things in context, remember *Benedict v. Ratner* from Chapter 2. The court held that an assignment of accounts as collateral was not effective, because it was fraudulent as to the other creditors, because they did not know the property would not be subject to their claims. Article 9 was subsequently enacted to, among other things, permit secured creditors to have security interests enforceable against other creditors (and bankruptcy trustees and buyers of the collateral), provided secured creditors gave notice, by perfecting the security interest. Filing a financing statement is a deceptively important task for a creditor and its lawyers.

2. *A* is the best answer. Mutai Bank did loan first. It also perfected first. A creditor's security interest perfects when it has attached and the creditor has done whatever is necessary to perfect. When Mutai Bank made its loan and filed on February 1, it had then attached (meeting the three requirements of security agreement, value, debtor having rights in the collateral), and perfected (by filing). As of that date, Kimetto Finance's security agreement had not attached, because Kimetto Finance had not yet given value. Rather, Kimetto Finance's security agreement attached and perfected on March 1, when it finally loaned money, giving value. But priority does not go to first to perfect or first to loan, contrary to B and C. As between perfected creditors, priority generally goes to the first to file or perfect. §9-322(a)(2). Mutai Bank's priority date is February 1. Kimetto Bank's priority date is January 1, giving it priority over Mutai Bank.

    That result may seem unfair, where Mutai Bank loses priority even though it loaned money to Baker Long Distance and perfected, before Kimetto Finance made its loan. But Article 9's rule provides a clear method of establishing priority. Mutai Bank, before lending, could simply have searched the UCC records, which would have disclosed that Kimetto Finance already established priority in Baker Long Distance's inventory and accounts. The date of filing is a public record, clearer and easier to establish than the dates of signing security agreements and making loans. Creditors must know the priority rules and act accordingly.

3. *C* is the best answer. In a priority dispute between two perfected creditors, the general rule is that priority goes to the first to file or perfect. But §9-234 gives special priority to a purchase money security interest (PMSI). If the collateral is not inventory or livestock, the PMSI takes priority as long as it is perfected no later than 20 days after the debtor receives the collateral. §9-234. Contrary to D, the rule applies to PMSI's generally, not just to a PMSI in consumer goods. Contrary to D, the creditor gets a grace period, if the collateral is not inventory or livestock, receiving priority as long as the creditor perfects within 20 days of delivery of the collateral. That grace period applies here, where the collateral is equipment.

    If the collateral is inventory or livestock, the PMSI creditor may still get priority, but to do so, before the debtor receives the collateral, must perfect and give the other creditor notice.

4. *C* is the best answer. A security interest generally "continues in collateral notwithstanding sale, lease, license, exchange, or other disposition thereof." §9-315(a)(1). There are several exceptions to that rule, but none of them apply here. The creditor could consent and release its security interest. Id. The security interest could be unperfected. §9-317(b). The transaction could be a consumer-to-consumer sale, §9-320(b) or a sale to a buyer in the ordinary course of business. §9-320(a). This question at

first might sound like a buyer in the ordinary course of business transaction. But that exception is narrower than it sounds, as set out in the list of qualifications after the *Western Limestone* case, culled from §9-320(a) and §1-201(b)(9). Applicable here is the requirement that the buyer purchase goods "from a person . . . in the business of selling goods of that kind." Khufu is in the construction business, not in the business of selling equipment. The buyer in the ordinary course rules does not protect all good faith buyers, contrary to A. Rather, it protects a buyer purchasing goods from someone in the business of selling such goods, such as someone buying construction equipment from a construction equipment retailer.

5. *C* is the best answer. A sale to a mere good faith buyer will be subject to the security interest, as the last question illustrated, contrary to D. But a sale to a buyer in the ordinary course of business will be free of the security interest, provided all the requirements of §9-320(a) and §1-201(b)(9) are met. Those requirements are met here, so Moulson would take free of the security interest. The sale breached the security agreement, but the buyer is protected as long as the buyer did not know that the sale breached the agreement. §1-201(b)(9). The question illustrates how the buyer in the ordinary course rule encourages customers to buy from merchants, by freeing them from wondering if the merchant's inventory is someone's collateral.

BANKRUPTCY AND ARTICLE 9

When a debtor enters the bankruptcy court seeking financial relief, a creditor is likely to get nothing unless the court recognizes the validity of the security interest held by that creditor in an asset of the debtor. Federal law in the form of the Bankruptcy Code allows the debtor's trustee in bankruptcy (or, in Chapter 11 reorganizations, a similar entity called the "debtor in possession") to use various theories, explored below, to attack the security interest. If those attacks fail, the creditor's rights in the collateral continue, and such a creditor is likely to retrieve the collateral (or its value) from the bankruptcy proceeding before it is over. It is the job of the creditor's attorney to be aware, from the creation of the security interest, of issues that might arise in bankruptcy and take appropriate steps to lessen their effect.

I. THE TRUSTEE'S STATUS

The filing of a bankruptcy petition creates an automatic stay of any further creditor collection activity. Bankruptcy Code §362. Thereafter, creditors must pursue whatever rights they have in the bankruptcy proceeding only.

The trustee in bankruptcy is given a number of useful rights in resisting or attacking creditors' claims. As we have seen, the so-called "strong arm clause" imbues the trustee with the state law status of a hypothetical judicial lien creditor who acquires a lien on all of the debtor's property as of the moment of the filing of the bankruptcy petition. Bankruptcy Code §544(a) (reprinted below). Because state law, here §9-317(a)(2) of the Uniform Commercial Code, allows such a lien creditor to avoid unperfected security interests, the trustee may do so too. In addition, §558 gives the trustee the benefit of whatever defenses the debtor would have had against the creditor's claim, so that, for example, if the debt is barred by the Statute of Frauds or a statute of limitations, the trustee may assert these matters. Under §544(b) of the Bankruptcy Code, the trustee is imbued with the rights and position of any unsecured creditor who has a claim against the estate. In the cryptic and often criticized opinion of Moore v. Bay, 284 U.S. 4 (1931), the Supreme Court, per Oliver Wendell Holmes, held, however, that the trustee gets better rights than the creditor represented because the trustee's claim is not limited to the amount of the actual creditor's claim but rather is the size of the entire estate.

§544. Trustee as Lien Creditor and as Successor to Certain Creditors and Purchasers

(a) The trustee shall have, as of the commencement of the case, and without regard to any knowledge of the trustee or of any creditor, the rights and powers of, or may avoid any transfer of property of the debtor or any obligation incurred by the debtor that is voidable by—

(1) a creditor that extends credit to the debtor at the time of the commencement of the case, and that obtains, at such time and with respect to such credit, a judicial lien on all property on which a creditor on a simple contract could have obtained such a judicial lien, whether or not such a creditor exists; . . .

or

(3) a bona fide purchaser of real property, other than fixtures, from the debtor, against whom applicable law permits such transfer to be perfected, that obtains the status of a bona fide purchaser and has perfected such transfer at the time of the commencement of the case, whether or not such a purchaser exists.

(b) The trustee may avoid any transfer of an interest of the debtor in property or any obligation incurred by the debtor that is voidable under applicable law by a creditor holding an unsecured claim that is allowable under section 502 of this title or that is not allowable only under section 502(e) of this title.

PROBLEM 113

Lew Sun, a Korean, moved to Chicago and opened a Korean restaurant called "Seoul Food." He had many unsecured creditors (food sellers, linen services, employees, etc.). On April 17, he applied to the International State Bank for a loan of $10,000, and signed a security agreement in favor of the bank, secured by an interest in Sun's equipment. On April 18, one hour before the bank filed the financing statement, Sun filed a bankruptcy petition in the federal court.

(a) Can the trustee avoid the bank's security interest under §544(a) of the Code?

(b) What result if the bank had filed its financing statement two seconds before the bankruptcy petition was filed?

(c) If the bank's interest had been a *purchase money security interest*, would the filing of the bankruptcy petition have cut off the usual 20-day grace period? See §546(b) of the Code, which follows.

> *§546. Limitations on Avoiding Powers*
> . . . (b)(1) The rights and powers of the trustee under section 544, 545, or 549 of this title are subject to any generally applicable law that—
>
> > (A) permits perfection of an interest in property to be effective against an entity that acquires rights in such property before the date of such perfection; or
> >
> > (B) provides for the maintenance or continuation of perfection of an interest in property to be effective against an entity that acquires rights in such property before the date on which action is taken to effect such maintenance or continuation. . . .

In re Duckworth

United States Court of Appeals, Seventh Circuit, 2014
776 F.3d 453

HAMILTON, Circuit Judge.

In these appeals we consider whether a secured lender can use parol evidence against a bankruptcy to save a security agreement from a mistaken description of the debt to be secured. The security agreement here said that the collateral secured a promissory note made on a given date. The date was a mistake. The borrower had executed a promissory note but two days after the stated date. This is the sort of mistake that can be corrected as between the original parties to the loan by reforming the instrument based on parol evidence.

We have previously held, however, that under Illinois' enactment of the Uniform Commercial Code a secured lender cannot use parol evidence *against a bankruptcy* to correct a mistaken description of the collateral in a security agreement. *In re Martin Grinding & Machine Works, Inc.*, 793 F.2d 592, 595 (7th Cir. 1986). Similarly, the First Circuit has held that a lender cannot use parol evidence against a bankruptcy to change or add to the debts secured by the security agreement, relying on the same provisions in Massachusetts' enactment of the UCC. *Safe Deposit Bank & Trust Co. v.*

Berman, 393 F.2d 401, 402–03 (1st Cir. 1968). The reasoning of these cases persuades us that the lender in these appeals was not entitled to use parol evidence against the bankruptcy to correct the mistaken description of the debt to be secured. We therefore hold that the security agreement did not give the lender a security interest in the specified collateral that could be enforced against the trustee. We reverse the judgments of the district courts and remand for further proceedings in the bankruptcy court.

I. Factual and Procedural Background

The parties filed cross-motions for summary judgment based on the following undisputed facts. On December 15, 2008, David L. Duckworth borrowed $1,100,000 from the State Bank of Toulon. The transaction was executed through a promissory note that was dated and signed on December 15 and an Agricultural Security Agreement dated two days earlier, December 13, 2008. The security agreement said that Duckworth granted the State Bank of Toulon a security interest in crops and farm equipment. The promissory note referred to the security agreement. The security agreement identified the debt to be secured, but the identification had a critical mistake. The security agreement said that it secured a note "in the principal amount of $_____ dated *December 13, 2008.*" But there was no promissory note dated December 13. Both the December 15 promissory note and the security agreement were prepared by the bank's loan officer.

In 2010, Duckworth filed a petition for bankruptcy protection under Chapter 7 of the bankruptcy code. Appellant Charles E. Covey was appointed trustee. The bank filed two complaints in bankruptcy court to initiate adversary proceedings. On cross-motions for summary judgment, the bankruptcy court held that the mistaken date in the security interest did not defeat the bank's security interest and that the security agreement of December 13, 2008 secured the note of December 15, 2008. The bankruptcy court issued two decisions in favor of the bank, one for proceeds from the sale of Duckworth's crops and another for proceeds from the sale of some of his farm equipment. The trustee appealed both bankruptcy court orders to the district court, where the appeals were assigned to different judges. Both district judges affirmed, and the trustee has appealed, in No. 14-1561 regarding the crop sale and in No. 14-1650 regarding the equipment sale. The issue before us is whether the mistaken date in the security agreement defeats the banks' asserted security interest in the crops and farm equipment.

II. Analysis

We review *de novo* a grant of summary judgment, meaning we decide the questions of law without giving deference to the decisions of the district court or the bankruptcy court. See *In re ABC-Naco, Inc.,* 483 F.3d 470, 472

(7th Cir. 2007). The trustee argues that the security agreement unambiguously identified the debt to be secured, but did so only for a nonexistent debt and therefore failed to grant a security interest to secure the note of December 15, 2008. Even if the mistake in the security agreement might be corrected as between the original parties to the loan, the trustee argues, parol evidence of such a mistake cannot be used against a bankruptcy trustee to save the faulty security agreement.

The bank argues that the security agreement is enforceable against the original borrower and should also be enforceable against the trustee. The bank relies on the terms of the security agreement itself, parol evidence of the original parties' intent, and Illinois' "composite document" rule to save its security interest. The bank also contends that its transaction with the debtor satisfied the minimum requirements for an enforceable security interest under Illinois' enactment of the Uniform Commercial Code and therefore the security interest is effective against the trustee.

We first parse the terms of the security agreement and conclude that it cannot be construed to secure the December 15, 2008 note. We then consider the parol evidence argument. We conclude that although the evidence could have supported reformation of the security agreement as between the original parties, the evidence cannot be used against the bankruptcy trustee to reform the security agreement or otherwise to correct the mistaken identification of the debt to be secured. Nor does the composite document rule save the bank's security interest here. Finally, we examine the governing statute, Article 9 of the Uniform Commercial Code, and determine that it directs us to enforce the agreement according to its terms, which fail to secure the debt to the bank.

A.   THE TERMS OF THE SECURITY AGREEMENT

The security agreement is governed by Illinois law, except where federal law might preempt it. Illinois adopts the familiar principle that an unambiguous contract is interpreted by the court as a matter of law without use of parol evidence. *Air Safety, Inc. v. Teachers Realty Corp.*, 185 Ill. 2d 457, 236 Ill. Dec. 8, 706 N.E.2d 882, 884 (1999).

The relevant provisions of the security agreement are unambiguous as applied to these facts. The security agreement grants the bank a security interest "to secure the Indebtedness," which is defined as "the indebtedness evidenced by the Note or Related Documents." The security agreement then defines the "Note" as "the Note executed by David L. Duckworth in the principal amount of $_____ dated December 13, 2008, together with all renewals of, extensions of, modifications of, refinancings of, consolidations of, and substitutions for the note or credit agreement." In the security agreement, the dollar amount of the loan was left blank.

The bank faces two textual obstacles in arguing that the terms of the security agreement secure the debt embodied in the December 15 promissory note. First, the security agreement refers clearly to a December 13 promissory note that the parties agree never existed. The promissory note that the Bank seeks to secure was signed and dated on December 15.

Second, the Bank cannot rely on the security agreement's "Related Documents" provision to incorporate the December 15 promissory note. The relevant definitions in the security agreement are essentially circular. The definition of "Indebtedness" points the reader to "Related Documents," which are defined as documents "executed in connection with the Indebtedness." The "Indebtedness" is defined in turn as the debt evidenced by the "Note or Related Documents," and the Note again is defined as "the Note executed . . . dated December 13, 2008." These circular definitions thus offer no escape from the mistaken date. On its face, the security agreement secures only a December 13 promissory note that never existed. The text of the security agreement does not incorporate the promissory note dated December 15 or the description of the debt contained therein.

B.   PAROL EVIDENCE AGAINST THE TRUSTEE?

To cure the mistaken date in the security agreement and connect it to the December 15 promissory note, the bank relies primarily on parol evidence, from outside the four corners of the document. The bank relies on the December 15 promissory note itself and testimony regarding the bank's and the borrower's intentions.

The bank offers two related theories for reading the security agreement as securing the December 15 note. First, the bank contends that parol evidence is generally admissible to assist in interpreting the security agreement, which it asserts is ambiguous. Second, the bank argues that we should use the composite document rule to read the security agreement and the December 15 note together because the two documents were executed as part of the same transaction. See, e.g., *Tepfer v. Deerfield Savings & Loan Ass'n*, 118 Ill. App. 3d 77, 73 Ill. Dec. 579, 454 N.E.2d 676, 679 (1983) (documents executed by same parties in course of same transaction are "construed with reference to one another because they are, in the eyes of the law, one contract"). Both arguments attempt to justify the use of evidence external to the security agreement itself.

The testimony of both the bank officer who prepared the documents and borrower Duckworth makes clear that the bank made a mistake in preparing the security agreement. We are confident that the bank would have been able to obtain reformation—even of an unambiguous agreement—against the original borrower if he had tried to avoid the security agreement based on the mistaken date. See *Fisher v. State Bank of Annawan*, 163 Ill. 2d

177, 205 Ill. Dec. 520, 643 N.E.2d 811, 814 (1994) (reformation action available where clear and convincing evidence shows parties made a mutual mistake); *Suburban Bank of Hoffman-Schaumburg v. Bousis,* 144 Ill. 2d 51, 161 Ill. Dec. 289, 578 N.E.2d 935, 939 (1991) (same); *Harley v. Magnolia Petroleum Co.,* 378 Ill. 19, 37 N.E.2d 760, 765 (1941) (same).

A bankruptcy trustee is in a different position, however. A bankruptcy trustee is tasked with maximizing the recovery of unsecured creditors. See *In re Vic Supply Co.,* 227 F.3d 928, 931 (7th Cir. 2000). To assist in this task, trustees may exercise the so-called strong-arm power: the trustee is deemed to be in the privileged position of a hypothetical subsequent creditor and can avoid any interests that a hypothetical subsequent creditor could avoid "without regard to any knowledge of the trustee or of any creditor." See 11 U.S.C. §544(a). The strong-arm power is a "blunt information-generating tool" that encourages lenders to give public notice of their security interests by harshly penalizing those who fail to do so. Jonathan C. Lipson, *Secrets and Liens: The End of Notice in Commercial Finance Law,* 21 Emory Bankr. Dev. J. 421, 450-51 (2005) (criticizing the strong-arm power, "a necessary evil," as perhaps "more troublesome for its over- and under-inclusiveness than for its basic goals"); see also Barkley Clark & Barbara Clark, *The Law of Secured Transactions Under the Uniform Commercial Code* §6.02(1)(a) (3d ed. 2011) ("The strong-arm clause is the ultimate Article 9 enforcer."); *id.,* §6.02(1)(b) ("As a matter of public policy, the [strong-arm] rules penalize secret liens and encourage lenders to give public notice of their security interests.").

The bank argues that constructive notice may still be imputed to a trustee using the strong-arm power. The concept of constructive notice comes from state real property law and defines the property rights of good faith purchasers. See *In re Crane,* 742 F.3d 702, 706-07 (7th Cir. 2013). A good faith purchaser cannot avoid the claims of creditors who have complied with state recording laws that provide public notice of the ownership of and liens on property. For that reason, constructive notice constrains a trustee who seeks to use the specific strong-arm power of a good faith purchaser of property. See 11 U.S.C. §544(a)(3); *In re Sandy Ridge Oil Co.,* 807 F.2d 1332, 1336 (7th Cir. 1986).

But the trustee here does not need to assume the role of a good faith purchaser to avoid the lender's interest. The trustee can use other strong-arm provisions and stand in the shoes of other subsequent creditors, to which the limitations of constructive notice do not apply. The trustee may avoid the bank's security interest by acting as a hypothetical judicial lien creditor. 11 U.S.C. §544(a)(1). Such a trustee, unconstrained by constructive notice, may "void a security interest because of defects that need not have misled, or even have been capable of misleading, anyone." *In re Vic Supply Co.,* 227 F.3d at 931.

We therefore must treat the trustee as if he were a hypothetical later lien creditor and ask if the bank has a valid security interest that could be asserted against such a creditor. We conclude that the bank's asserted security interest is not valid against such a later creditor. Such a creditor would be entitled to rely on the text of a security agreement, despite extrinsic evidence that could be used between the original parties to correct the mistaken identification of the debt to be secured.

We find guidance principally from our prior decision in *Martin Grinding* and the First Circuit's decision in *Safe Deposit Bank and Trust Co. v. Berman.* Those decisions emphasize the importance of third parties' ability to rely on unambiguous documents—even if the original parties can show they contain mistakes—to determine the validity and priority of security interests.

In *Martin Grinding*, we held that parol evidence about the original parties' intentions could not be used to correct a mistake in a security agreement by adding, over a bankruptcy trustee's objection, to the agreement's written list of the collateral securing a loan. The lender had failed to list inventory and accounts receivable as collateral in the security agreement. We enforced the unambiguous security agreement according to its terms:

> That the security agreement omits any mention of inventory and accounts receivable is unfortunate for the Bank, but does not make the agreement ambiguous. Since the security agreement is unambiguous on its face, neither the financing statement, nor the other loan documents can expand the Bank's security interest beyond that stated in the security agreement.

793 F.2d at 595. We recognized that the result was contrary to the intentions of the original parties. We explained, though, that the result should promote economy and certainty in secured transactions more generally, a central goal of Article 9 of the Uniform Commercial Code. *Id.* at 596 (Article 9 was intended to enable "'the immense variety of present-day secured financing transactions . . . [to] go forward with less cost and with greater certainty.'"), quoting Ill. Rev. Stat. ch. 26, ¶ 9-101 Uniform Commercial Code Comment (comment to version of UCC in effect in 1986).

The rigid rule allows later lenders to rely on the face of an unambiguous security agreement, without having to worry that a prior lender might offer parol evidence (which would ordinarily be unknown to the later lender) to undermine the later lender's security interest. *Martin Grinding*, 793 F.2d at 596-97. On the other hand,

> if parol evidence could enlarge an unambiguous security agreement, then a subsequent creditor could not rely upon the face of an unambiguous security agreement to determine whether the property described in the financing statement, but not the security agreement, is subject to a prior security interest. Instead, it would have to consult the underlying loan documents

to attempt to ascertain the property in which the prior secured party had taken a security interest. The examination of additional documents, which the admission of parol evidence would require, would increase the cost of, and inject uncertainty as to the scope of prior security interests, into secured transactions. *See California Pump & Manufacturing Co.*, 588 F.2d [717, 720 (9th Cir. 1978)]; *H & I Pipe & Supply Co.*, 44 B.R. [949, 951 (Bankr. M.D. Tenn. 1984)]. Therefore, although the rule excluding parol evidence works results contrary to the parties' intentions in particular cases, it reduces the cost and uncertainty of secured transactions generally.

Id. at 597 (footnote omitted).

In these appeals, the bank would have us limit *Martin Grinding* to prohibit use of parol evidence to correct mistakes only in identifying *collateral* but to allow its use to correct mistakes in identifying the *debt* to be secured. The bank notes that such identification of collateral is expressly required by the Illinois enactment of the Uniform Commercial Code, see 810 Ill. Comp. Stat. 5/9–203(b)(3)(A), while the statute does not similarly require identification of the debt to be secured.

We reject the bank's suggested limitation, finding persuasive guidance from our colleagues in the First Circuit in *Safe Deposit Bank and Trust Co. v. Berman*, 393 F.2d 401, which addressed a mistake in identifying the debts to be secured. In that case the borrower took out a series of loans over several years. All the promissory notes referred to the same original security agreement for collateral. The problem was that the original security agreement itself identified only a single promissory note as the debt to be secured. By the time the borrower declared bankruptcy, that single promissory note had been paid off. By the terms of the security agreement itself, therefore, there was no debt to be secured and thus no security interest.

Like the bank here, the lender argued that the notes showed that the parties intended to create a security interest securing all the later loans. The bankruptcy and district courts had agreed with the trustee, however, that the lender could not use parol evidence against the trustee to show that it had a security interest in the collateral to assure payment of the later loans.

The First Circuit affirmed, albeit "reluctantly because the result is commanded not by fireside equities but by the necessary technicalities inherent in any law governing commercial transactions." 393 F.2d at 402. The First Circuit noted that collateral could be used to secure future debts if the security agreement provided as much. (A so-called "dragnet" clause in a security agreement can include such later loans to the borrower, see UCC §9–204(c) (security agreement may provide that collateral secures "future advances or other value"), but the intent to secure later loans must be explicit in the security agreement.) The First Circuit held that the absence of such language could not be cured by parol evidence, at least as against the bankruptcy trustee. This was so even if the evidence showed that the original parties had intended to include such language. In other words, parol evidence could not be used to add a dragnet clause where the original security agreement did not include one.

Recognizing that its decision was contrary to the evident intent of the original parties to the loans, the First Circuit concluded that the more general effects of the lender's proposed cure would be worse than sticking to the text of the security agreement:

> In a commercial world dependent upon the necessity to rely upon documents meaning what they say, the explicit recitals on forms, without requiring for their correct interpretation other documents not referred to, would seem to be a dominant consideration. If security agreements which on their face served as collateral for specific loans could be converted into open-ended security arrangements for future liabilities by recitals in subsequent notes, much needless uncertainty would be introduced into modern commercial law.

393 F.2d at 404; accord, *Texas Kenworth Co. v. First Nat'l Bank of Bethany,* 564 P.2d 222, 226 (Okla.1977) (refusing to interpret security agreement as securing future advances of credit; "potential creditors who do inquire should be able to rely upon the security agreement itself in determining what obligations are secured").

In both *Safe Deposit Bank and Trust* and the case before us, the lender made a mistake and failed to ensure that the security agreement properly identified the debt to be secured. We do not see a sound basis for distinguishing between the mistaken identification of the debt in our case and the mistaken failure to add a "dragnet" clause in *Safe Deposit Bank and Trust.*

The bank points out that even a hypothetical later lender who finds the recorded financing statement has a duty to inquire further to see the security agreement itself. That is certainly correct, as far as it goes. But the bank argues that the later lender would be obliged to inquire still further. We see no basis for imposing on the later lender a legal duty to inquire beyond the face of an unambiguous security agreement, at the risk of losing the priority of its lien based on parol evidence concerning the dealings between the original parties.

The bank argues, though, that if it had been asked for the security agreement, it surely would have shown the later lender both the security agreement and the promissory note of December 15, despite the erroneous date in the security agreement. That reasoning is not consistent with *Martin Grinding* or *Safe Deposit Bank and Trust.* We also rejected the same argument in *Helms v. Certified Packaging Corp.,* 551 F.3d 675, 680 (7th Cir. 2008), where we reaffirmed that a subsequent creditor is justified in relying on the security agreement alone. In that case, the publicly filed financing statement listed collateral that was not specified in the security agreement itself. We held that the security agreement controlled. A creditor need look no further than the security agreement: "A prudent potential creditor would have requested a copy of the security agreement because that, and not what an employee of an existing creditor might tell the potential creditor over the phone, is the security interest that the parties to the security agreement had agreed to create." *Id.*

That argument applies with even more force where the parol evidence that a party seeks to use to enlarge the security interest consists of a separate and private document (the note of December 15) that is not identified in the security agreement, rather than a publicly available financing statement as in *Helms.* See also *Caterpillar Financial Services Corp. v. Peoples Nat'l Bank, N.A.,* 710 F.3d 691, 696 (7th Cir. 2013) (explaining that between two conflicting descriptions of the collateral, the "security agreement is controlling").

The bank also argues that we should overlook the erroneous date in the security agreement because it was just a small error that would have been easy to discover. We disagree. We find no limiting principle that would allow the courts or parties to distinguish reliably between small errors and big ones. Under the reasoning of *Martin Grinding, Helms,* and *Safe Deposit Bank and Trust,* parol evidence cannot be used to correct even the seemingly minor clerical error in the security agreement. We must hew to the "necessary technicalities inherent in any law governing commercial transactions," even when the result is harsh. *Safe Deposit Bank & Trust Co.,* 393 F.2d at 402. We therefore do not think that parol evidence, contemporaneously executed or not, can be used to undermine the ability of later lenders (or bankruptcy trustees) to rely on unambiguous security agreements.

C. THE BANK'S STATUTORY ARGUMENT

Seeking to steer clear of the parol evidence problem, the bank also contends that it has a security interest enforceable against the trustee because the transaction satisfies the statutory requirements for enforcing a security interest. The bank relies on Illinois' enactment of UCC §9-203(b), which provides in relevant part, and subject to exceptions that do not apply here:

[A] security interest is enforceable against a debtor and third parties . . . only if:

> (1) value has been given;
> (2) the debtor has rights in the collateral . . . ; and
> (3) . . . the debtor has authenticated a security agreement that provides
> a description of the collateral. . . .

810 Ill. Comp. Stat. 5/9-203(b). (Paragraph (b)(3) offers three alternative ways to satisfy its requirements by giving the secured party possession or control of the collateral, but they do not apply here.) The bank asserts that

its security interest is enforceable against the trustee because the bank gave value, borrower Duckworth had rights in the crops and farm equipment, and the parties authenticated a security agreement that described the collateral.

The trustee responds that another provision in the UCC, section 9-201, provides that the terms of a security agreement must be enforced as written: "Except as otherwise provided in the Uniform Commercial Code, a security agreement is effective according to its terms between the parties, against purchasers of the collateral, and against creditors." 810 Ill. Comp. Stat. 5/9-201(a). The trustee argues that the UCC thus points us to the terms of the agreement, and the bank must lose because those terms fail to secure the debt the bank relies upon.

The trustee has the better reading of the UCC. Section 9-203 cannot cure the security agreement's failure to identify correctly Duckworth's debt to the bank, at least against a later lender or the trustee. We have previously read these two sections of the UCC together, concluding that section 9-203's requirements for enforcing a security interest are an exception to section 9-201's general rule that a security agreement is effective according to its terms: "An agreement that violates section 9-203 may not be effective according to its terms." *In re Vic Supply Co.*, 227 F.3d at 932; see also UCC §9-201, official comment 2 ("It follows that subsection (a) does not provide that every term or provision contained in a record that contains a security agreement or that is so labeled is effective.").

Section 9-203 sets out minimum requirements that must be satisfied to enforce a security interest. It does not provide a mechanism for rescuing a lender from its mistakes in drafting a security agreement. A security interest that satisfies section 9-203's requirements may be enforced, but only according to the terms of the security agreement. The bank's argument to the contrary is puzzling. It urges that its interest must be "enforceable" under section 9-203. But enforceable how, if not according to the agreement's terms? Section 9-203 provides no gap-filling terms for when a security agreement fails. We see no reason to invent them merely because the bank made a mistake in preparing its security agreement. . . .

Accordingly, we hold that the mistaken identification of the debt to be secured cannot be corrected, against the bankruptcy trustee, by using parol evidence to show the intent of the parties to the original loan. Nor do the other loan documents themselves provide a basis for correcting the error against the trustee. Later creditors and bankruptcy trustees are entitled to treat an unambiguous security agreement as meaning what it says, even if the original parties have made a mistake in expressing their intentions. The judgments of the district courts are REVERSED and the cases are REMANDED for proceedings consistent with this opinion.

This case should remind you of the case earlier in the book, In re Motors Liquidation Company, in which a law firm accidentally filed a termination statement it did not mean to file and lost the client $1.5 billion. Here the amount of the loan was a mere $1.1 million, but still. . . .

II. PREFERENCES

As a debtor's financial situation deteriorates, many unfortunate things often occur before everything skids into bankruptcy. The rules against preferential transfers are designed to combat two evils: (1) a feeding frenzy by the creditors, as they seize everything in sight while there is still something to seize, and (2) the debtor's decision to pay off a favorite creditor and stiff the others.

A *preference* is a "transfer" (defined in the Bankruptcy Code to include the creation of a security interest in the debtor's property) made or suffered by the bankrupt to pay or secure a pre-existing debt within the 90-day period preceding the filing of the bankruptcy petition,[1] which has the effect of giving the transferee (the creditor) a greater payment than the creditor would get under the usual bankruptcy distribution. The trustee can avoid such preferential transfers under §547 of the Bankruptcy Code, reprinted below, if the debtor was insolvent at the time of transfer, which is presumed in the 90-day period. An Article 9 creditor who delays perfection until the 90 days before bankruptcy is frequently met with a trustee who is wielding §547 as a weapon.

If the creation of a security interest is deemed preferential, the trustee can cancel it, thus turning the preferred creditor into an unsecured (read *unpaid*) one. Other transfers of the debtor's property (for instance, a cash payment) are returned to the bankrupt's estate at the trustee's insistence.

§547. Preferences

(a) In this section—

(1) "inventory" means personal property leased or furnished, held for sale or lease, or to be furnished under a contract for service, raw materials, work in process, or materials used or consumed in a business, including farm products such as crops or livestock, held for sale or lease;

(2) "new value" means money or money's worth in goods, services, or new credit, or release by a transferee of property previously transferred

---

1. The preference period is *one year* before the filing of the petition if the transfer is to an *insider*, defined broadly in §101(31) of the Bankruptcy Code to include relatives, partners, co-habitors, attorneys, officers of corporations, and others.

to such transferee in a transaction that is neither void nor voidable by the debtor or the trustee under any applicable law, including proceeds of such property, but does not include an obligation substituted for an existing obligation;

(3) "receivable" means right to payment, whether or not such right has been earned by performance; and

(4) a debt for a tax is incurred on the day when such tax is last payable without penalty, including any extension.

(b) Except as provided in subsections (c) and (i) of this section, the trustee may avoid any transfer of an interest of the debtor in property—

(1) to or for the benefit of a creditor;

(2) for or on account of an antecedent debt owed by the debtor before such transfer was made;

(3) made while the debtor was insolvent;

(4) made—

(A) on or within 90 days before the date of the filing of the petition; or

(B) between ninety days and one year before the date of the filing of the petition, if such creditor at the time of such transfer was an insider; and

(5) that enables such creditor to receive more than such creditor would receive if—

(A) the case were a case under chapter 7 of this title;

(B) the transfer had not been made; and

(C) such creditor received payment of such debt to the extent provided by the provisions of this title.

(c) The trustee may not avoid under this section a transfer—

(1) to the extent that such transfer was—

(A) intended by the debtor and the creditor to or for whose benefit such transfer was made to be a contemporaneous exchange for new value given to the debtor; and

(B) in fact a substantially contemporaneous exchange;

(2) to the extent that such transfer was in payment of a debt incurred by the debtor in the ordinary course of business or financial affairs of the debtor and the transferee, and such transfer was—

(A) made in the ordinary course of business or financial affairs of the debtor and the transferee; or

(B) made according to ordinary business terms;

(3) that creates a security interest in property acquired by the debtor—

(A) to the extent such security interest secures new value that was—

(i) given at or after the signing of a security agreement that contains a description of such property as collateral;

(ii) given by or on behalf of the secured party under such agreement;

(iii) given to enable the debtor to acquire such property; and

(iv) in fact used by the debtor to acquire such property; and

(B) that is perfected on or before 30 days after the debtor receives possession of such property;

(4) to or for the benefit of a creditor, to the extent that, after such transfer, such creditor gave new value to or for the benefit of the debtor—

(A) not secured by an otherwise unavoidable security interest; and

(B) on account of which new value the debtor did not make an otherwise unavoidable transfer to or for the benefit of such creditor;

(5) that creates a perfected security interest in inventory or a receivable or the proceeds of either, except to the extent that the aggregate of all such transfers to the transferee caused a reduction, as of the date of the filing of the petition and to the prejudice of other creditors holding unsecured claims, of any amount by which the debt secured by such security interest exceeded the value of all security interests for such debt on the later of—

(A)(i) with respect to a transfer to which subsection (b)(4)(A) of this section applies, 90 days before the date of the filing of the petition; or

(ii) with respect to a transfer to which subsection (b)(4)(B) of this section applies, one year before the date of the filing of the petition; or

(B) the date on which new value was first given under the security agreement creating such security interest;

(6) that is the fixing of a statutory lien that is not avoidable under section 545 of this title;

(7) to the extent such transfer was a bona fide payment of a debt for a domestic support obligation;

(8) if, in a case filed by an individual debtor whose debts are primarily consumer debts, the aggregate value of all property that constitutes or is affected by such transfer is less than $600; or

(9) if, in a case filed by a debtor whose debts are not primarily consumer debts, the aggregate value of all property that constitutes or is affected by such transfer is less than $5,000.

(d) The trustee may avoid a transfer of an interest in property of the debtor transferred to or for the benefit of a surety to secure reimbursement of such a surety that furnished a bond or other obligation to dissolve a judicial lien that would have been avoidable by the trustee under subsection (b) of this section. The liability of such surety under such bond or obligation shall be discharged to the extent of the value of such property recovered by the trustee or the amount paid to the trustee.

(e)(1) For the purposes of this section—

(A) a transfer of real property other than fixtures, but including the interest of a seller or purchaser under a contract for the sale of real property, is perfected when a bona fide purchaser of such property from the debtor against whom applicable law permits such transfer to be perfected cannot acquire an interest that is superior to the interest of the transferee; and

(B) a transfer of a fixture or property other than real property is perfected when a creditor on a simple contract cannot acquire a judicial lien that is superior to the interest of the transferee.

(2) For the purposes of this section, except as provided in paragraph (3) of this subsection, a transfer is made—

(A) at the time such transfer takes effect between the transferor and the transferee, if such transfer is perfected at, or within 30 days after, such time, except as provided in subsection (c)(3)(B);

(B) at the time such transfer is perfected, if such transfer is perfected after such 30 days; or

(C) immediately before the date of the filing of the petition, if such transfer is not perfected at the later of—

(i) the commencement of the case; or

(ii) 30 days after such transfer takes effect between the transferor and the transferee.

(3) For the purposes of this section, a transfer is not made until the debtor has acquired rights in the property transferred.

(f) For the purposes of this section, the debtor is presumed to have been insolvent on and during the 90 days immediately preceding the date of the filing of the petition.

(g) For the purposes of this section, the trustee has the burden of proving the avoidability of a transfer under subsection (b) of this section, and the creditor or party in interest against whom recovery or avoidance is sought has the burden of proving the nonavoidability of a transfer under subsection (c) of this section.

(h) The trustee may not avoid a transfer if such transfer was made as a part of an alternative repayment schedule between the debtor and any creditor of the debtor created by an approved nonprofit budget and credit counseling agency.

(i) If the trustee avoids under subsection (b) a transfer made between 90 days and 1 year before the date of the filing of the petition, by the debtor to an entity that is not an insider for the benefit of a creditor that is an insider, such transfer shall be considered to be avoided under this section only with respect to the creditor that is an insider.

PROBLEM 114

On June 8, Business Corporation borrowed $80,000 from Octopus National Bank (ONB) and gave the bank a security interest in its equipment (worth $100,000). On July 18, ONB filed a valid financing statement in the proper place. The next day, Business Corporation filed its bankruptcy petition. Can the trustee destroy ONB's secured position and turn it into a general creditor under the theory that the delayed perfection is a preference? If ONB *had* perfected on June 8 but the debtor made some extraordinary payments to ONB in the 90-day period before the filing of the petition, could the trustee use §547 to make ONB pay that money back into the estate? See White & Summers §24-4(a). Finally, again assume that ONB had perfected on June 8 but that the collateral was only worth $60,000 (the debt was still $80,000, so the bank is undersecured). Would routine payments made to service this debt be preferential? See §547(c)(2); Union Bank v. Wolas, 502 U.S. 151 (1991).

PROBLEM 115

On November 1, the Piggy National Bank loaned Kermit $1,000 to buy a banjo he wanted for his nightclub act, making him sign a security agreement and a financing statement. He bought the banjo on November 15, and the bank filed the financing statement in the proper place on December 5. Kermit filed his bankruptcy petition the next day. Is the *transfer* of the security interest in his banjo a preference? See §547(c)(3). If the bank's security interest was not of the *purchase money* variety but was simply a loan made on November 1 secured by "equipment now owned or after-acquired, with the banjo bought by Kermit (using his own money) on November 15 and the bank filing its financing statement on December 5, what result? See §547(e)(2); White & Summers §24-4(a).

PROBLEM 116

In early 2020, John Carter borrowed $1,000 from the Barsoom World Bank; it was a *signature loan* (i.e., no collateral). On September 25, 2020, John made a $500 payment to the bank (assume that this payment is not in the ordinary course), but on October 4 he borrowed $300 more from the bank, giving it a security interest in his sword collection. The bank never filed a financing statement, and John filed a bankruptcy petition on November 8, 2020. How much, if anything, can his bankruptcy trustee recover from the bank? See §§544(a)(2), 547(c)(4); White & Summers §24-5.

The Moment of "Transfer." Sometimes it is obvious when a transfer of the debtor's property occurs (the debtor gives a diamond ring to a creditor on Monday at 3:00 P.M., for example), but where the transfer is accomplished by creating a security interest in the property, when does it occur? Section 547(e) has rules concerning this. For real property (other than fixtures), the transfer is said to happen when a bona fide purchaser could no longer prevail over the creditor, which in almost all cases is the moment of the filing in the real property records. See §547(e)(1)(A). For personal property and fixtures, §547(e)(1)(B) chooses the moment when a judicial lien creditor could not achieve priority over the creditor, which under §9-317 is the moment of perfection (usually the filing of a financing statement). However, even here the Bankruptcy Code gives the creditor a break that state law may not because it creates a 30-day grace period from the moment of attachment (the "time such transfer takes effect between the transferor and the transferee"). If perfection is accomplished during this federal grace period, a relation back occurs to protect the transfer from the trustee's attack. See §547(e)(2)(A).

III.   THE FLOATING LIEN IN BANKRUPTCY

Section 60 of the former Bankruptcy Act condemned as a preference the creation of a security interest within four months of the filing of the bankruptcy petition unless the creditor advanced new money for the collateral as it was acquired. A question of immense concern to creditors who lent against inventory or accounts receivable was whether their security interest in the collateral acquired in that four-month period would be preferential. Even though the UCC clearly permits after-acquired property to be covered automatically by the security interest, the Code is drafted so that the security interest cannot *attach* or be *perfected* until the debtor acquires an interest in the property and, arguably, *that* occurs within the four-month period; §§9-203, 9-308(a). Under both the prior and the current versions of the Bankruptcy Act, *perfection* of the security interest is the moment of "transfer" in preference disputes, and thus the argument is that the collateral first falling under the floating lien during the preference period is recoverable by the trustee as a preferential "transfer" securing an old debt.

Everyone crossed their fingers and waited for a federal appellate court to hear a bankruptcy challenge to an Article 9 floating lien. The Seventh Circuit spoke first. In Grain Merchants of Ind., Inc. v. Union Bank & Sav. Co., 408 F.2d 209 (7th Cir. 1969), the court upheld the floating lien's validity as to the property falling under it during the preference period, though the court noted that in the case at bar there was both inflow and outgo of collateral during the relevant time period, and the creditor had thus not improved its position by getting an increased amount of collateral prior to bankruptcy.

The Bankruptcy Code's solution to this after-acquired property/preference issue is found in §547(c)(5). The test found therein, while alarming at first view, is remarkably simple in operation. It commands the courts to compare the debt/collateral difference at two points: 90 days before the filing of the petition (or the first date within that period where a debt was owed if the loan was made within the 90-day period), and the date of the filing of the petition. There is a preference to the extent that the creditor's position has improved within this period.

PROBLEM 117

The Last National Bank had a perfected security interest in the inventory of the Epstein bookstore, which owed the bank $20,000. On March 1, the inventory was worth $8,000. On May 28, when Epstein filed for bankruptcy, the inventory was worth $20,000 because the store had purchased several new shipments for cash in the interim. What can the trustee do about the bank's claim? What if the bank first loaned Epstein $20,000 on May 1, when the inventory was worth $12,000, though worth $20,000 when the petition was filed on May 28th?

In re Smith's Home Furnishings, Inc.

United States Court of Appeals, Ninth Circuit, 2001
265 F.3d 959

CYNTHIA HOLCOMB HALL, Circuit Judge.

Plaintiff-appellant Michael Batlan ("trustee") appeals the district court's judgment affirming the decision of the bankruptcy court. Batlan filed an action to recover payments made by a chapter 11 debtor to defendant-appellee Transamerica Commercial Finance Corporation ("TCFC"). The bankruptcy court found that the payments were not avoidable transfers under 11 U.S.C. §547(b). We agree with the bankruptcy court and the district court that the trustee did not satisfy his burden of showing that TCFC received a greater amount by virtue of the payments than it would have received in a hypothetical chapter 7 liquidation.

FACTUAL AND PROCEDURAL BACKGROUND

Smith's Home Furnishings, Inc. ("Smith's"), sold furniture, electronic goods, and appliances at 19 stores in Oregon, Washington, and Idaho. TCFC was one of Smith's primary lenders for almost a decade. TCFC financed Smith's purchase of some merchandise (the "prime inventory"), consisting mainly of electronic goods and appliances. TCFC's loans were secured by a first-priority floating lien on the prime inventory and the proceeds from it. Thus, the prime inventory served as collateral for TCFC's loans to Smith's.

Under the loan agreements, TCFC extended credit to Smith's by granting approval to various manufacturers. After receiving approval, the manufacturers shipped merchandise to Smith's. When Smith's sold a product financed by TCFC, it paid TCFC the wholesale price of that product.

Smith's did not segregate its sales receipts. Instead, Smith's deposited all its sales proceeds into commingled bank accounts at the end of each day. First Interstate Bank ("the Bank"), Smith's revolving-line-of-credit financier, swept the accounts daily, leaving the accounts with overnight balances of zero. The next day, the Bank advanced new funds to Smith's if sufficient collateral was available. Smith's then paid its operating expenses and creditors, including TCFC.[2]

During 1994, Smith's suffered substantial losses. Consequently, in March 1995 TCFC reduced Smith's line of credit from $25 million to $20 million. Over the next few months, TCFC reduced Smith's line of credit twice more, down to $13 million by August. During the same period, TCFC required substantial pay-downs of Smith's debt; Smith's paid TCFC most of its available cash in a series of 36 payments, totaling more than $12 million, between May 24, 1995, and August 22, 1995.

On August 18, 1995, TCFC declared a final default, accelerated the entire debt due from Smith's, and sought a receiver for the company. For the first time, TCFC also sought to require Smith's to segregate the proceeds from its collateral.

Smith's voluntarily initiated bankruptcy proceedings under chapter 11 of the Bankruptcy Code on August 22, 1995 (the "petition date"). As of that date, Smith's owed $10,728,809.96 to TCFC. TCFC took possession of its collateral and liquidated it, receiving $10,823,010.58.

On October 11, 1995, the case was converted to a chapter 7 liquidation and Batlan was appointed as trustee. The trustee discovered the $12,842,438.96 in payments that Smith's had made to TCFC during the 90 days before the petition date (the "preference period"). Believing that the payments were preferential, he asked TCFC to return the money to the bankruptcy estate. When TCFC refused, the trustee initiated this adversary proceeding, seeking to avoid the payments as preferential transfers, under 11 U.S.C. §547(b), and to recover the money for the benefit of other creditors of Smith's, under 11 U.S.C. §550(a).

The parties stipulated that the payments met the first four elements of a preferential transfer under 11 U.S.C. §547(b)(1)-(4). . . . The parties proceeded to trial to determine whether the payments met the fifth element of the preferential transfer statute, 11 U.S.C. §547(b)(5), and whether TCFC could establish an affirmative defense under 11 U.S.C. §547(c)(5).

On September 10, 1998, the bankruptcy court ruled, in a letter opinion, that the trustee had failed to meet his burden of proof in showing that the payments were preferential transfers. The court reasoned that, because the value of the collateral on the petition date ($10,823,010.58) exceeded

---

2. Because of these procedures, the allegedly preferential payments, which we will describe below, were not made directly from the proceeds of the sales of TCFC's collateral.

the amount of TCFC's claim on the petition date ($10,728,809.96), TCFC was oversecured by $94,200.62. As a result, the court concluded that, because TCFC was a floating-lien creditor, the trustee was required to prove that TCFC was undersecured at some time during the preference period in order to avoid the transfers. The court also ruled that TCFC's collateral should be valued at liquidation value ($10,823,010.58) and that liquidation costs should be deducted from the liquidation value in computing the value of the collateral, but that the trustee had failed to present credible evidence of TCFC's liquidation costs. Because the bankruptcy court concluded that the trustee had not proved that the transfers were preferential, the court did not address TCFC's affirmative defense under §547(c)(5).

The trustee filed a motion for reconsideration. In response, the bankruptcy court amended its opinion to correct typographical and computational errors, but otherwise confirmed its judgment. The trustee timely filed an appeal to the district court, raising the same issues that it raises in this appeal. In a published opinion, Batlan v. Transamerica Commercial Finance Corp., 237 B.R. 765, 776 (D. Or. 1999), the district court affirmed the bankruptcy court's decision "in all respects." This timely appeal followed. . . .

DISCUSSION

I. "GREATER AMOUNT" TEST

This case requires us to interpret two sections of the Bankruptcy Code, 11 U.S.C. §§547(b)(5) and 547(g). 11 U.S.C. §§547(b) permits a trustee to "avoid any transfer of an interest of the debtor in property" when certain conditions are met. One of the conditions is that the transfer enable the creditor to receive more than such creditor would receive if:

> (A) the case were a case under chapter 7 of this title;
> (B) the transfer had not been made; and
> (C) such creditor received payment of such debt to the extent provided
> by the provisions of this title.

11 U.S.C. §547(b)(5). TCFC and the trustee dispute whether the 36 payments made during the preference period enabled TCFC, as a result of the 36 payments, to receive more than if the payments had not been made and TCFC had received payments only pursuant to a chapter 7 liquidation. Section 547(g) places the burden of proof on the trustee to show all of the conditions of §547(b). Thus, the trustee must show that the creditor received a greater amount than it would have if the transfer had not been made and there had been a hypothetical chapter 7 liquidation as of the petition date. If the trustee shows that TCFC received a greater amount by virtue of the 36 payments, then the payments are avoidable as preferential transfers. See In

re Lewis W. Shurtleff, Inc., 778 F.2d 1416, 1421 (9th Cir. 1985). The trustee contends that he satisfied his burden because: 1) the 36 payments plus the amount that TCFC received from the post-petition sale of its collateral is greater than the amount received from the post-petition sale of the collateral standing alone; and 2) TCFC has not traced the source of the allegedly preferential payments to sales of its collateral. We disagree with both of the trustee's arguments.

A.   THE ADD-BACK METHOD DOES NOT SATISFY THE TRUSTEE'S BURDEN WHEN
      THE PAYMENTS COME FROM COLLATERAL SECURED BY A FLOATING LIEN

The trustee tried to satisfy his burden under §547(b)(5) by adding the amount of the 36 payments to the amount TCFC received as a result of the post-petition sale of its remaining collateral. The trustee then compared this amount to the obviously smaller amount of the post-petition sale by itself and concluded that TCFC must have received a greater amount because of the payments. Some bankruptcy courts have used the same "add-back" method employed by the trustee to determine the status of a creditor on the petition date. See In re Al-Ben, Inc., 156 B.R. 72, 75 (Bankr. N.D. Ala. 1991) (adding alleged preferences to the amount of unpaid balance at the petition date to find the creditor's secured status); In re Estate of Ascot Mortgage, Inc., 153 B.R. 1002, 1018 (Bankr. N.D. Ga. 1993) (adding pre-petition amounts received to what would have been received under a chapter 7 liquidation).

We agree with the bankruptcy court and the district court, however, and conclude that the "add-back" calculation does not satisfy the trustee's burden in this case. Pre-petition transfers to a creditor that is fully secured on the petition date are generally not preferential because the secured creditor is entitled to 100 percent of its claims. See In re LCO Enterprises, 12 F.3d 938, 941 (9th Cir. 1993). This is not a hard and fast rule. As the bankruptcy court in this case noted, payments that change the status of a creditor from partially unsecured to fully secured at the time of petition may be preferential. See Porter v. Yukon Nat'l Bank, 866 F.2d 355, 359 (10th Cir. 1989). Moreover, a transfer may be avoided when the creditor is fully secured at the time of payment, but is undersecured on the petition date. See In re Estate of Sufolla, Inc., 2 F.3d 977, 985-86 (9th Cir. 1993). The trustee failed to show, however, that TCFC was undersecured *at any time* during the preference period. Instead, the evidence submitted showed that as of the petition date, the value of the collateral held by Smith's exceeded its indebtedness to TCFC. If TCFC was never undercollateralized, then TCFC could not have received more by virtue of the 36 payments than it would have received in a hypothetical liquidation without the payments.

It is important to understand that TCFC did not loan one fixed amount to the debtor; instead, TCFC held a "floating lien." A floating lien is a financing device where the creditor claims an interest in property acquired after the original extension of the loan and extends its security interest to cover further advances. The floating lien is a lien against a constantly changing mass of collateral for a loan value that will change as payments are received and further advances are made. See 3 Norton Bankr. L. & Prac. 2d §57.23. The cases the trustee cites applying the "add-back" method do not deal with floating liens. It is not correct to assume that the 36 payments gave TCFC more than it would have received if the payments had not been made. Instead, under a floating lien arrangement, those payments are used to liquidate part of the debtor's debt. Then, new credit under the floating lien is extended and is secured by new collateral. It is not enough for the trustee to show that the 36 payments plus the amount received upon dissolution exceeded the amount of TCFC's secured claim as of the petition date. Since collateral and indebtedness changed throughout the preference period, these values do not prove that TCFC received more by virtue of the payments than it would have received without them. Under §547(b)(5), the trustee must show that the amount of indebtedness under the floating lien was greater than the amount of collateral at some point during the 90-day period. See In re Schwinn Bicycle Co., 200 B.R. 980, 992-93 (Bankr. N.D. Ill. 1996) ("At no point in time did the collateral value fall below the outstanding debt, and therefore TIFCO was not preferred in having received payments on its secured debt.").

The trustee contends that the existence of the floating lien means that the burden is shifted to TCFC under §547(c)(5). Section 547(c)(5) provides an affirmative defense for creditors when the trustee has successfully demonstrated that the creditor received more from the payments than under a hypothetical liquidation. Section 547(c)(5) insulates the transfer of a security interest in after-acquired property, i.e., a floating lien, provided that the creditor does not improve its position during the preference period. In effect, the trustee contends that the existence of a floating lien means that he does not have to prove that the creditor was undersecured at some point during the 90-day period and therefore received more by virtue of the payments than the creditor would have if the creditor had waited for a chapter 7 liquidation.

We reject the trustee's argument. A floating lien does not shift the burden of showing avoidability to the creditor. The trustee still has to satisfy his burden under §547(b)(5). The Tenth Circuit has addressed the question of what needs to be shown by a trustee to avoid a transfer financed by the sale of inventory subject to a floating lien. See In re Castletons, 990 F.2d 551 (10th Cir. 1993). In *Castletons*, the creditor held a floating lien on the debtor's inventory, accounts receivable, and proceeds. The trustee sought to avoid the payments given by the debtor to the creditor during the preference period. The Tenth Circuit affirmed the district court's holding that the trustee failed to show that the creditor received more from the challenged payments than it would have received in a chapter 7 liquidation. It explained:

> [A]ll payments to [the creditor] came from assets already subject to its security interest. It is further uncontested that the nature of [the creditor's] security interest in debtor's assets was never altered during the preference period. Under these circumstances, it cannot be said, as §547(b)(5) requires, the transfers enabled [the creditor] to receive more on its debt than would be available to it in a Chapter 7 distribution.

Id. at 555. Essential to the court's holding was its recognition that the creditor held a floating lien:

> While the identity of individual items of collateral changed because of sales and subsequent acquisitions of new collateral, the overall nature of [the creditor's] security interest remained the same.

Id. at 556.

It is true that other courts have evaluated floating lien cases by proceeding directly to the §547(c)(5) affirmative defense without a discussion of the requirements of §547(b)(5). See In re Wesley Indus., 30 F.3d 1438, 1443 (11th Cir. 1994); In re Lackow Bros., Inc., 752 F.2d 1529, 1530-31 (11th Cir. 1985). But in those cases, the parties had stipulated or the bankruptcy court had found that the creditor was undersecured as of the petition date. In other words, the §547(b)(5) burden had already been satisfied so it did not need to be discussed. The trustee in this case never showed that TCFC was undersecured at any point during the 90-day period and the bankruptcy court determined that TCFC was fully secured as of the petition date. The trustee did not satisfy his burden. See Richard F. Duncan, Preferential Transfers, the Floating Lien, and Section 547(c)(5) of the Bankruptcy Reform Act of 1978, 36 Ark. L. Rev. 1, 20 (1987) ("[I]t is not necessary to reach the question of application of section 547(c)(5) until after the trustee has met his burden of proving all of the necessary elements of a preference under section 547(b)."); James J. White & Daniel Israel, Preference Conundrums, 98 Com. L.J. 1, 4 (1993) ("It is important to remember, however, that 547(c)(5) applies only to a creditor who is undersecured ninety days before bankruptcy. The creditor who is fully secured cannot be attacked under 547(b). There is no initial deficiency and later transactions cannot improve the creditor's position.").

B.   THE BURDEN OF TRACING THE FUNDS USED TO MAKE
THE PREFERENTIAL PAYMENTS IS ON THE TRUSTEE

The trustee contends that its use of the "add-back" method is correct because TCFC has not shown that the source of the allegedly preferential payments was sales of TCFC's collateral. In *Castletons,* it was undisputed that all of the preference period payments came from sales of assets subject to the creditor's floating lien. See In re Castletons, 990 F.2d at 555. In this case, however, the payments came from a commingled account that contained monies from the sales of other goods not subject to TCFC's lien. When Smith's made a sale, the proceeds were deposited into commingled bank accounts. Smith's bank swept the accounts daily, leaving them with zero balances overnight. Thus, the challenged payments were not made directly from the proceeds of the sales of TCFC's collateral. On the other hand, there is no evidence indicating that Smith's did not sell off enough of TCFC's collateral to account for all of the challenged payments. . . .

[W]e believe that it is part of the trustee's §547(b)(5) burden to trace the funds used to make the payments to sales of merchandise not subject to TCFC's liens. See In re Robinson Bros. Drilling, Inc., 6 F.3d 701, 703 (10th Cir. 1993) ("Under 11 U.S.C. §547(g), a trustee seeking to avoid an allegedly preferential transfer under §547(b) 'has the burden of proving by a preponderance of the evidence every essential, controverted element resulting in the preference.'") (quoting 4 Collier on Bankruptcy ¶547.21[(5)] at 547-93 (15th ed. 1993)); cf. In re Prescott, 805 F.2d 719, 726-27 (7th Cir. 1986) (placing burden on trustee to establish value of collateral and to show that value of collateral was less than the amount of indebtedness at time of transfer). One might argue that the creditor will be in a better position than the trustee to prove whether or not the alleged preferential payments came from the proceeds of the sale of its own collateral. On the other hand, in bankruptcy, it is the trustee who accedes to the debtor's books and records and has easier access and a better ability to divine the financial activities of the debtor in its last months of operation. Regardless of which side is better equipped to decipher the debtor's final financial actions, we hold that the language of the statute places the burden of demonstrating the source of such preferential payments squarely on the trustee.[3] See In re Lease-A-Fleet,

---

3. Our decision furthers the paramount policy behind §547: equality of distribution among creditors of the debtor. See In re Schwinn Bicycle Co., 200 B.R. 980, 993 (Bankr. N.D. Ill. 1996). If a floating lien creditor genuinely did not profit from a preference period transfer, then the creditor should not be forced to disgorge those payments. We agree with the dissent that §547 also tries to dissuade creditors from rushing to extract payments from the debtor shortly before bankruptcy. We do not think that our decision controverts this policy or that this is a case involving a race to the debtor's assets. The trustee offered no evidence that TCFC was less than 100 percent secured at the time of any of the 36 payments. For the payments it made to TCFC, the debtor received additional financing to keep its business afloat. Rather than encouraging a race to dismember the debtor, our decision to place the burden on the trustee to show that TCFC did not receive more by virtue of the payments than it would under a hypothetical liquidation encourages TCFC and other creditors to continue extending credit under floating liens.

151 B.R. at 348 ("It is therefore an unfortunate fact of life that a preference plaintiff must effectively prove a negative (that the defendant is not a totally secured creditor), even though the secured creditor is the party with most access to proof of the validity of its own security interests.").

Commingled funds or not, §547(b)(5) places the burden on the trustee to show that the payments at issue came from a source other than sales of TCFC's collateral. Here there is no suggestion that any sales of products funded by TCFC were not subject to TCFC's priority lien. Instead, both parties stipulated that TCFC held a valid security interest in Smith's property. It is true that the route the payment took to TCFC was indirect, but we are not prepared to release the trustee from his burden under §547(b)(5) simply because the payments did not, demonstrably, come directly from sale of TCFC's collateral. See In re Compton Corp., 831 F.2d 586, 591 (5th Cir. 1987) ("The federal courts have long recognized that '[t]o constitute a preference, it is not necessary that the transfer be made directly to the creditor.'") (quoting National Bank of Newport v. National Herkimer County Bank, 225 U.S. 178, 184, 32 S. Ct. 633, 56 L. Ed. 1042 (1912)). It is up to the trustee to show that the payments did not come from TCFC's collateral before he can use the add-back method to satisfy his §547(b)(5) burden. . . .

CONCLUSION

We affirm the decision of the bankruptcy court in all respects.
[The forceful dissent of Judge Graber is omitted.]

IV. FRAUDULENT TRANSFERS

Under §548 or §544(b) of the Bankruptcy Code, the trustee can avoid any "transfer" (including the creation of an Article 9 security interest) that is a *fraudulent transfer*. The law as to what is or is not a fraudulent transfer has been developing for centuries, but is generally summarized in the Uniform Fraudulent Transfer Act (UFTA), which most states have adopted. There, an existing or later creditor (and the bankruptcy trustee, per §544(b)) may avoid two types of fraudulent transfers: those where the transferee from an insolvent debtor does not give "reasonably equivalent value in exchange," and those where the transferor and the transferee have the *actual intent* to defraud the debtor's creditors.

Fraudulent conveyances may be easy to identify.

James H. Rice Co. v. McJohn

Supreme Court of Illinois, 1910
244 Ill. 264

On October 6, 1902, the James H. Rice Company, a corporation, filed its bill of complaint in the superior court of Cook county against Joseph McJohn and Edward McJohn, charging that on September 17, 1902, complainant recovered a judgment against said Joseph McJohn in the circuit court of Cook county for $1801.60; that prior to the rendition of the said judgment Joseph McJohn was the owner of certain real estate in Cook county, which was improved by a three-story brick building; that on September 20, 1902, an execution was issued upon said judgment and delivered to the sheriff of said county; that on August 7, 1902, prior to the rendition of the judgment but after the indebtedness upon which it was rendered had accrued, Joseph McJohn conveyed the said real estate to Edward McJohn for a pretended consideration of one dollar; that said conveyance was a mere sham and was made with intent to defraud complainant and other creditors of Joseph McJohn out of their just demands; that no consideration was paid by Edward McJohn therefor, and that the premises are now held by Edward McJohn in trust for Joseph McJohn and for the purpose of preventing a levy and sale of the premises under said execution; that Joseph McJohn has no personal or real estate liable to levy and sale, except the premises aforesaid, on which the sheriff could levy and realize said judgment; that the sheriff has frequently requested Joseph McJohn to pay said judgment or to turn out property upon which he could levy, but Joseph McJohn has refused to do so. The bill made Joseph McJohn and Edward McJohn defendants, and prayed that they might be required to answer and state the facts and circumstances attending the said conveyance, the amount paid thereon by Edward McJohn and the purpose of the conveyance; that upon a hearing the said conveyance and deed be set aside and declared null and void; that a receiver be appointed, with the usual powers and duties of a receiver; that the sheriff be directed to proceed to levy upon and sell the premises for the satisfaction of complainant's judgment, and for such other and further relief as equity may require.

[The court set aside the conveyance as "fraudulent and null and void."]

PROBLEM 118

When Arnold Austin retired as an international diplomat, he was famous but much in debt. He decided to make money by writing his memoirs, which were certainly best-seller material. He gave a security interest in the right to receive royalty payments from his publisher to his wife as collateral for "the

an arrangement by which Dr. Mohsen lends Aptix money, which Aptix uses to pay employee salaries and essential creditors in an effort to keep functioning. . . . Dr. Mohsen receives money back from Aptix on demand. . . . This setup allows . . . Aptix to pay unsecured creditors as it sees fit, while effectively avoiding its obligations toward a judgment creditor that holds a judgment lien.

Id. Thus, the district court concluded that the arrangement was "not as innocent as Dr. Mohsen suggests." Id.

On appeal, Mohsen takes issue with both the district court's factual findings and the legal principles it applied. Mohsen's factual challenge is fundamentally a reassertion of the argument rejected by the trial judge, namely that the granting of the security interest to Mohsen was intended to benefit not defraud creditors by keeping Aptix operational. Borrowing a concept from bankruptcy cases, Mohsen argues that the on-going operation of Aptix was a "legitimate supervening purpose" such that the confluence of three badges of fraud was insufficient to establish actual intent to defraud.

Mohsen's reliance on the concept of a "legitimate supervening purpose" is misplaced. The concept is typically applied in bankruptcy cases where courts have held that in assessing whether a transfer constitutes a fraudulent conveyance under 11 U.S.C. §548(a)(1), the confluence of several badges of fraud can establish "conclusive evidence of actual intent to defraud, absent 'significantly clear' evidence of a legitimate supervening purpose." Acequia, Inc. v. Clinton (In re Acequia, Inc.), 34 F.3d 800, 806 (9th Cir. 1994) (quoting Max Sugarman Funeral Home Inc. v. A.D.B. Investors, 926 F.2d 1248, 1255 (1st Cir. 1991)). Once multiple indicia of fraud are established, the burden shifts to the transferee to prove that there was a "legitimate supervening purpose" for the transfer at issue. Id. There is no bright line test for what constitutes a legitimate supervening purpose; the issue is simply whether the presumption of fraud has been adequately rebutted. See In re Bateman, 646 F.2d 1220, 1223 n.4 (8th Cir. 1981) ("The burden which shifts now upon a showing of reasonable grounds is not a burden of going forward with the evidence requiring the bankrupt to explain away natural inferences, but a burden of proving that he has not committed the objectionable acts with which he has been charged." (quoting Shainman v. Shear's of Affton, Inc., 387 F.2d 33, 37 (8th Cir. 1967))).

Here, Mohsen attempts to rebut the presumption of fraudulent intent by focusing on the reason that Aptix needed to borrow money from Mohsen, i.e. it could not obtain funding elsewhere, and its ultimate use of the money, i.e. to pay employees and other creditors. Although Mohsen's argument may explain why Aptix entered into the loan arrangement with Mohsen, it does not explain why it was necessary for Aptix to grant Mohsen a security interest in substantially all of its assets when Mohsen had never required such an interest for his past loans. It also does not address the district court's express finding that the arrangement was not as innocuous or well-intentioned as Mohsen suggests. Mohsen failed to rebut the circumstantial inference arising from the badges of fraud and, therefore, it was not clear error for the district court to conclude that Aptix granted the security interest with the actual intent to defraud Quickturn.

Mohsen's legal arguments are also without merit. First, he argues that California law protects the right of debtors to "pay one creditor in preference to another, or . . . give to one creditor security for the payment of his demand in preference to another." Cal. Civ. Code §3432. Mohsen fails to recognize, however, that the section of the California Civil Code on which he relies does not insulate debtors who make transfers with the intent to defraud creditors not party to the transaction. Kemp v. Lynch, 8 Cal. 2d 457, 460-61, 65 P.2d 1316 (1937) (a transfer that appears to be a lawful preference, but which is made with a fraudulent intent will be vitiated); Roberts v. Burr, 135 Cal. 156, 159, 67 P. 46 (1901) (stating that a debtor may pay one creditor in preference to another in the absence of fraud).

Similarly, Mohsen argues that Aptix did not have the requisite fraudulent intent because it entered into the security agreement in order to benefit some of its creditors. This argument reads §3439.04(a)(1) as if it requires that the debtor intend to defraud *all* of its creditors, whereas the language actually used in the statute mandates only that the debtor act with the actual intent to "defraud *any* creditor" (emphasis added).

Finally, Mohsen asserts a defense under Cal. Civ. Code §3439.08(a), which states that a "transfer or an obligation is not voidable under subdivision (a) of Section 3439.04, against a person who took in good faith and for a reasonably equivalent value or against any subsequent transferee or obligee." Mohsen argues that the security interest should not be voided because Aptix engaged in the security agreement in a good faith effort to stay in business and the amount of money loaned to Aptix exceeded the value of the security granted in return. This argument fails for two reasons. First, it appears that Mohsen did not invoke §3439.08(a) in the proceedings before the district court and he is therefore prevented from raising the statutory defense for the first time on appeal. Singleton v. Wulff, 428 U.S. 106, 120, 49 L. Ed. 2d 826, 96 S. Ct. 2868 (1976); United States v. Carlson, 900 F.2d 1346, 1349 (9th Cir. 1990). Even if this argument were properly before us, Mohsen only identifies evidence tending to show Aptix's good faith in entering into the transaction and points to no evidence showing that Mohsen himself acted in good faith as required by the statute. Cal. Civ. Code §3439.08(a). Mohsen's heavy reliance on the California case Annod Corp. v. Hamilton & Samuels, 100 Cal. App. 4th 1286, 123 Cal. Rptr. 2d 924 (2002) does not address the flaws in his argument.

In *Annod,* the court applied §3439.08 to find that a law firm had not engaged in a fraudulent transaction when it executed partnership draws pursuant to a pre-existing partnership agreement rather than pay an outstanding judgment for unpaid rent. 100 Cal. App. 4th at 1293-94. Mohsen makes much of the court's conclusion that the partners had received the draws in good faith in part because "if the draws were not paid, none of the former partners would have continued working and generating revenue for the struggling law practice." Id. at 1293. Mohsen asserts that under *Annod* transactions engaged in with the purpose of keeping a struggling business afloat cannot constitute fraudulent transactions. In making this assertion, Mohsen ignores the extensive additional evidence relied on by the court as the complete basis for finding that the partners acted in good faith. Id. at 1296 (focusing on evidence that the payments made were substantially less than previous draws, represented undermarket values for the services performed, and were consistent with the partner's significant efforts to increase funds available to creditors). *Annod* does not stand for the proposition that a transfer made to enable an enterprise to stay in business cannot constitute a fraudulent transaction. Contrary to Mohsen's assertions, the district court did not err as a matter of law in determining that Aptix's grant of a security interest to Mohsen was a voidable transaction under California law.

NEWMAN, Circuit Judge, dissenting.

I respectfully dissent. Dr. Mohsen loaned over nine million dollars to the company he had founded and operated, secured by the assets of the company. My colleagues hold that the purpose of making the secured loan was to defraud future creditors, based on two undisputed facts: that Dr. Mohsen expected an adverse attorney fee award in favor of Quickturn, and that his previous smaller loans to his company were unsecured. I cannot agree that the requirement of security for the larger loans establishes fraudulent intent. . . .

Precedent illustrates instances of fraudulent intent. In Kemp v. Lynch, 8 Cal. 2d 457, 460-61, 65 P.2d 1316 (1937) an ostensibly lawful preference made with "the understanding that it shall be a mere simulated transfer" was fraudulent. See also Bank of Cal. v. Virtue & Scheck, Inc., 140 Cal. App. 3d 1026, 1039, 190 Cal. Rptr. 54 (1983) (collecting cases) ("California courts have consistently treated a secret reservation in the grantor as potent evidence of fraud"). Unlike *Kemp,* here there was no simulated transfer, but regular monthly loans to meet payroll and other operating obligations. The facts of this case are more analogous to those of *Wyzard,* in which a secured loan was taken in order to pay an existing debt when it became known that an adverse judgment was imminent; the court held that there was no fraud in a transfer made "with recognition that the transfer will effectively prevent another creditor from collecting on his debt." *Wyzard,* 23 Cal. App. 4th at

1189-90 (concluding that the facts did not raise a triable issue of fact as to fraud, notwithstanding the existence of three factors of fraud); see also *Annod Corp.*, 100 Cal. App. 4th at 1299 (no triable issue of fact, despite three factors of fraud).

Aptix granted Dr. Mohsen a security interest; the money was needed and used for legitimate business purposes. The panel majority states that this "does not explain why it was necessary for Aptix to grant Mohsen a security interest" when "Mohsen had never required such an interest for his past loans." Maj. op. at 9. It is surely not fraudulent to obtain security for a loan of over nine million dollars, whatever the relationship between the lender and the recipient. Knowledge of a potential adverse judgment does not establish fraudulent intent when making a loan to meanwhile keep the company alive and operating. See *Wyzard*, 23 Cal. App. 4th at 1189 (a transfer in anticipation of liability, "with recognition that the transfer will effectively prevent another creditor from collecting on his debt," is not fraudulent).

V. NON-CONSENSUAL LIENS AND THE TRUSTEE

Section 547(b) of the Bankruptcy Code condemns as preferential all judicial liens acquired by a creditor within the 90 days preceding the bankruptcy filing if taken while the bankrupt was insolvent.

As for statutory liens (the garage mechanic, etc.), they are effective under §545 against the trustee if (a) they would be good against a BFP and (b) they do not arise only on insolvency. The reason for this last rule—statutory liens that arise only on insolvency are void against the trustee—is this: originally the Bankruptcy Code permitted the separate states to specify which general creditors would get priority payments when the bankrupt's estate was distributed. When that power was taken away from the states, the states battled back by rewriting their priority statutes as statutory lien statutes—providing, for example, that unpaid employees would have an automatic lien on the employer's assets if the employer became insolvent but not otherwise. Because Congress didn't want the states to be able to dictate priorities in a federal insolvency proceeding, §545 and its predecessor were redrafted to avoid this type of statutory lien.

CHAPTER 8   ASSESSMENT: MULTIPLE CHOICE QUESTIONS

1. Antonio Credit loaned $100,000 to Prospero, a chemist, secured by Prospero's patent rights. Antonio Credit was uncertain whether to perfect by filing in the relevant state UCC office or in the United States

The transaction here was a conditional sale in form, but a secured sale in substance, so Article 9 applies. To perfect, Sycorax Gallery could simply have filed a financing statement. It did not, and so was unperfected, meaning in bankruptcy it will become unsecured. Article 9 prevails over the party's agreement, so the painting was no longer Sycorax Gallery's property, contrary to A and B. Rather, it became Prospero's painting, subject to Sycorax Gallery's security interest. This question emphasizes a basic skill of any lawyer that deals with transactions.

3. *A* is the best answer. A creditor that receives payment may have to return it, if the debtor files bankruptcy within the next 90 days (or even one year, for insiders). Contrary to D, the bankruptcy trustee may recover some transfers of the debtor's property in the prebankruptcy period. This payment meets all the requirements of §547 of the Bankruptcy Code: a transfer of the debtor's property during the prebankruptcy period that put the creditor in a better position than would have otherwise occurred in bankruptcy. Without the payment, Caliban would have had a $40,000 claim secured by $25,000 in collateral, so would have been undersecured in bankruptcy by $15,000. With the payment, Caliban has a $25,000 claim, fully covered by $25,000 in collateral. None of the exceptions apply (not an ordinary course payment, not a contemporaneous exchange of value such as a cash sale, not followed by new value from the creditor, or any of the other exceptions in §547). Contrary to B, even innocent creditors are subject to the rule; no collusion or bad faith need be shown. An unsecured or undersecured creditor that gets payment may need to cross its fingers for the next 90 days.

4. *C* is the best answer. Section 547 does not authorize the bankruptcy trustee to recover all transfers of the debtor's property in the prebankruptcy period. A key requirement is that the transfer have preferential effect, enabling the creditor to receive more than the creditor would have in a liquidation bankruptcy. §547(c). An oversecured creditor, like Miranda, will be fully paid in bankruptcy. The payment did not make her better off than bankruptcy would have, unlike a payment to an undersecured or unsecured creditor. There are also several exceptions that protect some creditors who receive transfers with preferential effect. It is unnecessary to consider them here, where the transfer does not even meet the initial requirement of preferential effect.

5. *C* is the best answer. The niece was not a creditor, so the issue of preferential transfers or perfected security interests do not arise. But the trustee also has the power under Bankruptcy Code §548, to recover fraudulent transfers, broadly defined as any transfer made by the debtor, within two years before bankruptcy, while insolvent, without receiving reasonably

equivalent value. The transfer here meets all those requirements. Fraud need not be shown, contrary to B.

Note that in addition to §548, the bankruptcy trustee may also use state law to recover fraudulent transfers, such as transfers made with intent to hinder creditors. State law often permits the trustee to attack transfers made more than two years before bankruptcy.

CHAPTER 9

PROCEEDS

Should the debtor, with or without the blessing of the secured creditor, sell the collateral or trade it for some other item, the creditor wants its security interest transferred to whatever is left in its place when the collateral moves on. Article 9 phrases this as giving the creditor an interest in "proceeds" of the collateral. Consider, for example, a security interest in a retailer's inventory. As that inventory is sold in the usual course of business the creditor now is most concerned in reaching the payments given to the retailer. This right to proceeds is an important cog in the machinery of financing, and this chapter explores what the creditor must do to make sure the proceeds belong to that creditor.

I. THE MEANING OF PROCEEDS

Proceeds is defined in §9-102(a)(64) (*cash proceeds*, a subcategory of proceeds is defined in §9-102(a)(9)), and the priority rules for proceeds are contained in §9-315. Read those sections.

PROBLEM 119

When Rosetta Stone bought a new car from Champollion Motors, Inc., she traded in her five-year-old car, made a $200 down payment by giving the dealer her check, and signed a promissory note for the balance payable to the dealership. Rameses National Bank had a perfected security interest in Champollion Motors' inventory.

(a) Does that security interest continue in the car once it is delivered to Ms. Stone? See §9-320(a).

(b) Under §9-315(a) the bank's security interest will continue in *proceeds,* as defined in subsection (1). What are the proceeds of the car sale?

(c) Is the attachment of the creditor's security interest in the proceeds automatic, or must they be claimed in the original security agreement? See §9-203(f).

Farmers Cooperative Elevator Co. v. Union State Bank

Iowa Supreme Court, 1987
409 N.W.2d 178

LARSON, J.

Rodger Cockrum operated a farm and hog confinement operation in Madison County, Iowa. For several years financing for a substantial portion of the operation came from [Union] State Bank of Winterset (Union State). In February 1981, Union State loaned Cockrum a large sum of money and took a security agreement covering

> all equipment and fixtures, including but not limited to sheds and storage facilities, used or acquired for use in farming operations, whether now or hereafter existing or acquired; all farm products including but not limited to, *livestock, and supplies used or produced in farming operations whether now or hereafter existing or acquired. . . .*

(Emphasis added.)

In December 1983 and January 1984, Cockrum entered into several purchase money security agreements with Farmers Cooperative Elevator Company (CO-OP) for livestock feed. See Iowa Code §554.9312 (1983). For each transaction, CO-OP filed a financing statement with the Secretary of State, which stated:

> This is a purchase money security interest which covers Collateral described as all feed sold to Debtors by Secured Party and all of Debtors' feeder hogs now owned or hereafter acquired including . . . additions, replacements, and substitutions of such livestock, including all issues presently or hereafter

conceived and born, the products thereof, and the proceeds of any of the described Collateral.

Cockrum defaulted on his obligations to both Union State and the CO-OP. CO-OP commenced an action against Cockrum seeking possession of collateral. (International Barter Corporation was also joined as a defendant, but its petition under chapter 11 of the Bankruptcy Act stayed further proceedings against it, and it is not involved in the present action.)

Union State filed a statement of indebtedness and requested that its security interests be established as a first security lien on Cockrum's hog inventory and any sale proceeds therefrom. CO-OP responded by filing an amendment to its petition, joining Union State as a defendant and alleging that its right to the hogs is superior to Union State's.

On CO-OP's motion to adjudicate law points, the district court ruled that Union State's security interest in the hogs was prior and superior to the CO-OP's. CO-OP has appealed from that decision.

We first address CO-OP's argument that its interest in the livestock and proceeds therefrom is superior to Union State's under section 554.9312(4) [now §9-324(a) — Eds.]. That section provides:

A purchase money security interest in collateral other than inventory has priority over a conflicting security interest in the same collateral or its proceeds if the purchase money security interest is perfected at the time the debtor receives possession of the collateral or within twenty days thereafter.

"Purchase money security interests" are defined in section 554.9107 [now §9-103 — Eds.]:

A security interest is a "purchase money security interest" to the extent that it is
a. taken or retained by the seller of the collateral to secure all or part of its price; or
b. taken by a person who by making advances or incurring an obligation gives value to enable the debtor to acquire rights in or the use of collateral if such value is in fact so used.

Union State concedes that CO-OP held a purchase money security interest in the feed. The question, however, is whether such a priority interest continues in livestock which consume the feed.

In essence, one who takes a purchase money security interest under section 554.9107(a) is the equivalent of the old conventional vendor — a seller who has, in effect, made a loan by selling goods on credit. See J. White & R. Summers, Uniform Commercial Code §25-5, at 1043 (2d ed. 1980). Put more simply, a purchase money security interest "is a secured loan for the price of new collateral." Henderson, Coordination of the Uniform Commercial Code with Other State and Federal Law in the Farm Financing Context, 14 Idaho L. Rev. 363, 375 (1978). In this case, CO-OP took the purchase money security interests to secure the price of the feed, not the hogs. Consequently, by definition, CO-OP does not have a purchase money security interest in the hogs.

CO-OP, nevertheless, argues that their priority interest in the feed continues to be superior in the hogs pursuant to section 554.9203(3) because the hogs are "proceeds" of the feed. That section provides, "[u]nless otherwise agreed a security agreement gives the secured party the rights to proceeds provided by section 554.9306." Subsection 1 of section 554.9306 defines proceeds to include "whatever is received upon the sale, exchange, collection or other disposition of collateral or proceeds."

CO-OP contends that the "other disposition of collateral" language in section 554.9306 [now §9-315(a) — Eds.] includes ingestion and the biological processes involved when livestock consume feed, and as a result, fattened livestock are proceeds of the feed they consume. Such an argument was rejected in a case on all four hooves, so to speak. In First National Bank of Brush v. Bostron, 564 P.2d 964, 966 (Colo. App. 1977), the court emphasized that "[the livestock producer] received nothing when he disposed of the collateral by feeding it to the . . . cattle . . . the collateral was consumed, and there are no traceable proceeds to which the security interest may be said to have attached."

We agree with the result reached by the Colorado court. Ingestion and biological transformation of feed is not a type of "other disposition" within the contemplation of section 554.9306. For UCC purposes, the hogs are not proceeds of the feed.

CO-OP also argues that it should prevail over Union State pursuant to section 554.9315(1) [now §9-336 — Eds.], which provides in part:

> If a security interest in goods was perfected and subsequently the goods or a part thereof have become part of a product or mass, the security interest continues in the product or mass if
> a. the goods are so manufactured, processed, assembled or commingled that their identity is lost in the product or mass. . . .

CO-OP contends that its superior interest in the feed continued in the hogs because the feed became commingled with the hogs.

Section 9-315 of the Uniform Commercial Code is probably the least litigated and discussed section of article 9. See Hawkland Uniform Commercial Code Series §9-315:01, at 256 (1986) (hereinafter Hawkland). The only reported case examining this question is *Bostron*. There, the court concluded that cattle are neither a "product" nor a "mass" as these terms are used in the statute. The reference in subsection (a) to "manufactured, processed, assembled, or commingled" precludes any other interpretation. The feed which the cattle ate did not undergo any of these transformations, that is, it was not manufactured, processed, assembled or commingled with the cattle. . . . Once eaten the feed not only loses its identity, but in essence it ceases to exist and thus does not become part of the mass in the sense that the Code uses the phrase.

Bostron, 564 P.2d at 966.

Examining the *Bostron* decision and the question presented by the present case, one Uniform Commercial Code commentator has said:

Other than section 9-315, no Code provision clearly suggests a contrary result, and section 9-315 does not seem to apply since the goods have not been manufactured, processed or commingled. Rather, their identity has been lost through ingestion, a process apparently not contemplated by section 9-315.

Hawkland at 262.

When construing a statute, we search for an interpretation that is sensible, workable, practical and logical. Emmetsburg Ready Mix Co. v. Norris, 362 N.W.2d 498, 499 (Iowa 1985). CO-OP's argument, although creative, stretches the language of section 554.9315 beyond our interpretation guideposts.

Because of our disposition on the merits, we need not address Union State's procedural issues. We have considered all arguments raised and find no error.

Affirmed.

PROBLEM 120

Octopus National Bank (ONB) made a loan to Dairy, Inc., secured by Dairy's equipment. The equipment was then sold to Cheeseworks, Inc., which later sold the equipment to Buttercups, Inc. Was the money that Cheeseworks received as proceeds of the sale subject to ONB's security interest? See Border State Bank, N.A. v. AgCountry Farm Credit Servs., FLCA, 535 F.3d 779 (8th Cir. 2008).

While Article 9 does not usually apply to security interests taken in an insurance policy as collateral (the common law or other statutes regulate these transactions), insurance payments that qualify as *proceeds* are regulated by the Code; §9-109(d)(8). For example, if the collateral is a car that is destroyed in a traffic mishap and the car owner receives compensation from an insurance company, the insurance money is *proceeds,* and any security interest in the car attaches to these monies.

Helms v. Certified Packaging Corp.

United States Court of Appeals, Seventh Circuit, 2008
551 F.3d 675

POSNER, Circuit Judge.

Sarah Michaels, Inc., a manufacturer of bath products and a customer of a packaging manufacturer named Certified Packaging Corporation, declared bankruptcy together with affiliated corporations unnecessary to discuss separately. The trustee in bankruptcy brought an adversary proceeding against Certified seeking to avoid transfers that Michaels had made to that company to pay for packaging. The trustee obtained a default judgment for some $2 million but in an effort to collect the judgment collided with LaSalle Bank, which, as the assignee of a loan to Certified, claimed a security interest in Certified's assets. LaSalle in turn assigned its claim to CPC Acquisition, which is the successor to Certified and which has intervened in the bankruptcy proceeding to assert the priority of its lien over the trustee's judgment lien. For the sake of simplicity we'll pretend that LaSalle was and remains the lender to Certified and thus the adversary of the trustee in bankruptcy.

In December 2000, after LaSalle had made the loan, a fire broke out at one of Certified's plants and damaged equipment in it. The plant was shut down for several weeks, and the business losses resulting from the shutdown greatly exceeded the damage to Certified's property. Certified brought two lawsuits (both in Illinois state courts) in the wake of the fire. One was against its insurance broker, Rothschild, for negligence in having failed to list the plant on a business-losses insurance policy that Rothschild had procured for Certified. That suit was settled for $88,000 after deduction of attorneys' fees. The trustee contends that the settlement money should belong to the bankrupt estate, LaSalle that the money should belong to it as proceeds of the collateral damaged in the fire. The bankruptcy judge agreed with the trustee but was reversed by the district judge, and the trustee appeals.

Certified's other suit was against Commonwealth Edison and claimed that the fire had been due to Com Ed's negligence in maintaining one of its power lines. In that suit, which is pending, Certified seeks damages of $2,000,000 for property damage and business losses, the latter accounting for about 90 percent of the claimed damages. The bankruptcy judge, seconded by the district judge, ruled that the business-losses part of Certified's claim against Com Ed belongs to the trustee in bankruptcy, not to LaSalle. The cross-appeal challenges that ruling.

So we must decide whether the negligence claim against Rothschild for business losses, and the parallel claim against Certified, or either, or neither, are part of LaSalle's security interest. The issues are governed by the Uniform Commercial Code, as interpreted by the Illinois courts.

The loan agreement between LaSalle and Certified gave LaSalle a security interest in the equipment damaged in the fire. If a suit against someone who steals or damages collateral eventuates in an award measured by the diminution in the value of the collateral caused by the defendant's wrongdoing, so that the award restores the original value of the collateral, the award, like an insurance payment for damaged collateral, constitutes "proceeds" of the collateral and is therefore covered by the lender's security interest. UCC §§9-102(a)(64)(D) (proceeds include, "to the extent of the value of collateral, claims arising out of the loss, nonconformity, or interference with the use of, defects or infringement of rights in, or damage to, the collateral"), (E); McGonigle v. Combs, 968 F.2d 810, 828-29 (9th Cir. 1992); In re Wiersma, 324 B.R. 92, 106 (B.A.P. 9th Cir. 2005), reversed on other grounds, 483 F.3d 933 (9th Cir. 2007); In re Territo, 32 B.R. 377, 379-80 (Bkrtcy. E.D.N.Y. 1983); Richard F. Duncan et al., The Law and Practice of Secured Transactions: Working with Article 9 §2.05[3], pp. 2-57 to 2-58 (2008); R. Davis Rice, "McCullough v. Goodrich & Pennington Mortgage Fund, Inc.: Are Secured Creditors Really 'Secure' from Third Party Impairment of Collateral?," 59 S. Car. L. Rev. 455, 467-70 (2008); Lynn M. LoPucki & Elizabeth Warren, Secured Credit: A Systems Approach 205-06 (2d ed. 1998).

If Certified's suit against Com Ed succeeds, it will be as if Com Ed had converted some $200,000 of the collateral for LaSalle's loan and was therefore obliged to repay it; and "an action for conversion is a proper remedy for a secured party to bring against a third party when its collateral has been disposed of by the debtor." Taylor Rental Corp. v. J.I. Case Co., 749 F.2d 1526, 1529 (11th Cir. 1985); see also UCC § 9-315, comment 2; Bartlett Milling Co., L.P. v. Walnut Grove Auction & Realty Co., 665 S.E.2d 478, 488-89 (N. Car. App. 2008); Farmers State Bank v. Easton Farmers Elevator, 457 N.W.2d 763, 766 (Minn. App. 1990). And so the judgment obtained in that suit would constitute proceeds of the collateral up to its value. That is why LaSalle's entitlement to the property-damage component of Certified's claim against Com Ed is unchallenged, and it is why if Rothschild, the insurance broker, had failed to obtain insurance coverage for damage to the physical assets that secured LaSalle's loan, the claim against the broker rather than for loss of business would be a claim to proceeds of the collateral.

But the claim against Rothschild *was* for failure to obtain business-loss insurance, and we do not see how compensation for that failure can be considered proceeds of collateral. The usual proceeds of collateral are the money obtained from selling it. By a modest extension, as we have just seen, they are money obtained in compensation for a diminution in the value of the collateral. But replacing a business loss is not restoring the value of damaged collateral. There is no necessary relation between the value of collateral and a business loss that results from its being destroyed or damaged—as this case illustrates: the business losses exceeded the impairment of the value of the collateral ninefold. The claim of a secured creditor to the proceeds of collateral cannot exceed the value of the collateral. UCC §9-102(a)(64)(D), (E); In re Tower Air, Inc., 397 F.3d 191, 199 and n.10 (3d Cir. 2005); In re Stevens, 130 F.3d 1027, 1030 (11th Cir. 1997). Recall the qualification in the definition of proceeds in UCC §9-102(a)(64)(D): "to the extent of the value of collateral."

The district judge was therefore wrong to treat the $88,000 settlement of Certified's claim against Rothschild for failing to procure business-loss coverage as proceeds of damaged collateral. . . .

NOTE

When the collateral is gone but the debtor still has money, creditors may press various theories to claim it as proceeds of their collateral. Compare, e.g., BMW Financial Services, NA, LLC v. Rio Grande Valley Motors, Inc., 2012 WL 4623198 (S.D. Tex. 2012) (funds from settling lawsuit held to be proceeds of underlying franchise rights); In re Wright Group, Inc., 443 B.R. 795 (Bankr. N.D. Ind. 2011) (customers' payments to play golf were not proceeds of golf course equipment).

PROBLEM 121

Farmers' Friend Credit Association loaned Farmer Bean money secured by his crops. In 2020 the federal government paid Farmer Bean not to grow any crop that year. Is the government payment the "proceeds" of the crop? See PHI Fin. Serv. v. Johnston Law Office, 2016 WL 308944 (N.D. 2016); Annot., 79 A.L.R.4th 903.

II. PRIORITIES IN PROCEEDS

PROBLEM 122

The Aquarius Auto Audio Shop (AAAS) sold and installed stereo systems in cars. Its inventory was financed by the Canis Major Bank and Trust Co., which had a perfected security interest in present and after-acquired inventory. When Aquarius sold the systems, it sometimes was paid cash, sometimes extended credit without signed contracts, and sometimes made credit customers sign contracts promising payment and granting AAAS a security interest in the systems. When Aquarius needed further financing, it took a later loan from the Cassiopeia Finance Company, granting the lender a security interest in its accounts receivable and its chattel paper. Cassiopeia knew all about the prior loan and inventory security interest of the Canis Major Bank at the time it filed its financing statement in the proper place. Aquarius defaulted on both loans, and both secured parties claimed the accounts and chattel paper (only Canis Major claimed the inventory). Canis Major's theory was that the accounts and chattel paper were *proceeds* of the inventory. The chattel paper was in Cassiopeia's possession; it had not yet collected any of the accounts receivable. Who should prevail? See §§9-315, 9-330(a), 9-322(a) and (b); White & Summers §25-10(a). What result where the accounts receivable financer filed first?

PROBLEM 123

Shadrach Heating and Air Conditioning, Inc., borrowed $15,000 from the Meshach Merchants Financing Association (MMFA) in order to purchase a new furnace for its own home office. When one of its important clients needed an identical furnace in a hurry, Shadrach Heating sold it its own new furnace, which it installed in the client's place of business. The $17,000 check it received in payment was put into Shadrach's checking account (balance prior to this deposit: $81) with the Abednego State Bank. Thereafter, Shadrach made one further deposit of $5,000, followed a week later by a withdrawal of $5,040.

(a) Are proceeds from the furnace sale still in the bank accounts? See Universal C.I.T. Credit Corp. v. Farmers Bank, 358 F. Supp. 317 (E.D. Mo. 1973) (the general rule is that "in tracing commingled funds it is presumed that any payments made were from other than funds in which another had a legally recognized interest," called the *lowest intermediate balance* rule). Section 9-315(b) permits tracing of *identifiable* proceeds; see also Official Comment 3 to this section. Note §4-210(b).

(b) If Shadrach Heating defaults on its loan repayment to MMFA and also on an unsecured promissory note currently held by the Abednego State Bank, can the bank exercise its common law right of setoff and pay itself out of the checking account, or is its setoff right junior to MMFA's security interest in the proceeds? See §9-340.

(c) What can a creditor claiming an interest in proceeds do to protect itself from setoff by the debtor's bank?

(d) If the depositary bank has a security interest in proceeds deposited in the debtor's account, but honors a check that depletes the account, may it still recover the money as traceable and identifiable proceeds? See §9-315's Official Comment 7, §9-332(b), and In re Cumberland Molded Products, LLC, 2009 WL 2208582 (Bankr. M.D. Tenn. 2009).

HCC Credit Corp. v. Springs Valley Bank & Trust Co.

Supreme Court of Indiana, 1999
712 N.E.2d 952

SULLIVAN, J.

Lindsey Tractor Sales, Inc., sold 14 tractors to a customer and used the $199,122 proceeds to pay off the debt it owed Springs Valley Bank & Trust. Yet HCC Credit Corporation had financed Lindsey's purchase of the tractors and held a valid and perfected security interest in both the tractors and the proceeds from their sale. Because we hold that the payment to the bank was not in the ordinary course of the operation of Lindsey's business, HCC is entitled to recover the $199,122.

BACKGROUND

Lindsey Tractor Sales, Inc., purchased wholesale farm equipment from Hesston Corporation for resale in Lindsey's French Lick farm machinery sales and service business. At the times relevant to this case, HCC Credit Corporation provided financing for the purchases.

Written contracts governed the relationship between Hesston and HCC and Lindsey, including a security agreement. In the security agreement, Lindsey granted HCC a security interest in all the equipment it purchased from Hesston and in the proceeds from the sale of the equipment. Lindsey also agreed to pay HCC immediately for equipment sold from the proceeds of the sale. However, at no time did Hesston or HCC require Lindsey to deposit or segregate proceeds from the sale of Hesston products in a separate account.

The parties agree and the trial court found that the security agreement was binding and enforceable against Lindsey, that Lindsey understood the purpose and effect of the security agreement (including the requirement of paying for equipment immediately when sold), and that HCC had a valid and perfected security interest in the equipment and proceeds from the sale thereof.

In 1991, the Indiana State Department of Transportation agreed to purchase from Lindsey 14 Hesston tractors. Lindsey acquired the tractors from Hesston on credit provided by, and subject to the security agreement in favor of, HCC. Lindsey received payment from the State on August 15,

1991, and deposited the proceeds of $199,122 in the company's checking account at Springs Valley Bank & Trust. At the time of the deposit, Lindsey had $22,870 in other monies on deposit in the account. On the next day, August 16, 1991, Lindsey wrote a check on this account payable to the bank for $212,104.75.

Lindsey's payment to the bank of the proceeds from the sale of the tractors was applied to pay debts owed by Lindsey to the bank. These debts were evidenced by four promissory notes dated January 23, 1987, November 19, 1990, February 7, 1991, and February 13, 1991. All four represented previously refinanced debts and three of them were not yet due when they were paid on August 16. The bank and Lindsey did not discuss paying off the four notes with Lindsey prior to their payment, nor did the bank seize the account to pay the notes. More specifically, Lindsey did not tell anyone associated with the bank that $199,122 of the $212,104.75 used to pay off the notes was from the sale of Hesston products. On the other hand, during the previous eight years Lindsey had borrowed funds or refinanced debts in excess of 100 times with the bank. The average debt balance outstanding during that period was between $100,000 and $200,000. After the notes were paid with the proceeds from the sale of the tractors, Lindsey owed the bank between $2,000 and $15,000.

Lindsey filed a bankruptcy liquidation proceeding in December of 1991, and dissolved shortly thereafter.

In the trial court, HCC sought to recover the $199,122 in proceeds from the sale of Hesston tractors that the bank received from Lindsey. Each party moved for summary judgment, agreeing that there were no genuine issues of material fact. The trial court granted summary judgment in favor of the bank and the Court of Appeals affirmed. HCC Credit Corp. v. Springs Valley Bank & Trust, 669 N.E.2d 1001 (Ind. Ct. App. 1996).

DISCUSSION

I

Under both the terms of the security agreement between the parties and the provisions of Article 9 of the Uniform Commercial Code as adopted by our legislature, HCC had a valid and perfected security interest in the $199,122 proceeds from the sale of the tractors. See Ind. Code §26-1-9-306(2) [now §9-315(a) — EDS.] ("a security interest continues . . . in any identifiable proceeds including collections received by the debtor"). If this were the end of the matter, there is no question but that HCC would be entitled to the money: UCC Article 9 gives the "secured party, upon a debtor's default priority over 'anyone, anywhere, anyhow' except as otherwise provided by the remaining [UCC] priority rules." Citizens Natl. Bank of Whitley County v. Mid-States Dev. Co., 177 Ind. App. 548, 557, 380 N.E.2d 1243, 1248 (1978) (citing Ind. Code §26-1-9-201; other citations omitted).

But in promulgating the 1972 version of Article 9 of the Uniform Commercial Code, the National Conference of Commissioners on Uniform State Laws (NCCUSL) appended the following "official comment":

> Where cash proceeds are covered into the debtor's checking account and paid out in the operation of the debtor's business, recipients of the funds of course take free of any claim which the secured party may have in them as proceeds. *What has been said relates to payments and transfers in the ordinary course.* The law of fraudulent conveyances would no doubt in appropriate cases support recovery of proceeds by a secured party from the transferee out of ordinary course or otherwise in collusion with the debtor to defraud the secured party.

UCC §9-306 cmt. 2(c) (1972), 3 U.L.A. 441 (1981) (emphasis supplied). We will refer to this official comment in this opinion as "Comment 2(c)."

Although our legislature has never adopted the NCCUSL comments as authoritative, there seems to be general agreement that, at least to some extent, Comment 2(c) is an exception to the Indiana UCC's general priority rules. The bank argues that in this case, the proceeds were paid out of Lindsey's checking account in the operation of Lindsey's business and that the payment was made in the ordinary course without any collusion with the debtor. As such, the bank contends, Comment 2(c) operates to provide that the bank received the $199,122 free of any claim which HCC had in it as proceeds.[1] The trial court and Court of Appeals adopted this rationale. HCC now seeks transfer, arguing that its perfected security interest entitles it to the proceeds.

II

At a certain level of abstraction, this case requires us to assess the relative rights of a secured creditor to the proceeds of its collateral and of a third party to whom the debtor transfers those proceeds. Sound commercial policy considerations can be marshaled in support of both the rights of the secured party and the rights of the transferee.

---

1. As discussed under Background, supra, Lindsey deposited the proceeds from the tractors' sale into the business's checking account and then used those proceeds, along with other funds in the account, to pay the bank. The commingling of the proceeds with other funds does not cut off HCC's claim. It is well settled that in appropriate circumstances, "a secured party may trace 'identifiable proceeds' through a commingled bank account and into the hands of a recipient who lacks the right to keep them." Harley-Davidson Motor Co., Inc. v. Bank of New England-Old Colony, N.A., 897 F.2d 611, 620 (1st Cir. 1990) (collecting cases).

A

Commercial policy considerations supporting the rights of a secured party are well set forth by Judge Garrard in *Citizens National Bank*. In that case, the debtor sold collateral in which a party held a valid and perfected security interest. When the debtor deposited the proceeds in the debtor's bank account, the bank exercised a contractual right of set-off. In weighing the bank's right to set-off against the secured party's interest in the proceeds, the court found that a secured party should be able to rely on its compliance with the UCC's requirements for perfection and its search of the public recording system as against the unrecorded interest of the setting-off bank. 177 Ind. App. at 559, 380 N.E.2d at 1249. "Were this otherwise," Judge Garrard wrote, "a secured party with an interest in proceeds could not rely on recording." Id. Instead, he reasoned, the secured party would be required to take additional steps to insure full protection such as requiring special accounts or inquiring into loan transactions which are not a matter of public record. 177 Ind. App. at 559, 380 N.E.2d at 1250. "Putting such a duty on a secured party, as well as permitting a bank to prevail if that duty is not met, undercuts significant values of certainty, efficiency and reliance which are at the heart of the [UCC's] emphasis on public filing." Id.

The court also noted that while it might be a safe practice for a secured party to require that proceeds be payable to it before future advances to the debtor are made, "it is purposefully not required by the [UCC] for the maintenance of a proceeds security interest since it tends to curtail commercial practice and business operation." Id. In holding for the secured party, Judge Garrard concluded that if UCC Article 9 "is to be a comprehensive system for the perfection of security interests in personal property we see no reason for requiring special standards, with their increased costs, that must be met if a secured party is to prevail over a bank's right of set-off. The [UCC's] priority rules are sufficient." Id.

In *Citizens National Bank,* the conflicting interests were between the creditor's perfected security interest and the bank's right to set-off. In the case before us, the conflicting interests are between HCC's perfected security interest and the bank's asserted right as ordinary course transferee.[2] As such, the result in *Citizens National Bank* does not dictate the result here. But *Citizens National Bank* helps us understand the policy interests that favor enforcing HCC's perfected security interest that requiring secured parties

---

2. It is clear that the bank did not seize Lindsey's account for purposes of paying the four notes. Indeed, the trial court found that Lindsey did not consult with the bank before paying the notes and that the bank did not know that the funds it received were the proceeds of the sale of Hesston tractors or that HCC had any claim thereto.

to take steps beyond those specified in Article 9 to protect their interests "undercuts significant values of certainty, efficiency" and "tends to curtail commercial practice and business operation."

B

Just as Judge Garrard gives sound policy reasons in *Citizens National Bank* for enforcing perfected security interests, there are sound policy reasons for allowing third party transferees to retain proceeds of another's collateral. When he was a judge of the United States Court of Appeals for the First Circuit, Justice Breyer had occasion to address this subject: "If . . . courts too readily impose liability upon those who receive funds from the debtor's ordinary bank account—if, for example, they define 'ordinary course' of business too narrowly—then ordinary suppliers, sellers of gas, electricity, tables, chairs, etc., might find themselves called upon to return ordinary payments . . . to a debtor's secured creditor, say a financier of inventory." Harley-Davidson Motor Co., Inc. v. Bank of New England-Old Colony, N.A., 897 F.2d 611, 622 (1st Cir. 1990) (internal citation omitted).

Judge Breyer was also able to "imagine good commercial reasons for not imposing, even upon sophisticated suppliers or secondary lenders, who are aware that inventory financiers often take senior secured interests in 'all inventory plus proceeds,' the complicated burden of contacting these financiers to secure permission to take payment from a dealer's ordinary commingled bank account. These considerations," he continued, "indicate that 'ordinary course' has a fairly broad meaning; and that a court should restrict the use of tracing rules to conduct that, in the commercial context, is rather clearly improper." Id.[3]

Harley-Davidson makes a strong statement of the policy interests supporting the bank's claim to the $199,122. But it is interesting to note that despite Judge Breyer's conception of the commercial utility of a "fairly broad meaning" for "ordinary course," his court was unwilling to find that

---

3. We note that in their most recent revision of Article 9, the American Law Institute and National Conference of Commissioners on Uniform State Laws have proposed that this liberal approach be codified. A new section would be added to Article 9 providing that "transferee of funds from a deposit account takes the funds free of a security interest in the deposit account unless the transferee acts in collusion with the debtor in violating the rights of the secured party." UCC §9-329 [now §9-332(b) —Eds.] (1998). "Broad protection for transferees helps to ensure that security interests in deposit accounts do not impair the free flow of funds. It also minimizes the likelihood that a secured party will enjoy a claim to whatever the transferee purchases with the funds. Rules concerning recovery of payments traditionally have placed a high value on finality. The opportunity to upset a completed transaction, or even to place a completed transaction in jeopardy by bringing suit against the transferee of funds, should be severely limited." Revision of UCC Article 9, §9-329, cmt. 3 (Reporters' Interim Draft Aug. 7, 1997).

the transferee bank in the *Harley-Davidson* case was entitled to summary judgment.

III

Judge Garrard's opinion in *Citizens National Bank* and Judge Breyer's in *Harley-Davidson* each illustrates the way the UCC streamlines legal impediments to commerce: reducing the burden on perfected secured parties in the former and reducing the burden on ordinary course payees in the latter. But the drafters of the UCC recognized that these two efforts could come into conflict as they do in this case. Comment 2(c) is meant to resolve that conflict.

Comment 2(c) is not a statute and is not written in the form of a statute; it does not set forth a tightly-worded rule, followed by equally tightly-worded elements necessary to establish its application. Rather, it is a narrative collection of three sentences from which we conclude that a recipient of a payment made "in the ordinary course" by a debtor takes that payment free and clear of any claim that a secured party may have in the payment as proceeds. The Comment also tells us that the payment (1) will be in the ordinary course if it was made "in the operation of the debtor's business" but (2) will not be in the ordinary course if there was "collusion with the debtor to defraud the secured party." We do not take these two factors to be the equivalent of statutory elements but rather descriptive of two parameters for determining "ordinary course." That is, whether a payment was made in the ordinary course will be a function of (1) the extent to which the payment was made in the routine operation of the debtor's business and (2) the extent to which the recipient was aware that it was acting to the prejudice of the secured party.[4]

As to the routine operation of business parameter, payment of sales tax collections or F.I.C.A. withholdings would obviously be at the most routine end and a one-shot payment of subordinated debt not yet due would be at the least. At various points between these extremes would fall payments ordered by how routine they were to both debtor and transferee measured by such factors as their size, their frequency, whether the debtor received merchandise or services in return, whether the payment was on an

---

4. We explicitly reject the notion that Comment 2(c)'s "payments and transfers in the ordinary course" are the equivalent of UCC §1-201(9)'s "buyer in the ordinary course of business." Without giving extensive treatment to this point, we observe that §1-201(9)'s definition arises in the context of "buying" which is not always applicable in Comment 2(c) disputes (including this one). See ITT Commercial Fin. Corp. v. Bank of the West, 166 F.3d 295, 306 (5th Cir. 1999); Merchants Natl. Bank & Trust Co. v. United States, 202 Ct. Cl. 343 n.3 (1973). We also note that §1-201(9) contains a knowledge requirement on the part of the buyer which differs from that which we find required by Comment 2(c). . . .

obligation overdue, due or not yet due, etc. The cases have explored such payments as those for monthly marketing expenses, retainers to legal counsel by companies in financial difficulty, offsets against pre-existing debts, and periodic term loan payments in this or related bankruptcy contexts.

As to the awareness of prejudice parameter, it is hard to imagine the recipient of the monthly utility or rent payment having any knowledge that it was being paid with proceeds. At the other end of the spectrum is actual fraud in which debtor and recipient have colluded against the secured party.[5] Between these poles will fall payments where the recipient knows that a security interest exists but does not know that the payment is being made in violation of that interest; payments where the recipient had sufficient notice to put a reasonable recipient, exercising prudent business practices, on notice that something was awry; and payments where the recipient has information causing it to suspect strongly that a payment violates a secured party's interest, yet takes deliberate steps to avoid discovering more.

The nature of the relationship between the debtor and the transferee can give rise to a presumption of the transferee's awareness of prejudice, especially where the transferee itself is a lender. Such a secondary lender whose debt is subordinated to the secured party's or who has explicitly excluded the debtor's obligations to the secured lender in computing the debtor's borrowing base will generally be presumed to have actual knowledge of prejudice to the secured party. This occurs because the secondary lender has extended credit to the debtor with the express understanding that the secured party stands in a superior position to be repaid, at least in certain circumstances.

We reaffirm that a security interest continues in any identifiable proceeds of collateral including collections received by the debtor. Ind. Code §§26-1-9-201 & 306(2). We also reaffirm that Comment 2(c) is the law of Indiana: a recipient of a payment made "in the ordinary course" by a debtor takes that payment free and clear of any claim that a secured party may have in the payment as proceeds. And we hold that whether a transfer of proceeds is "in the ordinary course" requires an assessment of both (1) the extent to which the payment was made in the routine operation of the debtor's business and (2) the extent to which the recipient was aware that it was

---

5. Compare Commerce Bank, N.A. v. Tifton Aluminum Co., Inc., 217 B.R. 798, 803 (W.D. Mo. 1997) (transferee knew of the secured party's interest in the proceeds and that the secured party had informed the debtor that it was not authorized to use any of the proceeds); NCNB Texas Natl. Bank v. Standard Iron & Steel Co., Inc., 1990 WL 37929 (D. Kan. Mar. 16, 1990) (transferee privy to intimate knowledge of debtor's financial situation); Universal C.I.T. Credit Corp. v. Farmers Bank of Portageville, 358 F. Supp. 317, 324 (E.D. Mo. 1973) (debtor told the transferee bank that the secured party had revoked its floor plan financing arrangement and that debtor wanted the bank to be "safe" on its loan).

acting to the prejudice of the secured party. Because we agree that "imposing liability too readily on payees . . . could impede the free flow of goods and services essential to business," *J.I. Case*, 991 F.2d at 1277, we further hold that the transfer will be free of any claim that a secured party may have in it as proceeds unless the payment would constitute a windfall to the recipient. A windfall occurs in this context when the recipient has no reasonable expectation of being paid ahead of a secured creditor because of the extent to which the payment was made outside the routine operation of the debtor's business, because of the extent to which the recipient was aware that it was acting to the prejudice of the secured party, or because of both of these factors in combination.

While the determination of "ordinary course" is a question of law, sometimes an evaluation of the extent to which the payment was routine or the extent of the recipient's knowledge will require factual analysis. In such a situation, summary judgment would be inappropriate.

IV

Before applying these principles to the case before us, it is important to discuss J.I. Case Credit Corp. v. First National Bank of Madison County, 991 F.2d 1272 (7th Cir. 1993), a decision of the United States Court of Appeals for the Seventh Circuit applying Indiana law to a substantially identical problem. (*J.I. Case* served as the principal authority for the Court of Appeals in this case.)

As in the case before us, the debtor in *J.I. Case* deposited proceeds from the sale of secured agricultural equipment in his business checking account where it was commingled with funds from other sources. The debtor then used the commingled funds to pay creditors other than the secured creditor, including his bank lender. After careful analysis of whether these payments were "payments and transfers in ordinary course" within the meaning of Comment 2(c), the court concluded:

> [U]nder Comment 2(c), a payment is within the ordinary course if it was made in the operation of the debtor's business and if the payee did not know and was not reckless about whether the payment violated a third party's security interest.

991 F.2d at 1279. The court held that the payments were made in the ordinary course of business and the secured party was not entitled to recover them because both (1) the bank did not know that the debtor's payments violated the secured party's security interest (although the bank did know about the secured party's security interest) and (2) the bank did not receive payments from the debtor in reckless disregard of the fact that those payments violated the secured party's security interest. Id.; accord, ITT Commercial Fin. Corp. v. Bank of the West, 166 F.3d 295, 307 (5th Cir. 1999).

Without expressing any view as to the outcome of *J.I. Case,* it is clear that the Seventh Circuit's approach focussed exclusively on the awareness of prejudice parameter. . . . [W]e generally agree with this analysis. But the court did not independently examine the extent to which the debtor's payment to the bank was made in the routine operation of the debtor's business. For this reason, we decline to follow *J.I. Case.*

v

We hold that Lindsey's payment of $199,122 to the bank here was not a payment in the ordinary course of the operation of Lindsey's business. There is no disagreement as to the following facts. See Record at 19-20; 374; 418. The bank was aware that HCC had a valid and perfected security interest in Lindsey's tractor inventory. The bank took this into account in making its decision to extend credit to Lindsey and did not take a security interest in any of the collateral covered by HCC's security agreement. During the eight years prior to the payment at issue here, Lindsey had borrowed funds or refinanced debt in excess of 100 times with the bank and the average debt balance owed was between $100,000 and $200,000. Two of the notes Lindsey paid off represented a refinancing of approximately $225,000 in continuing debt carried by the bank. After the notes were paid off, Lindsey was in the unprecedented position of owing the bank only between $2,000 and $15,000. The bank's senior loan officer agreed with HCC's counsel that the $199,122 payment was "extraordinary" and constituted the largest ever made on any debt Lindsey owed the bank. The officer also said, "Anytime a significant loan balance is paid off you have to look at it as something that would not be a normal trade transaction, like paying interest or something like that."

The payment to the bank constituted the proceeds of collateral in which HCC had a valid and perfected security interest. The payment was used to liquidate a substantial secured debt which, for the most part, was not due. It was an extremely large payment, the likes of which Lindsey had never made before. And although the bank was not advised that the source of the payment it received constituted the proceeds of HCC's collateral, the bank knew of HCC's perfected security interest. As such, it had extended credit to Lindsey with the express understanding that HCC stood in a superior position to be repaid, at least in certain circumstances. We conclude that the payment was not in the ordinary course of Lindsey's business. For the bank to prevail would result in a windfall—a windfall because the bank had no reasonable expectation that Lindsey could or would liquidate its debt due the bank in advance of paying HCC for the tractors financed—at the expense of HCC which had taken all measures required by the UCC to protect its interest. As a result, the exception to the Indiana UCC's priority rules provided by Comment 2(c) does not apply and HCC, not the bank, is entitled to the $199,122.

CONCLUSION

Having previously granted transfer, thereby vacating the decision of the Court of Appeals, we now reverse the judgment of the trial court and remand this matter to the trial court with directions that summary judgment be entered for HCC and for any further proceedings that may be required.

NOTE

In a footnote the court states that the revised Article 9 has a section more explicitly protecting the transferee in the ordinary course in this situation. Read §9-332(b) and its Official Comments and decide if the case would have come out differently had that section then been in effect. See Banner Bank v. First Community Bank, 854 F. Supp. 2d 846 (D. Mont. 2012) (junior creditor that knowingly received funds from sale of senior creditor's collateral did not take free from security interest of senior creditor under §9-332(b), due to collusion with debtor).

PROBLEM 124

Octopus National Bank loaned $200,000 to Big Department Store and took a security interest in its inventory "now owned or after-acquired," which it perfected by filing a financing statement on July 5. Antitrust National Bank loaned $100,000 to Total Store, Inc., and took a security interest in its inventory "now owned or after-acquired," which it perfected by filing a financing statement on September 25. Without the consent of either creditor, the two retailers merged the following year, when the inventories of both were worth $300,000. The new entity was named Total Department Store. Which bank has priority in this situation? See §§9-102(a)(56), 9-203(d) and (e), 9-508 (and its helpful Official Comments), 9-325, 9-326, and the latter's Official Comments; White & Summers §25-11(a); Jean Wegman Burns, New Article Nine of the UCC: The Good, the Bad, and the Ugly, 2002 Ill. L. Rev. 29, 70-75.

Read §9-315(d) carefully, and work your way through the following Problem.

PROBLEM 125

On August 2, when the filed financing statement in favor of the Last National Bank covered "all business machines," the debtor engaged in the transactions listed below. Decide for each transaction if the bank should take action before August 23 or if the financing statement is sufficient as filed:

(a) The debtor traded a computer for another computer.

(b) The debtor traded another computer for a painting to be hung in the office.

(c) The debtor traded a duplicating machine for a used car (and state law requires a lien interest in a vehicle to be noted on the certificate of title as the sole means of perfection).

(d) The debtor sold a calculator to a friend for cash and that same day used the cash to buy a painting to hang in the office.

(e) The debtor sold an adding machine for $500 and put the cash in a bank account at a different bank; on August 2, that bank exercised its right of setoff against the account. See §9-340.

(f) The debtor sold a coffee maker for $200 and gave the money to a Salvation Army volunteer that same day; see §9-332(a).

PROBLEM 126

Balboa Bank & Trust Company floor-planned the inventory of Erickson Motors and perfected its security interest in the inventory (and proceeds) by filing in the proper place. See §9-311(d). Erickson Motors sold a car on credit to John Smith, who paid $1,000 down and signed a contract obligating him to pay $25,000 more. The car dealership assigned this contract and the promissory note Smith signed to the Cartier Finance Company, which took possession of these items and notified Smith he was to make future payments to Cartier. Smith made no payments at all because the car had serious mechanical difficulties, and eventually the parties cancelled the transaction and the car was returned to Erickson Motors on September 11. On September 12, a representative of Cartier Finance Company came to the dealership and took possession of the car, claiming it was *proceeds* from the contract of purchase, which Cartier still had. Balboa Bank objected and claimed a superior interest in the car, asserting its priority in the inventory of the dealership. Who prevails here? See §9-330(c) and its Official Comments 9 and 10.

For a complete review of priority problems, some involving proceeds and some not, read Official Comments 4 through 9 of §9-322. If you can understand them all, you are on top of the subject matter of this course.

CHAPTER 9   ASSESSMENT: MULTIPLE CHOICE QUESTIONS

1. Bond Manufacturing, in need of cash, sold some of its milling equipment for $10,000. At the same time, Bond Manufacturing missed a loan payment to Seizure Finance, who held a perfected security interest in Bond Manufacturings' equipment. Seizure Finance declared default

and demanded that Bond Manufacturing hand over the $10,000. Bond Manufacturing refused, contending that Seizure Finance was still entitled to go after its collateral in the hands of the buyer and had a security interest only in equipment, not cash. Is the $10,000 collateral of Seizure Finance?

    a. No, unless the security agreement grants a security interest in equipment and also cash.

    b. No, because the sale did not eliminate the security interest in the equipment.

    c. Yes, because the $10,000 is identifiable proceeds of collateral.

    d. Yes, under equitable considerations.

2. Bond Manufacturing had another piece of equipment, the Miller CNC, which it used to produce circuit boards. The machine was destroyed by fire, but was insured. The insurance company wrote Bond Manufacturing a check for the replacement value of the machine. Was the check proceeds of Seizure Finance's collateral?

    a. Yes, because it is payment for the time the machine was indisposed.

    b. Yes, because it is a product of the collateral.

    c. No, because it was not received upon sale or other disposition of the collateral.

    d. No, unless the security agreement covers checks.

    e. Yes, because it is insurance payable by reason of damage to the collateral.

3. Bond Manufacturing sold a piece of equipment, receiving $19,000. Seizure Finance did not pay attention for about a year, by which time the money had been spent, and was no longer traceable using accounting methods. Did Seizure Finance lose its security interest in those proceeds?

    a. No, the debtor cannot unilaterally destroy a security interest.

    b. Yes, the security interest continues only in identifiable proceeds.

    c. No, Seizure Finance would be entitled to claim as proceeds any cash Bond Manufacturing had.

    d. Yes, a security interest in proceeds in collateral lasts only 20 days.

4. Bond Manufacturing, increasingly entrepreneurial, traded another piece of manufacturing equipment for a sports car. Bond Manufacturing appeased the angry Seizure Finance by acknowledging that the car was proceeds of Seizure Finance's collateral, although the parties took no action to note the security interest on the certificate of title. Two months later, Bond Manufacturing finally staggered into bankruptcy. Seizure Finance had a security interest in the car, as collateral. But was it a *perfected* security interest (we know what happens to an unperfected security interest in bankruptcy)?

a. Yes. Seizure Finance had a perfected security interest in the collateral and so will have a perfected security interest in the proceeds, the car.

b. Yes, provided that Seizure Finance perfected its security interest by filing a financing statement.

c. No, this security interest in proceeds became unperfected after 20 days.

d. No, a security interest cannot be perfected in proceeds.

5. Boxcar Bank had a purchase money security interest in Furniture Retail's inventory. Paper Finance had a security interest in Furniture Retail's chattel paper. Furniture Retail often sold furniture on credit, receiving in return sales contracts under which the buyer promised to pay and put up the furniture as collateral. Furniture Retail delivered the contracts to Paper Finance, who kept them locked in a vault. If Boxcar Bank claimed such contracts as proceeds of inventory and Paper Finance claimed the contracts as chattel paper, who takes priority?

a. First to file or perfect.

b. Boxcar Bank, who had a purchase money security interest.

c. Paper Finance, as a chattel paper creditor.

d. The creditors would share equally.

ANSWERS

1. *C* is the best answer. When the collateral is sold (or otherwise disposed of), the creditor automatically has a security interest in identifiable proceeds. §9-315(a)(2). That right arises under the statute, and need not be included in the security agreement, contrary to A, although security agreements often include "proceeds" in the granting clause. Proceeds include anything acquired upon the sale, so the $10,000 sum is identifiable proceeds. The creditor is entitled to proceeds and, in general, retains the security interest in the collateral. §9-315(a)(1),(2). Contrary to B, the creditor has a right to proceeds even if it retained its security interest in the transferred collateral. That sounds as if the creditor's collateral will double in value, but in practice many factors prevent that. Some buyers take free of the security interest, some buyers would be difficult to track down, and often the proceeds are not tracked.

2. *E* is the best answer. Proceeds is broadly defined in §9-102(64) to include insurance payments for lost or damaged collateral.

3. *B* is the best answer. A practical limitation on the security interest in proceeds is that it applies only to "identifiable proceeds of collateral." Often, as here, a debtor receives proceeds of collateral but later they become untraceable. Creditors can protect against this in the security agreement, by getting a security interest in bank accounts or other collateral,

or requiring debtors to track proceeds (such as by having a lock-box account at a bank).

4. *C* is the best answer. If the security interest is perfected in collateral, the creditor has a security interest perfected in the proceeds—but only for 20 days, unless one of the following apply:

    i.   The creditor filed for the collateral and could have filed for proceeds category (and the proceeds were not acquired for cash proceeds);
    ii. the proceeds are identifiable cash proceeds; or
    iii. the security interest is perfected within 20 days,

    A security interest in a car cannot be perfected by filing, so (i) does not apply. The car is not cash proceeds, so (ii) does not apply. Seizure Finance could have complied with (iii) and remained perfected by getting its security interest noted on the certificate of title. But it did not, so its security interest is unperfected—and so ill-fated in bankruptcy.

5. *C* is the best answer. This question serves simply to illustrate a very specific priority rule. Section 9-330(a) provides:

    A purchaser of chattel paper has priority over a security interest in the chattel paper which is claimed merely as proceeds of inventory subject to a security interest if:

    > (1) in good faith and in the ordinary course of the purchaser's business, the purchaser gives new value and takes possession of the chattel paper or obtains control of the chattel paper under Section 9-105; and
    > (2) the chattel paper does not indicate that it has been assigned to an identified assignee other than the purchaser.

    Because inventory finance and chattel paper finance are important and potentially conflicting commercial practices, Article 9 provides a specific rule to resolve priority.

DEFAULT

In what is perhaps the only portion of secured transactions law where things can get exciting, Part 6 of Article 9 presents us with the rules on default and foreclosure. In this segment if a debtor ceases to make payments the creditor must take action to enforce its rights in the collateral. Even in our civilized times this can involve pitched battles during ugly encounters. For example in *Griffith v. Valley of the Sun Recovery & Adjustment Bureau*, 613 P.2d 1283 (Ariz. App. 1980), the repossessor was held liable in negligence for the actions of the debtor's neighbor who used a shotgun to shoot a bystander during a repossession melee. It is the job of the lawyers involved to make sure that everyone obeys the rules Article 9 lays down to ensure the process is fair to everyone, and, when things go awry, to know who bears what responsibility.

I. *PRE-DEFAULT DUTIES OF THE SECURED PARTY*

PROBLEM 127

Andy Doria was the owner of 100 shares of Titanic Telephone, which he pledged to the Morro Castle National Bank as collateral for a $10,000 loan. At the time of the pledge, the stock was selling for $100 a share.

(a) If the stock began to fall in value and if on November 4, when it was selling at $80 a share, Andy called the bank and told the bank to sell, is the bank responsible if it does not and the stock bottoms out at $1.50 a share? Read §9-207; see, e.g., Layne v. Bank One, Ky., N.A., 395 F.3d 271 (6th Cir. 2005).

(b) Would it help the bank's position if the pledge agreement contained a clause saying that the bank was not responsible for its own negligence in dealing with the stock? Read §1-302(b); see Brodheim v. Chase Manhattan Bank, N.A., 75 Misc. 2d 285, 347 N.Y.S.2d 394 (Sup. Ct. 1973); G. Gilmore, ch. 42.

(c) Andy's dealings with the bank became more complicated, and eventually the bank held, as pledgee, Andy's stocks in five different companies. One of these, Lusitania Foundry, offered a stock split option that had to be exercised by December 31, so Andy wrote the Morro Castle National Bank and, explaining that his records had become confused, asked the bank how many shares of Lusitania Foundry it held. The bank replied that it possessed 50 shares (this was a typographical error; it actually held 150). Andy tendered 50 shares of equivalent stock to the bank in exchange for a return of 50 shares of Lusitania Foundry, on which he then exercised the stock option, which proved very profitable. On January 3, Andy learned he owned 100 more shares that the bank held; it was too late to take the stock option on these shares. Does Andy have a cause of action against the bank under §9-207? Under §9-210? What damages can he recover? See §9-625(b) and (f).

(d) May a creditor in possession sell the collateral, in the absence of default or authorization in the security agreement? See Segovia v. Equities First Holdings, LLC, 2008 WL 2251218 (Del. Super. Ct. 2008).

PROBLEM 128

Mazie Minkus borrowed $2,000 from the Mount Brown State Bank and, as collateral, pledged to the bank her stamp collection (valued at $2,000). She used the money for a South American vacation. While she was away, the bank, which was located in an unstable geological area, was destroyed in an earthquake. The stamp collection went with it. Fortunately, the bank was fully insured by a policy with the Gibbons Insurance Company, which, inter alia, paid the bank $2,000 for the loss of the stamp collection. Gibbons then notified Mazie that she should pay the $2,000 debt to the insurance company, which was using the doctrine of subrogation to step into the shoes of the bank. Need she pay? See §9-207(b)(2); G. Gilmore §42.7.

II.   DEFAULT

State Bank of Piper City v. A-Way, Inc.
Illinois Supreme Court, 1987
115 Ill. 2d 401, 504 N.E.2d 737

WARD, J.

The plaintiff, State Bank of Piper City, filed a complaint in the circuit court of Iroquois County against the defendant, A-Way, Inc., to enforce its security interest in grain and the proceeds from sales of grain held by the defendant on account for a debtor of the plaintiff. The circuit court granted the defendant's motion to dismiss the complaint and denied the plaintiff's motion to vacate the order of dismissal. On the plaintiff's appeal, the appellate court reversed and remanded (135 Ill. App. 3d 1010), and we granted the defendant's petition for leave to appeal (103 Ill. 2d R. 315). . . .

In February 1982, the plaintiff was awarded a judgment in the amount of $131,083.91 against William C. Brenner upon his default on promissory notes that had been secured, under article 9 of the Uniform Commercial Code (UCC) (Ill. Rev. Stat. 1979, ch. 26, par. 9-101 et seq.), by a security interest in grain owned by Brenner which was stored in the defendant's warehouse. In a supplementary proceeding to enforce its judgment (Ill. Rev. Stat. 1981, ch. 110, par. 73), the plaintiff served the defendant with a citation to discover assets that it held on Brenner's behalf. The defendant responded by an affidavit acknowledging the accuracy of an attached ledger sheet with information regarding Brenner's account. The ledger sheet listed, inter alia, the number of bushels of grain the defendant held for him, 5,141.20, and the costs of drying and storing the grain. The plaintiff then moved for a citation order requiring the defendant to pay the plaintiff $5,141.20, confusing the number of bushels with their value, "as partial satisfaction for the judgment entered" in its suit against Brenner. The court held a hearing at which the defendant failed to appear, and allowed the plaintiff's motion. Acting upon the order, the defendant sold the grain, obtaining $11,310.64; of that amount, the defendant remitted $5,141.20 to the plaintiff and applied the balance to outstanding charges on Brenner's accounts.

Approximately eight months later, realizing its mistake, the plaintiff brought this action under article 9 of the UCC (Ill. Rev. Stat. 1979, ch. 26, par. 9-101 et seq.), to enforce its security interest in the proceeds of the grain sale over and above $5,141.20. The court dismissed the plaintiff's complaint on the grounds that the doctrines of merger and res judicata barred the suit. As stated, the appellate court reversed the dismissal.

The defendant first contends that the trial court properly dismissed the plaintiff's complaint under the doctrine of merger and that any rights the plaintiff had under the promissory notes of Brenner merged into the judgment, extinguishing any interest it had in the grain. "The general rule is, that by a judgment at law or a decree in chancery, the contract or instrument upon which the proceeding is based becomes entirely merged in the judgment. By the judgment of the court it loses all of its vitality and ceases to bind the parties to its execution. Its force and effect are then expended, and all remaining legal liability is transferred to the judgment or decree. Once becoming merged in the judgment, no further action at law or suit in equity can be maintained. . . ." (Doerr v. Schmitt (1941), 375 Ill. 470, 472, quoting Wayman v. Cochrane (1864), 35 Ill. 152, 154; Rock Island Bank & Trust Co. v. Stauduhar (1978), 59 Ill. App. 3d 892, 900.) Second, under principles of res judicata, it says, citing Hughey v. Industrial Com. (1979), 76 Ill. 2d 577, 582-583, that the plaintiff is barred from bringing the present action because the issue now raised could have been litigated in the citation proceeding.

The defendant's contentions have not been directly addressed by this court. We judge that, under the language of article 9 of the UCC (Ill. Rev. Stat. 1979, ch. 26, section 9-501(1)(5)) and from constructions in other jurisdictions, these contentions are without merit.

Section 9-501(1) [now §9-601 — Eds.] of the UCC serves to broaden the options available to a secured creditor upon a debtor's default. . . . Section 9-501(1) of the UCC states:

> When a debtor is in default under a security agreement, a secured party has the rights and remedies provided in this Part [concerning default]. . . . He may reduce his claim to judgment, foreclose or otherwise enforce the security interest by any available judicial procedure. . . . The rights and remedies referred to in this subsection are cumulative.

(Ill. Rev. Stat. 1979, ch. 26, par. 9-501(1).)

When a secured creditor has chosen to reduce his claim to judgment "the lien of any levy which may be made upon his collateral by virtue of any execution based upon the judgment shall relate back to the date of the perfection of the security interest in such collateral" (Ill. Rev. Stat. 1979, ch. 26, par. 9-501(5)) and serve as a continuation of the secured creditor's original perfected security interest (Ill. Ann. Stat., ch. 26, par. 9-501(5), Uniform Commercial Code Comment, at 322 (Smith-Hurd 1974)). Thus, a secured creditor's effort to collect its debt through the judicial process will not "operate to destroy his security interest vis-à-vis the debtor or to impair its priority [interest] over third parties" (2 G. Gilmore, Security Interests in Personal Property sec. 43.7, at 1209-1210 (1965); [citations omitted]).

The doctrine of merger does not, contrary to the defendant's argument, preclude a secured creditor from enforcing its security interest in the property given as collateral.

In Ruidoso State Bank v. Garcia (1978), 92 N.M. 288, 587 P.2d 435, cited above, a secured creditor earlier had brought suit to enforce its security interest in two vehicles which it had previously levied upon in satisfaction of a judgment against its debtors upon their default on promissory notes. The vehicles, however, had been released upon a trial court's finding that they were exempt property. Subsequently the secured creditor brought the suit involved. The debtors argued, inter alia, that by foreclosing on the notes the secured creditor caused the security agreements executed by the debtors to merge in the judgment, precluding their subsequent enforcement. The court rejected this contention, holding:

> Merger does not apply here for the reason that the Bank[, the secured creditor,] had two separate causes of action. It could sue and reduce the debt to judgment. In that case the debt would be merged into the judgment. However, the debt would be carried forward so that the Bank's rights under the security agreement would not be destroyed. The security agreements, under the statutory prohibition [i.e., under article 9 of the UCC], would not be merged into the judgment.

Ruidoso State Bank v. Garcia (1978), 92 N.M. 288, 290, 587 P.2d 435, 437....

Here even though the notes merged in the judgment precluding further action on the notes (Doerr v. Schmitt (1941), 375 Ill. 470, 472; Rock Island Bank & Trust Co. v. Stauduhar (1978), 59 Ill. App. 3d 892, 900), that merger did not preclude the plaintiff from bringing this action to enforce its security interest in the grain. That security interest was provided for in security agreements separate from and independent of the notes. The security agreements provided that upon the debtor's default the secured creditor "shall have all of the rights and remedies of a secured party under the Illinois Uniform Commercial Code," remedies which are, as previously stated, "cumulative." Furthermore, the "lien of any levy," which was made upon the grain pursuant to the plaintiff's judgment against Brenner, related back to the time of perfection of the security interest. (Ill. Ann. Stat. ch. 26, par. 9-501(5), Uniform Commercial Code Comment, at 322 (Smith-Hurd 1974).) Thus, the merger of the note in the plaintiff's judgment against Brenner and the plaintiff's citation to discover assets proceeding did not affect the plaintiff's security interest in the remaining grain-sale proceeds.

The defendant next contends that the plaintiff is barred under res judicata from bringing the present action against A-Way, Inc.:

> The doctrine of res judicata provides that "a final judgment rendered by a court of competent jurisdiction on the merits is conclusive as to the rights of the parties and their privies, and, as to them, constitutes an absolute bar to a subsequent action involving the *same* claim, demand or cause of action." (Emphasis added.) [Citation.] When res judicata is established

"as a bar against the prosecution of a second action between the same parties upon the same claim or demand . . . it is conclusive not only as to every
matter which was offered to sustain or defeat the claim or demand, but as
to any other matter which might have been offered for that purpose. . . ."
Housing Authority for La Salle County v. YMCA (1984), 101 Ill. 2d 246,
251-252.

Because of the provision under article 9 of the UCC for multiple and
cumulative remedies upon the debtor's default, res judicata will not bar a
secured creditor from exhausting his remedies under the UCC. . . .

Although the decisions cited involved successive actions against a
debtor in default, there is no reason not to apply the same principles to
situations, as here, involving third parties. Not to do so would defeat the
purpose of article 9 in providing a secured creditor with multiple remedies
upon a debtor's default.

That the order entered in the citation proceeding against the defendant was a final order (Illinois Brewing & Malting Co. v. Ilmberger (1910),
155 Ill. App. 417, 418) does not, under res judicata, preclude the plaintiff
from bringing the present action. The order was entered in execution of
the plaintiff's judgment against Brenner. Here, the plaintiff is acting in its
capacity as a secured creditor attempting to enforce its article 9 security
interest in the surplus proceeds from the sale of the grain, proceeds which
it mistakenly omitted in the citation proceeding. The action of the plaintiff in the citation proceeding does not bar the plaintiff from proceeding
here.

The defendant argues too that if the plaintiff is permitted to proceed
with this action it will suffer undue hardship because it has applied the
proceeds remaining from the sale to its other accounts of Brenner. The
argument appears to border on effrontery. The defendant in the argument admitted that it knew the amount of the plaintiff's judgment against
Brenner; that it was aware that the plaintiff had made a mistake in request-
ing that it pay the plaintiff 5,141.20 dollars instead of bushels; and that it did
not disclose to the plaintiff the amount it received from sale of the grain.
These may have been considerations in the defendant's not appearing at
the citation proceeding. If we were to conclude that fraud had been present,
which under our analysis we need not do, res judicata, of course, would not
be applicable. Hughey v. Industrial Com. (1979), 76 Ill. 2d 577, 583; McNely
v. Board of Education (1956), 9 Ill. 2d 143, 151-152.

For the reasons given, we hold that the trial court erred in dismissing
the complaint. The judgment of the appellate court reversing and remand-
ing the cause is affirmed.

Judgment affirmed.

The secured party's Part 6 Article 9 rights come into being whenever there has been a *default* by the debtor. The Code, however, does not define *default,* and the only judicially recognized form of default is failure to pay the debt on time; see Cofield v. Randolph County Commn., 90 F.3d 468 (11th Cir. 1996). Since the Code is silent on the meaning of the term, the security agreement must fill in the blanks. It is the lawyer's job to draft the security agreement so as to cover the possible exigencies with appropriate clauses triggering default and the ability to foreclose. One way to do this is by a specific definition of the term *default,* so that it includes not only failure to pay on time but also failure to perform any of the terms of the agreement. *Default* may also be defined to cover certain specific problems: death of the debtor, an assignment for the benefit of creditors, institution of any insolvency proceeding, impairment of the collateral, etc.

A practical point that debtors (and law students) sometimes overlook: Even if the debtor is making all the loan payments on time, there will be default if another default event specified in the security agreement occurs, such as failure to provide proof of insurance for the collateral or failure to pay other creditors on time (called a "cross-default clause"). See, e.g., Regions Bank v. Thomas, 422 S.W.3d 550 (Tenn. Ct. App. 2013) (failure to provide proof of insurance on collateral was default under loan contract, permitting repossession and sale of aircraft).

If through inadvertence, mistake, or deliberate bad faith the creditor repossesses when there is no right to do so, the creditor is guilty of conversion (and breach of contract) and will have to pay all damages caused thereby. In re Martin Specialty Vehicles, Inc., 87 Bankr. 752, (Bankr. D. Mass. 1988).

Some security agreements provide simply that default is the failure to observe the conditions and promises of the security agreement and then include an acceleration clause similar to this one:

> The parties agree that if at any time the secured party deems itself insecure because in good faith it believes the prospect of payment or performance is impaired, it shall have the right to declare a default and accelerate payment of all unpaid sums or performance or, at its option, may require the debtor to furnish additional collateral.

Read §1-309 carefully.

PROBLEM 129

When Mr. and Mrs. Bankruptcy bought a mobile home from Nervous Motors, Inc., they signed a purchase money security agreement in favor of the

Subsequently, but before Purchaser's first monthly installment became due, Commercial felt itself insecure, and it directed the Automobile Recovery Bureau of St. Louis, Missouri to repossess the automobile. On June 22, 1966—four days before Purchaser's first monthly installment was due and at a time when he was not in default—the repossessing professionals, without notice, demand, communication, or correspondence with Purchaser, removed his locked automobile from the front of his house in the dead of night, [and] delivered it to Commercial[2] along with Purchaser's personal property. . . .

OUT OF THE VERBAL WILDERNESS

The skillful Trial Judge having been aware that this contract . . . was not written for those who run to read discerned its true meaning by recognizing its true sequential structure. Unlike Commercial which assumes that the right to accelerate without notice or demand is synonymous with the right to repossess without notice or demand, the Judge carefully distinguished between the two. Acceleration, he charged, was permissible without notice or demand. But upon acceleration Commercial then had to make demand or give notice to Purchaser so that the admitted failure of notice/demand . . . made Commercial's repossession an unlawful conversion.

The Court's instruction tracked the terms of the contract correctly. Though under clause [i][b] (note [2], supra) "Time Balance" might from acceleration become due at any time without notice, if Commercial felt itself insecure, the very next provision in the contract provides "[ii] Purchaser agrees in any such case [a] to pay said amount to Seller, *upon demand*, or, [b] at the election of Seller, to deliver vehicle to Seller." (Emphasis added.) Clause [ii][a][b] with its alternative stated in the disjunctive does not speak in terms of rights which Commercial has. Rather it speaks in terms of *actions* which Purchaser must take depending on the choice opted by Commercial.

---

2. Purchaser did not have the slightest idea that his car had been repossessed. He notified the police that it was missing, in the belief that it had been stolen, and it was the police who finally uncovered what had actually transpired.

Even the austere stipulation vividly portrays Commercial's conduct and presages its predicament:

> On June 22, 1966, Automobile Recovery Bureau, St. Louis, Missouri, at the telephone direction and request of Commercial Credit Corporation, without notice, demand, communication or correspondence with plaintiff, some time during the night, took the locked 1966 Ford Galaxie automobile off the street in front of plaintiff's home, and delivered the car to Commercial Credit Corporation at St. Louis, Missouri. Commercial Credit Corporation had no communication, either written or oral, with plaintiff prior to taking the automobile. Commercial Credit Corporation requested, ordered, authorized and directed the repossession of the 1966 Ford Galaxie 500 automobile from Vern Klingbiel because it felt itself, or vehicle, insecure.

It could require Purchaser to pay off in full or it could require redelivery. But before Purchaser was bound to do either Commercial had first to indicate which course was required. The two words, "upon demand," are not only conspicuous, they are unavoidable.

Not yet overborne, Commercial would further have us construe the contract so as to declare that no notice was necessary prior to repossession by falling back on clause [iii][b] which provides: "[iii] This mortgage may be foreclosed [a] . . . or [b] Seller may, without notice or demand for performance or legal process, . . . lawfully enter any premises where Vehicle may be found, and take possession of it."

This is equally unavailing. At the outset, this clause follows—does not precede—but follows clause [ii] which, [a][b] as we have held, calls for notice/demand before Purchaser is required to act upon a declared acceleration. Equally important, in the sequential structure of the contract this refers only to a *foreclosure*. This means that there must be a default on the part of the Purchaser. This can take the form of Purchaser's failure to perform as in [i][a] or an acceleration under [i][b]. Certainly in the case of predefault acceleration, as a result of the manner in which this contract is constructed, clause [ii][b] in effect calls for notice/demand to precipitate a default. The failure or refusal of Purchaser after such notice/demand would, of course, be a [i][a] default, thus setting in train the foreclosure provisions of [iii][a] or [b], including *at that stage* even the most stealthy repossession by night riders. But this privilege is not available by skipping from [i][b] to [iii][b] over the head of [ii][a][b]. . . .

We think there was evidence, if believed by the jury, to warrant the inference of more than simple inadvertence or a technical conversion. There was first the circumstance of the stealthy retaking without notice of any kind, although notice clearly was called for as we have held. At that time Purchaser was not in default. Further, Purchaser's own personal property was taken along with the automobile. This was never returned to him, nor did he receive recompense for it. In fact, Commercial never even contacted Purchaser to inform him of the repossession. He had to find out through his own effort and investigation. There are many other factors unnecessary to catalogue which sustain the punitive damage finding.

This leaves only the objection to the Court's instruction on actual damages. Clearly there was sufficient evidence to cover the three elements submitted by the Court for the loss of value of the automobile, Purchaser's personal property, and the loss of the vehicle for an intervening period.

The objection is pointed at the term "actual value" rather than market value of the car. Assuming, but not deciding that it was error, such error was harmless. The "actual" damages awarded totalled $770. Of this sum $120 was for the loss of Purchaser's personal property, which Commercial fully concedes is correct. Purchaser's testimonial estimate of the loss from the loss of use of the car, which clearly is a permissible element of damages, was approximately $500. Thus, this leaves only $150 for the loss of value of the automobile itself. This modest recovery does not demonstrate any harm.

Affirmed.

NOTE

On default, the debtor's attorney should read the security agreement carefully to see if expressly or impliedly it gives the debtor a right to notice before repossession. Conversely, the secured party's attorney should make sure the security agreement avoids statements like "upon demand," which may give rise to such an implication.

Where a bank pursued its foreclosure remedy under the guise of a state attachment procedure that was clearly unconstitutional, the plaintiffs in Guzman v. Western State Bank of Devil's Lake, 540 F.2d 948 (8th Cir. 1976), took the unusual step of suing under the Civil Rights Act, 42 U.S.C. §1983, and recovered nearly $10,000 in actual damages and $30,000 in punitive damages. The court expressly found the bank guilty of bad faith.

PROBLEM 130

Natty Birdwhistle bought a car with money borrowed from Carpe Diem Finance Company (which perfected its interest in the car). The security agreement provided that "time was of the essence" and that the acceptance by the finance company of late payments was not a waiver of its right to repossess. Natty always paid 10 to 15 days late. One month, Carpe Diem Finance had had enough, and it sent a man out who took the car (using a duplicate set of keys) from the parking lot of the factory where Natty worked. Has a default occurred? See §1-303(d) and (f); Moe v. John Deere Co., 516 N.W.2d 332 (S.D. 1994); G. Gilmore §44.1, at 1214: "[C]ourts pay little attention to clauses which appear to say that meaningful acts are meaningless and that the secured party can blow hot or cold as he chooses." If Carpe Diem's conduct has waived the right to repossess if Natty is late, what can it do to reinstate the "time is of the essence" clause? See §2-209(5); TCF Equipment Finance, Inc. v. New Door of New York Corp., 33 Misc. 3d 1213(A), 2011 WL 5041795 (N.Y. Sup 2011).

NOTE ON CREDIT INSURANCE AND DEFAULT

If the debtor has died or become ill or disabled, so that the credit insurance taken out at the time the original contract was signed should pay the debt, there is authority for the proposition that the secured creditor must look first to the credit insurance before repossessing. Owens v. Walt Johnson

Lincoln Mercury, Inc., 281 Or. 287, 574 P.2d 642 (1978); Corbin v. Regions Bank, 574 S.E.2d 616 (Ga. App. 2002).

III.   REPOSSESSION AND RESALE

Section 9-609 authorizes the secured party to skip going through judicial processes and to repossess the collateral on the debtor's default if this can be done without a "breach of the peace." For the meaning of that elusive term, see White & Summers §26-7; Census Fed. Credit Union v. Wann, 403 N.E.2d 348 (Ind. App. 1980); Comment, Breach of Peace and Section 9-503 of the Uniform Commercial Code—A Modern Definition for an Ancient Restriction, 82 Dick. L. Rev. 351 (1978); Annot., What Conduct by Repossessing Chattel Mortgagee or Conditional Vendor Entails Tort Liability, 99 A.L.R.2d 358. Grant Gilmore:

> In the financing of business debtors repossession causes little trouble or dispute. In the underworld of consumer finance, however, repossession is a knock-down, drag-out battle waged on both sides with cunning guile and a complete disregard for the rules of fair play. A certain amount of trickery seems to be accepted: it is all right for the finance company to invite the defaulting buyer to drive over to its office for a friendly conference on refinancing the loan and to repossess the car as soon as he arrives. It is fairly safe for the finance company to pick up the car on the street wherever it may be parked, although there is always a danger that the buyer will later claim that he had been keeping a valuable stock of diamonds in the glove compartment. But the finance company will do well to think twice before allowing its man to break into an empty house, even though a well-drafted clause in the security agreement gives it the right to do exactly that. And if the housewife, who is invariably pregnant and subject to miscarriages, sits on the sofa, stove, washing machine or television set and refuses to move, the finance company man will make a serious mistake if he dumps the lady or carries her screaming into the front yard. Juries love to award punitive damages for that sort of thing and the verdict will often be allowed to stand.

G. Gilmore §44.1, at 1212-1213.

For many types of collateral, the creditor is unlikely to use self-help repossession. Repossessing the inventory of a store or the equipment on a construction company would be difficult without breaching the peace, unless the debtor cooperates. But one type of collateral is often left unattended on public streets overnight: vehicles. Some two million cars are repossessed each year. Many of the reported judicial decisions on repossession involve cars.

Smith v. AFS Acceptance, LLC

United States District Court, Northern District of Illinois, 2012
2012 WL 1969415

ELAINE E. BUCKLO, District Judge.

Plaintiffs Rosalind Smith and Rashai Jackson sued defendants AFS Acceptance, LLC ("AFS") and Equitable Services, Inc. ("Equitable") for various statutory and common law claims arising out an incident that occurred on August 16, 2010. . . . AFS has moved to dismiss the claims against it: (1) violation of Article 9, §609(b)(2) of Illinois' Uniform Commercial Code ("Repossession Statute") (Count II); (2) negligence (Count III); and (3) willful and wanton behavior (Count IV). In addition, Equitable has moved to dismiss all five claims against it: (1) violation of the Fair Debt Collection Practices Act, 15 U.S.C. §1692 (Count I); (2) violation of 810 ILCS 5/9-609(b)(2) (Count II); (3) negligence (Count V); (4) willful and wanton behavior (Count VI); and intentional infliction of emotional distress (Count VII). For all the following reasons, both motions are denied in part and granted in part.

AFS's Motion to Dismiss

AFS argues that I should dismiss Count II, which alleges a violation of the Repossession Statute, because plaintiffs failed to allege facts establishing an agency relationship between AFS and Equitable. Plaintiffs respond that, regardless of the relationship between AFS and Equitable, AFS is liable for the actions taken on its behalf.

Under the Repossession Statute, a secured party, after default, has the right to take possession of the collateral without judicial process so long as the secured party "proceeds without breach of the peace." 810 ILCS 5/9-609(b)(2). Comment 3 to the Repossession Statute states, "In considering whether a secured party has engaged in a breach of the peace, however, courts should hold the secured party responsible for the actions of others taken on the secured party's behalf, *including independent contractors* engaged by the secured party to take possession of collateral." 810 ILCS 5/9-609, Comment 3 (emphasis added). According to Comment 3, a secured party may be liable for the actions of another, even if no agency relationship exists. Here, plaintiffs allege that AFS loaned money to Smith for the purchase of the vehicle. Plaintiffs also allege that Equitable acted on AFS's behalf. Thus, plaintiffs' allegations are sufficient to claim that AFS, as a secured party, may be liable under the Repossession Statute for the actions of Equitable. *See Thompson v. Gateway Financial Services, Inc.*, No. 10 CV 7658, 2011 WL 1429207, at *2 (N.D. Ill. Apr. 14, 2011) (relying on Comment 3 to find that the secured party may be liable for actions taken by independent contractor with no agency relationship); *Williams v. Republic Recovery Service, Inc.,* No. 09 C 6554, 2010 WL 3732107 at *3-4 (N.D.Ill. Sept. 16, 2010) (same). Thus, Count II stands. . . .

Equitable's Motion to Dismiss

Equitable moves to dismiss the FDCPA claim against it. First, it argues that plaintiffs have failed to provide sufficient facts to show that Equitable is a "debt collector" under the Act. Plaintiffs respond by pointing to Section 1692a(6) which states that "[f]or the purpose of section 1692f(6) of this title, ["debt collector"] also includes any person who uses any instrumentality of interstate commerce or the mails in any business the principal purpose of which is the enforcement of security interests."15 U.S.C. §1692a(6). At this stage, plaintiffs' allegations that Equitable is a "debt collector" for purposes of §1692a(6) is sufficient.

Section 1692f(6) prohibits "[t]aking or threatening to take any nonjudicial action to effect dispossession or disablement of property if—(A) there is no present right to possession of the property claimed as collateral through an enforceable security interest; (B) there is no present intention to take possession of the property; or (C) the property is exempt by law from such dispossession or disablement."Plaintiffs allege that defendants "did not have a present right to possession of the vehicle" because Equitable's "attempt to repossess the vehicle "constituted a 'breach of the peace' in violation of 810 ILCS 5/9-609(b)(2)." Am. Compl. ¶27. "In other words, if the debt collector violated the self-help repossession statute, by breach of the peace or otherwise, then the collector had no present right to possession of the property under §1692f(6)."*Fleming-Dudley v. Legal Investigations, Inc.,* No. 05 C 4648, 2007 WL 952026, at *5 (N.D. Ill. Mar. 22, 2007).

The Illinois Commercial Code allows a secured party to use self-help repossession "without judicial process, if it proceeds without breach of the peace."810 ILCS 5/9-609(b)(2). Under Illinois law, "breach of the peace" as used in the statute "connotes conduct which incites or is likely to incite immediate public turbulence, or which leads to or is likely to lead to an immediate loss of public order and tranquility."*Chrysler Credit Corp. v. Koontz,* 277 Ill. App. 3d 1078, 214 Ill. Dec. 726, 661 N.E.2d 1171, 1173 (Ill. App. Ct. 1996)."Whether a given act provokes a breach of the peace depends upon the accompanying circumstances of each particular case."*Id.* at 1174.

Plaintiffs allege that the vehicle was parked in a driveway at Rosalind Smith's mother's house. "Unknown Repossession Agents" backed a tow truck up the driveway and "began to hook the vehicle up."Am. Compl. ¶11. One of Rosalind's children noticed the agents hooking the vehicle up to the tow truck. Rosalind's mother and children, including Rashai Jackson, ran outside to see what was going on. When Rosalind's mother asked the agents what was going on, they told her they were taking the vehicle for nonpayment of the loan. Then, Rashai Jackson opened the door to the vehicle and got into it. The agents continued to hook the vehicle up to the tow truck and then raised the rear of the vehicle with Rashai still in the vehicle and with the door of the vehicle open. The agents started to tow the vehicle out of the driveway with Rashai still in the vehicle. Rosalind then yelled for the agents to stop towing the vehicle and to put it down because her daughter was in the vehicle. Rosalind then jumped into the vehicle with her daughter. The agents continued to tow the vehicle out of the driveway and into the street. Police officers were called to the scene and told the agents to stop towing the vehicle and the agents complied. Rosalind and Rashai exited the vehicle. The police officers told the agents to return the vehicle to its original place in the driveway. Throughout this incident, Rosalind's mother, children, and individuals from neighboring residences yelled at the agents to stop towing the vehicle away with individuals in the vehicle and the vehicle's doors open.

I conclude that plaintiffs have put forward sufficient allegations concerning a "breach of the peace" to survive a motion to dismiss. While plaintiffs certainly played a role in any breach of the peace, Equitable's employees, despite the fact that plaintiffs jumped into the vehicle, raised the rear of the vehicle and actually towed the vehicle away from the driveway with two individuals in the vehicle and the doors open. All this was done while plaintiffs' family members and neighbors yelled at the agents to stop towing the vehicle. Equitable makes much of the fact that the plaintiffs themselves played a role in any breach by first jumping into the vehicle, but totally fails to address the fact that its own employees continued to tow the vehicle down the street *with the two women in the back*. In addition, they did so with a group of people yelling at them to stop. Finally, the police were called to the scene to restore order. Equitable has put forward no cases like this one where both parties contributed, in part, to the breach of the peace. The language of the statute states that the secured party can repossess secured property so long as the secured party "proceeds without breach of the peace." Nothing in this language suggests that the fault for any breach must lie solely with the party doing the repossessing, and Equitable has failed to present any authority to the contrary.

Thus, plaintiffs' claim under the FDCPA and Smith's standalone claim for a violation of 810 ILCS 5/9-609(b)(2) survive Equitable's motion to dismiss. And, as above, the claim under 810 ILCS 5/9-609(b)(2) is limited to Smith, as Jackson was not a debtor or an obligor. . . .

Finally, plaintiffs allege a state law claim of intentional infliction of emotional distress against Equitable. To state a claim for intentional infliction of emotional distress, plaintiff must show that: "(1) defendant's conduct was extreme and outrageous; (2) the defendant intended to inflict severe emotional distress or knew that there was at least a high probability that his conduct would inflict severe emotional distress; and (3) the defendant's conduct did cause severe emotional distress."*Naeem v. McKesson Drug Co.,* 444 F.3d 593, 604-05 (7th Cir. 2006).

"Conduct is extreme and outrageous only if the conduct has been so outrageous in character and so extreme in degree as to go beyond all possible bounds of decency."*Van Stan v. Fancy Colours & Co.,* 125 F.3d 563, 567 (7th Cir. 1997) (internal quotations and citations omitted). The standard for determining whether one's conduct is outrageous is whether an average person in the community would find the conduct outrageous. Restatement (Second) of Torts, §46, cmt. d, at 73 (1965). The Seventh Circuit has also suggested that the following factors may be considered: whether the defendant had control or power over the plaintiff, whether the defendant reasonably believed its goal was legitimate and whether the defendant was aware that the plaintiff was peculiarly susceptible to emotional distress. *Franciski v. Univ. of Chi. Hospitals,* 338 F.3d 765, 769 (7th Cir. 2003).

While this is a close call, plaintiffs IIED claim survives Equitable's motion to dismiss. The conduct alleged—towing two women down the street with the doors opened—is sufficiently outrageous in nature as to constitute a basis for recovery under intentional infliction of emotional distress. There is no suggestion that the tow truck operators were unaware of the women's presence in the vehicle, and thus the most likely explanation of the agents' behavior is that they intended to severely frighten the women. An average member in the community could certainly think it outrageous for tow truck operators to proceed with a repossession with two individuals in the vehicle. I acknowledge that the two women jumped into the car, likely in an attempt to stop the towing. A reasonable person could conclude, however, that what followed on the part of the towing agents was "extreme in degree." As Equitable points out, the tow truck operators arrived at the scene with the "legitimate" goal of repossessing the vehicle. However, a defendant's "reasonable belief that his objective is legitimate does not provide a defendant carte blanche to pursue that objective by outrageous means."*McGrath v. Fahey,* 126 Ill. 2d 78, 127 Ill. Dec. 724, 533 N.E.2d 806, 809 (Ill. 1998). The tow truck operators obviously exerted control over the plaintiffs in that they controlled the time and location in which plaintiffs could safely exit the vehicle. Given the facts (as alleged by plaintiffs), plaintiffs' claim survives at this stage.

For all of the foregoing reasons, AFS's motion to dismiss [28] is granted in part and denied in part. Likewise, Equitable's motion to dismiss [38] is granted in part and denied in part.

Particularly in consumer debtor cases where the repossession violates Article 9 of the Code will the complaint allege, as the one in the case above did, violation of other statures or common law tort theories. Most states have a Consumer Sales Act (called by various names) that give injured consumers actual damages, punitive damages and attorney fees, and the federal government has the Fair Debt Collection Practices Act, 15 U.S.C. §1692, which does the same thing for outrageous behavior in debt collection.

QUESTION

This court clearly holds that if the secured party hires an independent contractor to repossess then the secured party is liable for whatever misconduct the independent contractor commits. But what if the debtor sues the independent contractor itself for committing a breach of the peace or other forbidden activity during the repossession? Does §9-609 create liability in that case? See Nelson v. BMW Fin. Serv. NA, 2015 WL 8328073 (D. Minn. 2015).

PROBLEM 131

Don Jose was in charge of repossession for Carmen Motors. One Monday morning, the dealership told him that cars owned by four debtors (Escamillo, Micaela, Zuniga, and Morales) were to be picked up because the buyers had missed payments. Look at §9-609, and answer this question: is Carmen Motors required to give the debtors *notice* that they are in default before repossessing? Don Jose visited each of the debtors with the following results:

(a) Don Jose found Escamillo's car parked in his driveway at 2:00 A.M.; he broke a car window, hot-wired the car, and drove it away. Has a breach of the peace occurred? See Giles v. First Virginia Credit Services, Inc., 560 S.E.2d 557 (N.C. App. 2002). What if Escamillo heard the window break, rushed out, and began yelling? May Don Jose continue the repossession, or must he quit? If he goes away, may he try again later that night? See Wade v. Ford Motor Credit Co., 8 Kan. App. 2d 737, 668 P.2d 183 (1983) (any debtor protest breaches the peace, but second try allowed);. Chrysler Credit Corp. v. Koontz, 277 Ill. App. 3d 1078, 1081 (1996) (mere "Don't take it" statement by the debtor not enough to make repossession breach the peace).

(b) Don Jose showed up at Micaela's house accompanied by his brother (an off-duty sheriff who was wearing his sheriff's uniform). Don Jose told Micaela that he was repossessing the car, and she said nothing. Has a breach of the peace occurred? See Official Comment 3 to §9-609; Stone Mach. Co. v. Kessler, 1 Wash. App. 750, 463 P.2d 651 (1970) (*constructive force* also constitutes a breach of the peace); accord First & Farmers Bank v. Henderson, 763 S.W.2d 137 (Ky. App. 1988) ($75,000 punitive damages). See also In re Bolin & Co., LLC, 437 B.R. 731 (D. Conn. 2010) (the presence of a police officer did not breach the peace where the officer was not there to help with the repossession).

(c) When no one was at home, Don Jose broke into Zuniga's garage through the use of the services of a locksmith. The garage lock and door were undamaged. A clause in the contract provided that the secured party had the right to enter the debtor's premises to remove the property. Does the repossession comply with §9-609? See §9-602(6); Pantoja-Cahue v. Ford Motor Credit Co., 375 Ill. App. 3d 49, 872 N.E.2d 1039 (2007); White & Summers §26-7.

(d) Don Jose phoned Morales and said that the car was being recalled because of an unsafe engine mount. Morales brought the car in that morning. When the time came to pick up the car, Don Jose simply smiled, said "April Fool; it's been repossessed!" and refused to return it. Is the repossession valid? Compare Cox v. Galigher Motor Sales Co., 213 S.E.2d 475 (W. Va. 1975), with Ford Motor Credit Co. v. Byrd, 351 So. 2d 557 (Ala. 1974), commented on in 40 Ohio St. L.J. 501 (1979).

Repossession Technology. Automobile repossession in the 21st century has developed a new tactic employing a "starter interrupt device." This invention allows the creditor to push a button on a computer and suddenly the car won't start. The debtor is usually called immediately and told that the car can be reactivated by making a payment, which (with kids who need to get to school, or a boss at work looking at empty desk) the debtor usually does immediately. Often the repossession has beeps that warn the debtor that the repo is coming soon, and, in theory, the debtor has also been given a code that can be punched into the car's computer to restore the vehicle to mechanical health for a 24-hour period even without a payment (very useful in emergencies). To avoid accidents the starter interrupt device is not supposed to work when the car is running (though stories circulate of cars swerving uncontrolled through traffic or stalled at traffic lights turning green). Enthusiastically embraced by creditors, this quasi-evil innovation has most often been used in subprime automobile financing, but is now expanding into more general application, and may soon be exposing supposedly well-to-do drivers who can't get out of their reserved parking spaces at work.

Hilliman v. Cobado

New York Supreme Court, 1986
499 N.Y.S.2d 610

HOREY, J.

By an order to show cause the plaintiff has brought on a motion for injunctive relief. In particular the plaintiffs seek an order of this court that the defendant return 26 cattle which the defendant seized and removed from the plaintiffs' farm premises. While not specifically denominated as a motion brought under the provisions of CPLR 6301 it is clear that the motion in issue falls within the parameters of that section.

The factual background giving rise to the motion is this: the defendant sold the plaintiff a herd of cattle. Sale was initially to be effected under an instrument denominated a "collateral security mortgage" dated February 1, 1984. Under the terms of this instrument the sale was secured by a mortgage on the farm realty of the plaintiff purchaser. However, before delivery of the cattle, the defendant demanded additional security interest in the cattle to be sold.

As a consequence of this demand a second instrument entitled "chattel mortgage" dated February 8, 1984 was executed by plaintiffs. Under the terms of this instrument the defendant was given a chattel mortgage interest in "68 cows and 1 bull."

Both instruments had the same provisions for payment of the indebtedness (sale price) which was $48,200. Payment was to be made by plaintiff by even monthly payments of $1,000. Interest was provided at 11% per annum.

After the delivery of the cattle to the plaintiff, the plaintiff under a claim of right culled a number of the cattle delivered. The defendant took exception to this practice. As a result of negotiations a third instrument was executed. This was also denominated a "chattel mortgage." It is dated June 20, 1985. Under the terms of this instrument the collateral is recited to be "37 replacement cows." The balance due was fixed at $39,552.77. Provision for payment of this reduced amount continued as previously provided, viz., $1,000 per month with the balance drawing interest at 11% per annum. The court regards it as significant that the plaintiff has never been in default on the required contract payments. . . .

After the second chattel mortgage no specific default was alleged by the defendant. Inferentially it appears that he continued to be disturbed by the plaintiff's practice of culling poorer cattle from the herd. Suddenly without any prior warning, the defendant Cobado and two deputy sheriffs arrived at the premises of the plaintiff, Szata. Mr. Szata, a cripple, proceeding with the aid of a cane and his wife went out of their home to meet Cobado and the deputies. It was then that the deputies advised Mr. and Mrs. Szata that Cobado "was here to repossess the collateral under the terms of the security agreement."

Mr. Szata immediately replied that he was not in default and that Cobado was to leave the premises immediately and could not have the cattle.

Mr. Szata attempted to engage Cobado in conversation to no avail. Cobado simply turned and ran to the barn saying "to hell with this we're taking the cows."

Cobado entered the barn and started releasing the cattle from their stanchions.

A brief conversation ensued between Deputy Buchardt and Mr. and Mrs. Szata. Deputy Buchardt told them that Cobado had a violent temper and a reputation for violence. The Deputy also told Mr. Szata that if he (Szata) got out of line he would be arrested.

After an unfruitful attempt to call their attorney, Mr. and Mrs. Szata went to the barn and again told Cobado to stop. Cobado simply laughed at them and continued to release the cattle and drive them around in the barn.

At this time while Cobado was beating the released cattle and trying to herd them through a small opening in the barn door a Fay Hilliman, the mother-in-law of Mr. Szata and the mother of Mrs. Szata arrived at the barn. She joined the Szatas in ordering Cobado to desist. Cobado ignored them and continued to push the cattle through the barn opening.

Before the cattle were loaded onto the trucks assembled, Lt. Ernie Travis of the Cattaraugus County Sheriff's Department appeared on the scene. He advised Cobado that if he, Cobado, left with the cattle he would be arrested. Cobado ignored the warning and when he left with the cattle he was arrested for possession of stolen property. Later Mr. Szata was charged with fraudulent sale of mortgaged property. As of the argument of the motion at bar no disposition had been made of either criminal charge. . . .

The second instrument executed, viz., the first chattel mortgage dated February 8, 1984, securing "68 cows and 1 bull" contained the following provisions for seizure, to wit:

> In conjunction with, addition to or substitution for those rights, secured party, at his discretion, may (1) *enter debtor's premises peaceably* by secured party's own means or with legal process and take possession of the collateral, or render it unusable or dispose of the collateral on the debtor's premises and the debtor agrees not to resist or interfere. . . .

(p. 2 chattel mortgage dated February 8, 1984.) Italics added.

The third instrument, executed, viz., the second chattel mortgage dated June 20, 1985 contains an identical provision for seizure as that in the chattel mortgage of February 8, 1984, set forth above.

The quoted provisions from the two chattel mortgages follow an immediate prior contract provision also referable to default and repossession which provided that upon default "the *secured party will have all the rights,* remedies and privileges *with respect to repossession,* retention and sale of the collateral and disposition of the proceeds *as are accorded to a* secured party by *the applicable section of the UCC* respecting 'default' in effect as of the date of the security agreement."

This court finds nothing in conflict between the clause in each chattel mortgage providing the secured party with the right to enter "debtor's premises peaceably" and the immediate prior provision in those chattel mortgages stating that the secured party has those rights as to repossession which are accorded under the UCC. This is for the reason as we have seen that the repossession rights granted under the UCC may only be exercised "without breach of the peace" §9-504 UCC [now §9-609—EDS.]

Since the motion turns to consideration of "breach of the peace" we look to decisional law for definition of that term.

In People v. Most, 171 N.Y. 423 (Ct. of Appeals 1902, Opn. by Vann, J.), our highest court stated that a breach of the peace was well known at common law. The court then defined it as follows:

> It is a disturbance of public order by an act of violence, or by any act likely to produce violence, or which by causing consternation and alarm, disturbs the peace and quiet of the community.

171 N.Y. 423 at 429.

The right to self help by way of repossession is an assignment of the exclusive power of the sovereignty of a state. This is true because it represents a delegation of the exclusively governmental function of resolving disputes. See generally Sharrock v. Dell Buick, 45 N.Y.2d 152 at 162 and Fuentes v. Shevin, 407 U.S. 67 at 93. The delegation of the right of repossession to a secured party is not a carte blanche one. Rather it is specifically limited and exercisable only without a breach of the peace. Its exercise should be strictly confined to those situations, rare as they may be, when the repossession can be accomplished peaceably. Physical confrontation or the threat thereof is not necessary to effect a breach of the peace.

Certain it is that in ignoring the order of the purchasers to desist and remove himself from the premises; in ignoring the admonition of Lt. Travis of the Sheriff's Department to desist; in demonstrating his contempt for all restraint by his statement "to hell with this we're taking the cows"; by proceeding to release the cows, beating and herding them to the trucks, without heed of the warning that his continuance would result in his arrest, the defendant Cobado not only engaged in conduct which was likely to produce violence and consternation but did in fact produce violence, consternation and disorder.

This court finds as a matter of fact and law that the retaking of the plaintiff's cattle was a "breach of the peace."

Accordingly the decision of the court is that the defendant Cobado forthwith at his cost and expense redeliver the cattle repossessed by him to the plaintiff inclusive of any calves born to those cattle during his possession thereof.

PROBLEM 132

Octopus National Bank (ONB) financed Mary Melody's purchase of a new car, in which it perfected its security interest. The loan agreement provided that on default, the bank had all the rights listed in Part 6 of Article 9 of the UCC and that the parties agreed that the bank would not be liable for conversion or otherwise if there were other items in the car at the time it was repossessed. Mary missed a payment, and ONB's agent took the car in the dead of night from its parking place in front of her home. She protested the next day, claiming that her golf clubs were in the trunk. ONB looked there but couldn't find the clubs. When she sued, ONB defended on the basis of the security agreement's exculpatory clause. Is it valid? See Ford Motor Credit Co. v. Cole, 503 S.W.2d 853 (Tex. Civ. App. 1973). If ONB finds the clubs and returns them promptly on her demand, is the bank still guilty of conversion? See Thompson v. Ford Motor Credit Co., 324 F. Supp. 108 (D.S.C. 1971).

PROBLEM 133

Repossession agent Paul Chambers, seeking to repossess a particular Ford Expedition, parked in a tow truck near the debtor's house. He saw the debtor back the Expedition out of the driveway and then leave it on the street with its motor running, while the debtor went back into the house. Chambers quickly towed the car off. Less than a minute later, he stopped to check the Expedition and saw two children in the backseat. He immediately drove the Expedition back to the debtor's house and returned the children and the vehicle to the now-distraught debtor. Did Chambers violate Article 9? See Chapa v. Traciers & Assocs., 267 S.W.3d 386 (Tex. App. 2008).

PROBLEM 134

Octopus National Bank declared a default on Jessica Napoleon's car loan, and Napoleon showed up at ONB to surrender the vehicle. May ONB decline to take it and instead just sue Napoleon for the debt? See §9-601 and Chemtex, LLC v. St. Anthony Enters., 490 F. Supp. 2d 536 (S.D.N.Y. 2007).

It is important to remember that if the debtor files a petition in bankruptcy, §362 of the Bankruptcy Code creates an automatic stay of any creditor collection activity. This automatic stay forbids not only repossession but also even more prosaic attempts to collect the debt, such as dunning letters. The automatic stay does not depend on formal court notice that the bankruptcy petition has been filed; it is in effect from the moment of the filing. Creditor action taken without knowledge of the filing must be undone on learning that the debtor's bankruptcy has already occurred. But any true information that reaches the creditor from whatever source that the bankruptcy has been filed invokes the protection of the automatic stay. Deliberate creditor conduct thereafter violating the stay would not only be in contempt of court, but could also lead to the invocation of §362(k): "An individual injured by any willful violation of a stay provided by this section shall recover actual damages, including costs and attorneys' fees, and, in appropriate circumstances, may recover punitive damages." Let the lender beware.

PROBLEM 135

Wonder Spa gave Antitrust National Bank (ANB) a security interest in its accounts receivable and chattel paper in return for a loan. When Wonder Spa missed two payments in a row, ANB notified the spa's customers that future payments should be made directly to the bank. Does the bank have this right? Read §9-607 and its Official Comment 2; see §9-406(c). If the spa stops opening its doors, need its former customers keep paying ANB? (The spa contracts did not mention the possibility that the contracts would be assigned.) See §9-404(a); G. Gilmore, ch. 41. The ability of customers to raise defenses against the finance company is bound up in the law of negotiable instruments—see Unico v. Owen, 50 N.J. 101, 232 A.2d 405 (1967), the leading case—and special consumer protection statutes, e.g., Uniform Consumer Credit Code §3.404, and regulations such as the FTC's Holder in Due Course rule, 16 C.F.R. §433 (1975); Annot., 39 A.L.R.3d 518. Section 9-403(e) carefully preserves any other rule of law that protects consumers from waiving their rights to assert their defenses against assignees of their obligations.

After repossession, the secured party may in some circumstances (§§9-620 to 9-622, explored below) simply keep the collateral and give up further remedy (this is called *strict foreclosure*). More typically the repossessing creditor will resell the collateral and, if the resale does not pay the debt in full, then sue the debtor for any *deficiency* (or, if the resale more than pays the debt, return the *surplus* to the debtor[3]).

Section 9-610 and the sections that follow it regulate the resale. Note that in most cases §9-611(c) dictates that the secured party must give the debtor *notice* of the time and place of the sale. The reason for this notice is twofold: On getting it, the debtor may elect to use the §9-623 right of redemption (about which more later), or the debtor can attend the sale or send potential buyers who will enter real bids and, by actively competing in the bidding, bring a fair price for the collateral. The notice requirement is much litigated: What must it say, whom must it go to, and what happens if it is not given? These issues are raised by the Problems below, which also consider another §9-610 matter, the §9-610(b) mandate that "every aspect of a disposition of collateral, including the method, manner, time, place, and other terms must be commercially reasonable." As to the meaning of *commercially reasonable*, see G. Gilmore §44.5.

PROBLEM 136

After Nightflyer Loan Company had repossessed Lynn Brown's car, it decided to advertise it for bids in a local newspaper. Is this a private or a public sale? See Official Comment 7 to §9-610. How much in advance of the resale must she be given notice? See §§9-611, 612. What should the notice say? See §9-614 (for the notice to be given to non-consumer debtors, see §9-613). Must

---

3. You can imagine how often this happens. "Like neutrinos, surpluses are believed to exist but are never observed," White & Summers §26-13 at 1357.

it state whether it is a public or private sale? See Boulevard Bank v. Malott, 2013 WL 324041 (Mo. App. 2013). If the car were to be sold in an Internet auction, would it be sufficient to give notice of the web address of the auction and the physical address of the auction company? See Moore v. Wells Fargo Constr., 903 N.E.2d 525 (Ind. App. 2009).

After the resale, Nightflyer simply sent her a statement saying that the amount she now owed was $3,200. She is unsure how Nightflyer came up with this figure, and comes to you, her attorney/cousin, for advice. What are her rights here? See §§9-616, 9-625(c) and (e). The price obtained at the resale seems suspiciously low to her. How relevant is that? See §9-627(a). She suspects that the reason the sale brought so little is that the only bidder was Nightflyer Loan Company itself. Can they do that? See §§9-610(e), 9-615(f), and 9-626(a)(5); White & Summers §26-10(d). If she succeeds in reducing the amount she owes, can she also get actual damages for the harm they have caused her? See §9-625(d); White & Summers §26-13(e).

PROBLEM 137

Mr. and Mrs. Miller decided to open a restaurant, for which purpose they needed $80,000. They went to Apocalypse National Bank, which agreed to loan them the money if they (1) got a surety, (2) signed an agreement giving the bank a security interest in the restaurant's equipment and inventory, and (3) pledged to the bank additional collateral having a value of $20,000 or more. The Millers got Mrs. Miller's father (Mr. Stuhldreher) to sign as surety; they signed the security agreement; and they borrowed $20,000 worth of stock from Mr. Miller's cousin, Mr. Layden. The stock was registered in Layden's name at the time it was pledged to the bank, but the bank had it reregistered in the bank's name so that it could be sold easily in the event of default. The bank did, however, file its financing statement in the appropriate office. Subsequently, the Millers borrowed another $5,000 from Northbend Credit Union, which also took a security interest in the restaurant's equipment, and filed a financing statement. The restaurant then became involved in an unfortunate food poisoning incident, and business fell off dramatically. The Millers (who were in the midst of a divorce) missed two payments on the loan. The bank sent its collection agent, Mr. Crowley, out to the restaurant, and he repossessed the assets he found there. Mr. Crowley sent a written notice to Mr. Miller (who he knew was now living in a hotel), telling him that the stock would be sold on the open market (no specific date given) and that the restaurant equipment would be sold at public auction on December 1 at the offices of the Crowley Collection Agency. Crowley phoned Mr. Stuhldreher (the surety) and told him the same thing. He sent a written notice to Mr. Layden (the stock owner), but the letter came back marked "Moved—No Forwarding Address." If asked, either Mr. or Mrs. Miller would have supplied Crowley with

Layden's new address. Crowley sold the stock for $10,000 on the open market (that was its current selling price) and auctioned off the restaurant equipment on December 1 for $500 (only one bid was received—Crowley himself was the bidder; he later resold the equipment to other restaurants for $10,000). Crowley turned over the proceeds from the two sales ($10,500 total) to Apocalypse National Bank, which then brought suit against the Millers and Mr. Stuhldreher for the deficiency. Answer these questions:

(a) Is a surety entitled to a notice under §9-611? That is, is he a *debtor*? Read §§9-102(a)(28)(A), 9-102(a)(72), 9-611(c). Was Mr. Layden a *debtor* too? See Official Comment 2a to §9-102. Does the *oral* notice to Mr. Stuhldreher satisfy §9-611(b)? See §§1-201(b)(36), 9-102(a)(7), and 9-611's Official Comment 5.

(b) Were any parties entitled to notice of the *stock* sale? See §9-611(d). How about the sale of the equipment? See §9-611(c). If no notice was sent to Northbend Credit Union before the equipment was sold, did Mr. Crowley himself take free of its security interest when he bought the equipment at the foreclosure sale? See §9-617. Did the buyer take free of its security interest when he bought the equipment from Crowley? See §2-403(1).

(c) Is the notice sent to Mr. Miller sufficient as to Mrs. Miller? See Tauber v. Johnson, 8 Ill. App. 3d 180, 291 N.E.2d 180 (1972).(d) Does §9-611 require the creditor, to whom a notice is returned by the post office, to take further steps to notify the debtor? See Official Comment 6; Auto Credit of Nashville v. Wimmer, 231 S.W.3d 896 (Tenn. 2007).

(e) Since the restaurant equipment is also named as collateral on the junior filed financing statement, must the bank notify that secured party of the resale? See §9-611(c) and (e).

(f) Who has the burden of proof as to the commercial reasonableness of the sales? See §9-626(a)(2).

(g) If Crowley had given the equipment sale no publicity, has a *public* sale occurred, and, if so, was it *commercially reasonable*? See §9-610, Official Comment 7.

(h) When a secured party repossesses goods and sells them at a foreclosure sale, will this give rise to the Article 2 sales warranties being made to the purchaser at the sale? See §§2-312, 9-610(d) and (e), and the latter's Official Comment 11.

R & J of Tennessee, Inc. v. Blankenship-Melton Real Estate, Inc.

Court of Appeals of Tennessee, 2005
166 S.W.3d 195

ALAN E. HIGHERS, J.

This case involves a lawsuit filed by a secured party against a guarantor seeking a deficiency judgment following a foreclosure sale. The guarantor argued that the secured party was not entitled to a deficiency because he was given inadequate notice and the sale was conducted in a commercially unreasonable manner. Following a hearing, the trial court awarded the secured party a deficiency judgment. We reverse and remand to the trial court for further action consistent with this opinion.

I.   Factual Background and Procedural History

On February 23, 2000, Walden Blankenship ("Mr. Blankenship"), as acting president of Blankenship-Melton Real Estate, Inc. ("Blankenship-Melton"), entered into a loan transaction with the Bank of Henderson County (the "Bank"). In exchange for the Bank loaning Blankenship-Melton $40,133, Blankenship-Melton executed a security agreement granting the Bank a security interest in a 1999 Bryant boat, a New Holland tractor, a 1999 Ford F150 truck, and a 1994 mobile home. The agreement called for Blankenship-Melton to pay off the loan by June 18, 2000.

The collateral used to secure the loan was purchased by Blankenship-Melton prior to entering into the loan in question. According to Mr. Blankenship, Larry Melton, a director of Blankenship-Melton, purchased the truck new for an amount between $23,000 and $24,000, and the vehicle's title listed Blankenship-Melton as the owner. Mr. Blankenship purchased the tractor used as collateral, as well as a tiller, a bush hog, and a boom pole, for an amount between $17,000 and $18,000. Mr. Blankenship also stated that Blankenship-Melton paid approximately $15,000 for the double-wide mobile home when they purchased it. At the time the loan agreement was entered into in February of 2000, the Bank estimated the value of all of the collateral to be at least $40,000.

Contemporaneously with the execution of the promissory note, Mr. Blankenship executed a guaranty agreement promising to remain personally liable on the promissory note owed to the Bank. The guaranty agreement identified Mr. Blankenship's home address as "2820 Shady Hill Road, Lexington, TN, 38351." In addition, Larry Melton and his son, Steve Melton, the secretary of Blankenship-Melton, also executed personal guarantees to secure the loan. The Bank renewed the loan on two separate occasions, extending the due date for six months each time. At some point, the loan went into default. During this period of time, Mr. Blankenship asserted that he communicated with the Bank and asked the Bank to foreclose on the collateral. Stan Reynolds, a representative of the Bank, did not recall Mr. Blankenship making such a request. Regardless of this dispute, Mr. Blankenship never personally paid any amounts toward the outstanding loan amount.

Johnny Melton is the majority shareholder and president of R & J of Tennessee, Inc. ("R & J" or "Appellee"). Larry Melton and Steve Melton approached Johnny Melton explaining that this particular note had come due and asked for help with some outstanding loans Blankenship-Melton owed to the Bank. On November 6, 2001, Johnny Melton, acting as agent for R & J, purchased the promissory note from the Bank for $26,455.39. At the time R & J purchased the promissory note from the Bank, Blankenship-Melton was already in default on the loan, and the Bank had already begun to institute foreclosure proceedings on the collateral. In addition, only the truck, tractor, and mobile home were left as collateral to secure the note.[4] When R & J purchased the note, Steve Melton had been living in the trailer which was used as collateral, and he never paid rent to Blankenship-Melton during his periods of occupancy. Larry Melton had possession of the Ford truck and drove it on a daily basis. The tractor remained in Larry Melton's possession and was stored at his personal residence. According to Johnny Melton, at the time R & J purchased the note, the tractor was inoperable due to mechanical problems.

In June of 2002, Johnny Melton, acting as agent for R & J, began the foreclosure process. On June 11, 2002, Johnny Melton sent a notice to Mr. Blankenship indicating that the collateral would be sold at a public sale on June 21, 2002. According to Johnny Melton, Steve Melton and Larry Melton continued to use the collateral during this period of time. R & J sent the notice of sale by certified mail to Mr. Blankenship at the address listed in the promissory note. Mr. Blankenship, however, had subsequently moved and conceded that he never notified the Bank of his new home address. According to Johnny Melton, similar notices were also sent to Larry Melton and Steve Melton. Johnny Melton also posted a copy of the notice of sale at R & J's office, the courthouse, and on the collateral. The envelope containing the notice to Mr. Blankenship, which was introduced as an exhibit at trial, indicated that the postal service attempted to deliver the notice to Mr. Blankenship at his old address on June 13 and 18, 2002. Despite having not received a return receipt indicating successful delivery of the notice, R & J went ahead with the sale of the collateral on June 21, 2002. On June 28, 2002, the postal service returned the notice to R & J marked "not deliverable as addressed."

On the date of the public sale, only Johnny Melton, on behalf of R & J, and Larry Melton were present, and only Johnny Melton placed a bid on the collateral. R & J purchased the mobile home for $8,000, the Ford truck for $11,000, and the tractor for $1,000. Johnny Melton stated that he used

---

4. Prior to assigning the promissory note to R & J, the Bryant boat was sold and the proceeds applied toward the outstanding debt. As a result, the Bank released the boat as collateral securing the loan.

his previous experience in the banking industry and mobile home business to assess the value of each item of the collateral at the time of the sale. On August 26, 2002, Johnny Melton, on behalf of R & J, filed a lawsuit against Mr. Blankenship in the General Sessions Court of Henderson County, seeking a deficiency judgment in the amount of $13,388.40 pursuant to the personal guaranty. The general sessions court found in favor of Mr. Blankenship, and R & J appealed the decision to the Circuit Court of Henderson County. Following a de novo bench trial, the circuit court entered a deficiency judgment against Mr. Blankenship in the amount of $10,847.29.

Mr. Blankenship filed a timely notice of appeal to this Court and presents the following issues for our review:

I.   Whether Appellant, Walden Blankenship, was given statutorily sufficient notice regarding the public sale of the collateral pursuant to section 47-9-611(b) of the Tennessee Code;

II. Whether Appellee, R & J of Tennessee, failed to dispose of the collateral in a commercially reasonable manner under section 47-9-610(b) of the Tennessee Code and to exercise good faith pursuant to section 47-1-203 of the Tennessee Code;

III. Whether Appellee, R & J of Tennessee, exercised reasonable care pursuant to section 47-9-207(a) of the Tennessee Code in preserving and exercising custody of the collateral used to secure the loan at issue; and

IV. Whether the trial court erred in finding that no evidence was introduced at trial regarding the condition and value of the tractor on the date of the foreclosure sale as it relates to Appellee's bid.

In addition to the issues raised by Appellant, we are also asked to review the following issue raised by Appellee:

V.   Whether Appellant, Walden Blankenship, waived the objections to the foreclosure sale which he now raises on appeal according to the terms of the personal guaranty.

For the reasons contained herein, we reverse the decision of the trial court. . . .

III.   WAIVER OF OBJECTIONS

R & J asserts on appeal that Mr. Blankenship has waived his right to contest the sufficiency of the foreclosure sale and notice based upon the terms of the personal guaranty. The applicable provision of Tennessee's version of the Uniform Commercial Code provides:

124 S.W.3d 116, 120 (Tenn. Ct. App. 2003) (citing Bradley v. McLeod, 984 S.W.2d 929, 933 (Tenn. Ct. App. 1998)). In applying this standard this Court has stated: It is clear that a finding of an abuse of discretion cannot be based simply upon an appellate court's determination that it would have decided the question differently. Whiton v. Whiton, No. E2000-00467-COA-R3-CV, 2002 WL 1585630, at *7, 2002 Tenn. App. LEXIS 512[,] at *21 (Tenn. Ct. App. July 18, 2002). Rather, this standard requires that we determine "whether the lower court's exercise of its discretion went beyond the bounds of a fair exercise of discretion." Id. Davis v. Estate of Johnnie Rex Flynn, No. E2001-02480-COA-R3-CV, 2002 WL 31174229, at *9, 2002 Tenn. App. LEXIS 702, at *23 (Tenn. Ct. App. Sept. 30, 2002). The federal complaint was filed on June 21, 2002, and the trial in this matter occurred on July 28, 2003. We presume that Mr. Blankenship received service of the federal complaint prior to the trial of this matter in the court below. "The moving party must demonstrate that the new evidence was not known prior to or during the trial and that it could not have been ascertained by the exercise of reasonable diligence." Collins, 916 S.W.2d at 945; see also Seay, 654 S.W.2d at 399. Accordingly, we find that the trial court did not abuse its discretion in denying Mr. Blankenship's motion partially based on the information contained in the federal complaint. In turn, we are constrained to reviewing only the evidence presented at trial when determining whether the notice sent to Mr. Blankenship was sufficient under section 47-9-611(b) of the Tennessee Code.

The official comment to section 47-9-611(b) provides that "[t]he notification must be reasonable as to the manner in which it is sent, its timeliness (i.e., a reasonable time before the disposition is to take place), and its content." Tenn. Code Ann. §47-9-611 cmt. 2 (2003). Mr. Blankenship does not contest that R & J failed to send the notice in a timely fashion. See Tenn. Code Ann. §47-9-612. Rather, he contests whether the notice was sent in a reasonable manner when it was addressed to an address where he no longer lived. In addition to the timing of the notice, the reasonableness of the notice also encompasses a consideration of where the notice was sent. Commercial Credit Corp. v. Cutshall, 1979 WL 30031 (Tenn. Ct. App. 1979).

Section 47-9-611 of the Tennessee Code "leaves to judicial resolution, based upon the facts of each case, the question whether the requirement of 'reasonable notification' requires a 'second try,' i.e., whether a secured party who sends notification and learns that the debtor did not receive it must attempt to locate the debtor and send another notification." Tenn. Code Ann. §47-9-612 cmt. 6 (2003). We begin by examining the definitions of the key terms contained in section 47-9-611(b) of the Tennessee Code. The term "send" is defined as follows:

"Send," in connection with a record or notification, means:

(A) to deposit in the mail, deliver for transmission, or transmit by any other usual means of communication, with postage or cost of transmission provided for, addressed to any address reasonable under the circumstances; or

(B) to cause the record or notification to be received within the time that it would have been received if properly sent under subparagraph (A).

Tenn. Code Ann. §47-9-102(75) (2003). The definition section applicable to Tennessee's version of Article 9 does not define "notice," but we find guidance in the general definition section of the Code, which provides:

A person "notifies" or "gives" a notice or notification to another by taking such steps as may be reasonably required to inform the other in ordinary course whether or not such other actually comes to know of it. A person "receives" a notice or notification when:

(A) It comes to his attention; or

(B) It is duly delivered at the place of business *through which the contract was made or at any other place held out by him* as the place for receipt of such communications[.]

Tenn. Code Ann. §47-1-201(26) (2003) (emphasis added).

The policy justifications for providing notice to a debtor are equally applicable to a secondary obligor, and can be stated as follows:

We think the provision for notice in connection with a sale is intended to afford the debtor a reasonable opportunity (1) to avoid a sale altogether by discharging the debt and redeeming the collateral or (2) in case of sale, to see that the collateral brings a fair price. A notice that does not afford him this reasonable opportunity is not reasonable notification and a sale under it is not commercially reasonable.

Intl. Harvester Credit Corp. v. Ingram, 619 S.W.2d 134, 137 (Tenn. Ct. App. 1981) (citing Mallicoat v. Volunteer Fin. & Loan Corp., 57 Tenn. App. 106, 415 S.W.2d 347, 350 (1966)).

In support of his argument that the notice given was not reasonable, Mr. Blankenship relies on our decision in Mallicoat v. Volunteer Finance & Loan Corp., 57 Tenn. App. 106, 415 S.W.2d 347 (1966). In *Mallicoat,* the secured party sent a notice of sale to the debtor by certified mail, but the notice was returned to the secured party undelivered. *Mallicoat,* 415 S.W.2d at 349. After receiving the returned notice, the secured party continued to conduct a sale of the collateral and sued the debtor for a deficiency judgment. Id. In finding the notice in that case insufficient under the predecessor statute to section 47-9-611, we stated:

In view of the undisputed proof in this case that the debtor did not receive the notice and that the secured creditor was aware that he had not received it, it is our opinion the creditor not only failed to show a compliance with the Act but that the record affirmatively shows a lack of compliance and a conscious disregard of the debtor's right to notice. The property was not perishable. The debtor lived in Knoxville where the creditor had its place of business and sold the property. In addition, the creditor had information as to where the debtor was employed and where his parents lived. Yet, the sale was allowed to proceed without any further effort to comply with the notice requirement.

Id. at 350; see also First Tenn. Bank Natl. Assn. v. Helton, No. 03A01-9501-CV-00026, 1995 WL 515658, at *2, 1995 Tenn. App. LEXIS 339, at *5-6 (Tenn. Ct. App. May 23, 1995).

Courts throughout the country vary as to whether the secured party has the burden of proving that the debtor or a secondary obligor received actual notice of a pending sale. See Richard C. Tinney, Annotation, Sufficiency of Secured Party's Notification of Sale or Other Intended Disposition of Collateral Under UCC §9-504(3), 11 A.L.R.4th 241, §§14-16 (2003). Many of our sister states interpret the notice provision to require only that the creditor send notice. See Underwood v. First Ala. Bank of Huntsville, 453 So. 2d 742, 745 (Ala. Civ. App. 1983); Hall v. Owen County State Bank, 175 Ind. App. 150, 370 N.E.2d 918, 925 (1977); McKee v. Miss. Bank & Trust Co., 366 So. 2d 234, 238 (Miss. 1979); Commerce Bank of St. Louis v. Dooling, 875 S.W.2d 943, 946 (Mo. Ct. App. 1994); First Natl. Bank & Trust Co. of Lincoln v. Hermann, 205 Neb. 169, 286 N.W.2d 750, 752 (1980). Our decision in *Mallicoat,* however, demonstrates that Tennessee requires more than a mere "sending" in order for a secured party to be in compliance with the statute. James J. White & Robert S. Summers, Uniform Commercial Code §26-10, at 987 (1972).

At the other end of the notice spectrum, we have held that the notice requirement is satisfied when the following occurs:

> The sending of notice, certified, return receipt requested, is commercially reasonable. When a plaintiff forwards notice to the debtor's proper address, certified, return receipt requested, and the notice is received at that address and returned signed by someone at the address, it is reasonable for plaintiff to assume that the defendant received the notice.

Caterpillar Fin. Services Corp. v. Woods, No. 89-326-II, 1990 WL 15230, at *3, 1990 Tenn. App. LEXIS 117, at *7-8 (Tenn. Ct. App. Feb. 22, 1990). Our case law makes clear that "the creditor will not be forced to take responsibility for lost mail or the debtor's refusal to accept properly delivered mail." Nationsbank v. Clegg, No. 01-A-01-9510-CH-00469, 1996 WL 165513, at *5,

1996 Tenn. App. LEXIS 214, at *14 (Tenn. Ct. App. Apr. 10, 1996). Yet, we have also made clear that:

> While absolute proof of receipt of notice may not be required in every instance, a creditor, who only makes one attempt to contact the debtor, and is left uncertain of receipt of the notice, has not fulfilled its obligation to the debtor when it proceeds with a disposition less than two weeks from mailing its first notice.

Id. 1996 WL 165513, at *5, 1996 Tenn. App. LEXIS 214, at *15-16.

We disagree with Mr. Blankenship's assertion that section 47-9-611(b) requires the secured party to prove that the secondary obligor actually received the notice. See Commercial Credit Corp. v. Cutshall, 1979 WL 30031 (Tenn. Ct. App. 1979). Based on the facts presented to the trial court below, however, we find the trial court's holding that notice in this case was sufficient under the statute to be erroneous as a matter of law. We are mindful that Mr. Blankenship bears some responsibility for not receiving notice in this case. See The Cent. Trust Co. of Northeastern Ohio v. Snair, No. CA-5818, 1982 WL 5437, at *1, 1982 Ohio App. LEXIS 15214, at *2-3 (Ohio Ct. App. June 23, 1982); Gen. Motors Acceptance Corp. v. Horn, No. 5861, 1978 WL 216247, at *3, 1978 Ohio App. LEXIS 11155, at *5 (Ohio Ct. App. July 20, 1978). However, R & J sent the notice to Mr. Blankenship on June 11, 2002, and conducted a sale ten days later on June 21, 2002, without receiving any indication as to whether the notice actually reached Mr. Blankenship. We find, therefore, that this amounts to unreasonable notice under the statute and reverse the trial court's holding on this issue. See Nationsbank v. Clegg, No. 01-A-01-9510-CH-00469, 1996 WL 165513, at *5, 1996 Tenn. App. LEXIS 214, at *15-16 (Tenn. Ct. App. Apr. 10, 1996).

V. Commercial Reasonableness of the Sale of the Collateral

Lack of reasonable notice to a secondary obligor is one factor bearing upon whether the sale of the collateral was commercially reasonable. See Mallicoat v. Volunteer Fin. & Loan Corp., 57 Tenn. App. 106, 415 S.W.2d 347, 351 (1966); Gen. Motors Acceptance Corp. v. Middleton, No. 02A01-9103-CH-00033, 1991 WL 206517, at *4, 1991 Tenn. App. LEXIS 820, at *7 (Tenn. Ct. App. Oct. 16, 1991). "However, notice by itself is not conclusive on the question of whether a sale was commercially reasonable." Decatur County Bank v. Smith, No. CAW1999-02022COAR3CV, 1999 WL 1336042, at *3, 1999 Tenn. App. LEXIS 864, at *9 (Tenn. Ct. App. Dec. 27, 1999). We note that the remaining issues presented by Appellant for our review focus upon whether Appellee conducted the sale of the collateral in a commercially reasonable manner. Accordingly, we will discuss these issues collectively in this section of the opinion.

"After default, a secured party may sell, lease, license, or otherwise dispose of any or all of the collateral in its present condition or following any commercially reasonable preparation or processing." Tenn. Code Ann. §47-9-610(a) (2003). As a secured party conducting a public sale, R & J also had the right to purchase the collateral at the sale. Tenn. Code Ann. §47-9-610(c)(1) (2003). In carrying out the sale of the collateral R & J was bound by two standards. "First, in exercising his rights upon default the secured party is bound by the good faith requirement applicable throughout the Uniform Commercial Code." *Decatur County Bank*, 1999 WL 1336042, at *3, 1999 Tenn. App. LEXIS 864, at *6 (citing Tenn. Code Ann. §47-1-203). The second requirement that R & J was bound to follow addresses the procedures used in selling the collateral and provides:

> Commercially reasonable disposition. Every aspect of a disposition of collateral, including the method, manner, time, place, and other terms, must be commercially reasonable. If commercially reasonable, a secured party may dispose of the collateral by public or private proceedings, by one (1) or more contracts, as a unit or in parcels, and at any time and place and on any terms.

Tenn. Code Ann. §47-9-610(b) (2003); see also Am. City Bank of Tullahoma v. W. Auto Supply Co., 631 S.W.2d 410, 419 (Tenn. Ct. App. 1981). This Court has defined "commercially reasonable" as follows:

> The requirement that the property be disposed of in a "commercially reasonable" manner seems to us to signify that the disposition shall be made in keeping with prevailing trade practices among reputable and responsible business and commercial enterprises engaged in the same or a similar business.

Mallicoat v. Volunteer Fin. & Loan Corp., 57 Tenn. App. 106, 415 S.W.2d 347, 350 (1966); see also Tenn. Code Ann. §47-9-627(b) (2003). The trial court found that R & J conducted the sale in good faith and in a commercially reasonable manner. We disagree.

Like notice, review of a sale of collateral to determine whether it was conducted in good faith and in a commercially reasonable manner is an inquiry dependent upon the facts of each case. In reviewing the facts of this case, we are cognizant of the following:

> Rather than viewing in isolation specific details of the sale of the debtor's collateral, it is the aggregate of circumstances in each case which should be emphasized in reviewing the sale. The elements of manner, method, time, place and terms cited by the Uniform Commercial Code are to be viewed as necessary and interrelated parts of the whole transaction.

In re Four Star Music Co., Inc., 2 B.R. 454, 463 (Bankr. M.D. Tenn. 1979) (citations omitted).

This court has often looked to the following factors when attempting to ascertain whether a foreclosure sale was conducted in a commercially reasonable manner:

> Although the statute has not attempted to define the parameters of the term "commercially reasonable," case law has specified six factors by which the statute requirements may be measured:
>   (1) the type of collateral involved; and
>   (2) the condition of the collateral; and
>   (3) the number of bids solicited; and
>   (4) the time and place of sale; and
>   (5) the purchase price received or the terms of the sale; and
>   (6) any special circumstances involved.

Decatur County Bank v. Smith, No. CAW1999-02022COAR3CV, 1999 WL 1336042, at *2, 1999 Tenn. App. LEXIS 864, at *7-8 (Tenn. Ct. App. Dec. 27, 1999) (quoting In re Four Star Music Co., Inc., 2 B.R. 454, 461 (Bankr. M.D. Tenn. 1979)). "The burden of proving that a sale of collateral is commercially reasonable under these statutes is on the secured party seeking the deficiency judgment." *Decatur County Bank*, 1999 WL 1336042, at *3, 1999 Tenn. App. LEXIS 864, at *7.

Mr. Blankenship argues that the timing of the sale demonstrates it was conducted in a commercially unreasonable manner. In support of his position, he points to the fact that R & J delayed in conducting a sale of the collateral for seven and one-half months after purchasing the note. Mr. Blankenship notes that at the time R & J purchased the note it had already been in default for some time.

The official comment to section 47-9-610 of the Tennessee Code provides:

> *Time of Disposition.* This article does not specify a period within which a secured party must dispose of collateral. This is consistent with this article's policy to encourage private dispositions through regular commercial channels. It may, for example, be prudent not to dispose of goods when the market has collapsed. Or, it might be more appropriate to sell a large inventory in parcels over a period of time instead of in bulk. Of course, under subsection (b) every aspect of a disposition of collateral must be commercially reasonable. This requirement explicitly includes the "method, manner, time, place, and other terms." *For example, if a secured party does not proceed under section 9-620 [§47-9-620] and holds collateral for a long period of time without disposing of it, and if there is no good reason for not making a prompt disposition, the secured party may be determined not to have acted in a "commercially reasonable" manner.* See also section 1-203 [§47-1-203] (general obligation of good faith).

Tenn. Code Ann. §47-9-610 cmt. 3 (2003) (emphasis added). Mr. Blankenship directs our attention to this Court's holding in Nationsbank v. Clegg, No.

01-A-01-9510-CH-00469, 1996 WL 165513, 1996 Tenn. App. LEXIS 214
(Tenn. Ct. App. Apr. 10, 1996), where we stated:

> Of concern to this Court is the fact that the secured parties in this
> instance permitted an automobile to sit idly for over 13 months after default.
> The UCC does not state particular time limits for a secured party to take pos-
> session of the collateral, or to proceed with a sale following the taking of pos-
> session. The determination of whether delay is commercially unreasonable
> requires consideration of all surrounding circumstances, including market
> conditions, the possible physical deterioration of the collateral, its economic
> deterioration through obsolescence, and the time required to assemble the
> collateral and prepare it for sale. . . .
>
> We have found no evidence in the record, or other authority which
> indicates that the 13 month delay in selling the automobile, a depreciating
> asset, is "in keeping with the prevailing trade practices among reputable firms
> engaged in similar business activities," in Tennessee. Thus, the delay appears
> unreasonable to this Court. . . .
>
> In exercising its rights upon default, Nationsbank is bound by the good
> faith requirement applicable throughout the Uniform Commercial Code.
> Tenn. Code Ann. §47-1-203. American City Bank of Tullahoma v. Western
> Auto Supply, 631 S.W.2d 410, 420 (Tenn. App. 1981). The obligation of good
> faith required the secured parties in this instance to have sold the car with
> greater haste.

Nationsbank, 1996 WL 165513, at *3-4, 1996 Tenn. App. LEXIS 214, at *8-10
(citations omitted).

In response, R & J contends that, unlike the facts in *Nationsbank,* the
collateral in this case did not sit unused during the period leading up to the
sale. To the contrary, Larry Melton continued to drive the truck, and Steve
Melton continued to live in the mobile home. Only the tractor remained
unused since it was inoperable at the time of the foreclosure sale.

"The policy of the Uniform Commercial Code, as to the disposition of
collateral, is to balance and protect the rights of both debtor and creditor,
while maximizing the recovery from the disposition of the collateral for the
benefit of all parties." *Nationsbank,* 1996 WL 165513, at *3, 1996 Tenn. App.
LEXIS 214, at *8 (citations omitted). Upon reviewing the entire record, we
find that the evidence clearly preponderates against the trial court's finding that the sale of the collateral conducted by R & J in this case was commercially reasonable. Once a debtor or secondary obligor raises the issue
of the commercial reasonableness of a sale, the secured party, in this case
R & J, bears the burden of proving that the sale was carried out in a commercially reasonable manner. Decatur County Bank v. Smith, No. CAW1999-
02022COAR3CV, 1999 WL 1336042, at *3, 1999 Tenn. App. LEXIS 864, at
*7 (Tenn. Ct. App. Dec. 27, 1999). R & J failed to carry this burden at trial.

In addition to the failure to provide adequate notice, R & J failed to offer a reasonable explanation as to why it waited in excess of seven months to conduct a sale of the collateral, during which time Larry Melton and Steve Melton were allowed to continue using the collateral. See *Nationsbank*, 1996 WL 165513, at *3-4, 1996 Tenn. App. LEXIS 214, at *8-10. Contrary to R & J's position, we note that use of the items of collateral in this case would cause them to depreciate more rapidly, not less. Mr. Blankenship also raises a related issue regarding R & J's handling of the collateral after it purchased the note in question. Mr. Blankenship asserts that, by allowing Steve Melton and Larry Melton to continue to use the collateral over the seven and one-half months before the sale, R & J increased the amount of the deficiency. According to Mr. Blankenship, in addition to constituting bad faith on the part of R & J, this amounts to a violation of section 49-9-207(a) which provides, in relevant part, as follows:

> *Rights and duties of secured party having possession or control of collateral.* —
> (a) DUTY OF CARE WHEN SECURED PARTY IN POSSESSION. Except as otherwise provided in subsection (d), a secured party shall use reasonable care in the custody and preservation of collateral in the secured party's possession.

Tenn. Code Ann. §47-9-207(a) (2003). We agree with Mr. Blankenship that the actions by R & J relating to the use and custody of the collateral constitute an additional factor demonstrating that the disposition of the collateral in this case was commercially unreasonable. See Farmers & Merchants Bank v. Barnes, 17 Ark. App. 139, 705 S.W.2d 450, 453 (1986) (holding a sale of collateral commercially unreasonable where the collateral remained in the custody of the original owner who was permitted to continue using it for six months prior to the sale); The Bank Josephine v. Conn, 599 S.W.2d 773, 775 (Ky. Ct. App. 1980) (finding a sale of collateral commercially unreasonable where the secured party did not dispose of the collateral for four to five weeks after repossessing it, thereby allowing it to deteriorate further prior to the sale).

We also agree with Mr. Blankenship that R & J's actions in allowing Larry Melton and Steve Melton to continue to use the collateral prior to the sale constituted bad faith. Johnny Melton's own testimony, indicating that Larry Melton and Steve Melton also continued to retain possession of the collateral after the sale, supports this conclusion:

> *Q:* Who keeps the vehicle for you, Mr. Melton?
> *A:* Larry Melton still takes care of it.
> *Q:* Yes. The tractor, where is the tractor at?
> *A:* It's still at their place.

Q: At the Melton place?
A: At the Melton place.

. . .

Q: Where is the mobile home at currently?
A: It's still on the property where it was.

. . .

Q: Is Mr. Larry Melton living in that mobile home?
A: Not that I'm aware of.
Q: Who is living in it?
A: Steve is living in it.
Q: Okay. Steve Melton?
A: Uh-huh.

Providing notice of a public sale to the general public corresponds with additional factors related to the procedures employed by the secured party in conducting the sale. When a secured party undertakes to dispose of the collateral by public sale, advertising of some sort should be conducted in order to increase competitive bidding and maximize proceeds. Gezon Motors v. Gould, 1976 WL 23727 (Mich. Dist. 1976). Although R & J posted a notice of sale at the courthouse and on the collateral, the record also indicates that R & J never advertised the sale in a public newspaper or utilized an experienced auctioneer. See First Tenn. Bank Natl. Assoc. v. Helton, No. 03A01-9501-CV-00026, 1995 WL 515658, at *3, 1995 Tenn. App. LEXIS 339, at *7-8 (Tenn. Ct. App. May 23, 1995); see also U.S. v. Warwick, 695 F.2d 1063, 1073 (7th Cir. 1982); Benton v. Gen. Mobile Homes, Inc., 13 Ark. App. 8, 678 S.W.2d 774, 776 (1984). Given the nature of the collateral, this is another factor indicating the sale was not conducted by R & J in a commercially reasonable manner. Leasing Serv. Corp. v. Broetje, 640 F. Supp. 51, 53 (E.D. Wash. 1986) (finding a public sale commercially reasonable, despite the fact that the secured party was the only bidder present, where the secured party properly notified the debtor and advertised the sale in newspapers in the area of the sale); Kobuk Engg. & Contracting Services Inc. v. Superior Tank & Constr. Co-Alaska, Inc., 568 P.2d 1007, 1011 (Alaska 1977) (holding that a sale was not commercially reasonable where the secured party merely gave a copy of the notice to the court clerk for posting on a bulletin board and did not advertise in the newspaper in the area where the collateral was to be sold); The Bank Josephine v. Conn, 599 S.W.2d 773, 775 (Ky. Ct. App. 1980) (stating that a sale was commercially unreasonable where the secured party failed to prove where he posted notices, did not advertise in any newspapers, and was the only bidder at the sale).

In addition to being the only bidder at the sale, R & J also valued the collateral instead of seeking an independent appraisal. Johnny Melton did testify that he had prior experience in the banking and mobile home industries which he used to value the collateral. We note that an independent appraisal may not be required in every case. When coupled with the other facts present in this case, however, R & J's failure to do so in this instance is an additional factor indicating that this sale was not conducted in a commercially reasonable manner. See In re Cummings, 147 B.R. 738, 746 (D.S.D. 1992) (holding that a secured party failed to conduct a sale in a commercially reasonable manner where he did not obtain an appraisal, exerted minimal effort to notify potential buyers, and failed to give notice to the debtor); In re Thomas, 1973 WL 21424 (W.D. Va. 1973) (stating that the fact that the secured party failed to obtain an independent valuation of the collateral by a third party was a factor supporting the commercial unreasonableness of the sale); Kobuk Engg. & Contracting Services, Inc. v. Superior Tank & Constr. Co., Alaska, Inc., 568 P.2d 1007, 1011 (Alaska 1977) (expressing the opinion that, had the secured party conducted an independent appraisal of the collateral, a finding of commercial reasonableness would be more likely); Jefferson Bank & Trust Co. v. Horst, 599 S.W.2d 201, 203 (Mo. Ct. App. 1980) (finding a public sale of a mobile home commercially reasonable where the secured party obtained an independent appraisal).

The aggregate of circumstances in this case demonstrates that the sale of the collateral conducted by R & J was not conducted in good faith or in a commercially reasonable manner as required by Article 9 of Tennessee's Uniform Commercial Code.

VI. Effect of Failure to Conduct a Commercially Reasonable Sale and Provide Sufficient Notice

Because R & J failed to provide Mr. Blankenship with adequate notice under section 49-9-611, Mr. Blankenship may be entitled to certain statutory damages. Tenn. Code Ann. §47-9-625 (2003). We remand this case to the trial court and instruct the court to determine what damages, if any, Mr. Blankenship is entitled to pursuant to section 47-9-625 of the Tennessee Code due to R & J's failure to provide adequate notice. . . .

On remand, the trial court must also conduct an additional inquiry. Tennessee follows the "rebuttable presumption rule" which governs a creditor's failure to comply with Tennessee's version of the Uniform Commercial Code.

Under Tennessee law, in the event the creditors foreclose upon security interest in collateral and conduct a commercially unreasonable sale, there is a presumption that the debtor is damaged to the extent of the deficiency claimed. The fact of an unreasonable sale does not result in the extinguishment of any deficiency whatsoever. Federal Deposit Insurance Corp. v. Morgan, 727 S.W.2d 500 (Tenn. Ct. App. 1986). This presumption shifts the burden of proving to the creditor the amount that should reasonably have been obtained through sale conducted according to the law. ITT Industrial Co. v. Rector, 1982 WL 170990 (Tenn. Ct. App. 1982)]. The presumption is a presumption of law, and is a burden shifting device, requiring the party who is in a better position, to go forward with the evidence. Where evidence is presented sufficient to rebut the presumption, creditors are entitled to recover the deficiency. Id. Decatur County Bank v. Smith, No. CAW1999-02022COAR3CV, 1999 WL 1336042, at *3, 1999 Tenn. App. LEXIS 864, at *9-10 (Tenn. Ct. App. Dec. 27, 1999). "It is the burden of the secured party to rebut this presumption and failure to rebut the presumption with evidence of fair market value in the record results in denial of the secured party's claims for deficiency judgment." In re Frazier, 93 B.R. 366, 372 (Bankr. M.D. Tenn. 1988) (citations omitted); see also Fed. Deposit Ins. Corp. v. Morgan, 727 S.W.2d 500, 502 (Tenn. Ct. App. 1987) (citing United States v. Willis, 593 F.2d 247, 260 (6th Cir. 1979)); Empire S., Inc. v. Repp, 51 Wash. App. 868, 756 P.2d 745, 750-51 (1988).

At trial, the parties presented conflicting testimony regarding the value of the collateral on the date of the foreclosure sale. In rendering a judgment below, the trial court listed the proceeds from the foreclosure sale in its tabulation of the deficiency owed R & J, but the court failed to state whether this amount constituted the fair market value of the collateral on the date of the sale. Therefore, we are unable to determine what the fair market value of the collateral was on the date of the foreclosure sale and whether R & J overcame the presumption that the amount received at the sale equaled the debt owed. See In re Frazier, 93 B.R. at 372. On remand, the trial court is instructed to determine whether R & J presented sufficient proof in this regard and is entitled to a deficiency judgment. See Provident Employees Credit Union v. Austin, 1981 WL 138032 (Tenn. Ct. App. 1981). If the trial court determines that

R & J has overcome the presumption and is entitled to a deficiency, then the trial court is instructed to determine whether the deficiency should be offset by any damages due Mr. Blankenship pursuant to section 47-9-625 of the Tennessee Code. See Gen. Motors Acceptance Corp., 1991 WL 206517, at *4, 1991 Tenn. App. LEXIS 820, at *11-12.

VII. CONCLUSION

For the foregoing reasons, we reverse the trial court's decision. We remand this case to the trial court with instructions to determine whether the Appellant is entitled to damages against Appellee consistent with this opinion. We also instruct the trial court to determine whether Appellee is entitled to a deficiency and, if so, the amount that the deficiency should be offset by Appellant's damages, if any, consistent with this opinion. Costs of this appeal are taxed against Appellee, R & J of Tennessee, Inc., for which execution may issue if necessary.

To the extent that this case holds that the creditor must do any sort of checking to see that the notice was actually received, it was overruled by Auto

Credit of Nashville v. Wimmer, 231 S.W.3d 896 (Tenn. 2007) ("To require every creditor to verify receipt of notification in every situation would place an unreasonable burden on them, making secured transactions in this state unduly cumbersome").

PROBLEM 138

Car dealers sometimes engage in a shady practice called "yo-yo financing." The buyer is persuaded to take a "spot delivery" of the car being purchased, but is warned that the deal is off if the seller is unable to secure financing for the buyer. If the financing goes through, well and good, but if not the buyer must surrender the car or work out some other means of payment, and, if necessary the seller will hunt the car down and bring it back to the dealership using a spare set of keys and then sell it to some other customer. Is this an Article 9 transaction? See §2-401(1). If so, is the car dealer at risk of damages under §9-625(c)(2) if no notice is given of the subsequent resale of the car? See Cappo Management V, Inc. v. Britt, 282 Va. 33, 711 S.E.2d 209 (2011). If the customer, on learning of the failure of the financing, voluntarily returns the keys to the dealership, is any subsequent sale of the car governed by the repossession rules of Article 9? If the car dealer resells the car, must the car dealer return the first buyer's down payment (if any)? See §9-615(d). Another issue that has arisen with yo-yo financing is whether the purchaser of the car has any ownership interest in it so that the dealership's security interest could even attach during the period when it is unclear if financing will be forthcoming; see In re Byrd, 546 B.R. 434 (Bankr. D. Idaho 2016).

Yo-yo financing is sometimes called "bait and switch" financing because the buyer thinks he/she has bought a new car only to be told to return it because the financing mysteriously fell through. When the buyer returns to the dealership, a new deal is often offered with worse terms for the buyer. If the buyer won't return the car, threats are often made that police will be called, the buyer's employer will be informed (or the base commander if the buyer is in the service), etc. Out and out fraud and lies are common. Courts may take a dim view of these practices—witness the Supreme Court of Virginia's opinion cited above. For an expanded discussion of yo-yo financing, see http://www.edmunds.com/car-loan/dont-fall-prey-to-spot-delivery-scams-and-yo-yo-financing.html.

PROBLEM 139

The Bunyan State Bank held a perfected security interest in the logging equipment of the Blue Ox Timber Company. When Blue Ox defaulted on its loan repayment, Bunyan repossessed the equipment. The sale was held the next day in the middle of a snowstorm. The equipment sold for very little (there was only one bidder, and he complained that it was hard to know the condition of the equipment because it was so dirty, being covered with mud from the backwoods). Bunyan sued Blue Ox for the amount still due. Answer these questions:

(a) Was the notice period too short? See §9-612. See, e.g., In re MarMc Transp., Inc., 469 B.R. 84 (Bankr. D. Wyo. 2012). Would if affect the notice requirement if the collateral were perishable, such as a load of tomatoes? See §9-611(d)?

(b) Is the secured party required to wash the collateral prior to sale? See §9-610(a); Weiss v. Northwest Acceptance Corp., 274 Or. 343, 546 P.2d 1065 (1976); Timothy R. Zinnecker, The Default Provisions of Revised Article 9 of the Uniform Commercial Code: Part I, 54 Bus. Law. 1113, 1149-1151 (1999).

(c) Did it violate §9-610(b) to conduct the sale in the snowstorm? Liberty Natl. Bank & Trust Co. v. Acme Tool Div. of the Rucker Co., 540 F.2d 1375 (10th Cir. 1976).

PROBLEM 140

When you explained to your client, Repossession Finance Company, all the rights that debtors have when the creditor seizes the collateral and resells it, the president of the company asked you to draft a clause in the security agreement waiving these rights. How should you do this? See §9-602 and its Official Comment. Can guarantors (as opposed to the primary debtor) waive these rights? See §9-602, Official Comment 4; Kraenzler v. Brace, 321 Wis. 2d 265, 773 N.W.2d 481 (2009).

PROBLEM 141

Facade Motors granted a security interest in its inventory to Octopus National Bank (ONB), which duly perfected by filing a financing statement in the proper place. Subsequently Facade Motors granted an identical security interest to Nightflyer Finance Company to get short-term credit. When Facade failed to repay the second debt, Nightflyer repossessed the inventory and sold it. Must it somehow account to ONB for the proceeds of the resale? Does the buyer at the resale take free of the security interest of the senior creditor? See §§9-608 (and its Official Comment 5), 9-615(g), and Official Comment 5 to §9-610; note §§9-617, 2-312, 9-610(d) and (e). How can the resale creditor avoid making the warranty in §2-312?

Penalties for Non-compliance. Amazingly, under the prior version of Article 9, it was unclear what the penalty was for a secured party who did not follow the required rules when disposing of the collateral, and the states reached differing results, with many resolving the matter by non-uniform statutes. Some courts held that failure to comply resulted in a forfeiture of the creditor's right to collect a *deficiency* (the difference between the amount owed and the amount realized at the foreclosure sale)—this was called the *absolute bar* rule. Others (like the Tennessee decision reprinted above) allowed a deficiency but made the creditor overcome a *rebuttable presumption* that had the rules been followed, there would have been no deficiency and allowed the creditor to pursue the debtor for the amount still due only if the creditor could overcome this presumption by adequate proof.

PROBLEM 142

Facade Motors repossessed the car that Portia Moot used in her law practice but failed to send her any notice of the foreclosure sale, which brought only half the amount she still owed on the car. May it still sue her for the deficiency? See §9-626(a) and its Official Comments. What are Portia's rights? See §9-625. If Portia had purchased the car for her *personal* use, what is the rule? See §9-626(b). Why would the drafters have done this?

Coxall v. Clover Commercial Corp.

Civil Court, City of New York, 2004
4 Misc. 3d 654, 781 N.Y.S.2d 567

JACK M. BATTAGLIA, J.

On October 21, 2002, Jason Coxall and Utho Coxall purchased a 1991 model Lexus automobile, executing a Security Agreement/Retail Installment Contract. The "cash price" on the Contract was $8,100, against which the Coxalls made a "cash down payment" of $3,798.25 and financed the balance of $4,970. Apparently simultaneously with the sale, the Contract was assigned to Clover Commercial Corp., whose name was printed on the top and at other places. Although Majestic Capital Inc. is designated as the "Seller" and "Dealer" in the assignment, at trial the parties referred to the seller of the automobile as Jafas Auto Sales. Title to the vehicle was put in Jason Coxall's name.

The Coxalls were required by the Contract to make monthly payments of $333.68 each, beginning November 21, 2002. No payments were made, however, because Jason Coxall experienced mechanical difficulties with the vehicle soon after purchase. On February 19, 2003, Clover Commercial took possession of the vehicle, and on the next day mailed two letters to Jason Coxall; in one, Clover told Mr. Coxall that he could redeem the vehicle with a payment of $5,969.28, exclusive of storage charges and a redemption fee; in the other, Clover gave Mr. Coxall notice that the vehicle would be offered for private sale after 12:00 noon on March 3, 2003.

On March 3, 2003, the Lexus was sold back to Jafas Auto Sales for $1,500. On April 22, 2003, Clover Commercial wrote to Jason Coxall demanding that he pay a "remaining balance" of $4,998.09.

Jason Coxall commenced Action No. 1 with a Summons with Endorsed Complaint dated April 29, 2003 that states the nature and substance of the cause of action as "automobile illegally repossed [sic]," and seeks damages of $8,000 with interest from February 19, 2003. Clover Commercial was served on May 2, and filed its Answer on May 20. Despite the filing, the action was placed on the Part 12 calendar for inquest to be held on June 27.

Meanwhile, with a Summons and Verified Complaint dated June 16, 2003 and filed on June 25, Clover Commercial commenced Action No.2 against Jason Coxall and Utho Coxall, seeking $4,630.62 with interest from October 21, 2002 plus reasonable attorney fees. The Verified Complaint alleges that "Plaintiff is the holder for value of a promissory instrument dated 10/21/02 duly executed and delivered and/or guaranteed by the defendant(s)." These documents show Clover Commercial's attorney to be E. Hope Greenberg, the same attorney who signed Clover's Answer in Action No. 1 approximately one month earlier. . . .

[The trial court ruled in favor of the creditor, but on appeal this court found that the notice was only given to one of the two debtors and that the resale of the car had not been proven by the creditor to be commercially reasonable, particularly in light of the low sale price and other suspicious circumstances. The court then turned to a consideration of the effect of these failures on the creditor's ability to continue its pursuit of the debtors.]

DEFICIENCY

When the secured party has disposed of the collateral in a commercially reasonable manner after sending reasonable notification to the debtor, the debtor will be liable for any deficiency if the proceeds of the disposition are not sufficient to satisfy the debt and allowed expenses. (See Revised UCC §9-615[(d)]; see also Former UCC §9-504[(2)].) Former Article 9 was silent, however, on whether the secured party that had failed to send reasonable notification or had not disposed of the collateral in a commercially reasonable manner or both, as here could obtain a deficiency judgment against the debtor. . . .

"Three general approaches emerged. Some courts have held that a noncomplying secured party may not recover a deficiency (the 'absolute bar' rule). A few courts held that the debtor can offset against a claim to a deficiency all damages recoverable under former Section 9-507 resulting from the secured party's noncompliance (the 'offset' rule). A plurality of courts considering the issue held that the noncomplying secured party is barred from recovering a deficiency unless it overcomes a rebuttable presumption that compliance with former Part 5 would have yielded an amount sufficient to satisfy the secured debt." (Official Comment 4 to Revised UCC §9-626.)

In New York, the departments of the Appellate Division were not in agreement as to which of the approaches to follow, with the Second Department alone adopting the "absolute bar" rule. [Citations omitted.]

Revised Article 9 resolves the conflict and uncertainty for transactions other than consumer transactions by adopting the "rebuttable presumption" rule. (See Revised UCC §9-626[a][3].) The limitation of the "rebuttable presumption" rule to non-consumer transactions "is intended to leave to the court the determination of the proper rules in consumer transactions," and the court "may continue to apply established approaches." (Revised UCC §9-626[(b)].)

It is clear, therefore, that the "rebuttable presumption" rule is now the law in the Second Department for non-consumer transactions. The question remains, however, whether the "absolute bar" rule is to be applied in these actions, involving, as they do, a consumer transaction. A review of the legislative history provides no guidance. The Report of the New York State Law Revision Committee that accompanied Revised Article 9 through enactment states only that, "[w]ith respect to consumer defaults, Revised Article 9 makes no recommendation whatsoever, leaving the courts free to shape a remedy as is appropriate in each case." (The New York State Law Revision Commission, 2001 Report on the Proposed Revised Article 9, at 158.)

Up to now, New York courts have not distinguished between consumer and non-consumer transactions in fashioning rules where the enforcement provisions of Article 9 were silent, suggesting that the "rebuttable presumption" rule will be adopted for all transactions. But at this time, for a court sitting in the Second Department, there is an "absolute bar" rule that has not been legislatively displaced by Revised Article 9.

Having found, therefore, that Clover Commercial failed to comply with both the reasonable notification and commercially reasonable disposition requirements of Article 9, the "absolute bar" rule precludes it from recovering a deficiency from the Coxalls. Even if, however, the "rebuttable presumption" rule were to be applied, the result would be the same. Clover introduced no evidence of "the amount of proceeds that would have been realized had [it] proceeded in accordance with the provisions of" the Code relating to disposition of the collateral. (See Revised UCC §9-626[(a)][(3)][(B)].)

Specifically, Clover Commercial provided no evidence as to the fair market value of the Lexus on the date of the sale, either by reference to "blue book" value, appraisal, sales of similar vehicles or other measure. (See Long Island Trust Co. v. Williams, 133 Misc. 2d at 754, 507 N.Y.S.2d 993; see also Central National Bank v. Butler, 294 A.D.2d at 882, 741 N.Y.S.2d 643 ["certified appraised value"]; Kohler v. Ford Motor Credit Co., Inc., 93 A.D.2d at 208, 462 N.Y.S.2d 297 ["book value of the vehicle"].) Moreover,

Clover's witness, Adam Greenberg, acknowledged that Clover considered the Lexus to be of sufficient value to serve as collateral for the secured debt, which, at the least, was the amount financed, $4,970.

Although Clover Commercial cannot recover for any deficiency, it may recover "the sums owed to it prior to the repossession as well as the repossession charges." (See Avis Rent-A-Car System, Inc. v. Franklin, 82 Misc. 2d at 67, 366 N.Y.S.2d 83.) Clover's failure to comply with the enforcement provisions of Article 9 "would not discharge the [Coxalls] from all liability under the contract." (See Stanchi v. Kemp, 48 A.D.2d at 974, 370 N.Y.S.2d 26; see also Bank of China v. Chan, 937 F.2d 780, 788 [(2d Cir. 1991)].) At the time of repossession, three monthly payments of $333.68 were unpaid for a total due of $1,001.04; and the Contract provided for a 10% late charge for each payment not made when due, for an additional charge of $100.11. Clover is entitled, therefore, to $1,101.15 for payments in default and related late charges.

The Contract also provides that the debtor must pay the "cost of repossession, storage and preparation for sale" and "an attorney's fee of up to 15% of the amount due . . . unless the court sets a smaller fee." Clover Commercial includes $325 in its computation of the deficiency, which apparently is intended as a charge for repossession, storage, and preparation charges, but, unlike the late charge, the amount is not specified in the Contract, and no evidence was submitted to explain or support it. Similarly, there was no evidence to support an award of attorney fees. (See Orix Credit Alliance, Inc. v. Grace Industries, Inc., 261 A.D.2d 521, 521-522, 690 N.Y.S.2d 651 [2d Dept. 1999].)

Coxall's Claim Against Clover

Jason Coxall no longer has his Lexus. His down payment was $3,798.25, and he owes $1,101.15 for overdue payments. In effect, approximately four months' use of the vehicle has cost him approximately $5,000, not including alleged repair and towing expenses. Of course, "the debtor who precipitated the sale by defaulting on a debt is certainly not to be freed lightly from default." (Siemens Credit Corp. v. Marvik Colour, Inc., 859 F. Supp. at 692.) Nonetheless, does Mr. Coxall have a remedy for Clover Commercial's failure to comply with Article 9, beyond being relieved of any liability for a deficiency?

"Under common law, prior to the enactment of the Uniform Conditional Sales Act, the seller was under no obligation upon the retaking of the goods on buyer's default to make return of partial payment or any part thereof." (Laufer v. Burghard, 146 Misc. 39, 42, 261 N.Y.S. 364 [Sup. Ct., Erie County 1932].) "A retaking of the property by a conditional vendor is not a rescission of the contract so as to require the vendor to place the buyer in a former position and return the consideration received under the contract." (Id. at 45, 261 N.Y.S. 364.) If, however, the repossessing seller failed to comply with obligations imposed by statute after taking possession, a return of all or part of the payments made by the buyer was mandated. (See Rivara v. James Stewart & Co., 241 N.Y. 259, 262, 267, 149 N.E. 851 [1925], aff'd, 274 U.S. 614, 47 S. Ct. 718, 71 L. Ed. 1234 [1927]; La Rocca Builders, Inc. v. Sanders, 230 A.D. 594, 597, 245 N.Y.S. 262 [1st Dept. 1930].)

Under Article 9, "a person is liable for damages in the amount of any loss caused by a failure to comply" with the statute. (Revised UCC §9-625[(b)]; see also Former UCC §9-507[(1)].) "Damages for violation of the requirements of [the statute] . . . are those reasonably calculated to put an eligible claimant in the position that it would have occupied had no violation occurred." (Official Comment 3 to Revised UCC §9-625.) There are, however, both supplements to and limitations on this general liability principle.

"[A] debtor . . . whose deficiency is eliminated or reduced under Section 9-626 may not otherwise recover . . . for noncompliance with the provisions . . . relating to enforcement." (Revised UCC §9-625[(d)].) This provision "eliminates the possibility of double recovery or other overcompensation," but "[b]ecause Section 9-626 does not apply to consumer transactions, the statute is silent as to whether a double recovery or other over-compensation is possible in a consumer transaction." (Official Comment 3 to Revised UCC §9-625.) Respected commentators "argue that double recoveries should be denied in consumer cases too." (See White and Summers, Uniform Commercial Code, §25-13, at 919 [5th ed. 2000].[6])

The law in New York under Former Article 9 allowed a debtor to recover any loss resulting from the secured party's noncompliance, even though the secured party was deprived of recovery for a deficiency because of noncompliance. (See Liberty Bank v. Thomas, 222 A.D.2d 1019, 635 N.Y.S.2d 912 [4th Dept. 1995].) Here again, since Revised Article 9 does not displace existing law for consumer transactions, this Court must apply the pre-revision law. At the least, denial of a deficiency to the noncomplying secured party should not preclude the debtor's recovery of the statutorily-prescribed minimum damages. (See Matter of Calvin Angel, 142 B.R. 194, 198-99 [S.D. Ohio 1992]; Wilmington Trust Co. v. Conner, 415 A.2d 773, 781 [Del. 1980].)

Revised Article 9, like its predecessor, "provides a minimum, statutory, damage recovery for a debtor . . . in a consumer goods transaction" that "is designed to ensure that every noncompliance . . . in a consumer-goods transaction results in liability." (See Revised UCC §9-625[(c)]; Official Comment 4 to Revised UCC §9-625; Former UCC §9-507[(1)].) The debtor may recover "an amount not less than the credit service charge plus 10 percent

6. [Now §26-13 at 1358 (6th ed. 2010) — EDS.]

of the principal amount of the obligation or the time-price differential plus 10 percent of the cash price." (Revised UCC §9-625[c].) The statute "does not include a definition or explanation of the terms" used in the damage formula, but "leaves their construction and application to the court, taking into account the . . . purpose of providing a minimum recovery." (Official Comment 4 to Revised UCC §9-625.)

Here, according to the Contract, the time-price differential is $1,036.24 and 10% of the cash price is $810, for a total statutory damage recovery of $1,846.24. Mr. Coxall is entitled to this recovery even if he sustained no actual loss from Clover Commercial's failure to comply with Article 9. (See Davenport v. Chrysler Credit Corp., 818 S.W.2d 23, 31-32 [Tenn. App. 1991]; Erdmann v. Rants, 442 N.W.2d 441, 443 [N.D. 1989]; First City Bank-Farmers Branch, Texas v. Guex, 677 S.W.2d 25, 29 [Tex. 1984].) But, although Clover Commercial failed to comply with both the requirement for reasonable notification and the requirement for a commercially reasonable disposition, it is obligated for only one statutory damage remedy. (See Dunn v. Security Pacific Housing Services, 1996 Del. Super Lexis 428, *10-*11 [Super Ct., New Castle]; Crosby v. Basin Motor Co., 83 N.M. 77, 79, 488 P.2d 127, 129 [1971].)

Mr. Coxall would also be entitled to the value of the personal property that, he says, was contained in the vehicle when it was repossessed, but which has not been returned to him. (See Fitzpatrick v. Bank of New York, 125 Misc. 2d 1069, 1076, 480 N.Y.S.2d 864 [Civ. Ct., Queens County 1984].) But Mr. Coxall introduced no admissible evidence of that value.

DISPOSITION

In Action No. 1, judgment is rendered in favor of Jason Coxall against Clover Commercial for $745.09, representing the difference between Mr. Coxall's statutory damages of $1,846.24 and Clover's Commercial's damages for breach of the Contract of $1,101.15, with interest from March 3, 2003, plus costs. . . .

———————————

Military Loans. Ever since the Civil War federal law has appreciated that those called to military active duty have a reduced income and may have significant difficulty meeting current payment obligations. Consequently, the Servicemembers Civil Relief Act, 50 App. U.S.C. §§501 et seq., has broad rules covering all loans to servicemembers, protecting them, for example, from default judgments, evictions, and termination of various benefits such as life insurance without adequate notice. It converts all existing loan interest rates to a maximum of 6 percent during the period of active duty, and excuses any requirement for ever paying the excused interest (so that payments reduce principal). Many states have statutes protecting members of the military in their financial dealings, and these statutes frequently give terrific protection to service personnel during their military career.

IV. REDEMPTION AND STRICT FORECLOSURE

Centuries of property law have established the right of the defaulting debtor to recover the collateral by curing the default. The courts of equity first enforced this right of *redemption,* and it has become a common maxim that the courts will not permit anything to "clog the equity of redemption." See G. Gilmore §43.2; Indianapolis Morris Plan Corp. v. Karlen, 28 N.Y.2d 30, 268 N.E.2d 632, 319 N.Y.S.2d 831 (1971).

PROBLEM 143

When Paul Morphy borrowed $2,000 from the Lasker State Bank in order to finance a trip to Iceland, the bank made him sign an agreement giving the bank a security interest in Paul's private yacht. He agreed to repay the loan at the rate of $200 a month. He took the trip and on his return made the first payment on time. He failed to make the second payment on the due date, and the next day the bank repossessed the yacht. Paul raced to the bank with the late payment. He had $200 in cash, which he tendered. The bank refused to take the money. The bank's loan officer, a Mr. Anderssen, pointed to an acceleration clause in the security agreement that made the entire amount due if a payment was missed. Anderssen demanded the total unpaid balance. Need Paul pay off everything? See §9-623 along with its Official Comment 2. There is pre-revision authority for the proposition that misdescription of the redemption rights bars any action for the deficiency. First Natl. Bank v. DiDomenico, 302 Md. 290, 487 A.2d 646 (1985).

Strict foreclosure occurs when the creditor repossesses the collateral and simply keeps it in satisfaction of the debt. No deficiency is sought. The debtor (or other creditors having junior security interests) may not be pleased with strict foreclosure in all situations. Read §§9-620 to 9-622.

PROBLEM 144

Art Auctions, Inc. (AAI), sold Dudley Collector a $5,000 painting by Smock Pallet, a famous artist. Dudley paid $1,000 down and agreed to pay over $1,000 a month thereafter. The finance charge was $151.20; the annual percentage rate was 18 percent. The contract contained a clause saying that in the event of default, AAI could repossess the painting and keep it without reselling it or, at its option, could resell it and sue for the deficiency. Dudley made three more payments and then missed the last one, being temporarily short of funds. AAI, without notice, sent one of its agents to Dudley's home. Dudley's teenage son let the agent in, and he simply removed the painting from the wall and walked out, saying, "Thank you." Dudley immediately tendered $1,000 to AAI and demanded the painting. AAI refused (the painting is now worth $20,000). Four months later, Dudley filed suit. What is the basis of his cause of action, and to what relief is he entitled? See §§9-620(e) and (f), 9-625(b) and (c).

Here the creditor will make a huge profit by the use of strict foreclosure. Is that relevant? See McDonald v. Yarchenko, 2013 WL 3809512 (D. Or. 2013). Must the notice of strict foreclosure inform the debtor of the need to object within 20 days? See Born v. Born, 320 P.3d 449 (Kan. App. 2014).

If Dudley had made only one payment and then defaulted, causing AAI to repossess, could AAI have sent him a proposal that it would keep the painting and forgive *half* the remaining debt only? See §9-620(g).

PROBLEM 145

When Repossession Finance Company declared a default and repossessed all the office equipment of attorney Portia Moot, as allowed by the security agreement, the company then did nothing with the collateral except let it sit in a storage room for 17 months. Finally, it conducted a resale with appropriate notices and then sued Portia for the deficiency. She defended by arguing that actions speak louder than words and that, in effect, by doing nothing for such a long period, the finance company had constructively elected strict foreclosure and had forfeited any right to a deficiency. Is this correct? See Official Comment 5 to §9-620; Jefferson Loan Co., Inc. v. Session, 397 N.J. Super. 520, 938 A.2d 169 (2008) (failure to resell the repossessed vehicle for four years deemed "commercially unreasonable"); but see Key Equipment Fin. v. Southwest Contracting, Inc., 2015 WL 5159073 (D. Colo. 2015) (resale almost two years after repossession held commercially reasonable where explainable).

Reeves v. Foutz & Tanner, Inc.

New Mexico Supreme Court, 1980
94 N.M. 760, 617 P.2d 149

Sosa, C.J.

These suits were brought as separate actions but were consolidated by the Court of Appeals because the issues were essentially the same. The trial court held for plaintiffs, the Court of Appeals reversed, and we reverse the Court of Appeals.

Plaintiffs Reeves and Begay are uneducated Navajo Indians whose ability to understand English and commercial matters [is] limited. Each of them pawned jewelry with the defendant whereby they received a money loan in return for a promise to repay the loan in thirty days with interest. The Indian jewelry left with defendant as collateral was worth several times the amount borrowed. The plaintiffs defaulted and defendant sent each of them a notice of intent to retain the collateral, though Reeves claimed she never received notice. The retention was not objected to by either plaintiff. Defendant then sold the jewelry in the regular course of its business.

The question we are presented with is whether a secured party who sends a notice of intent to retain collateral, in conformance with §9-505 of the Uniform Commercial Code [now §9-620—Eds.], may sell the collateral in its regular course of business without complying with §9-504 [now §9-610—Eds.]? We decide that the secured party in this case could not sell the collateral without complying with §9-504.

The Uniform Commercial Code provides a secured party in possession with two courses of action upon the default of the debtor. Section 9-504 provides generally that the secured party may sell the collateral, but if the security interest secures an indebtedness, he must account to the debtor for any surplus (and the debtor must account for any deficiency). Section 9-505(2) provides the secured party with the alternative of retaining the collateral in satisfaction of the obligation. Under this section, the secured party must give written notice to the debtor that he intends to keep the collateral in satisfaction of the debt. The debtor is then given thirty days to object to the proposed retention and require the sale of the property according to §9-504.

In the present case we will assume that defendant gave proper notice to both Reeves and Begay of its intention to retain the collateral and that neither objected within thirty days. The trial court found that the defendant, in accordance with its normal business practice, then moved the jewelry into its sale inventory where it was sold to Joe Tanner, president of defendant corporation, or to Joe Tanner, Inc., a corporation owned by Joe Tanner and engaged in the sale of Indian jewelry. There was no accounting to plaintiffs of any surplus. The trial court also found that the defendant did not act in good faith in disposing of the jewelry, taking into consideration the relative bargaining power of the parties.

The defendant argues that the trial court should be reversed because it applied §9-504. It essentially argues that once it complied with §9-505(2) and sent the notice of intent to retain, it could do as it pleased with the property once the thirty days had elapsed without objection. The debtor-creditor relationship terminates, they claim, and the creditor becomes owner of the collateral.

The plaintiffs argue that the trial court was correct in applying §9-504 to require that any surplus from the sale of collateral be returned to the debtor. They urge that the intention of the secured party should control and where he intended to sell the collateral and did sell the collateral in the normal course of business, he must comply with §9-504 which governs sales of such collateral.

Neither party to this action has cited a case which has dealt directly with the issue here, but amicus has referred us to a Federal Trade Commission case on the subject where it was stated:

> In the Draftsmen's Statement of Reasons for 1972 Changes in Official Text, the Draftsmen summarized the purpose of §9-505 as follows:
>> Under subsection (2) [9-505(2)] of this section the secured party may in lieu of sale give notice to the debtor and certain other persons that he proposes to retain the collateral in lieu of sale.
>> The foregoing language strongly suggests that waiver of surplus and deficiency rights under §9-505 is appropriate only when prompt resale of repossessed collateral in the ordinary course of business is not contemplated by the creditor. . . . That being so, use of §9-505 by an automobile dealer, particularly one not disposed to pursue deficiency judgments, would appear calculated solely to extinguish surplus rights of consumers, which we do not believe was the intended purpose of §9-505.

In the Matter of Ford Motor Company, Ford Motor Credit Company, and Francis Ford Inc., 93 F.T.C. Rep., 3 C.C.H. Trade Reg. Rep. 21756, 21767 (FTC Docket No. 9073, Sept. 21, 1979). The Commission went on to say that a creditor of this type is not foreclosed from using §9-505(2) so long as he intends to retain the collateral for his own use for the immediately foreseeable future, rather than to resell the collateral in the ordinary course of business. We agree with the approach used by the Federal Trade Commission.

The Court of Appeals reasoned that once the creditor elected to retain the collateral, and followed the mechanics of §9-505, the property became his to keep or to sell. We do not find fault with this reasoning, but it misses the point. Defendant can do as he pleases with the property, but where he intends to sell the property in the regular course of his business, which is in substance selling the property as contemplated by §9-504, he must account for a surplus in conformity with §9-504.

The defendant also argues that plaintiffs could have objected to the retention, thus forcing a sale in compliance with §9-504. But because there was never any actual intent to retain under §9-505(2), the failure of plaintiffs to timely object does not foreclose their claim. Moreover, the fact that plaintiffs could have objected means nothing in this context; their objection would only have served to cause a sale of the goods, which sale was already intended by defendant.

The defendant also argues that the trial court erred in finding that it acted in bad faith. We need not reach this question because bad faith was not material to the trial court's conclusions of law and judgment, which we find to be proper.

The defendant next claims error in the fact that the trial court allowed interest on the judgment from November 1, 1974. The date is the approximate day on which the loss took place and is apparently not controverted. The amount due the plaintiffs was a sum certain once the jewelry was sold, as calculated according to the provisions of §9-504. It was not error for the court to allow prejudgment interest or to allow interest as a portion of the damages. Sundt v. Tobin Quarries, 50 N.M. 254, 265, 175 P.2d 684, 690-691 (1946).

The judgment of the trial court is affirmed.

QUESTION

Is this case right? Does the court mean that any time the creditor elects to use §9-620, that creditor is forbidden the right to resell the collateral in the ordinary course of its business? After this decision, and assuming the court would reach the same result under the revision of Article 9, can it be said that §9-620 is a dead letter in New Mexico?

CHAPTER 10   ASSESSMENT: MULTIPLE CHOICE QUESTIONS

1. Ickx purchased a Le Mans hybrid car on credit from Formulaic Motors, signing a security agreement, which provided that default would occur upon failure to make scheduled payments, upon failure to maintain insurance, or upon other events. Ickx made all payments in timely fashion but carelessly let the insurance expire. One morning, the car had disappeared from in front of Ickx's home. Ickx reported the car stolen to the police, who responded that Formulaic Motors had repossessed the car. Repo agents routinely keep police informed of their activity, to avoid misunderstandings when they spirit vehicles away. Can Formulaic Motors legally repossess Ickx's car, when Ickx has not missed a single payment?
   a. No, Formulaic Motors violated Article 9 by making a commercially unreasonable repossession.
   b. No, a creditor cannot repossess the car where the debtor is not in default in payment.
   c. Yes. Upon default as defined by the parties, the creditor may take possession of the collateral.
   d. Yes. Until paid for, the car belongs to the seller, Formulaic Motors.

2. Ickx contends that, even if Formulaic Motors was entitled to repossess the car, it was required to give him prior notice. There was no emergency that

prevented giving him notice and a car is not perishable goods, like fruit. Did Formulaic Motors violate Article 9 by failing to give prior notice?

  a. Yes, to take possession of the collateral, a creditor must give notice and proceed in a commercially reasonable manner.
  b. Yes, Article 9 requires good faith in all aspects, which would include giving prior notice of taking possession.
  c. No. Prior notice of repossession is not required by Article 9.
  d. No. Formulaic Motors can deal with its collateral as it pleases at all times.

3. Formulaic Motors repossessed the car of another defaulting debtor, Lauda. The security agreement provided that Formulaic Motors was permitted to use any means necessary to get the car, in the event of default. Formulaic Motors' agent broke through the garage door with an axe at 3 A.M., smashed the driver's side window of the car, pushed away Lauda, who had jumped out of bed, and warned neighbors with a megaphone not to intervene. Is Formulaic Motors in violation of Article 9?

  a. No. Its actions were authorized by Article 9 and the contract between the parties.
  b. Yes. It breached the peace and the contract provision that authorized such actions would not be effective.
  c. No, creditors are entitled to repossess the collateral, including taking any necessary measures.
  d. Yes. A creditor must get a court order in order to take possession of the collateral.

4. Formulaic Motors sent Prost notice that it would conduct a private sale of Prost's car, which Formulaic Motors had repossessed. The car had a market value of about $30,000 and the debt was $20,000. Formulaic Motors sold the car to a favorite customer for $21,000, applied $20,000 to the debt and gave Prost the surplus of $1,000. Prost is not satisfied. Is Formulaic Motors liable to Prost?

  a. No. Prost had notice the car was to be sold, so could have prevented the sale by paying off the debt.
  b. No. As with real estate foreclosure, sales of collateral are usually low-ball sales.
  c. Yes. Formulaic Motors failed to sell the collateral in a commercially reasonable manner.
  d. Yes. Formulaic Motors cannot sell someone else's car.

5. Jacob Finance held a security interest in the inventory of Marvelous Products, but with a subordinate position to another creditor, Esau Finance, who had filed an earlier financing statement. When Marvelous Products failed to make several payments, Jacob Finance took possession

of the inventory. Before selling, Jacob Finance gave all required notices, including notice to Esau Finance. Jacob Finance sold the inventory and applied the proceeds of the sale to pay off most of the debt. Esau Finance demanded that Jacob Finance hand over enough of the sale proceeds to pay off Esau Finance, because Esau Finance had priority. Is the junior creditor required to give the senior creditor first cut of the proceeds of the collateral sale?

a. Yes, that is exactly what priority means.

b. No. The junior creditor may apply the proceeds to its own debt, and if there is money left over, return it to the debtor.

c. Yes, the senior creditor is entitled to all of the sale proceeds.

d. No. Article 9 is strictly first come, first served.

ANSWERS

1. *C* is the best answer. The creditor may take possession of the collateral upon default. Default is not defined in Article 9, rather should be defined by the parties in the security agreement, which is normally drafted by the creditor. Contrary to B, the parties may define default to go well beyond a failure to make timely payments. There was a default here under the security agreement, so Formulaic Motors was entitled to take possession. Contrary to A, unlike an insecurity clause that requires the creditor to be insecure about its chances of being repaid, which would require a good faith or reasonable belief that the collateral was at risk, this default clause required only a lapse in the insurance.

2. *C* is the best answer. When a creditor *sells* the collateral, the creditor must give prior notice and proceed in a commercially reasonable manner. §9-610, §9-611. But those requirements do not apply to the preliminary act of taking possession, contrary to A. Rather, §9-609 permits a creditor to take possession, provided it does so without a breach of the peace. Repossession without notice is a common commercial practice permitted by Article 9, so would not be a violation of the obligation of good faith, contrary to B.

3. *B* is the best answer. This question illustrates two key rules. First, on default, a creditor may take possession of the collateral, without judicial process, provided there is no breach of the peace. §9-609. Second, most of the creditor's obligations with respect to default, such as the requirement that there be no breach of the peace in a repossession, may not be effectively varied in the parties' security agreement. §9-602(6).

   The requirement that there be no breach of the peace eliminates self-help repossessions for many creditors. If the collateral is inventory locked in a store or jewelry in the debtor's bedside drawer, then taking possession without the debtor's consent would require a breach of the peace. Such creditors are not out of luck. The debtor should abide by its contract and hand over the collateral. If not, creditors are well-versed in obtaining rapid judicial relief.

One important category of collateral, however, has wheels and is often left sitting invitingly on the street: vehicles. The creditor must still avoid breaching the peace. What constitutes a breach of the peace is often hard to determine. Is taking the car at 2 in the morning a breach of the peace, because neighbors might think it's a theft, or no breach, because it's a quiet time when likely no one will notice? This question used an extreme set of facts to make sure that there was a breach of the peace.

4. *C* is the best answer. A creditor may sell the collateral after default, contrary to D, but must do everything in a commercially reasonable manner. §9-610. Giving notice that a sale will occur is not sufficient, contrary to A. "Every aspect of a disposition of collateral, including the method, manner, time, place, and other terms, must be commercially reasonable." §9-610(b). Selling the car at a sub-market price to a favored party, without any bidding or attempt to get better offers, would not even be close to a commercially reasonable sale.

Formulaic Auto will be liable for damages. See §9-625. Another issue is whether Prost will get the car back. A good faith buyer at an Article 9 sale takes free of the debtor's interest, even if the creditor violated Article 9. If the buyer was reasonably unaware of Formulaic Motor's violation, then the buyer may have acted in good faith. If the buyer knew Formulaic Motor was selling it someone else's car at a submarket price, then the buyer may have acted in bad faith.

5. *B* is the best answer, which may be a surprise until we review the relevant rules. When a creditor sells the collateral, the creditor must apply the proceeds to, in order, the expenses of sale, the creditor's debt, the debt of creditors *subordinate* to the selling creditor (none, in this case) and give any surplus to the debtor. §9-615(a). The selling creditor is not obliged to give anything to creditors who have priority to the selling creditor. In this case Jacob is not required to give any sale proceeds to Esau. It sounds illogical that the junior creditor may sell the collateral without giving any proceeds to the senior creditor, until we consider the effect of the sale. When a creditor sells the collateral, the buyer takes the property free of the interests of the selling creditor, any creditor subordinate to the selling creditor, and the debtor. §9-617(a). The interests of creditors senior to the selling creditor are unaffected and remain with the collateral in the hands of the buyer. In other words, the junior creditor cannot sell the collateral free of the senior interest, but does not have to give any of the sale proceeds to the senior creditor, who keeps its interest in the collateral. So in this case, Jacob sold the inventory subject to

Esau's security interest but does not have to give any money to Esau, who can still seize the inventory and sell it if there is a default (and a default sale of the inventory no doubt triggered a default under Esau's security agreement).

Another rule comes into play. A selling creditor (Jacob) would violate the warranty of title unless it informed the buyer of Esau's security interest before the sale, or the parties agreed to exclude that warranty. §9-610(d). Potential buyers would naturally discount the price they were willing to pay, because they would still have to see that Esau was paid off, to own the collateral free of claims. The best practice, if a junior creditor is selling, is to enter into an agreement with the senior creditor beforehand, in order to sell the goods free of all security interests for the best price.

* This reference is to 1-105 in the original, pre-Revision version of Article 1.